Robert Heinecken
and the Art
of Appropriation

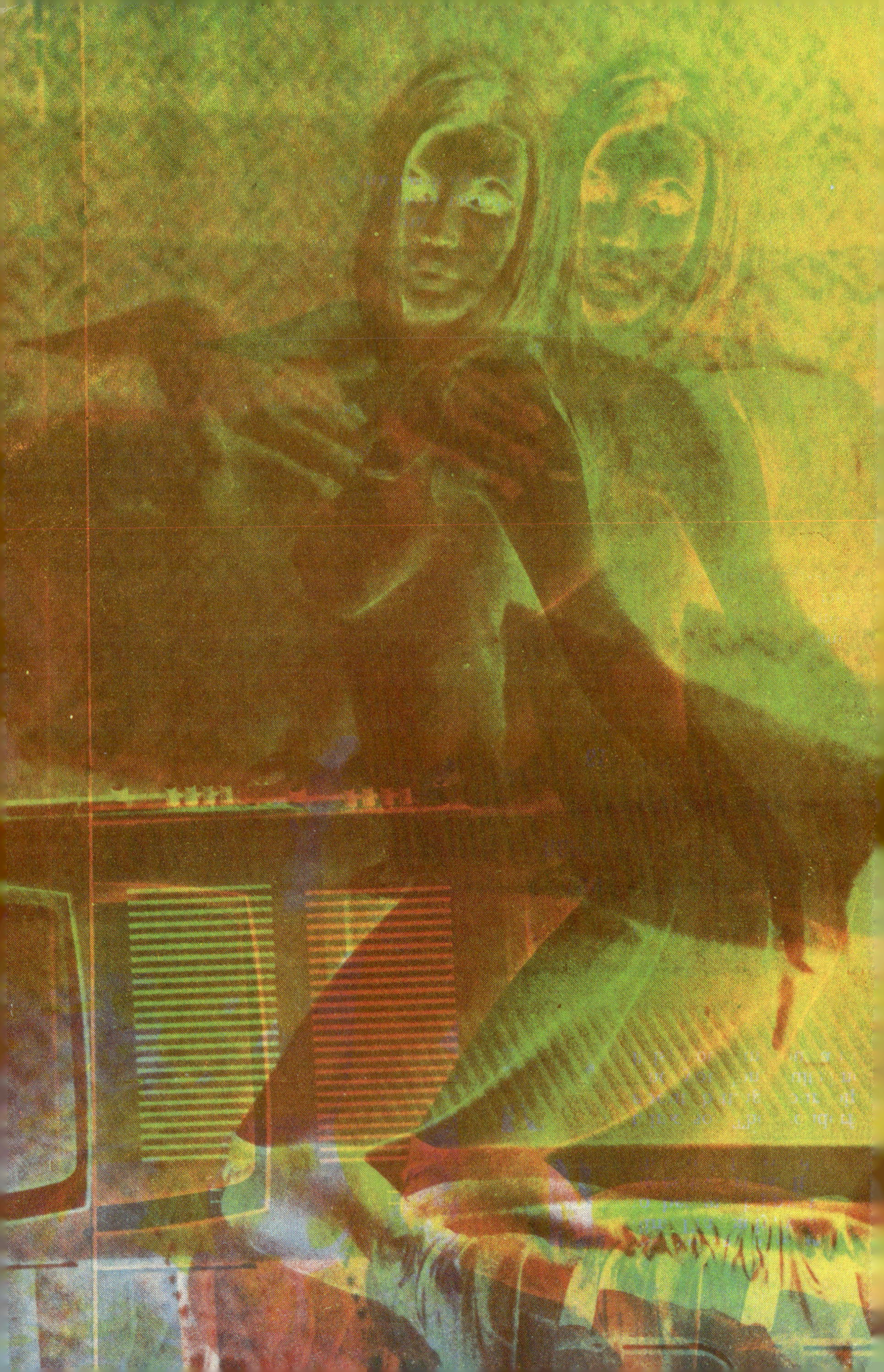

Robert Heinecken and the Art of Appropriation

Matthew Biro

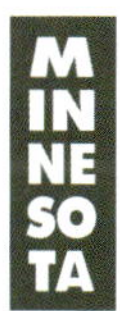

UNIVERSITY OF MINNESOTA PRESS

MINNEAPOLIS // LONDON

The University of Minnesota Press gratefully acknowledges the financial assistance provided for the publication of this book by the College of Literature, Science, and the Arts at the University of Michigan.

Cover art and frontispiece pages ii and vi: Robert Heinecken, *Mansmag: Homage to Werkman and Cavalcade* (1969). Offset lithography on bound paper, comprising 24 four-color lithographs (including covers recto and verso). 8 ¾ x 6 ⅝ inches (22.2 x 16.8 cm). Edition of 120, pages 11–12. Private collection. Copyright 2022 The Robert Heinecken Trust, Chicago.

Published by the University of Minnesota Press
111 Third Avenue South, Suite 290
Minneapolis, MN 55401–2520
http://www.upress.umn.edu

Cover and interior design by Frances Baca

ISBN 978-1-5179-0463-0 (hc)
ISBN 978-1-5179-0464-7 (pb)
Library of Congress record available at https://lccn.loc.gov/2021061644.

Printed in Canada on acid-free paper

The University of Minnesota is an equal-opportunity educator and employer.

28 27 26 25 24 23 22   10 9 8 7 6 5 4 3 2 1

To Bev

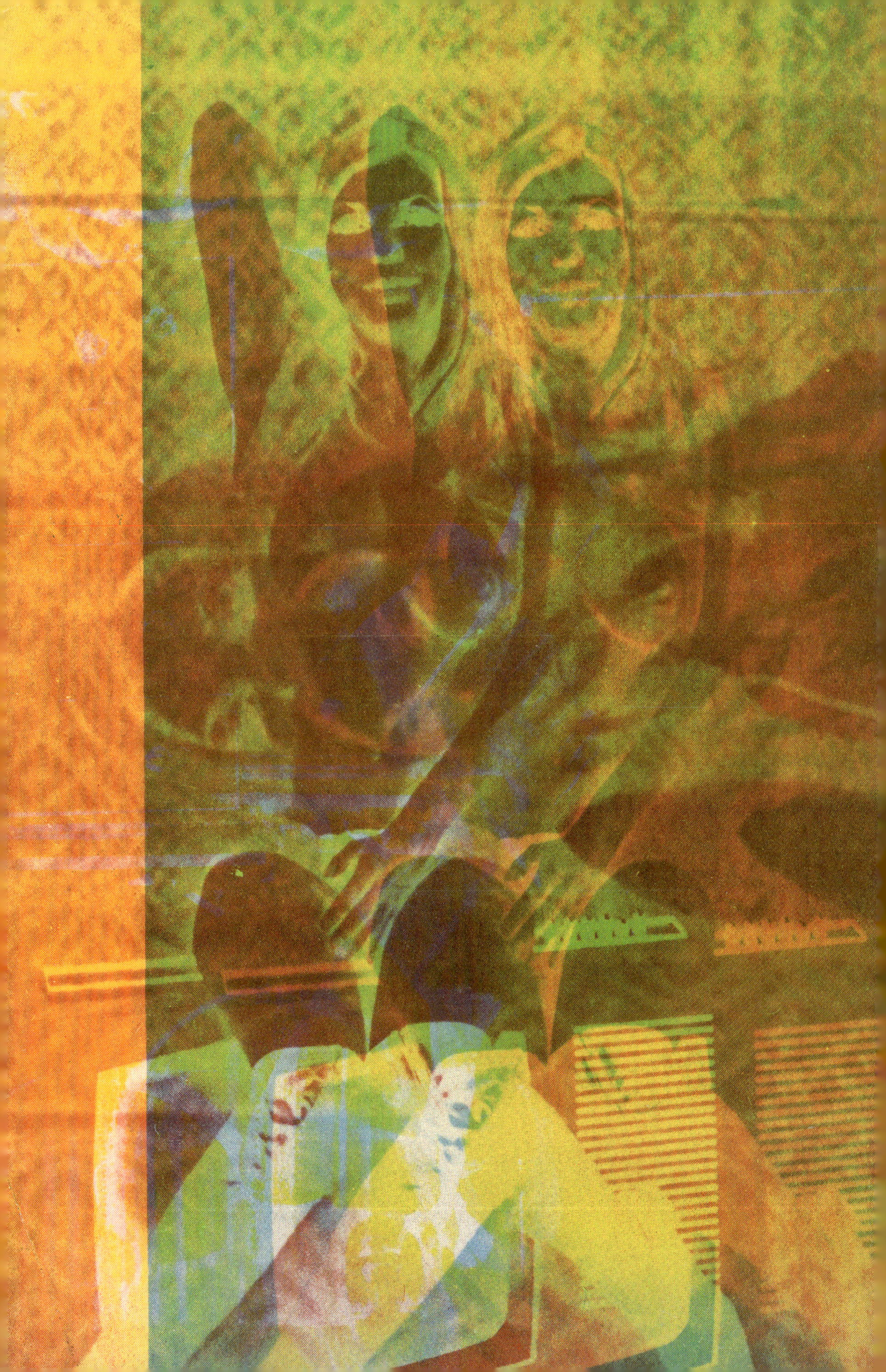

CONTENTS

Art, Photography, and the Consumption of Identity

This book considers the work of Robert Heinecken, the American artist active in Los Angeles and Chicago between the late 1950s and the late 1990s. Although most closely associated with the photogram technique and with photography, Heinecken (1931–2006) worked in a variety of media from (photographically derived) painting and sculpture to collage, installation, performance, and time-based work with TVs and slide projectors. He also consistently created artist's books, works that explored the systems of representation in which he existed. As a result, his creative activities speak to central issues in the evolution of contemporary art since the 1960s, most notably, its increasing hybridization and conceptual character as well as its focus on cultural critique and the mass media. Almost exclusively, Heinecken appropriated—rephotographed or otherwise reproduced—images rather than shooting them directly from life; and his work was concerned with consumer ideologies and how individual and collective identities were constructed through the press, television, and advertising.

Despite the fact that he made work that was consciously in dialogue with the history of twentieth-century avant-garde art and the tradition of postwar neo–avant-garde practices that it engendered, Heinecken was identified with the medium of photography, a classification that subsequently limited his recognition during his lifetime. Before the 1980s, as A. D. Coleman has argued, art photography and contemporary art existed in largely separate worlds in the United States and Europe in terms of exhibitions, criticism, and the market.[1] Even during the 1960s and 1970s, highly acclaimed photographers were not held in the same regard as highly acclaimed painters or sculptors, or even the new forms of "post-studio" (land, performance, or conceptual) artists that emerged then. Although photography was becoming more and more a part of contemporary art (a trajectory that stretched back to the historical avant-garde since the second decade of the twentieth century), advanced art photography in the 1950s and 1960s was largely "straight" and formalist. Artistic photography was thus anti-appropriationist and of little interest to contemporary artists who used photography in relation to other media or the critics and historians who wrote about them.[2] Only with the rise of postmodernism and such breakthrough figures as Cindy Sherman, Richard Prince, and Barbara Kruger could an artist work primarily as a photographer and be accepted as an artist first as opposed to an "art photographer."[3] This latter condition, unfortunately, was Heinecken's fate, despite the fact that he did not for the most part produce traditional types of art photographs.[4] Because he was identified with a medium that was still considered secondary by the American art world before the late 1970s, his achievements were easy to dismiss or ignore.

Although he was viewed with some suspicion in the photography world during the second half of his career, it is important to recognize what an innovator Heinecken was when compared to the dominant practitioners of the medium at the time he began working. First and foremost, he developed a practice that was radically distinct from the then-ascendant modes of "straight photography" that had emerged in art photography beginning in the teens. Straight photographers like Paul Strand and Edward Steichen, and, slightly later, Edward Weston, Ansel Adams, Imogen Cunningham, and others on the West Cost, practiced a type of modernist photography that stressed in equal measures the truth of the (represented) subject and the truth of the medium.[5] Straight photography emerged as a response to pictorialism, the photographic movement centered around Alfred Stieglitz in the late nineteenth and early twentieth centuries: a circle of creative practitioners who used the disruption of photographic realism as means of conveying an artistic impression as well as the photographer's subjectivity. By way of contrast, straight photographers wanted to capture their world in a way that emphasized the objectivity and surface qualities of the subject or thing represented; and they did so through medium-specific properties of photographic realism such as detail, clarity, contrast, depth of field, fine grain, a wide tonal range, and a smooth black-and-white surface.[6] Committed—like the pictorialists—to the role of the photographer as an artist, they avoided topicality or newsworthiness in what they chose to represent and instead pursued formal composition and craft as a means of creating a heightened awareness of vision, an awareness that was for them central to the artistic character of their photographs. Practiced in a "pure" and historically informed fashion, and no longer emulating other media like painting and literature, straight photography was understood to reveal the simultaneous truth of the object (a sense for the formal structure of the people and things depicted) and the truth of vision (a heightened self-consciousness about the intentionality of vision, its interpretive nature, and its specific relationship to the medium of photography).

Heinecken's appropriationist sensibility was very different from that of the modernist—and, in many ways, realist—straight photographers who emerged in the 1920s and whose ideas still dominated art photography in the 1960s. He rejected their emphasis on craft and the originality of the photographer's vision as encoded in the idea of previsualization.[7] And he disagreed with their belief that the truth of photography always began with objective inquiry, in the photographer's efforts to accurately represent the external world.[8] In addition, his art contained many characteristics that linked his practice to that of contemporaneous news and documentary photographers: an interest in topicality, world events, subject matter, and narrative, for example, as well as a choice of themes that tended toward the sensational.[9]

By the 1960s, documentary photography was very well established and diversified as both a concept and a set of practices. It extended from news and advertising photography and photojournalism, on the one hand, to the varied and more "personal" social documentary practices of figures like Walker Evans, Robert Frank, Diane Arbus, and Gary Winogrand, on the other.[10] Heinecken was in certain ways like Frank or Arbus in that he was focused on his contemporary society and he used photography to represent his world and its values in a critical light. But unlike Frank and Arbus, Heinecken understood that to be a documentarian did not mean that he had to remain tied to the physical world and the activity of moving through it in search of real people, settings, and events to record. Instead, aware of documentary's close ties to propaganda (where it was used to make falsehoods seem more credible), and of the photograph's ability to lie, Heinecken took the manufactured world of mass culture as his subject, using the medium of photography to critically analyze the ideologies inherent in the images to which he was most drawn. Although he rejected the realism of both straight photography and contemporary news and documentary photography, Heinecken was serious about recording his world and its social conditions.

The Corporeal and the Conceptual

As an appropriationist photographer, Heineken does not seem like an artist who would be interested in using his everyday life and biography—much less his mundane entertainments and diversions—as a springboard for more general critical representations. Heinecken, as we generally understand him, was primarily—as he called himself—a "photographist," an artist who used photographs and other photographic materials as opposed to an art photographer who took photographs to present a vision of the world.[11] A critical observer of society, he eschewed the camera and instead focused on common myths or stereotypes through the selection and transformative reproduction of preexisting images. He was the opposite of the straight photographers, who concentrated on their own subjective vision vis-à-vis a real (and objectively existing) world that their camera could capture. And he was also different from most documentary photographers, who, no matter how personal their vision, remained tied to the external world and the social or psychological manifestations that their cameras could uncover.

At the same time, although he generally avoided unmediated subjectivity and expressivity in his art, preferring to produce work that highlighted ideologies and systems, Heinecken intermittently but consistently used his own body and specific life experiences as content in his practice. He also more generally focused on his own predilections and tastes; the images that we see in Heinecken's work, in other words, are representations that he seemed to enjoy and collect. And because there is a highly pronounced corporeal—even sexual—character to Heineken's forms and iconography, his art seems expressive of straight male identity. Despite its conceptual character, it does not appear scientific or objective, and its subjects seem psychological and pleasure-seeking rather that philosophical, pertaining to the instincts rather than intellect. Suggestive of a particular point of view—a gaze that seemed both stereotypically male and intensely heterosexual—some of Heinecken's works were found by his audiences to be tremendously offensive.

"The most highly developed sensibility I have," Heinecken said in a famous interview, "is sexual, as opposed to intellectual or emotional."[12] And perhaps for this reason, from the very beginning of his career he maintained that the "figure, because of its human, erotic, sensual and psychological connections, remains my primary subject interest and is the vehicle for the formal content of the work."[13] Heineken's sexual sensibility often got him into trouble—in part because of the stereotypicality of the pornographic material that he appropriated, and in part because the figure on which he concentrated the most was the female one. Despite the fact that he also sometimes employed homosexual or gender-bending images (or manipulated his iconography to imply the same), his art projected an intensely male and heterosexual gaze for the vast majority of his audiences, and beginning in the 1970s, he began to be criticized for this despite his works' ironic and radically deconstructive aspects.

Already in 1979, while recognizing Heinecken's affinities to the "structuralist" approach of postmodern photography in New York, photographer and critic Martha Rosler reduced his work to mere "pussy porn," marketed by prominent photography galleries.[14] This appellation, although later dropped from Rosler's text, has, as Colin Westerbeck notes, "probably done more than anything else to bias an entire generation against Heinecken's work."[15] In 1983, curator and critic Carol Squiers developed

Rosler's characterization, arguing that Heinecken was a reactionary and pornographic photographer in a revolutionary guise—an argument that would soon be articulated by Allan Sekula as well. As Squiers put it, Heinecken "reproduced pornographic imagery for a middle-class gallery audience, which in that context could be taken as critical commentary while it reaped the benefits of titillating, aestheticized display. Thus he could capitalize on the stimulation value while appearing to perform the revolutionary actions of bringing forbidden subject matter into the gallery and challenging the conventions of good photography at the same time."[16] As a result, since the 1980s, Heinecken's work caused heated discussion in photography circles and beyond. As Mark Alice Durant noted in 2003:

> There are few artist/educators of his stature who have so thoroughly balanced the public and private responsibilities of those roles, yet he still endures critical ridicule. In 1992, Heinecken was chosen "Honored Educator" by the Society for Photographic Education at its national conference held that year in Washington, DC. In a scathing *Afterimage* review of the entire conference, the writer singled out this gesture towards Heinecken's academic career as a symbol of all that was wrong with the conference in particular and the organization in general. Referring to Heinecken as a "misogynist photographer," the writer reported on the "disappointment and disgust" expressed by the Women's Caucus of SPE at Heinecken's selection. I later asked him how he felt about this personal attack. He replied that he did not know whether to be more insulted at being called a "misogynist" or a "photographer."[17]

Both the attack and the response were typical for Heinecken. He was accused of affirming ideologies he purported to criticize, and he refused to disagree, preferring instead to articulate a response that encouraged further dialogue and inquiry.[18]

For photographers like Durant, who were influenced by Heinecken in the 1970s, there was "something fundamentally performative about Heinecken's persona. He excelled in playing various "masculine" roles: the military man, the family man, the artist bohemian, the hippie hedonist, the paternal professor, the bastard boyfriend, the barroom philosopher. His artwork was equally staged, taking on provocative roles in opposition to generally accepted guidelines of proper photographic art."[19] Heinecken could serve as a lightning rod for feminist—and other forms of political—critique in part because he performed his masculinity so overtly and thus seemed so tightly identified with his male-gaze-type subjects. But this critique ignored Heinecken's appropriations that did not fit the artist-as-pornographer role, nor did it acknowledge the fact that Heinecken's response to criticism was to direct attention back to the connections that his work made between the photographic medium and the construction of human sexual desire. Although he admitted to not being able to assess the ultimate value of his porn-based output, Heinecken felt compelled to explore the genre.[20] And although it may be uncomfortable to confront, part of the importance of Heinecken's art lies in the light it shines on the ways in which lens-based technologies and mass reproduction transformed human sexuality between the 1960s and the 1990s.

While it is important to acknowledge the problematic messiness of Heinecken's art, its corporeal and libidinal side, we cannot simultaneously ignore his consistent conceptualism: his predilection for ideas, systems, and language, which, like many West and East Coast artists of his generation, Heinecken inherited from Dada and surrealism. Heinecken was always very analytical when speaking or writing about his art, and he favored avant-garde strategies like chance, appropriation, and montage because they allowed him to ask sociological and anthropological questions of his culture. Similarly, like many avant-gardists he loved humor, in part because it allowed him to adopt a critical stance to his subjects.

Summarizing the general tendencies of his art, he wrote:

> I am interested in what I term gestalts; picture circumstances which
> bring together disparate images or ideas so as to form new meanings
> and new configurations. Often this involves the integration of words and
> typographic elements. In this vein, it is the incongruous, the ironic and the
> satirical which interest me, particularly in socio/political or sexual/erotic
> contexts. I sometimes visualize myself as a bizarre guerrilla, investing in
> a kind of humorous warfare in which a series of minimal, direct, invented
> acts result in a maximum extrinsic effect, but without consistent rationale.
> I might liken it to the intention of making police photographs in which
> there is no crime involved—but with that assumption.[21]

An artist who used media technologies for political, ironic, and conceptual purposes, Heinecken rephotographed the male gaze—and U.S. culture more generally—like the scene of a crime.

The Evolution of the Hair of the Artist as Aviator

Since its advent, one of the central questions attending the photograph was whether it was a document or art or something in between. And in many ways, Heinecken's importance lies in how complexly he engaged with this question, exploring the photograph as a simultaneous emanation of the real and as a vehicle of expression, representation (in the sense of symbolization or allegorization), and ideology. This complexity is prominently on display, for example, in *The Evolution of the Hair of the*

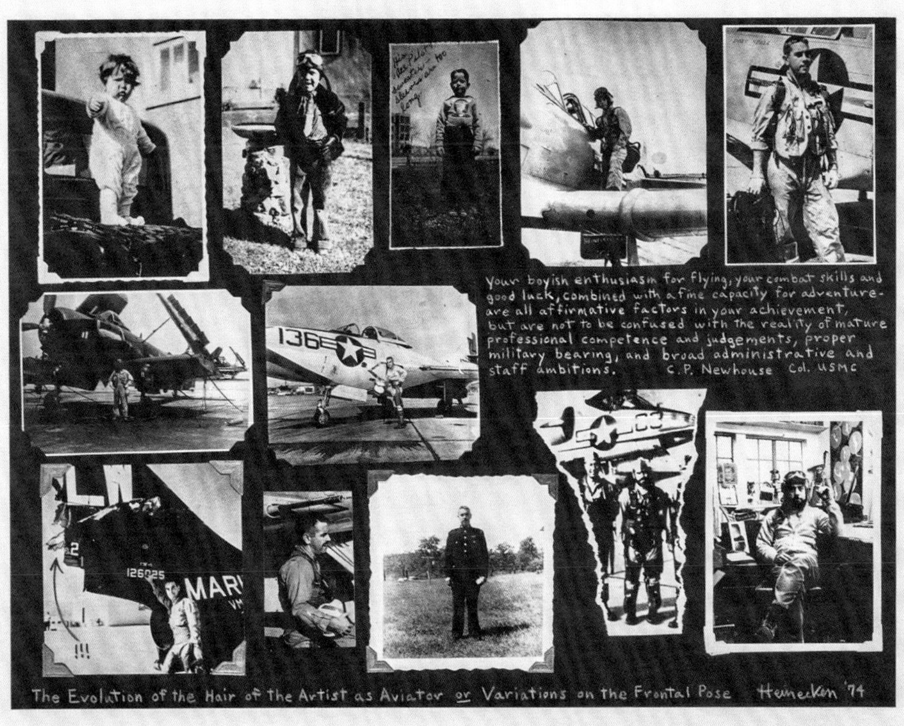

PLATE I.1. Robert Heinecken, *The Evolution of the Hair of the Artist as Aviator or Variations on the Frontal Pose* (1974), from the *Colors* portfolio (1975). Offset lithograph, 13 ⅞ x 17 ⅛ inches (35.24 x 43.5 cm); image on paper of 16 x 20 inches (40.64 x 50.8 cm). Private collection. COPYRIGHT 2022 THE ROBERT HEINECKEN TRUST, CHICAGO.

Artist as Aviator or Variations on the Frontal Pose, a work that exists in multiple forms, including the original collage of twelve gelatin silver prints on board with handwriting, an edition of offset lithographs, and an edition of gelatin silver prints with an internal dye-diffusion transfer (Polaroid SX-70) print adhered, all made in 1974 (Plate I.1).[22]

As suggested by the title, the three tight irregular rows of snapshots all represent the artist at various stages of his life from toddlerhood to his early forties, and they document Heinecken's longstanding engagement with aviation. The first three images show Heinecken as a boy and suggest an enduring interest in flight and the military, a message conveyed by the uniforms he wears as well as his outstretched arms in the first picture. The majority of the images represent the artist when he was a Marine pilot between 1953 and 1957. In this chronological grouping, we see him in a flight suit and standing in front of the jets he flew, often holding his body with rigid military bearing. The last image shows Heinecken as an artist in his Los Angeles studio in the early 1970s. Although he is relaxed and bearded, the aviator's cap that he wears suggests a continuing identification with the role of the pilot.

Upon initial examination, *The Evolution of the Hair of the Artist as Aviator* seems to possess a strong amateur documentary character. As a whole, the assemblage of images suggests a page in a photographic scrapbook, one of the classic formats that people traditionally used to create visual records of their lives in the nineteenth and twentieth centuries. Many of the photographs are mounted with photo corners, and as is common in photographic scrapbooks, text is used to identify and explain the images. The work is documentary in that the juxtaposed images seem to accurately depict different moments in Heinecken's life, revealing what he looked like, how he carried himself, as well as something of his class position and the institutions of which he was a part. The work is also documentary in that it seems to reproduce an official military text evaluating Heinecken during his service in the Marines. A handwritten paragraph, sandwiched between the top and bottom rows of photographs on the right-hand side of the image, suggests an official performance evaluation from a superior officer: "Your boyish enthusiasm for flying, your combat skills and good luck, combined with a fine capacity for adventure—are all affirmative factors in your achievement, but are not to be confused with the reality of mature professional competence and judgments, proper military bearing, and broad administrative and staff ambitions. C. P. Newhouse Col. USMC." Because it is somewhat critical, Colonel Newhouse's evaluation is not the type of text that people would typically put in their scrapbooks. In the context of Heinecken's life and the professional choices that he made, the citation makes sense, since the evaluation seems to describe personality traits that suit an artist more than a career military man.

Heinecken spoke prolifically about his life and its relationship to his art, and in the context of his biography, *Evolution,* created in the year that the artist turned forty-three, depicts his journey from childhood to mature adulthood. As we learn from his massive, two-volume autobiographical narrative, produced under the auspices of UCLA's Oral History Program, the question of masculinity loomed large in his development. Robert Friedli Heinecken was born on October 29, 1931, in Denver, Colorado, to Friedli Wilhelm Heinecken, an itinerant Lutheran minister, and his wife, Mathilda (Moehl) Heinecken.[23] When Robert was eight, his father left the family, running away with a woman from his congregation to live in the South Pacific, where he worked as a civilian contractor for the U.S. military. Three years later, in 1942, Friedli reunited with the family he abandoned, remarried Robert's mother, and moved everyone to Riverside, California, where Heinecken spent his adolescent years. Although he was recognized as bright and talented in writing and drawing since a very early age, Heinecken did not do well in school, perhaps because of his conflicted relationship to his father; his early college experiences at

Riverside Junior College and UCLA between 1949 and 1952 were marred by inconsistency and some failures.[24] In addition, despite his father's religious occupation, Heinecken decided he was not religious, and although he continued to attend his father's church while living at home, he was adamant about his atheism. Heinecken's developmental years thus display ambivalence about his own goals and abilities as well as the role that his father's example should play in his life.

In early 1953, while facing expulsion from UCLA and the loss of his student deferment, Heinecken took a test to become a Marine Corps pilot and was accepted into the program. He was on active duty between 1953 and 1957 and in the reserves until 1966. During this time he got married to his high school sweetheart, Janet Storey, and started a family.[25] Their twin children, Geoffrey and Kathe, were born in 1955, and their youngest daughter, Karol, was born in 1959.[26] Heineken credited becoming an aviator with helping him overcome his early aimlessness and recklessness and learning to live a more confident and directed life: it gave him a value system. Perhaps even more important, it seemed to allow him to transcend his fears about forming a traditional American family and forging a path in life. After leaving active duty, he returned to UCLA, earning his BA in art in 1959 and his MA in 1960, with a thesis on graphic design.[27] In light of this biographical history, *Evolution* seems to matter-of-factly depict the formative years of Heinecken's life before he became an artist.

Despite its documentary character, *Evolution* is also an artwork. Its artistic nature is conveyed by the features that mark it as different from the norm: its semicritical caption, the long span of time covered by the personal photographs (which seems too broad for a typical scrapbook layout), and the formally and tonally balanced arrangement of the work's variously shaped photographic elements. Furthermore, as a close examination of any of the three permutations of *Evolution* reveals, there is a carefully composed play between different levels of photographic representation in the work as a whole, a reflexivity that also marks the arrangement as art. In the collage, for example, many of the photo corners are mass reproduced (they are part of the photograph), while others are real, a contrast that emphasizes the heterogeneous nature of the photographic elements: some are original prints while others are copies. The lithograph deemphasizes this play slightly, but even here the spectator is made aware of differences between supposed originals and copies through the second-to-last image, which has noticeably fewer tonal values than the others, a sign of information being lost through photomechanical reproduction. Finally, in the gelatin silver print, a close-up SX-70 portrait of Heinecken is affixed to the photographic surface: a new, supposedly unique image of the artist is added to the work, although it too is a photograph of a photograph.[28]

With certain differences, *Evolution*'s title and its thematic selection of photographs evoke the typological and sociological concerns of U.S. conceptual art in the 1960s and 1970s, as exemplified by many of the mass-produced artist's books of Ed Ruscha as well as Dan Graham's *Homes for America,* a conceptual photo-text piece, which existed in multiple forms between 1965 and 1970.[29] Like these artworks, *Evolution* used photography and text in a deadpan and slightly ironic way to reveal general visual types—and by implication stereotypes—that supported the artist's everyday reality. While Ruscha and Graham focused their typological gaze on vernacular U.S. architecture, Heinecken concentrated on the human body. By disclosing the banal, seemingly mass-produced forms that governed distinct configurations of American society, Heinecken, like Ruscha and Graham, helped to shed light on the growing commodification of everyday life since the 1960s.[30]

As Heinecken's title spells out, two distinct characteristics are being compared in the artwork across time: the author's hairstyle as well as his enactment of a social convention, the striking of a specific pose for the camera. Hair is a primary attribute through which a person expresses his or her identity (in that it can be styled as a marker of gender, ethnicity, class, or subculture, for example), and Heinecken's juxtapositions of different haircuts and patterns of facial hair reveal their power as carriers of sexual, social, and political meaning.[31] Likewise, to pose for a picture is to construct oneself, to present oneself (more or less successfully) in terms of ideals with which one identifies.[32] Because of its slightly absurd (or, at least, particular) focus, however, it is clear that Heinecken's presentation of photographs and text is not scientific or even strictly autobiographical. Instead, as its title in conjunction with its formal self-reflexivity suggests, it is an artistic call to reflection on the ways in which technologies of mass reproduction both record and produce a sense of self. In light of Heinecken's family history, *Evolution* can be seen as tracing a series of masculine performances: Heinecken's varied self-presentations as he moved from boyhood emulations of real and imagined role models through different life stages, first as a military man and eventually as a countercultural artist.

Appropriation

Although *Evolution* used personal photographs, many of which were collected by Heinecken's mother, the rephotographed nature of a number of *Evolution*'s images reveals Heinecken's strategy of appropriation, which was nearly always a significant characteristic in his work. (Indeed, in comparison to the rest of his oeuvre, *Evolution* is decidedly more subtle in its appropriationist aspects.) As Heinecken understood it, appropriation was a strategy whereby he could construct a cultural critique; it was a type of process or working method by means of which he could sift through consumer culture and use his own tastes and predilections to examine the construction of postwar identity in the United States.

As a term for a set of related practices, *appropriation* has multiple meanings.[33] In the most literal sense, it denotes taking or copying something rather than making it oneself, actually acquiring it in some cases, or rephotographing it, or otherwise tracing an identifiable, culturally recognized source. Since the second decade of the twentieth century, appropriation has been a key strategy in contemporary art, first in the work of avant-garde artists like Marcel Duchamp and Hannah Höch, and later, after World War II, in the art of the neo–avant-garde, conceptual, and postmodern movements, not to mention today.

As exemplified by Duchamp's readymades *The Bicycle Wheel* (1913) and *Fountain* (1917), appropriation could be used to turn the mass-produced object into an auratic work of art, thereby revealing art's conceptual and institutional nature.[34] Shocking to their initial audiences, Duchamp's readymades—simple manufactured objects presented as works of art—reminded the spectator of how the creative act was a function of a larger network of relations between artist and beholder, and that it was mediated through institutions such as the press, museums, galleries, schools, and universities. By subverting an object's use value and insisting on its "art coefficient," its surplus or fetish value, defined by Duchamp as precisely that of which the artist was not aware and thus could not intend, the Duchampian readymade called on its audiences to reconceive art.[35] Now anything could be an artwork, simply because the artist chose, designated, or named it as such.

Duchamp's nominalization of art, his reduction of an object's art status to the artist saying it is such, undermined the longstanding notion of a hierarchy of the different aesthetic media (a hierarchy that placed painting and sculpture on the pinnacle). Art could be made from everything, and it did not require traditional skills of representation or craft. Violating all concepts of originality, authenticity, and uniqueness, it thus stood outside traditional criteria of aesthetic judgment such as taste and connoisseurship. The Duchampian readymade also called on its audiences to regard art as a commodity and thus to think about the work's legal definition and position in the marketplace. The Duchampian readymade was thus fundamentally nonpartisan: it equally supported left- and right-wing politics, because it projected a social and economic understanding of the work of art, an understanding that positioned the work in relation to questions of audience, value, influence, and development through the technologies of mass reproduction.

"If I had a hero," Heinecken said of Duchamp, "it would be him, as opposed to anybody else."[36] And he recognized the revolutionary nature of the readymade to rest on its destruction of modernism's traditional criteria of originality, style, and the artist's hand, and its revelation of the institutional context that allowed something to be perceived as art.[37] But Heinecken also noted his distance from the readymade concept: "I'm interested in that you see something, and you already know what it is, but it's been transformed in some way. It's not by the context of a gallery or an exhibition but by superimposition, making it negative, or altering it in some way. But you still know that it's something which hasn't been invented by me."[38] The point, for Heinecken, was for the spectator to recognize his Duchampian Dadaist gesture and its questioning of the nature of art, but also to engage with the artwork's status as a social document and the significance of what it represented. For this reason, contrary to Craig Owens's definition of the term in his influential theory of postmodernism, *appropriation,* as it was employed in Heinecken's work, never entailed the full erasure of the appropriated object's original meaning or context.[39]

The Arbitrariness of the Visual

Picasso's *Still Life with Chair Caning,* the first cubist collage, presents another aspect of avant-garde appropriation—its acknowledgment of the arbitrary nature of visual signification, and the fact that, through avant-garde art, vision can be fragmented and recombined, and the optical field formed like language.[40] Although he never referred to Picasso or Cubism directly, this was another key insight on which Heinecken's work depended. With a very reduced color palette, Picasso's breakthrough mixed-media work depicts an ambiguous collection of objects on a table covered with a tablecloth. In the center we see what appears to be a wine glass, its contour traced as if the beholder is simultaneously viewing it from many angles. On the left a folded newspaper emerges from behind the glass, evoked by a black, gray, and white rectangular element (again with multiple outlines suggesting different viewing angles) along with the letters *Jou,* for "Journal," floating in front of it. Monochromatic forms that suggest a smoker's pipe appear to float against or through the newspaper and letters. Finally, on the right, painted outlines and shading imply a cut lemon, a knife, a piece of cake or a scallop shell on a plate (or a napkin with a scalloped edge), and a placemat as well as the side and front corner of what might be a sturdy table. Below the painted objects, which partially occlude it, an oilcloth appears. A cheap, mass-produced item that would commonly be used to cover a table, the oilcloth has an extremely realistic chair-caning pattern printed on it. Through its positioning, material, and motifs, it simultaneously evokes a tablecloth and a chair seat tucked below a glass table. Finally, a real mariner's rope—evoking a table's bumper—serves to frame the composition, delimiting the visual field as well as echoing elements within it.

As suggested by this cubist collage, Picasso used appropriation, not to fully subvert the tradition of art and representation up until that point as did Duchamp, but rather to further multiply the signifying systems through which he constructed his (in certain ways still traditional) representation. Beginning in 1908, Picasso, along with Georges Braque, started to break down the tradition of realistic representation in the West through a form of painting retroactively termed *analytic cubism*.[41] Their visual interrogation of realistic representation since the Renaissance proceeded through a painterly dialogue that progressively flattened the picture space, reduced the color palette, blended solid with void, separated contour from shading, multiplied light sources, and introduced written language into the painterly field. Becoming more and more complex, analytic cubism fostered an attentiveness in its viewers to the medium of painting and to the conventions of representation, all the while maintaining semirecognizable images of the external world in the forms of portraits and still lifes. Traditional genres of painting were evoked to demonstrate the painter's radical departure from all conventions of realistic depiction, while at the same time the artworks engendered an awareness of how human vision assembles disparate optical elements into unities based on previously learned and commonly held expectations.

Still Life with Chair Caning marked the shift to cubism's so-called "synthetic" phase, where instead of analyzing vision, Picasso and Braque constructed images of the world that included elements that formerly possessed completely different identities. As we see in Picasso's *papier collés*, appropriation was used to increase the play between different types of representation. Analytic cubism already undermined the primary conventions of visual depiction—the distinctions between figure and ground, line and color, solid and void, plane and recession, openness and closure—and added language or writing, a radically distinct mode of signification, to painting. It remained for synthetic cubism, however, to introduce real-world objects, something that Picasso often did in ways that contradicted their original identities. As Rosalind Krauss, Yve-Alain Bois, and others have subsequently argued, this meant that synthetic cubism introduced a diacritical or semiological understanding of signification into art, a sense that the meaning of a work was always the function of a network of differences, a relationship between everything that appears and other possibilities existing in the common culture that had not been chosen. For this reason, elements in cubist collages often played multiple roles: the same newspaper collage element, for example, could simultaneously represent a bottle, depth, and reflection. In addition, elements often also signified their opposite: depth was communicated by the flattest elements in the artwork, or "atmosphere" and "luminosity" by the elements that were the most solid and least transparent. As a result, for the first time in modern art "a metalanguage of the visual" was presented.[42]

The cubists, however, never carried out the radical implications of their appropriative strategies. Neither Picasso nor Braque renounced representation completely to embrace full abstraction; as William Rubin points out, unlike later forms of collage, the *papier collés* were in certain ways still "governed by the classical principle of the unity of medium."[43] Appropriation, in Picasso's case, brought the real into the domain of art, revealing how everyday life could be cut, pasted, and become part of new representations. It remained for Duchamp to use the strategy to radically break with the tradition of Western art itself and its dominant conventions of realistic (and even quasi-abstract) representation, its hierarchy of media, and its reliance on forms of skill and craft that needed to be learned and mastered. Likewise, it remained for the Dadaists and the surrealists to develop the implications of collage and montage, a related practice that emerges in conjunction with most, if not all, methods of appropriation.

Like cubist painting, Heinecken's photo-based artworks rely on the arbitrariness of the visual. Particularly in his photograms and other works that superimpose images with text, different formal elements play multiple representational roles, and we get a sense that what we see depends on a network of oppositions that remains outside or on the margins of what is apparent. It is this sense of visual play, not unlike the movement of linguistic *différance* analyzed by Jacques Derrida and others, that gives many of Heinecken's works their uncanny sense of constant change and metamorphosis. In addition, as we shall see, Heinecken's art also benefited in other ways from cubism's linkage of the visual with the textual. This linkage acknowledged not only the fact that the visible environment was becoming more and more superimposed with text but also the idea that photography was helping people to dissect and reconfigure the visible world, allowing it to function more like a written language. This insight, implicit in cubism and made much more overt in Dadaism and surrealism, would be developed and elaborated in radically new ways in Heinecken's art.

Montage

If the act of appropriation forms a kind of "cut," a taking of a piece of something that already exists and separating it from its original context, then montage—the joining of at least two different elements together into a new formal configuration—emerges as an essential second step after nearly every appropriative act. Having studied the histories of art and photography in graduate school in California, Heinecken was well aware—already early in his career—of Dadaist and surrealist art.[44] Dada art, as he understood it, was a particularly important source of precedents or exemplars: artworks and other forms of cultural production that exemplified the range of signifying strategies that different types of montage could create.[45] Between the First and Second World Wars, Hannah Höch, John Heartfield, Man Ray, and others explored various methods of combining preexisting elements from radically different orders of reality, suturing together fragmentary representations of the real (photographic depictions of people, nature, and everyday life) with symbolic elements drawn from mass culture (printed texts, collective emblems, common phrases, and logos), sometimes also adding real objects as well as overlays created through traditional modes of art-making (e.g., painting, drawing, lithography, and the like). Through a wide variety of photographic media, they demonstrated how reality could be analyzed and shaped like a language; montage, as they practiced it, became a highly effective means of bringing social and political content into art as well as everyday life.

As the Dada artists and their contemporaneous audiences realized early on, montage could be oriented in constructive as well as deconstructive directions. On the one hand, as suggested by the early (all-over) compositional forms of Berlin Dada photomontage, such as Hannah Höch's *Cut with the Kitchen Knife Dada through the Last Weimar Beer-Belly Cultural Epoch of Germany* (1919–20) or George Grosz and John Heartfield's *Life and Work in Universal City, 12:05 Noon* (1919), the artist could create a fairly open-ended conjoining of elements, a suturing of disparate materials that supported multiple meanings that alternate depending on the viewer's specific focus. Because these works were packed with a multitude of different recognizable objects, and their constellations of elements permitted so many divergent selections or groupings, they could confirm a multiplicity of distinct, sometimes conflicting readings, something that was also the case with Berlin Dada assemblage. Furthermore, because they were so obviously edited and reassembled, these photomontages and found-object sculptures could induce their spectators to go beyond the mere identification and cataloging of visual and textual fragments, impelling them to develop overarching interpretations that elucidated the artist's possible positions vis-à-vis his or her various subjects. Viewers treated these montage-based works, in other words, as rich artistic statements, messages that needed to be completed in the minds of their beholders.

In addition to being deconstructive, promulgating conflicting lines of interpretation, Dadaist photomontage and assemblage also demonstrated that the conceptual order did not exhaust the beings and objects it subsumed. By combining visual and textual fragments so as to produce ambiguity, these works promoted the belief that the real world could not be reduced to the status of a photographic, sculptural, or written representation. In other words, by creating conflicting chains of metaphoric association that precluded the establishment of a single dominant reading, the incisive juxtapositions of the Dada artists preserved nature's difference from all forms of material representation. Since the visual and textual elements did not go together seamlessly or form well-known concepts or objects, it was difficult for the works' various beholders to think about their conjunctions of elements apart from the conflicting particulars they represented. Thereby, the richness and opacity of reality were retained—an experience of the world as necessarily surpassing the various characterizations and classifications that human beings projected on it.

While Dadaist montage strategies attempted to create a nonhierarchical relationship between elements that actively undermined any single reading or overarching interpretation, both the commercial and the communist photomontage artists that emerged after the Dada artists took another tack. Instead of promoting a plethora of equally valid (and divergent) readings, they toned down the inherent dissonance of photomontage and instead organized the work's elements so as to promote a much simpler and more identifiable message. Although they did not get rid of ambiguity and secondary readings altogether, they tended to subordinate these characteristics in favor of clarity and the repetition of a central message. Like the Dadaists, they cut and recombined elements of reality to envision their lives anew, but their representations juxtaposed image and text in ways that reinforced one another and sought support in their viewers' common concepts and expectations.[46]

This more constructive form of montage can be seen, for example, in John Heartfield's black, white, and gold book cover design for *So macht man Dollars* (1931), the German translation of Upton Sinclair's *Mountain City*, originally published in 1930 (Plate I.2). Sinclair's book was a muckraking novel that criticized American capitalism through a main character, Jed Rusher, who will do anything to get rich. Heartfield communicates Rusher's dog-eat-dog rise to the top of the oil business through the central symbol on the front cover: a very solid-looking gold dollar sign on which three men climb. The lower two figures appear to be middle-class businessmen of different ages (the younger man is situated below the older one), while the figure on top seems of a higher economic level. Thus the capitalist drive to accumulate more and more wealth is made literal

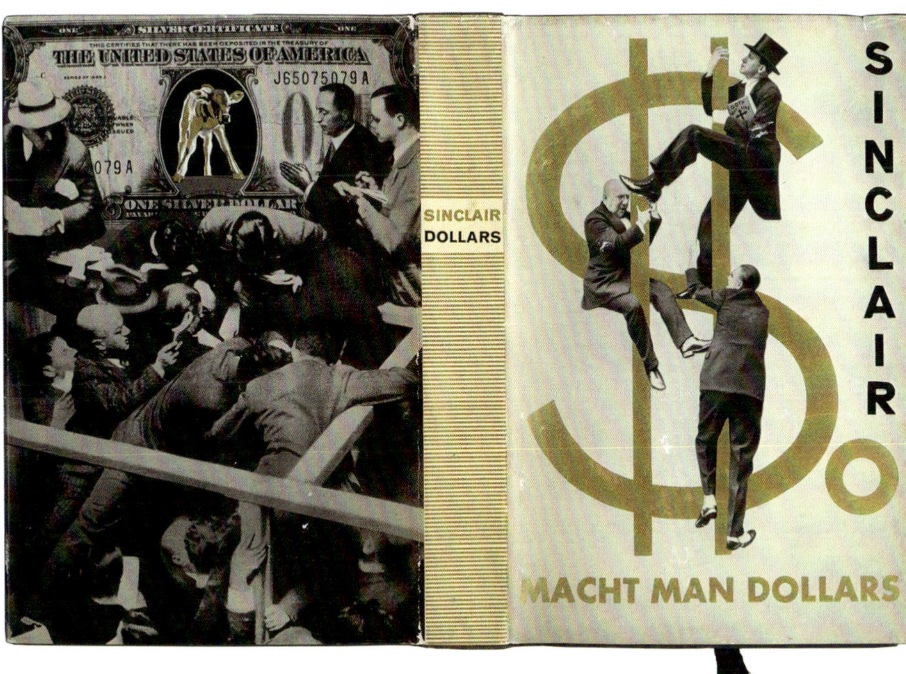

PLATE I.2. John Heartfield, dust jacket for the German translation of Upton Sinclair's *Mountain City, So macht man Dollars* (Berlin: Malik, 1931). Coated color paper, 5 x 15 inches (12.7 x 38.1 cm). Sammlung Jürgen und Waltraud Holstein, Berlin. COPYRIGHT THE HEARTFIELD COMMUNITY OF HEIRS / ARTISTS RIGHTS SOCIETY (ARS), NEW YORK / VG BILD-KUNST, BONN 2022.

through the depiction of an ascent that seems to take into account commonly accepted differences that have to do with both age and class.

The dollar sign does double duty in the book's overall design: in addition to serving as an object on which different men climb, it also forms the initial letter of the German title (the *S* in "So"), which was not a literal translation of the original English but, rather, a statement of the socialist book's major theme, "How to Make Dollars." As an image of a dollar sign, the *S* seems solid, since it appears as a scaffolding or structure on which men battle one another to ascend. When read as a letter, the form seems more ethereal, part of another realm that communicates an additional meaning. *So* is a complex word, having multiple meanings in German. As it is used on the cover, its meaning is probably closest to "thus" or "in this way," and as a result it functions as a shifter in Roman Jakobson's sense of the term: namely, as an "indexical symbol," a word that refers to a conventional meaning assigned to it by the linguistic code of which it is a part as well as to the specific message or utterance in which it functions (its specific speech context, in other words).[47] Operating as a hinge between the visual and the linguistic (a form that simultaneously indicates two different media of communication), the hybrid first word of the title refers to the image of the struggling men that surrounds it as well as to the novel's narrative as a whole. It suggests that this is how one makes money: by stepping on, climbing over, grabbing at, and ultimately overcoming one another. Finally, the dollar sign as *S* also mirrors the first letter of the author's last name, thus functioning as a brand or logo for Sinclair, whose full name is spelled out to the left of the front cover image and on the book's spine.

The back cover features a dollar bill with a golden calf superimposed directly over the portrait of George Washington. Money, Heartfield suggests through a series of cuts and splices, has become a false idol. A praying man and a reporter frame the bill on the right, while on the left a seemingly more sinister character, a stock speculator or a gambler (as suggested by the paper in his hands), turns away from the professional men's gaze. These figures evoke Heartfield's contemporary world and reveal different institutions—the church, the stock market, and the modern mass media—that are involved in different ways in the overall flow of capital. A scrum of men pushing one another within the confines of a set of rails appears below the bill and its attendant figures, echoing the battle of the three men on the front of the dust jacket. While the rails evoke the constraints of the modern bureaucratized world, the scrum, viewed from slightly above, evokes a Hobbesian war of all against all as well as— because of the figures that look down on it from above—a spectator sport. Overall, the complexity of Heartfield's photomontage is staggering, particularly since it continues to project a fairly clear message about the novel's main subject.

Postmodernism in the 1980s

Weimar-era montage, in both its deconstructive and constructive forms, tended to be allegorical, that is, figurative, moralizing, and multireferential. As Walter Benjamin defined it in relation to German culture, Weimar allegory dealt with examples of moral development: lives lived and lost, decisive moments, and questions of choice. He called it violent and weakly redemptive to emphasize the tragic character of human nature and history, and he insisted that the systems of knowledge through which allegories were understood were always multiple and nonabsolute. Postwar montage exhibits similar traits, and its employment in Heinecken's work presents particularly vivid as well as varied examples of allegorical signification.

In the early 1980s, Craig Owens adopted the idea of Benjaminan allegory to stand for the fundamental characteristics of postmodern art. Along with Douglas Crimp, Owens developed an account of allegorical montage that has proven to be quite influential, despite its limitations. In Crimp's case, the concept evolved out of his analyses of the photographic practices of Troy Brauntuch, Jack Goldstein, Sherrie Levine, Richard Prince, and Cindy Sherman, among others, whose postmodernism was a result of their strategies of appropriation—their selection and reuse of preexisting images or styles drawn from both popular and high culture.[48] Such work, according to Crimp, was socially critical because it contradicted such bourgeois concepts as the unique personality (the self-made and self-aware subject), originality (the basis for art both as personal expression and as a marketable commodity), and the real (a stable world "out there," independent of representation). In addition, because it effaced the strict lines of demarcation that modern artists attempted to draw between fine art and mass culture, postmodern photography and other art practices also undermined modern art, in that they impaired modernism's attempt to create a separate and autonomous sphere of culture, one that remained aloof from the problems of everyday life. All photography, according to Crimp, was potentially disruptive of modernism when it entered the museum—since here photographs undermined the primacy of painting and sculpture, the "traditional" modernist media, thereby attacking modernism's essentialism and autonomy. But allegorical photographic montage was even more antimodernist, in that it indicated modernism's full incorporation by the mass media as well as a fundamental dissolution of its model of the subject.

Owens related all postmodern art—photographic as well as otherwise—even more directly to Walter Benjamin's theory of allegory,[49] which he connected to post–abstract expressionist art, in particular, minimalism, conceptual art, land art, performance, and certain developments in photography in the 1970s and 1980s.[50] Like Crimp, Owens believed that appropriation was central to the practice of postmodernism, a strategy that for him criticized the concept of "authoritative" meaning, the clear or univocal interpretation of any particular visual sign.[51] But the list of postmodern characteristics was also more complex for Owens than it was for Crimp. In particular, Owens connected postmodernism to site specificity (works that opened themselves up beyond their particular material structures by constructing a dialogue with their physical environments), impermanence (a type of artistic practice that criticized the notion of the uniqueness and autonomy of art), accumulation (works that appeared as collections of fragments, thus rejecting all ideas of overall structure or self-sufficiency), discursivity (the interplay of image and text), and hybridization (the mixing of multiple media and the refusal of the artist to specialize within a single mode of practice).[52] At the heart of postmodernism's "allegorical impulse," according to Owens, was a doubling of one text by another—a superimposition that did not create mere ambiguity, but rather diametrically opposed readings that opened the work up to an infinite play of meaning and contexts.[53] As a result, postmodern works problematized the activities of reference and signification, encouraging their viewers to reflect on the constructed and socially produced character of subjectivity, representation, and the real.

Although excluded from influential critical accounts of postmodern photography in the 1980s, Heinecken's work, as we shall see, engages complexly with the tradition of allegorical montage as it developed between the 1920s and the 1990s.[54] Paralleling Crimp and Owens, his work demonstrates allegorical photographic montage to be critical of the status quo—a practice that overturned traditional concepts of art, life, and human nature. In contrast to Owens's position, and closer to Benjamin's theory of allegory, Heinecken's appropriative montage did not necessarily replace the fragment's "original" meaning with an entirely new "supplemental" one. The photograph's documentary character was never completely obliterated in Heinecken's work. Instead, as will be demonstrated, Heinecken's photographic montages consistently inspire documentary or journalistic inquiry—which encourages the investigation of subject matter and the seeking of knowledge about the world—in conjunction with wild and abstract fantasy, a response that undermines clear stereotypes and strict oppositions. As Heinecken suggested, it is not only the deconstruction of ideology and institutional critique that artworks must inspire but also engagement with the production of identity in the libidinally charged, site-specific, and representationally mediated contexts of everyday life.

Surrealism

As Heinecken's work reminds us, a photograph is generally an abstraction of something real—an image that is both fact and fiction, a representation based on a person or thing that existed, but one that has also been filtered and changed, frozen in time, stripped of life and essential information, and as such capable of signifying just about anything. By playing between art and document, works like *Evolution* emphasize this fact, and accordingly, their importance for contemporary art since the 1970s lies in their ability to render the transformation and objectification of both people and the environment palpable.

Throughout his career, Heinecken was keenly aware of Dadaism and the tradition of montage between the 1910s and the 1960s.[55] Understanding the revolutionary nature of Duchamp's readymades, he admired the French artist's conceptual process, which could turn anything into art but which also remained identifiably Duchamp's, without resorting to what was for Heinecken the false unification of an identifiable visual style.[56]

Duchamp's model of the readymade, of selecting something in the world and calling it art, allowed Heinecken to explore photography as a primary medium for radical and self-reflexive aesthetic inquiry. From nearly the beginning of his career, Heinecken viewed photography through an awareness of the historical avant-garde, and he always practiced photography as a critical and montage-based art. And although Heinecken sometimes disavowed the term, Duchamp appears to have been the artist who best helped him understand the strategy of appropriation as a means to collapse the distinction between art and everyday life.[57] Moreover, like the cubists, Heinecken also seemed highly aware of the arbitrariness of the visual sign and the fact that montage allowed artists to reconfigure the world and structure it like a language. Forms, colors, even recognizable elements taken from reality could be used to simultaneously signify meanings that were completely different from their ordinary, commonly accepted ones, and the same image field could contain multiple configurations that would allow the spectator to see dissimilar realities superimposed. Cognizant of the complex tradition of photomontage, Heinecken also knew that montage could be used both constructively and deconstructively, either to reinforce conceptual stereotypes or to break them down through an interplay of conflicting interpretations.

Heinecken was furthermore highly aware of the relationship between photography and the human psyche, a relationship that the surrealists began to explore in the 1920s in relation to Sigmund Freud's and Georges Bataille's models of individual and collective identity. Like the Dadaists, the surrealists were social critics: they attacked (social, political, and artistic) opponents in their contemporary world, and they practiced a bohemian lifestyle that they hoped would become a harbinger of a new type of human existence. Unlike the Dadaists, the surrealists had more developed models of human identity. Some of them, under the influence of Freud, divided human identities into conscious and unconscious aspects, or they understood the individual along the lines of Freud's structural model as possessing an id, or instinctual side, an ego, or conscious and rational aspect, and a superego, or internalization of society's laws and stereotypes. Other surrealists, under the influence of Bataille, explored the individual as both evolved and base, calculating (economic) and suicidal.[58] Thus, the surrealists' attack on bourgeois morality was subtler than that of the Dadaists. It was more general and less directed at specific targets, more subterranean, and it used photography to address the viewer's unconscious and instinctual side by capturing everyday reality and rendering it uncanny.

The photomontage *Ingres's Violin* (1924) by the American Man Ray, then living and working in Paris, exemplifies many of the strategies that

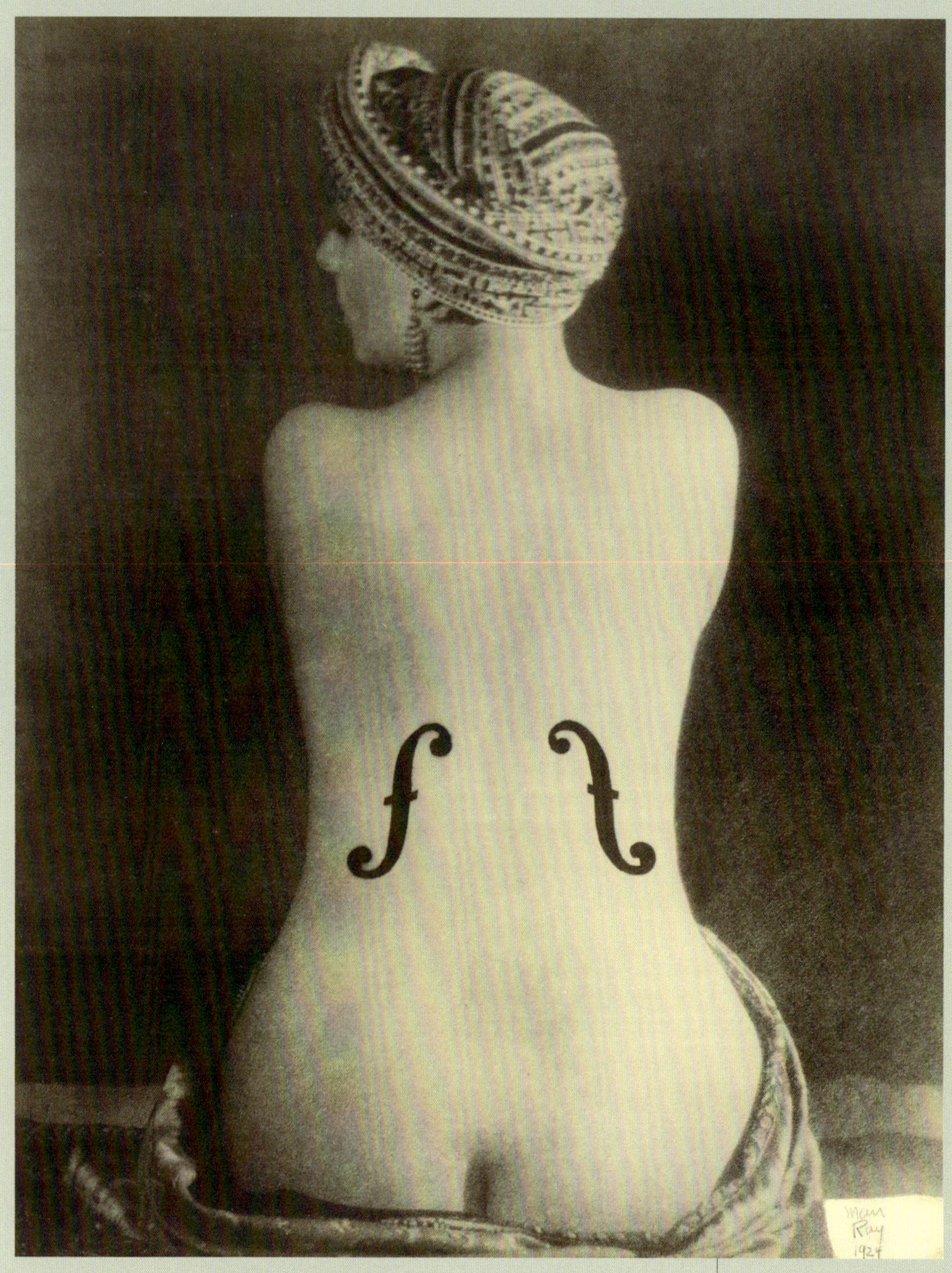

PLATE I.3. Man Ray, *Le Violon d'Ingres (Ingres's Violin)* (1924). Gelatin silver print, 11 ⅝ x 8 ¹⁵⁄₁₆ inches (29.53 x 22.7 cm). The J. Paul Getty Museum, Los Angeles. COPYRIGHT MAN RAY 2015 TRUST / ARTISTS RIGHTS SOCIETY (ARS), NY / ADAGP, PARIS 2022.

the surrealists used to evoke a sense of the uncanny (Plate I.3). Here we see a seminude young woman, wearing a turban and earrings, shot from behind, against a mostly dark background. Half-turning as if to meet the spectator's gaze, she presents her naked back to the viewer, covered only by a cloth that encircles her hips and buttocks. Two *f*-shaped lines, evoking the sound holes of a violin, are drawn in ink on her back. This gesture makes the work a photomontage, as well as a reference to cubism, and perhaps also to the breakthroughs that this earlier movement achieved in its merging of language with vision. Through its subject and motif (a racy and even quasi-pornographic harem scene), the photograph also refers to French orientalist history painting, for example, that of Jean-Auguste-Dominique Ingres, whom Man Ray cites in his title.

The photomontage's self-reflexive references to the history of art emphasize the work's position vis-à-vis modernist and avant-garde art: its allegiances to Ingres, Picasso, and Duchamp, as well as its differences from them. *Ingres's Violin* also addresses the spectator's body through a combination of eroticism and violence, which, through iconography and implied narrative, it joins with political issues such as French colonialism and sexual inequality. The young, attractive, and nearly nude body of the model, Kiki de Montparnasse (Alice Prin), is presented as a beautiful object to be consumed. Symmetrically framed against a blanket, she appears as an idealized image drawn from a colonial male sexual fantasy. Available and unresisting, she titillates, and in this regard the artwork is like contemporaneous pornography, most particularly, the colonial postcards of women and harem scenes taken in French Algeria.[59] Like these pornographic works, the model is positioned in a way that invites the spectator to look: a posture of display that does not challenge the gaze of the onlooker. At the same time, the *f*-shaped sound holes suggest cuts or gouges in her flesh and thus horrific violence. They magically turn her body into another object and thus make her seem hollow and doll-like, both living and dead.

Very importantly, the violence of the image cuts both ways. The woman is violated, but as she appears in the photomontage she also is alive and monstrous and, as such, a figure that threatens the patriarchal male gaze behind most pornography, a mode of looking that seeks to objectify that which it regards. The image also destabilizes the everyday reality conveyed through the photographic process by combining multiple time periods: a romanticized colonial past of the nineteenth century and the much rawer (but still colonial) contemporary moment, as suggested by the woman's bobbed haircut peeking out from below her turban. Even the dark blanket at which she stares—identifiable as such by a white band that runs behind her hips—creates an inexplicable and disturbing overtone by suggesting childhood punishment: a scenario in which a misbehaving young person is forced to sit and face a wall for an extended period of time.

This conflation of sexuality and violence in Man Ray's photomontage, as well as its mixing of the present with the past, and its evoking of childhood experiences, was intended to produce a sense of uncanniness. In Freud's famous conceptualization, the uncanny was a mental state in which the familiar and the unfamiliar were combined. We experience something as uncanny when we have doubts about whether it is alive or dead, as is the case with wax-work figures, dolls, and automatons, or in confrontations with mechanical processes, which because of their purposeful animation or some other quality seem somehow alive, yet also irreducibly alien.[60] Epileptic seizures and manifestations of insanity could also produce a sense of the uncanny, as did anything that evoked fundamental fears from childhood or anxieties about sexuality.[61] The uncanny created a sense of mental breakdown, of the dissolution of a stable sense of self.[62] For this reason, the double was a primary figure of uncanniness; this mental state could be given visual form through mirrors and shadows, shades that evoked the paranormal and witchcraft, and signs that conjured up the experience of death.[63]

Fundamentally, the uncanny marked the return of an atavistic attitude in modern life, a sense that the ordinary, secular, and rationalized world was pervaded by nonhuman intentions and ghostly forces. Through uncanny experiences, the individual was made aware of repressed fears and desires, unconscious material drawn from both the individual and the collective past.[64] The uncanny was thus a bridge to our forgotten childhoods as well as to vestiges of a primitive mind.[65] Most characteristically, the uncanny marked the reappearance of something familiar and well established in consciousness, a memory that had been estranged by the process of repression on either a psychic–individual or a cultural–historical level.[66] It provoked a temporary attitude that could be seen as either infantile or neurotic: "The over-accentuation of psychical reality in comparison with physical reality."[67] And it occurred either when repressed infantile complexes became reanimated through some experience or when primitive beliefs that we believed to be outmoded seemed once again to be confirmed by the physical world.[68]

As suggested by *Ingres's Violin,* surrealists like Man Ray used photomontage to render the body uncanny in ways that conveyed both violence and corporeal metamorphosis. Inspired in part by the constructive trajectory of photomontage, the surrealist photographers can be seen as emphasizing a relative simplicity, clarity, and intelligibility in their superimposition strategies in comparison to those employed by the Dada artists.

Unlike the Dadaists, the surrealists tended to make their own photographs rather than appropriating mass-reproduced photographic source materials, something that tended to preserve their representations' indexical relationships to their real-world subjects. Unlike the Dadaists, the surrealist photographers did not seek to overload their photomontages with a plethora of conflicting image fragments that completely violated a sense of unified space and time. Thereby, the surrealists sought to preserve the physical presence of their photographic subjects to a greater degree and thus to employ the indexical power of their medium to present reality as both literal and allegorical at the same time. Unlike the Dadaists, who used photomontage to construct more obviously artificial interpretations of reality (ones that attacked opponents and attempted to reveal social tendencies), the surrealists endeavored to represent the world as permeated by the same shifting play of presence and absence that characterized written language.[69] By using photomontage in this way—to both evoke and resist a sense of the arbitrariness of the visual sign—they presented reality as written or coded, thus creating a sense of uncanniness that was central to their art.

As suggested by his many references to surrealism over the course of his career, Heinecken was highly aware of surrealist photomontage, and it was from artists like Man Ray that Heinecken developed his own highly original practice of rendering mass media images uncanny. Heinecken's importance, we will see, lay in his ability to employ insights gained from the history of avant-garde art to an analysis of American mass culture between the 1960s and the 1990s. Specifically, he explored his own desires—for sex, information, entertainment, and a plethora of consumables like food, alcohol, and cigarettes—in relationship to photographic stereotypes culled from the mass media. To construct one's identity through consumption, as Heinecken understood it, was to fantasize and satisfy one's personal desires through visual representations and to enjoy a sense of individuation by means of mass-produced products.[70] Heinecken's great insight was to discern the growing interconnections between materialism and self-fashioning in U.S. culture and to reveal how photography as both a technology and an institution produced reification but also its critique.

The Technological Uncanny

Like the artists of the historical avant-garde before him, part of Heinecken's major significance lay in the fact that his work elaborated—like few others—the technological uncanny that was coming more and more to permeate his contemporary moment. Heinecken associated being a pilot with both empowerment and death, something that can be seen in *Organic Airplane* (1957), a tight shot of a jet fighter silhouetted against a cloud-streaked sky, with a second plane flying in the background (Plate I.4). Captured from an unfamiliar angle, the larger plane is almost unrecognizable: we slowly make out part of its dark hulking body, a small portion of the wing where it meets the fuselage, and the canopy that covers the cockpit. Because of the framing and the lack of detail produced by the dark exposure of the plane's body, the main form seems, as the title suggests, organic. And by imagining it as a human body, captured from a strange and nonstandard close-up angle, we can read it as a recumbent nude, recorded from a position somewhere below the figure's right arm, or as a representation of the nude's point of view as she gazes down at the front of her torso. And through this oscillation, the image cycles between the real and the imaginary, exposing the arbitrariness of signification in relation to an uncanny image that also evokes a pilot's viewpoint and thus yet another way in which technology can be seen to merge with the body.

Heinecken attributed some of his success as an artist to his training as an aviator. As he put it:

> When I went into the service I had flunked out of school. I was, for my age, quasi-alcoholic. I had no goals, no nothing, except to keep moving somehow. So, you go from that state of mind to eighteen months later when I'm commissioned in the Marine Corps. I got my wings, and I'm completely confident, completely ready to do whatever life is going to be . . . . [T]he confidence that comes from a program like that is invaluable.[71]

"You can't say being able to fly a jet fighter has anything to do with being an artist," he elaborated, "except there is something to it about confidence and knowing that you can be put up against certain daily problems. Every day is a problem when you get into that airplane. It's never perfect."[72] To make art, as Heinecken suggested, was to confront a set of complications that changed regularly: to establish parameters, make choices, and then to immediately follow through and execute what one has decided to do. And although the Korean War had ended by the time he graduated, the pilot's confidence that Heinecken applied to his creative work was a faith forged in confrontations with death, clashes that occurred during years of training exercises, first in flight school and then as a Marine flying instructor. As Heinecken recalled, his aviator training was fraught with peril. There were two situations in which he could have been killed.

> It was just that close. So, I did the right things in both instances. But right up until the last moment of getting out of the situation, you don't know. . . . You're on the radio all the time with the people, and they have the tapes.

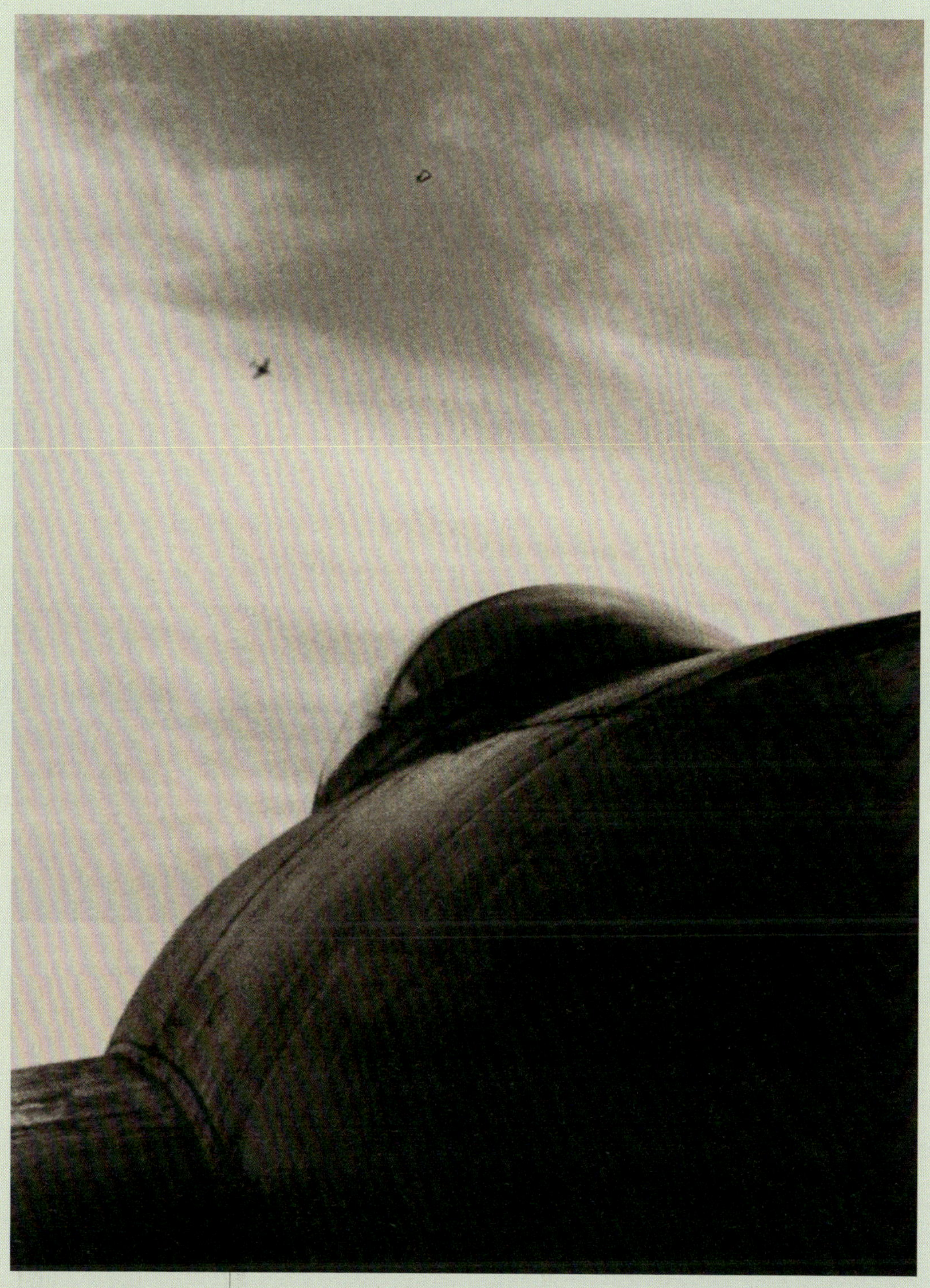

PLATE I.4. Robert Heinecken, *Organic Airplane* (1957). Gelatin silver print, 19 ½ x 14 ⅜ inches (49.53 x 36.51 cm). Proof 1/3. Collection of Geoff Heinecken.

I'm praying and I'm screaming like, "Get me out of this and I'll do this and I'll"— Which I had no idea I was saying. But when you sit down and play the tape, you're saying, "Who's that idiot talking?" And that's you talking, right? That was amazing to me. I have no memory of that, because you're just panicked. You're thinking you're going to die. And so, you fall back suddenly on what? Twenty years before that you would have had this notion that there was a life after death and that you had to be a good person.[73]

Heinecken had already rejected his father's Christianity by the time he was a teenager,[74] so what he had to fall back on were the same technologies that were endangering him in the first place: uncanny tools he controlled that promised both mastery and danger. He thereby learned to rely on his training—his military schooling through which he practiced conforming his body and mind to machines that let him extend his powers far beyond what he was physically capable of doing on his own.

Heinecken's first near-death experience occurred when he nearly ran out of fuel at the end of a long training flight right after his (much more experienced) training partner had just crashed and died. Once Heinecken finally landed, his engine cut out in less than a minute due to lack of fuel, emphasizing the closeness of his brush with death.[75] "During this time period," he reminisced,

> if you took four airplanes up, which was what we would do typically, two of them would lose the radios, one would lose hydraulic power. None of these were bad things, they just happened. . . . That airplane lands with two or three systems that have gone, but their backup systems have taken— You know, it doesn't worry you, because that's the way it is. But the fighter is a very complicated machine. And these were old airplanes, actually. They had just come back from Korea.[76]

Despite all the preparations and training of Heinecken and his fellow pilots, technologies could fail, and the flight controllers who oversaw the exercises could make mistakes. According to the artist, who was perhaps exaggerating, in the eighteen months that he was in his training squadron, it lost about eight airmen out of a total of thirty.[77]

Heinecken's second near-death experience occurred when the plane flying next to him in a practice dogfight collided with his jet, killing the other plane's pilot and forcing Heinecken to make a crash landing on a short and underequipped emergency landing strip in the desert behind Palmdale, California. With no canopy, radio, or oxygen mask, and with a charged but undeployed ejector seat, Heinecken had to cut his engines and glide into a landing, knowing all the while that his seat could deploy on impact with the ground and kill him.[78] Once again, he believed that his training routines saved him: "The whole thing is like two or three minutes.

I mean, things are happening like that [knocks]. It's just all procedural logic which you're trained with. If this does this, then you do this. If that does that, then you do this, and so on."[79] His plane could easily have killed him, but his training enabled him to control the situation and survive. "The whole military experience, at least in aviation," as Heinecken recalled,

> is that you're always in training for the next step of what you're going to do. When you go into combat it's different, and you have regular things—no, real things—to do every day. But until that happens, it's like going to school. Everyday you're learning another thing, you're advanced into another position relative to the flight situation. All kinds of ratings have to be fulfilled, like instrument ratings, carrier landings, gunnery ratings—you know, it's a school is really what it is—every day, except you're paid to do it, and it's interesting and it's dangerous.[80]

A confidence in one's training and experience and an immersion in new technologies that recognizes both their instrumentality and their uncanniness were necessary parts of the pilot's makeup. And such was the attitude that Heinecken brought to his art.

As his recollections suggest, Heinecken saw technology as radically uncanny: as powerful, pleasurable, dangerous, mysterious, and only partially controllable. And this sense of a technological uncanny seems to permeate *Organic Airplane* as well, with its connotations of both violence and sexuality. Indeed, there is something that is very personal about *Organic Airplane*, something that is the case not simply because the image relates to Heinecken's personal history, the life and individual story that he was in the process of making. The image strikes the viewer personally, because it hits us physically, through its formal, almost modernist composition, and, more important, through its uncanny mixing of the human with the inhuman. Both familiar and alien, *Organic Airplane* resists all attempts to comprehend it; we cannot, for example, really be sure if the picture was taken in the air or on the ground. By addressing unconscious or atavistic aspects of our personalities, Heinecken's mysterious representation of what could even possibly be a dogfight makes the questions it raises about the interchange between technology and the body seem to matter to us in a very personal way.

Heinecken's exploration of the technological uncanny in his art linked him to the theoretical models surrounding postmodern photography in the 1980s and 1990s (namely, those of Crimp and Owens), but they also distinguished him from them. As these critics argued, technologically based forms of representation like photography, video, and film were radically changing the ways in which people in the United States understood themselves as well as how they formed social groupings and performed their habitual behaviors and practices. Relationships between individuals and mass-produced objects and images were coming more and more to substitute for the one-on-one relationships with one another, and vanguard artists were confronting this issue through hybrid and montage-based allegorical art. Through appropriation, artists could grapple with the specific ideals and behaviors that mass-market consumer capitalism encouraged, while critically revealing the media and institutions through which art and identity were formed. The supposedly self-aware and centered subject of modernism was a fiction, undermined from within by the play of unconscious psychic forces, and from without by socially constructed stereotypes promoted by the media, the state, and consumer society at large. By revealing this situation—a result of individuals' ever-increasing linkages to broader systems of technological production, reproduction, and control—artists could help further the breakdown of traditional forms of racial-, gendered-, sexual-, and class-based identity and promote the development of new, nonnormative modes of existence and belonging.

At the same time, Heinecken's refusal to exempt self-reference from his art—his intermittent but continuing indication of his own position as a white, male, heterosexual artist, and former military man, situated within the thriving university system of the United States—also distinguishes his work from the New York–based models of postmodernism. In New York, with the exception of Cindy Sherman, the appropriations of the postmodern photographers seemed less tied to the artist's own body, interests, and life story; in Heinecken's version of the technological uncanny, the individual's own position as a consumer and as a social and professional actor could not be elided. Perhaps because of the prominence of white male heterosexual actors and values in art well into the 1970s, Crimp and Owens could genuinely celebrate a loss of focus on the individual in art, as they saw this (antimodernist) move as a means of opening up the necessary space for new modes of behavior and existence to form. For Heinecken, on the other hand, struggling with similar issues more than a decade and a half earlier, art needed to possess greater personal reference, since according to his understanding of the technological uncanny, one could only comprehend the social construction of different forms of identity by relating them to one's own specific situation and desires. And although it is true that Heinecken's work was sometimes focused during the 1960s and 1970s on the construction of white masculinity in the U.S. context, his oeuvre as a whole was never exclusively concentrated on male or even white subjectivity. Particularly as his practice developed in the 1980s and 1990s, Heinecken created more and more nonmasculine, racialized, and hybrid imagery. Indeed, what makes Heinecken's work so relevant today is the way it reveals how hybrid identity can be produced through consumption and the mass media. It is also relevant because it demonstrates how radically unstable masculinity's patriarchal and heterosexual norms really were by the 1960s and 1970s. Even his most male-centered work—the pornographic appropriations of the 1970s—radically deconstructed the straight male gaze.

In this book I will examine Heinecken's art and life chronologically, moving from his early gelatin silver photographs and photograms to his lithographs, collages, Kodalith transparencies, magazines, paintings, installations, books, and time-based artworks, as well as his numerous experiments with different types of photographic and printmaking technologies. Although Heinecken's art will be the primary focus, this text includes biographical points of reference inspired by the personal meanings that are contained within his creations—in addition, of course, to connecting Heinecken's work to his society and politics, to the history and meaning of twentieth-century art, and to contemporaneous theoretical discourses on the mass media and identity. In particular, Heinecken's art will be analyzed as a self-critical exploration of how his particular sense of "selfhood"—identity—was constructed through the elements of mass culture that he appropriated or otherwise consumed. Heinecken was an important artist, I argue, because of the formal and conceptual innovations he developed in the course of this process: devices and strategies that speak to the history of twentieth-century art. But he was also a key figure because of his interrogation of identity through visual culture—his understanding, in other words, that selfhood and vision were inextricably intertwined.

While *identity* is a term that can be used to indicate one's sense of selfhood, the word's meaning is much broader. Over the past twenty years, the term has grown significantly in popularity, coming to replace terms like *subjectivity* and *existence* as the preferred nomenclature to indicate who a person is as well as their relationship to more general categories of collective belonging. We commonly talk of *personal identity* as well as *collective identity*, *identity formation*, and *identity politics*; the divergent meanings that these formulations encompass suggest that the term *identity* covers a very broad and potentially conflicting range of definitions. As it will be used here, *identity* is understood as both inwardly and outwardly defined. It is used to indicate how we identify ourselves using collective categories such as gender, ethnicity, race, sexuality, nationality, profession, culture, religion, body type, health status, generation, and the like, as well as how we define ourselves in terms of our particular life histories as they encompass significant moments, actions, events, and affiliations. It will also be used to indicate how we are defined from without by other people and institutions in our societies, sometimes against our will.

Although Heinecken did not use the term in any clear-cut or programmatically defined way, it seems clear from his art, writings, and interviews that, like many intellectuals and artists at the time, he rejected the traditional view of subjectivity as a fixed and unchanging essence and instead embraced a notion of identity as socially constructed and mutable. In part because of the popularization of existentialism and psychoanalysis in the United States after World War II, artists like Heinecken were drawn to the idea that who a person was as an individual was the result of a process of self-development in which they produced their identity in dialogue with social roles and values. Freud's concept of identification provided one springboard for such a notion. Sartre's—with its debt to Heidegger's—was another. Central to all postwar concepts of identification was a sense of identity as produced both consciously and unconsciously and suspended between unity and disunity. It is this notion of identity that Heinecken developed so impressively in his art, connecting it to theories, practices, and examples that defined central forms of "Americanness" during the last four decades of the twentieth century.

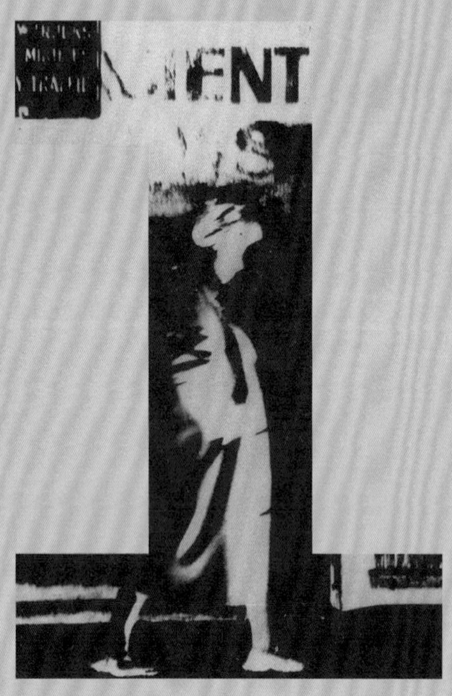

ARTIST AND EDUCATOR

Criticizing the American Family Ideal through 35mm Photography

HEINECKEN was a profound interrogator of photography's development between the 1960s and the 1990s. It is thus initially surprising that he rarely took his own photographs. The exception to this rule was his earliest work made between 1960 and 1965. These photographs, which were all shot with a 35mm camera, were his "straightest" or least manipulated. But even they combined opposites such as the organic with the technological or applied techniques of "bad photography" such as shooting against the light, motion blur, and over- and underexposure in order to make people and things look unfamiliar and strange. In other early 35mm photographs, Heinecken projected text, cartoons, or photographs onto nude models as another way of disrupting the reality effect of his photographs and bringing language and contradiction into his images. In still others, he used his children's dolls to stage psychologically charged tableaus that rendered American consumer culture uncanny.

As this chapter will demonstrate, Heinecken's early 35mm work explored the materialist and consumerist "family ideal" of the United States in the 1950s and early 1960s, a set of beliefs and values that supported suburbanization, procreation, material consumption, and the growth of the American middle class. Aware of the rapid assimilation of every aspect of public and private life into the burgeoning stream of representations created by the mass media, in these works Heinecken criticized the dominant values and stereotypes by which he seemed to orient and conduct his own existence: ideas about male and female behavior, parenting, and the U.S. conduct of the Vietnam War. Documenting a time during which he transitioned from the military (and the flying and control of airplanes) into academia (with a dual role as teacher and artist), they demonstrate a sociologically and historically informed perspective, one that sought to disclose the larger institutions, messages, and values that seemed to subtend his everyday behaviors and choices. While questioning the military ideal that had guided his early adulthood, Heinecken came more and more to interrogate the suburban family and the various roles that individuals were called to play within it.

Street Photography

Some of Heinecken's earliest works are unpopulated street photographs. Shot in dilapidated corners of West Los Angeles, these images of signs and graffiti consistently juxtapose multiple systems of representation.[1] *Why,* circa 1962, depicts a plaintively written interrogative inscribed on a concrete wall on which an irregular row of wooden boards has been nailed (Plate 1.1). On one level the image bears certain affinities to straight photography: it is detailed, geometrically composed, and quasi-abstract, a

balance of different lines, forms, and patterns. On another level the image is like contemporaneous documentary photography, in that it appears to present a detail from the social world in order to depict urban decay in a critical light: the words on the building seem to question its dilapidated state of being.[2] On a third level the image poses self-reflexive and semiotic questions in that it juxtaposes image with text. It thus provokes its spectators to attend to two different types of representational meaning and to synthesize them as components of a larger hybrid message. And on a final level the image is irreverently ironic: the graffiti seems to question—and thus protest against—the destruction of the urban fabric; however, through the tagging of the building, the unknown graffitist has only made the situation worse.

U.U., circa 1962, like *Why*, represents the world through a quasi-surrealist eye, mixing the image with language (Plate 1.2). Through its close-up selection of an anonymous urban detail, the photograph evokes the city's mystery, and—through the dried organic matter and the faded letters—it also stresses the metropolis's connections with decay and death. In addition, like *Why*, *U.U.* is sharply focused and formally composed, intent on a detail of modern life that most people would normally overlook, in this case an insignificant corner between a wall and a curb in which twigs and leafy detritus have collected. Two uppercase *U*s appear on the wall to the right of the dilapidated corner; they suggest horseshoe brands, gang signs, and, when read out loud, an uncanny ululation.

Evoking an unholy synthesis of Eugène Atget and Brassaï (Gyula Halász), *U.U.* allegorizes a melancholy urban condition by focusing the spectator's attention on the traces of human lives in an otherwise empty, perhaps industrial location in West Los Angeles.[3] And by playing between sense and nonsense, as well as mixing the organic with the manufactured, *U.U.* transforms Los Angeles into an uncanny space of mystery and hidden possibilities. Implicitly, by representing urban decline, the photograph also criticizes the rapid growth of the suburbs that had begun already in the 1950s.

When Heineken retired from active service in the Marines in 1957, he returned to UCLA, where he studied art, earning his BA in 1959 and his MA in 1960. At this time, he concentrated on printmaking and graphic design, while working as a designer and art installer at UCLA's Art Galleries (now called the New Wight Gallery). During his second stint at UCLA, Heinecken, as he recalled, "stumbled upon" photography through a classroom assignment; after he joined the Department of Art at UCLA as an instructor in 1960, he began to teach the medium around 1961 for the university extension program in downtown Los Angeles. During the next two years he designed and initiated a photographic curriculum for the department, and when appointed as an assistant professor in 1962, he began overseeing a regular series of courses in photography. A few years later, around the time he received tenure in 1967, Heinecken created a formal graduate program in photography at UCLA in which he taught until 1991.[4]

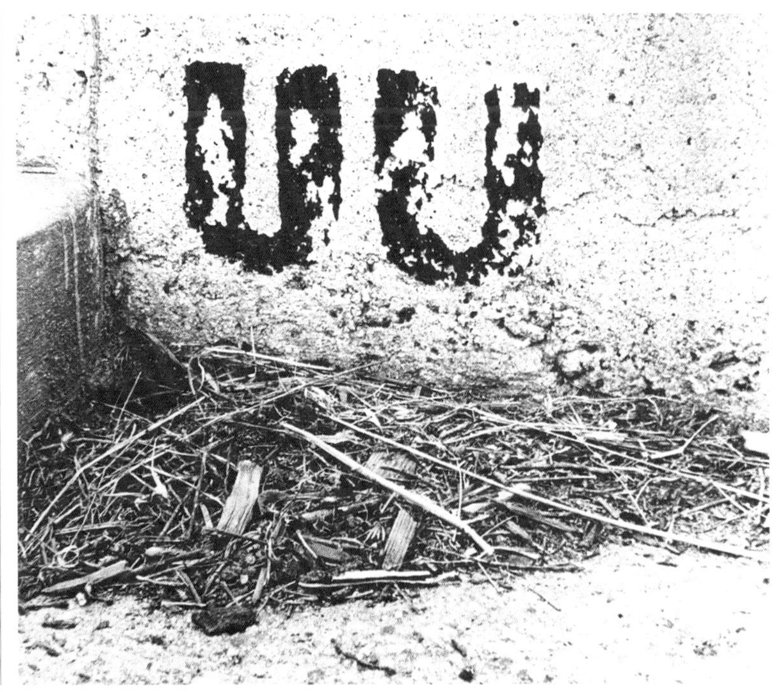

Between 1957 and 1966, Heinecken also served in the Marine Corps Reserve, an important source of income at the time for his growing family. Married in 1955, he and his wife, Janet Storey, had their first children, twins, in the same year. Thus for most of his early career as an art student and then as a young artist and professor at UCLA, Heinecken also raised a family, splitting household duties with Janet, who worked as a nurse in the UCLA hospital system.[5] In light of this, another striking aspect of the artist's early street photography is how ambivalent it seems about LA's booming economy in the early 1960s—something that benefited Heinecken and his family tremendously as the artist transitioned from military to civilian life. As Heinecken's street photography reminds us, even as the city developed and prospered, there were always areas of decline and neglect.

During the years Heinecken served as a pilot, began a family, and started to practice photography as an art form, Los Angeles was in fact undergoing rapid development. Its population, economy, and city limits were all expanding, fueled in particular by the area's aerospace, defense, and media industries, as well as by the metropolis's growth as a hub for international trade.[6] As numerous scholars have noted, LA became increasingly decentralized in the 1950s and 1960s, with a rising number of its citizens moving to the suburbs, living in housing developments, and commuting to work by car.[7] Feeling the threat of the Cold War, Americans in Los Angeles—as well as elsewhere—were turning inward, focusing on their immediate families and the satisfactions of consumerism and material comforts. Robert, Janet, and their children were no different; part of the quickly expanding middle class, they were building a family in a context of rapidly rising wealth and prosperity.

Works like *Why* and *U.U.* thus seem to criticize the postwar economic growth and suburbanization that were characteristic of Los Angeles in the 1950s and 1960s, using surrealist strategies such as unusual cropping or image–text dichotomies to emphasize the loss of place and uniqueness that was occurring in the city at this time.[8] Heinecken had studied art history at UCLA, and so he was well aware that both art and photography had long histories.[9] Surrealist practice, with its focus on ambiguity and allegory, provided him with a convincing alternative to the straight photographic practices dominant in San Francisco and in the world of art photography as a whole.[10] It allowed him to counter their powerful vision of the West Coast as sublime nature with uncanny street photographs that depicted the city but also suggested the growth of suburban culture. And its example would guide Heinecken as he turned to the exploration of other genres of photographic practice.

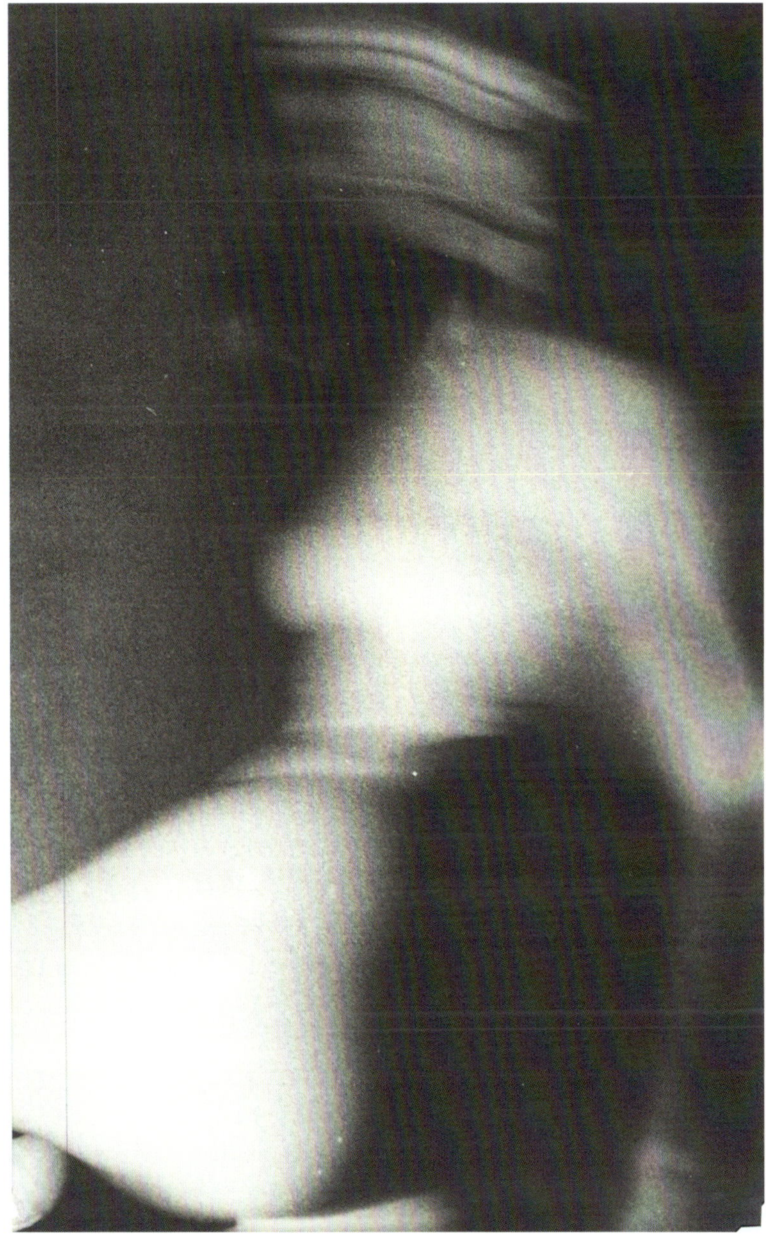

Figure Studies

In addition to producing quasi-surrealistic street photographs, which evoked the flight from the urban center that was part of the 1950s family ideal, Heinecken also created abstract studies of human figures starting around 1962; these were nude—often female—forms, transformed in one way or another through aspects of photographic technology. *Twisted Figure* (1964) seems to combine characteristics of traditional nineteenth-century nude photography—the staged pose as well as the turbanlike form on the woman's head—with features of twentieth-century photojournalism (Plate 1.3).[11] Its motion blur, for example, suggests Tom Howard's famous spy camera photograph of Ruth Snyder's electrocution on July 12, 1928, at Sing Sing Prison that was printed the next day on the front page of the *New York Daily News,* under the sensationalistic headline "DEAD." *Equivocal Figure* (1964), on the other hand, uses extreme soft focus to render a standing figure abstract and strange, while *Vertical Figure* (1962–64) and *Figure on Film* (1962–64) employ overexposure and high contrast to a similar effect on reclining nudes. In these and other works such as *Soft Figure* (circa 1962), there is an interest in exploring the human form as it transforms through photographic representation into something more abstract and allegorical. By melting or dissolving the human figure, these photographs evoke the violence that accompanies all acts of allegorical appropriation and the use of preexisting forms for poetic or artistic purposes.[12]

In a way resembling his critical approach to street photography, Heinecken dissolved the human form for diagnostic purposes in his figure studies, emphasizing how technology could distort the body in order to represent broader social changes that were transforming his world. As he was well aware, photography could always be used—often in conjunction with text—to define a person's physical and mental capacities and to assign them qualities and behaviors based on markers that suggest broader concepts of race, gender, class, and sexual orientation.[13] Citing photography's history—through its appropriation of the genre of the nude—while rendering corporeality fluid, Heinecken's figure studies thus opposed this stereotyping tendency inherent in the medium. Instead of defining the body, they dedifferentiated it. Making human physical nature ethereal, they suggested that people were inherently protean, always ready to take on new forms. Thereby they also implied that the concepts and stereotypes by which persons regulate themselves in societies—legal definitions, social roles, ideals of living, and the like—ultimately always do violence to some aspects of their physical beings by slowing or freezing their development.

As an artist with social and political concerns, Heinecken was always interested in the ways in which his own life conformed to the dominant ideologies of his time as well as how it diverged from them. Believing that he had changed the course of his life by following a masculine ideal as constructed by the U.S. military, Heinecken quickly became focused on the new personal and collective paradigms that were to guide his civilian life. As Elaine Tyler May has argued, the United States was strongly influenced by a "family ideal" in the late 1940s and 1950s, a set of norms and values that supported capitalism, suburbanization, and social and political conformism, while promising personal satisfaction through sexuality, material consumption, and procreation.[14] After the conclusion of World War II, U.S. couples began to form families and have babies at a significantly younger age and more rapid rate than at any other time in twentieth-century history. Creating a postwar "baby boom" that would last into the 1960s, this generation of men and women were noted for their social and political conservatism as well as their acceptance of traditional gender roles, with the husband acting as breadwinner and family patriarch and the wife serving as a compliant and fertile homemaker. Unlike the previous two decades, when the Depression and the Second World War legitimated women working outside the home, women of the 1950s and early 1960s were encouraged to devote themselves to the family sphere, just as men were persuaded to dedicate themselves to the success of the large corporations and new industries that were developing rapidly after the war. As recompense, the house in the suburbs became a well-stocked container for pleasure and self-development, and reproduction was valorized as serving both familial and national causes.[15]

This ideal, of course, was not equally obtainable. African Americans were barred from suburban homeownership in the 1950s, an important source of postwar prosperity.[16] Significantly, white European immigrants were allowed into the suburbs, thus diluting the WASP stamp on whiteness; as a result, the suburban middle-class lifestyle became more widely distributed around the United States.[17] In addition, the domestic ideal did not make both genders equally happy. The women of this era were nearly twice as likely as men to report unhappiness or declare that they would have made different life choices if given a second chance.[18] But at the same time, the ideal, at least for those who could attain it, represented real material advantages. It justified and supported the postwar economic boom that significantly raised the economic status of millions of families, and it alleviated anxiety about the Cold War, through materialistic display and the enjoyment of what was deemed to be a superior lifestyle in comparison to the rest of the world. As a result, the men and women of this generation largely stayed married to one another despite their disappointments and letdowns.

In certain ways, Robert and Janet were typical of the postwar parents of the baby boom generation who subscribed to this domestic ideal. They married early and began a family almost immediately, and after initially living in various types of military and university housing, they moved to a suburban single-family home in the Beverly Glen section of Los Angeles in 1960.[19] On the surface, moreover, they were both "organization men," to paraphrase the operative term from William H. Whyte's bestselling book of pop sociology from 1956, a work that criticized what the author saw as the outer-directed, corporatist mindset of American businesses at the time, which was an outlook that went hand in hand with the 1950s family ideal.[20] In terms of their chosen professions, in other words, the Heineckens were team players, employed by large, hierarchically run corporations. In other ways, they fell outside this materialist domestic ideal that—as May argued—supported a Cold War ideology: they were both employed and, as the children grew older, husband and wife shared child-care responsibilities. Moreover, instead of becoming a commercial pilot and embarking on a high-income profession, Heinecken instead chose to become an artist—a conceptualist who would teach photography at a major university and use it to explore his social and cultural situation. As Heinecken's figure studies perhaps already suggest, this was a situation in which the physical body's relationship to the images and ideologies that regulated American society was an area of growing concern.

The American Image Ideal

At the same time as he was making gelatin silver photographs that were indebted to both surrealism and the documentary tradition, Heinecken also developed one of the first fine art photography programs in Los Angeles, a program in which he taught between 1962 and 1991. The same principles that guided his photography practice were central to his teaching philosophy: he aimed to encourage experimentalism and a dedication to the principle that photography was a fine art as opposed to a merely technical discipline.[21] As he put it in "The Photograph, Not a Picture of, But an Object about Something" (1965), his first published description of the UCLA photography program: "The specific course content of the photography area at UCLA is fixed by artistic intention and any application of the work to vocational, pedagogical, or commercial aims is coincidental to that which is taught."[22] Supplemented by a print collection, a photography book and periodical library, and an exhibition program that encompassed both historical and contemporary photography, Heinecken's critique-based courses were designed to enable students to "evolve a body of work in which the images are related one to another and finally form a group of prints which can be seen and understood as personal images."[23]

The key to making photographs as art, Heinecken believed, was to let go of the photograph's supposed "objectivity" and instead treat it as a complex material object that "seeks to trigger a response, not simply to identify subjects and situations."[24] The photograph was both intentional and anti-intentional: chosen and therefore informed by the photographer's subjectivity, but also indexical and thus a trace of something external to the artist's perception and volition.[25] "The found object idea in sculpture,"

Heinecken noted, "is very close to a photographic concept. It depends on associative and formal meanings which reside in objects and surfaces, which when put together in such a way as to allow closure on various levels, become meaningful. Both ideas depend on actuality as well as on interpretation."[26] As he noted later in reference to his pedagogy, "when you make the photograph you learn something about the difference from what the photograph is to whatever else there is, drawing or reality or whatever. I was always very interested in having people understand that. If they never understood anything else, that it was not a passive tool. . . . Because it's like eyeglasses. . . . Or a hearing aid or whatever."[27] And although he encouraged photographic practices that were radically different from his own, he also believed in involving his students in group projects through which they could learn more about the nature of the medium as a whole.

Heinecken's most elaborate educational project was "The American Image Ideal" (1963), which combined his interest in the documentary and sociological functions of photography with his concentration on self-reflexivity and critique of the mass media.[28] A collaboration between Heinecken and ten of his students, including Bill Abel, Darryl Curran, Pat O'Neill, and Amy Yutani, the "American Image Ideal" was a multihour slide presentation, originally shown on four consecutive nights, at the International Design Conference in Aspen in 1963. (A shorter version of the show was reprised once at UCLA during the same year.) The work consisted of three slide projectors that threw an array of images appropriated from magazines, movies, comics, and commercial signage onto a large screen, and a tape-recorded soundtrack comprising music, dialogue, and sound effects such as hoofbeats and horse whinnies. The constantly changing triptych of images presented a typology of American life: recognizable individuals such as presidents like JFK, and movie stars like Marilyn Monroe; social types such as cowboys, businessmen, soldiers, astronauts, and teenagers; aspirational products such as hot rods, homes, and electronics; and parades, rallies, and images of sporting events and other forms of mass entertainment. Appropriated media photographs that evoked sexuality and violence were also included, as were images that referred to contemporaneous events like the Cold War and religious and racial tensions in American society. The soundtrack presented different voices elaborating on their "image" of the United States, as well as its "ideal," the values they thought the United States actually possessed.

The project was based on sociological research and analysis.[29] According to a brochure that Heinecken prepared for the premiere, he and his team based the presentation on interviews they conducted with foreign exchange students at UCLA about topics having to do with the relationship between the American image and the American ideal, a distinction they derived from the contemporaneous media theory of the American historian Daniel Boorstin. Among the questions they asked the foreign students were: "What does the American teenager look like?" "Does the Negro have freedom? Equal rights?" "Give as many adjectives or nouns which describe the U.S. in your mind. How are American products thought of in your country?" "Does America stand for peace or war?" "Did you feel that the American image abroad was a true reflection of America?" Taking these interviews as their jumping-off point, Heinecken and his team then created more than one thousand Kodak Kodachrome slides, which, as he put it, were "capable of confirming, qualifying, or contradicting these foreign impressions of America." Although the responses by the foreign students formed the major portion of the soundtrack that accompanied the slide presentation, the authors didn't simply try to represent what the foreign students saw as America but included their own impressions of it as well, using their selection and sequencing of images and dialogue to emphasize the United States as "a country of contrasts."

Although based on documentary research, the presentation was not clearly or scientifically structured, and its effect was ultimately nondidactic and nonprescriptive. As can be seen from the more than one-hundred-page score that has been preserved in the Heinecken Archive at the Center for Creative Photography, a document that details the progression of images and themes on each projector as well as the effects, dialogue, and music on the soundtrack, "The American Image Ideal" did not present a well-defined argument or spell out a central interpretation of American life. Instead, it encouraged its audience to make up their own minds about the viewpoints and images presented over the course of the performance. Just as Heinecken collaborated with his students to create the project (Curran and the others conducted all the interviews and each was responsible for one or more of the image sequences), the presentation's audiences were invited to assume an active role vis-à-vis the work and draw their own conclusions.

Significantly, "The American Image Ideal" distinguished between representations of everyday life and news events in the U.S. media and the underlying values—or lack of values—that these representations supposedly revealed. Although, as the work implied, the mass media was an important channel through which dominant ideologies were transmitted (and perhaps even formed), it was not the only source for community values and a shared sense of common purpose in America. Images could also provide clues to values that were different from the dominant ideologies promulgated by the mass media; as such, they could perhaps lead engaged spectators to discover new principles and concerns. As Heinecken put it, "The presentation is dedicated to the premise that everything can be better than it is, and that it is necessary to distinguish between what is an illusion and what is an ideal."[30]

"The American Image Ideal" suggested that mass culture was a source of enlightenment as well as illusion. The path to understanding was through critical analysis: the mass media's illusions, in other words, could only be decoded through direct confrontation and dialogue. In this way, the slide presentation supported and amplified the ideas behind Daniel Boorstin's book *The Image: A Guide to Pseudo-Events in America* (1961), which Heinecken cited as an influence.[31] As Boorstin argued, the increasing pace of the news in combination with the growing integration of text and image in the public sphere created a new situation in the United States and other advanced societies: a multimedia space in which news gathering was increasingly being supplanted by news making. With the rise of "pseudo-events" or news made for the camera—things like corporate anniversary celebrations, interviews, press conferences, and, eventually, dedicated news shows on broadcast television—a second illusionary world was constructed by the mass media. This was an American public sphere that was both more vivid and detailed than ever before as well as one that promised to satisfy citizens' ever-increasing expectations for information, quality of life, entertainment, and personal satisfaction. And although this illusionary world was ultimately a false one, promoting incorrect assumptions and eventually dissatisfaction, overcoming it could only take place by means of a historical analysis of the media's most important and frequently communicated illusions, values that affected individuals as well as U.S. society as a whole.

Boorstin distinguished between images and ideals, arguing that images destroyed values: moral or ethical ideals for which people should strive. In contrast to moral values, images were "synthetic, believable, passive, vivid, simplified, and ambiguous."[32] By this the historian meant that images were fabricated: created—like brand names, trademarks, and "corporate images"—to make an impression or serve specific ends. They hid their constructed nature; they presented nothing out of the ordinary that would cause their consumers to strive for something different or to contest the reality that these images were created to maintain. The basis of their appeal lay in their sensuousness—their vivid and concrete nature—as well as the fact that they simplified what they represented, editing out its undesirable qualities. Like advertisements, they were not objective; instead, they represented their subjects as good or, at the very least, attractive. Finally, images were ambiguous, floating somewhere between truth and falsity, imagination and reality, and thus inoffensive, believable, and easily adapted to new purposes. Pleasurable and consumable, they blurred our distinctions and confused our desires.

Ideals, other the other hand, were more like ideas, perfect forms existing only in the mind. Produced by a long tradition of human development, they did not serve particular ends, nor were they simplified and comfortably ambiguous, as were images. Most important, they did not defend or maintain the status quo; instead, they provided a moral or ethical standard against which people measured their world as well as their own conduct. As Boorstin put it, "Images are means. . . . An ideal, on the other hand, has a claim on us. It does not serve us; we serve it. If we have trouble striving toward it, we assume the matter is with us, and not with the ideal."[33] Unfortunately, according to Boorstin, in his contemporary U.S. society, the world of images had almost completely displaced the former sphere of ideals. As a result America had transformed itself from a land of dreams into a country of illusions—from a country in which people pursued new democratically selected ideals into a terrain in which nothingness, unreality, and moral stasis reigned.[34]

In addition to exemplifying his very experimental and open-ended approach to teaching art photography, "The American Image Ideal" thus also revealed Heinecken's affinities with contemporaneous media theory in the United States. As Boorstin argued, it was perhaps by examining how the United States projected its image abroad that the country might best overcome the world of illusion that it had projected around itself.[35] Heinecken and his team seem to have taken this argument to heart. By attempting to distinguish America's images from its ideals, they sought to construct a more egalitarian concept of U.S. identity, an understanding of the interaction of common tropes and values that would guide and coordinate Americans on both an individual and collective level. "The American Image Ideal" furthermore revealed many of the concerns that would guide Heinecken's art during its entire development: a documentary, quasi-sociological focus on mass media as a technology that helped to form both individual and collective identities; a concentration on imagery that because of its sexual or violent nature tended to affect spectators' bodies as well as their minds; and a consistent approach to composition that emphasized dialectical relationships and the linkage of opposites into larger "gestalts," constructions made from conjunctions of appropriated elements.

The Textual Body

Because it brings commercial signage and text together with the human body, *Venice Alley* (1963) marks an important transitional moment in Heinecken's artistic evolution in the early 1960s (Plate 1.4). During the first few years of his photographic practice, he made his own exposures,

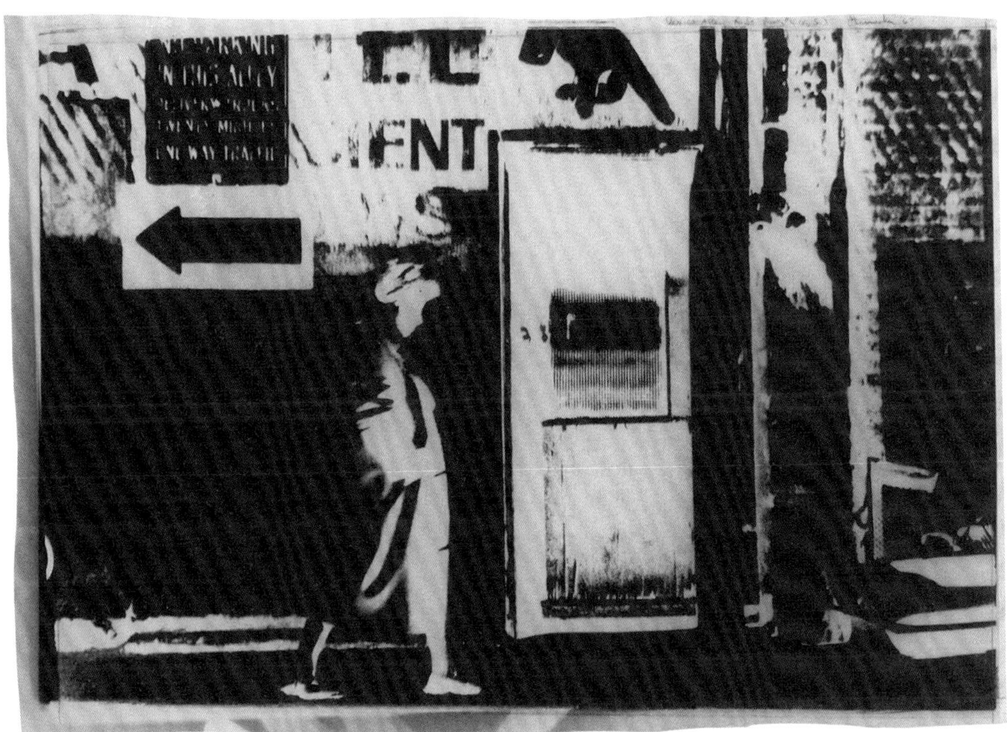

and when he shot human figures, he tended to separate them from their environments. He photographed empty street scenes and architecture, or he recorded the human figure in the studio, abstracting it in various ways through high contrast, blur, and under- or overexposure. His interests in the human body and in social and critical content were separated, in other words, cordoned off in parallel photographic projects.

In *Venice Alley,* which Heinecken produced in 1963 as both a gelatin silver print and an etching, body and text were brought in conjunction with one another, thereby allowing social content to be juxtaposed with corporeal form.[36] Here, in this high-contrast, visually ambiguous image, an indistinct skirted figure striding to the right seems to follow the directions of a disembodied hand with a pointing index finger extending in from the top of the photograph; she ignores the arrow behind her, which points in the opposite direction. Texts—both legible and illegible—appear on the wall behind her, which is also punctuated by geometric elements that evoke doors, windows, and perhaps steel fencing. Recalling the surrealist practice of depicting the city as both dangerous and marvelous, as a "forest of signs" (to use André Breton's term), pointing to an underlying instinctual and irrational play of forces, *Venice Alley* is significant in the context of Heinecken's development because it brings the body into his street photography for the first time, linking the human form to environmental text and symbols that convey social and political content.[37] After multiple iterations of *Venice Alley*, Heinecken turned away from street photography altogether. Instead, he began to focus much more closely on the human form, which—recalling his interest in graffiti and signage in the street photographs—he superimposed with different types of images and texts.

In his concern for the textual body, the body as permeated by language, images, and symbols, Heinecken can be linked to shared artistic tendencies in LA since the late 1950s. Although San Francisco could claim to be California's preeminent art city before World War II, the relative status of the two metropolises shifted in the 1950s, as key figures in the Dada and surrealist tradition—for example, Man Ray and Marcel Duchamp—began to exhibit and sometimes live in Los Angeles. These founding fathers of the historical avant-garde were drawn to the city by the collectors Walter and Louise Arensberg, who had moved there from New York in 1921 and had amassed a significant collection of modern and avant-garde art, with a particular emphasis on Dada and surrealism. Promoters of contemporary art, the Arensbergs made their collection accessible to young artists and writers, for example, Walter Hopps, who became an influential curator and director, cofounding the important Ferus Gallery in 1957 and later serving as the director of the Pasadena Museum of Art (now the Norton Simon Museum), between 1962 and 1967.[38] The presence of these and other figures brought energy and an awareness of the history of modern art to the developing art scene and collectors' market in Los Angeles, and they helped the metropolis become an important incubator for neo-Dada and neosurrealist practices.

As Peter Plagens had noted in 1974, "assemblage is the first home-grown California modern art."[39] Comprising figures as diverse as Wallace Berman, George Herms, Bruce Conner, Jess (Burgess Collins), Edward Kienholz, Noah Purifoy, and Betye Saar, the tendency was well represented in both Los Angeles and San Francisco in the late 1950s and 1960s.[40] West Coast assemblage was most generally associated with found object sculpture. Examples of such work include Berman's *Veritas Panel* (1956), which consisted of two door-like rectangles connected by metal hinges as well as paint, photographs, knobs, dowels, a stone, a mirror, and fragments of paper sheets containing handwriting; and Kienholz's *Roxy's,* a massive, ribald installation of hybrid manikins and furniture first shown at the Ferus Gallery in 1962. In both cases, the found objects were used compositionally and symbolically as elements of larger works, which explored social, political, and intellectual content, and which used their nonart components to criticize the modernist values of originality, subjectivity, expressivity, and the handmade.

As a tendency, however, assemblage went beyond sculpture, comprising multiple media, including collage and film.[41] *Tricky Cad* (1954–59), Jess's string of surreal mash-ups of the Dick Tracy comic strip, which morph Chester Gould's original drawings and texts into incomprehensible poetic combinations, exemplify the complexity of assemblagist collage.[42] Conner's *A Movie* (1958), on the other hand, an amalgam of found cinematic footage sourced from newsreels, B-movies, stag films, and novelty reels, has long been cited as a demonstration of assemblage's great contribution to film.[43] In general, West Coast assemblage was characterized by the use of appropriation and montage for poetic or social critical ends. Focused on everyday life and the detritus of contemporary consumer society, it distinguished itself from New York abstract expressionism as well as pop art on both coasts through its "dirtiness"—in facture as well as content—and, often, its politics.[44]

As Richard Cándida Smith has argued in a reading that accords with this text's model of allegorical signification, California assemblage began "with the artist insisting that the objects in a piece [had] at least two immediately visible meanings. They . . . continue[d] to index their original historical character while signaling the alternative images that the artist's vision . . . [had] revealed."[45] Unlike New York–based artists such as Robert Rauschenberg who used found objects and appropriated, mass-reproduced images in the 1950s and 1960s to raise aesthetic questions having to do with the practices of painting and sculpture in relation to the tradition of modernist formalism, "California-based artists used the medium instead to express highly personal feelings about race relations, the militarization of U.S. society, capital punishment, abortion laws, the displacement of sexual desire into violence and pornography."[46] As a result, assemblage on the West Coast also proved to be a hospitable medium for Black artists like Noah Purifoy, John Outterbridge, and Betye Saar, who were developing "a distinctive African American aesthetic" rooted in the specific communities whose everyday objects and images they appropriated.[47] Like these fellow LA artists, Heinecken was positioned outside the "professional" art world that was centered in New York; like them, he was more connected in terms of interests to the specific, nonart communities of which he was a part, as well as to the particular stereotypes of individual and collective identity that circulated within them.

Heinecken was friends with Wallace Berman from the early 1960s until the latter's untimely death on his fiftieth birthday in 1976.[48] Although Heinecken was not part of Berman's inner circle of artists and poets, they talked frequently about art.[49] It is thus possible that Heinecken, who was almost five years younger than Berman, was inspired by the older artist's thinking and practice.[50] At the very least, Heinecken's artistic activities share a number of similarities with West Coast assemblage as practiced by Berman. These similarities include a focus on language and the combination of image and text. Steeped in San Francisco Beat culture as well as jazz music and surrealist thought, Berman's assemblages commingled texts, photographs, and objects in ways that encouraged free association and stream of consciousness that take place in a reader's mind in response to noninstrumental or poetic language. And as suggested by "The American Image Ideal," as well as many other works, Heinecken did likewise, amalgamating word and image in a manner that contradicted the standard ways of seeing and reading things. Assemblage, as Heinecken and Berman practiced it, had a literary and conceptual bent that put it at odds with the dominance of formalism in painting and sculpture in the 1950s and early 1960s.

In addition, the two artists shared an interest in the mass media as a channel through which consciousness and identity were constructed as well as (potentially) contested. In 1964, Berman began to use a Verifax machine—an early form of photocopier—to make collages, thereby suggesting that even the most nonartistic technologies of mass reproduction could serve as instruments of art.[51] As he developed this series, Berman hit upon an iconic motif—a hand holding a transistor radio—that he used repeatedly to create grids containing other appropriated images. Recycled from a Sony ad published in *Life* magazine on June 12, 1964, this recurring frame emphasized Berman's vision of art as a simultaneously mechanical and spiritual medium.[52] A double-sided concept of art is suggested by the fact that images appeared in the space normally reserved for the receiver's speaker and thus seem drawn—like radio waves—from the air. In conjunction with the Hebrew letters that he also sometimes employed in these works—forms that were inspired by Berman's (loose) understanding of the Kabbalah and the tradition of Jewish mysticism—these highly associative icons suggested a magical, nonlinear realm underlying the administered society represented by the grids of radios. Although Berman's Verifax collages implied that the mass media formed a frame around everyday life (and thus in some ways determined a person's possibilities for understanding and being), they also suggested that the media was a conduit to the unknown, a force that could potentially disrupt the status quo. And it was this sense of the mass media as a purveyor and disrupter of stereotypes that appealed to Heinecken as well.

Berman was also important to Heinecken because of his example as a printmaker and publisher. Between 1955 and 1964, Berman issued *Semina,* an unbound, small-circulation magazine that was disseminated through the mail to his friends.[53] Produced on a hand press and published sporadically, nine editions of the journal—none of them ever totaling more than three hundred copies—eventually appeared. (Heinecken even worked on a few.)[54] Each issue consisted of a folder or container assembling poetry, drawings, collages, and photographs created by Berman and his circle as well as poets and artists that he admired from the past. Bringing the assemblage principle into the magazine format, *Semina* was modeled on earlier avant-garde magazines like *Transition, Dial, Broom,* and *View,* as well as Duchamp's great multiple, *Box in a Valise* (1941–66), a portable museum containing reproductions of the artist's major works. Like Berman, Heinecken would use the magazine format to explore his artistic concerns; like Berman, he would employ appropriation and (sometimes) collaboration to expand the possibilities of his art.

Slide Projections

The West Coast assemblage practices represented by Berman helped to legitimate the new directions in which Heinecken was taking U.S. photography, routes that "The American Image Ideal" had begun to explore. These trajectories—which included appropriation, montage, public performance, and mass media critique—were to occupy him for the rest of his career. In order to merge the photographic body with (often language-based) conceptuality and history, a concern that began with *Venice Alley,* Heinecken drew on the corpus of slides that were developed for the Boorstin-inspired slide presentation to make his next body of work.[55] Largely distancing himself from the act of taking the photograph, he used a slide projector to shine images and texts from "The American Image Ideal" onto nude models, who then photographed one another.[56] The resulting gelatin silver prints, produced in 1964 and 1965, all exploited the doubling effect of the projected image to transform the nude into a destabilizing object of social and political critique.

World War I Figure (1964) presents a good example of the psychosocial concerns that guided Heinecken's series. Here we see a tightly cropped image of a woman that shows only her back and buttocks (Plate 1.5). A phalanx of soldiers shot from a high angle merges with her flesh, their forms bleeding over onto a wall that she faces. The men are captured in furious movement, while the woman seems calm, passive, and almost inert. The soldiers, furthermore, become lighter where they combine with her figure, suggesting that as the line of forms touches her body, it becomes assimilated by it. This ambiguous double image provokes a series of disquieting interpretations. On one level, it seems to suggest that warfare arises from either sexual or infantile desire. The phalanx of men, pushing forward into the woman's body, imply both heterosexual activity—possibly even rape—as well as a metaphoric return to the womb.

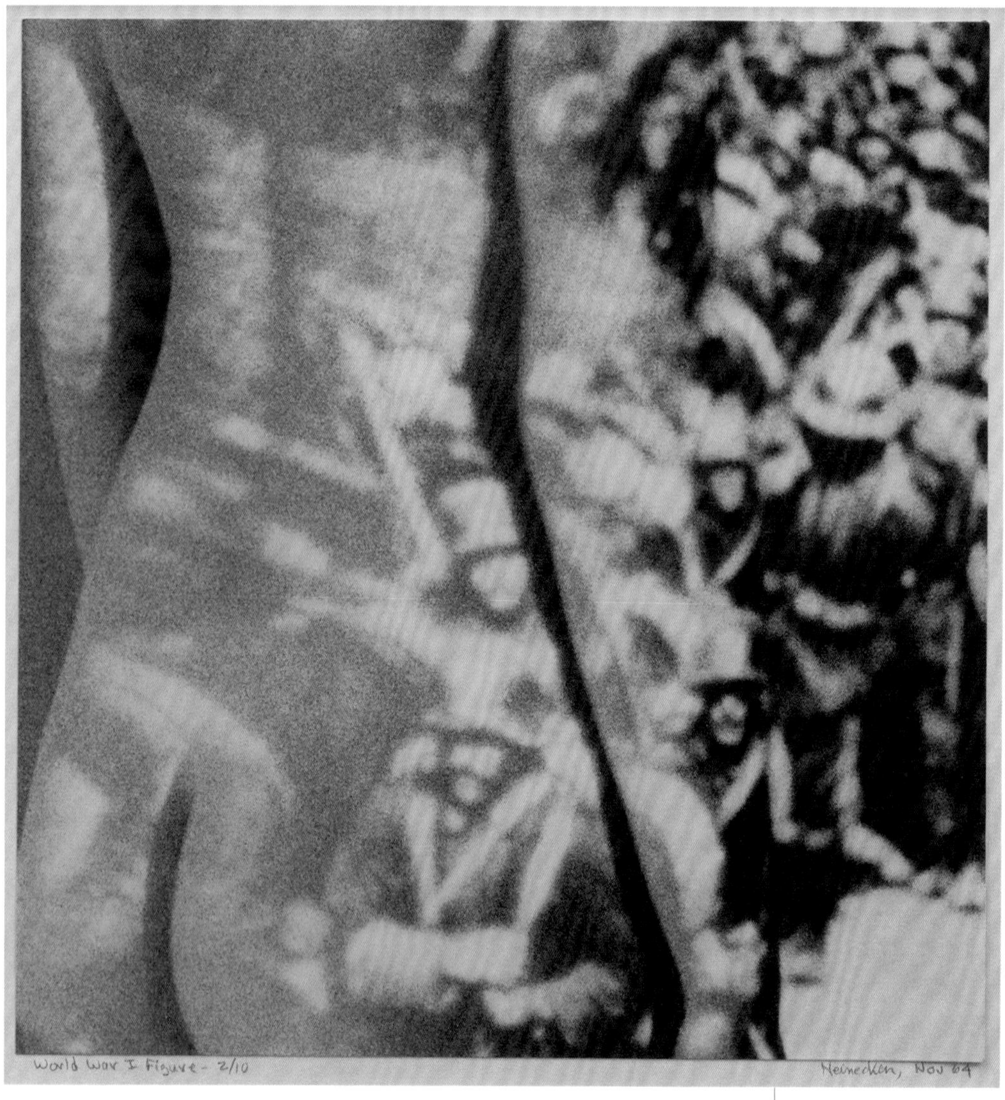

PLATE 1.5. Robert Heinecken, *World War I Figure* (1964). Gelatin silver print, 9.25 x 9.25 inches (23.5 x 23.5 cm). Private collection. COPYRIGHT 2022 THE ROBERT HEINECKEN TRUST, CHICAGO.

On a second level, because the photograph presents a single body composed of many, it recalls perhaps the most iconic representation of the social body, Abraham Bosse's frontispiece for Thomas Hobbes's *Leviathan* (1651). Created with input from the philosopher, Bosse's etching emblematized Hobbes's central thesis that societies were formed on the basis of a social contract. By ceding certain freedoms to a higher power—the sovereign who is represented by the composite figure as a whole—human beings raised themselves out of a state of nature, wherein, although they can do anything they want, human life in aggregate is "solitary, poor, nasty, brutish, and short."[57]

Despite his military background, Heinecken was critical of warfare—at least, this is what *World War I Figure* suggests. Although he had never experienced actual combat, he was struck by the images of violence that emerged from the Vietnam conflict, particularly those, like Eddie Adams's *Saigon Execution (General Nguyen Ngoc Loan Executing a Viet Cong Prisoner Nguyen Van Lém)* (1968), that undermined military ideals such as valor, honor, and discipline. Looking back on his career, Heinecken recalled being deeply affected by images of Vietnam War violence in the 1960s and 1970s and feeling that he had to engage with them in his art.[58] And even in these early photographs in which he began to juxtapose the human body with images, symbols, and texts, there seems to be an implicit criticism of the military mindset.

By the time Heinecken began to make his slide-projection photographs, images of Vietnam War violence had already begun to appear in the mainstream press—for example, in the context of its growing coverage of the war, *Life* magazine presented long articles on Vietnam in 1963 and 1964 that included color images of Viet Cong war dead and the torture of prisoners by South Vietnamese allies of the United States.[59] Men like Heinecken who served in the military would be aware of the connections among war, prostitution, and rape even before the Vietnam War had brought these issues to greater public consciousness by the end of the decade.[60] Furthermore, as suggested by Stanley Kubrick's brilliant comedy *Dr. Strangelove* (1964), the conflation of military violence with male sexuality had become a theme for cutting-edge filmmakers as well. In *World War I Figure,* Heinecken's approach to this subject (which would become much sharper over the next decade) was supported by his Bosse- or Arcimboldo-like merging of the woman's large body with the many smaller bodies of the soldiers, which raised these issues in combination with questions about the individual's relationship to his or her society. As a result, the photograph seemed to attack the masculine ideals that were promulgated by the U.S. military during the Cold War, ideals that had helped to guide the artist's life between the mid-1950s and mid-1960s.

Heinecken's superimposition of human forms in such a way as to suggest the constitution of one larger body out of many smaller ones also spoke to another important concern that was then driving the development of his art. If, as Bosse's frontispiece implies, the social body was formed from many individual ones, then what other analogies also held between the individual and the collective? Did collective life require a sense of self—a center of agency—just as the individual did? Could one speak of collective fears or collective desires? Heinecken's turn to the mass media as his primary subject seemed designed to explore these questions. By analyzing American images and the ideals that they replaced and obscured, he hoped to discern the common concepts, icons, and symbols that helped to construct U.S. identity on an individual and a collective level. In this series, by superimposing images and texts over the human form, he intended to discover how the body was formed in the image of something larger than itself.

Then People Forget You (1965) demonstrates this interest in exploring how collective ideals were imprinted on individual bodies at the same time as it helps to distinguish Heinecken's concerns from those of Berman (Plate 1.6). A close-up, tightly cropped photograph of a woman's torso viewed from the front, it presents its subject superimposed with a sentence that—because it is projected—follows the contours of her body. The image recalls an untitled collage by Berman from 1964 depicting a torso of a nude woman framed within an advertisement for a portable Sony TV.[61] A Sator Square or ancient Latin palindrome is inscribed between her breasts. This form, which constitutes the same words when read from left to right or right to left as well as from top to bottom or bottom to top, was sometimes believed to hold magical properties. In the context of Berman's collage, it implies the existence of a mystical realm made accessible through the modern technology represented by the portable television set. Although Heinecken's image does not include a depiction of the outer edges of a television set—a strategy to which he would turn less than a decade later in order to place his destabilizing montages squarely in the context of network programming—the format of the photograph recalls the standard 4:3 aspect ratio of TVs at the time.[62] The contrast between the almost-glowing white form of the woman and the deep black background into which her body disappears recalls the exaggerated

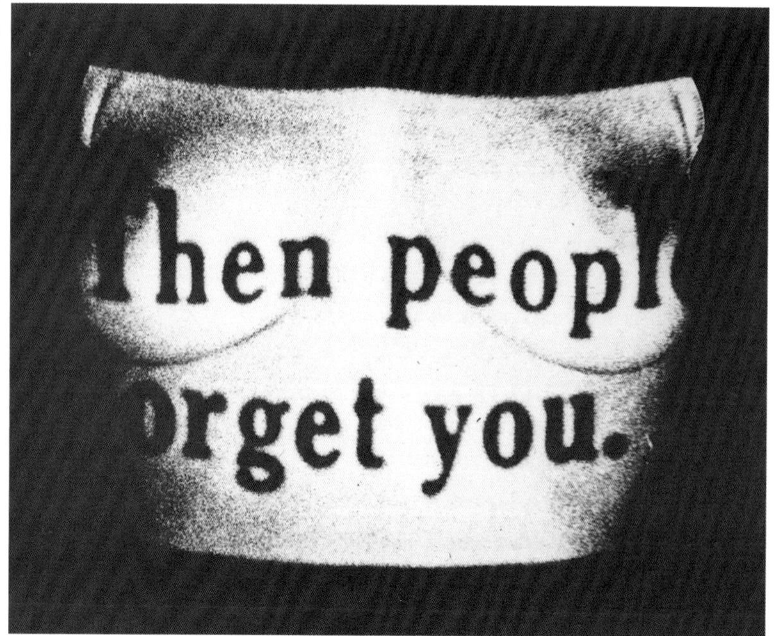

PLATE 1.6. Robert Heinecken, *Then People Forget You* (1965). Gelatin silver print, 10 ½ x 12 15⁄16 inches (26.7 x 32.8 cm). Collection Center for Creative Photography, The University of Arizona. COPYRIGHT 2022 THE ROBERT HEINECKEN TRUST, CHICAGO.

contrasts that result when images are photographed on television screens. For these reasons, Heinecken's representation evokes Berman's TV images. In Heinecken's photograph, on the other hand, the text seems mundane and advertisement-like, and thus very different from Berman's mystical Sator Square. Instead of suggesting the spiritual transcendence of everyday life, it emphasizes the power of the media to construct stereotypes and to define and regulate the body.

The superimposed caption (and title of the work) suggests the limited attention span of the U.S. television audience; when combined with an image of a woman's breasts that has been cropped so that her head is obscured, it evokes the media's fixation on sexuality and the depersonalization that results from this focus. As implied by how closely the text follows the contours of the woman's physical form, advertising creates a second skin around us, cloaking our bodies in stereotypes and ideologies. Despite the visual similarities, Heinecken's treatment of the text-inscribed female nude is thus very different from Berman's. As Claudia Bohn-Spector puts it: "While Berman's image seeks to lift popular and pornographic imagery out of its crassly pedestrian contexts and imbue it with mystery, Heinecken deliberately underscores its commercial status, uncovering the significant contradictions and ironies inherent in modern media iconography."[63]

In *E Pluribus Unum* (1965), Heinecken's overarching concerns were perhaps made even clearer (Plate 1.7). Here the famous seal of the United States with its Latin phrase meaning "Out of many, one" is superimposed with a nude torso. The woman is seated and the American eagle, with arrows and olive branch clutched in its talons, seems almost tattooed on her body. As was the case with *Then People Forget You*, the motif echoes Berman's cropping of the female nude in his untitled collage as well the more famous examples of female—and sometimes male—torsos in the surrealist art of Man Ray and René Magritte. In the work of these latter two artists, the female nude was often truncated, a strategy that made the form multistable, evocative of both a body and a face at the same time. This treatment can be seen, for example, in Magritte's *Rape*, which he produced as both a drawing and a painting in 1934, and Man Ray's gelatin silver print *Torso* (1923), one of many photographs that the artist produced during his career with the same title and motif.[64] For the male version of this trope, see Man Ray's *Minotaur* (1935).

The surrealists cropped the human body for a number of different reasons. In the first place, it made the body seem more like a classical sculpture, thus evoking the traditional ideal of beauty—still in effect in the nineteenth century—from which they were intentionally deviating.[65] In addition, by truncating the human form, they evoked war and mutilation,

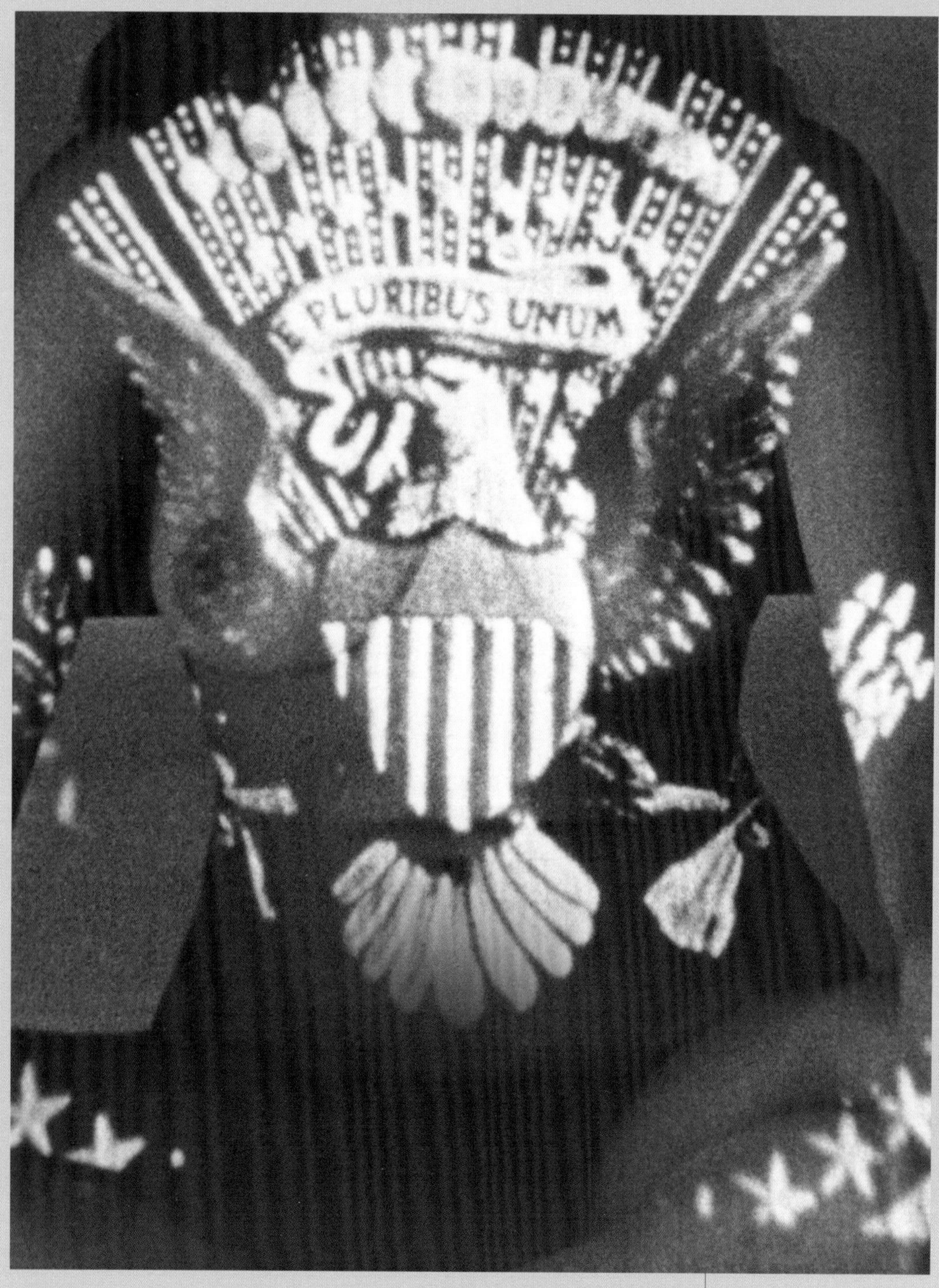

PLATE 1.7. Robert Heinecken, *E Pluribus Unum* (1965). Gelatin silver print, 9 ¾ x 7 ⅜ inches (24.76 x 18.73 cm). Collection Center for Creative Photography, The University of Arizona. COPYRIGHT 2022 THE ROBERT HEINECKEN TRUST, CHICAGO.

thereby recalling the trauma of World War I. Furthermore, by forming an image that equally suggested both life and death—a living person and an inanimate sculpture—they helped to create the sense of uncanniness that was central to their revolutionary project. Superimposing the head (or site of reason and cognition) with the body (the source of instinct and emotion), they undermined traditional distinctions that helped human beings understand themselves. Moreover, by creating a double image, a representation that could be read in different ways, they destabilized the human form, implying that the body was less comprehensible and perhaps more mutable than commonly thought. And through these various strategies, they sought to represent a play of psychic or instinctual forces existing beneath the surface of everyday reality: multiple points of conflict ready to erupt at any moment and undermine the stability of the military and family ideals that Heinecken used to guide and regulate his life.

E Pluribus Unum drew on these surrealist strategies of truncating and doubling the human form for similar reasons and with equal success. It projects an uncanny amalgam of sexuality and violence, suggesting that the body and the world are unstable, riven by history and instinct. Matter, even sentient matter, it reminds us, can always be transformed. The seal evokes U.S. currency, implying that the body is always for sale, a commodity like any other. Its motto performs the same function as the citation of Bosse's visual strategy in *World War I Figure*. It reminds the viewer that the social body is formed out of many individual ones; in turn, it emphasizes that society helps to constitute individuals through the imprinting of collective stereotypes. An allegorical image presenting the commodification of the human body, *E Pluribus Unum* challenged the guiding values of U.S. life while pointing to the surrealist concerns that would motivate the further development of Heinecken's art.

Dolls

The 1960s were a time of intense experimentation for Heinecken, during which he explored a vast variety of different photographic strategies to raise questions about the social construction of human identity—people's relationships to both images and ideals. Exemplifying this versatile experimental approach, Heinecken began taking photographs of his children's dolls in 1965, creating staged tableaus in which mass-produced commodities were arranged to suggest ambiguous human narratives and relationships. The resulting gelatin silver prints, which evoke advertising and surrealism, depict a dark theatrical world in which distinctions between living and dead, adult and child, and art and mass culture have all

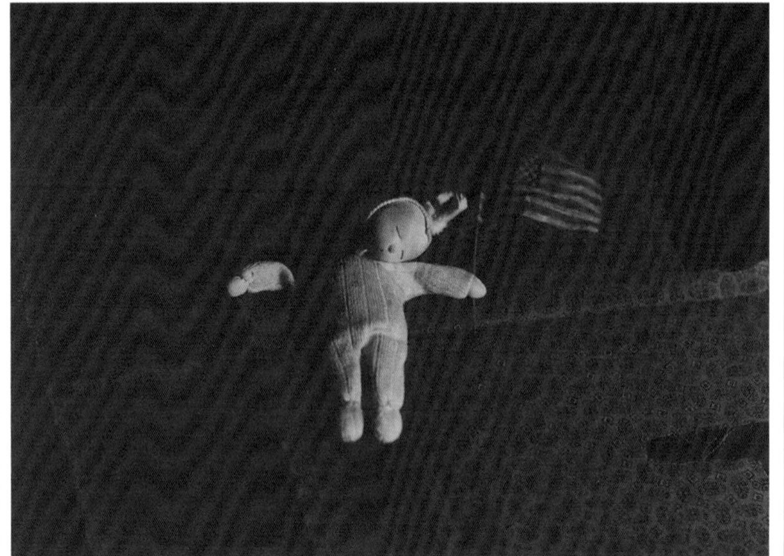

but broken down. In contrast to the slide projections with their textual and allegorical bodies, these doll photographs eschew written language, and instead they explore the social construction of identity through assemblages of objects that relate directly to the artist's family life. (Some of the figures were simply appropriated from Heinecken's children and used without further alteration; others were purchased and manipulated specifically for the photographs.)[66] Using these half-personal, half-readymade objects to explore how American society socialized its young, Heinecken posed questions about the role of parenting and the 1950s and 1960s family ideal in a media-saturated, war-torn world.

All American Doll (1965) depicts a ghostly and recumbent baby doll lying on a patterned cloth, its head turned to one side, an American flag in its hand (Plate 1.8). The doll's sprawled posture, the darkness of the image, and the slight aerial perspective make the scene seem foreboding or ominous. We are prompted to ask if the figure is asleep, unconscious, or dead, and to question what exactly has transpired. The horizontal form is clearly a baby; it lies as if it were shot with a bullet, the flag clutched in its loosening fingers. But the figure also suggests an adult soldier holding his country's standards, an important visual trope of war photography, as exemplified by popular works like *Raising the Flag on Iwo Jima* (1945) by Joe Rosenthal, and Yevgeny Khaldei's *Raising a Flag over the Reichstag* (1945), which was directly inspired by Rosenthal's image.[67] And by conflating the child with the adult—as well as confusing the distinction between living and dead—*All American Doll* raises a moral dilemma that was affecting more and more Vietnam-era families: Should your child serve in the Vietnam War?

In the year Heinecken made his doll photographs, Geoffrey and Kathe, his twins, turned ten, and his youngest daughter, Karol, celebrated her sixth birthday.[68] His children were thus not old enough to become fodder for the U.S. "military-industrial complex"—to use the important trope that President Dwight D. Eisenhower had popularized through his farewell address on January 17, 1961—and so this dilemma was not an actual one for Heinecken. Yet there seems to be an intention behind Heinecken's doll photographs to examine the toys with which his children played and how these objects—playthings formed in light of the American images that Boorstin argued had taken the place of the country's moral code—affected their future development. And despite Heinecken's good experiences as a Marine pilot during peacetime, and the fact that he credited his military training for making him a confident and capable adult, *All American Doll* suggests that by the mid-1960s, the artist was beginning to view the military in a rather different light. By 1966, Heinecken had left the Marine Corps Reserve; like many Americans who had supported the armed forces in the 1950s, he was horrified by the rising death toll of the Vietnam War, a tragedy that was being made more palpable than ever before by a flood of violent images from Southeast Asia disseminated by the news media. And in *All American Doll,* he evokes the tradition of war photography to prompt his audiences to think more critically about the values that U.S. children assimilated through the toys with which they played.

Dolls evoke children, and by raising questions of childhood playacting in conjunction with the adult theme of sacrificing oneself in war for the presumed good of one's country, Heinecken's series recalled the similarly age-mixing treatment of dolls by surrealist photographers like Hans Bellmer. Bellmer was best known for his gelatin silver photographs of *poupées* (French for "dolls")—homemade manikins that he built out of diverse materials and photographed in various states of assembly and undress.[69] Always female, Bellmer's poupées were youths not children, and they possessed sexual characteristics suggesting a stage of physical development slightly beyond puberty. Typically, Bellmer further sexualized his creations through clothing and dress: he favored stockings, negligees, and Mary Jane shoes, and he garbed his dolls so as to accentuate their erotic connotations. More disturbingly, he consistently violated the poupées' bodies, depicting them with missing or extra body parts, or with flesh made of mismatched or crudely grafted components. Simultaneously evoking sexual violence and uncontrolled genetic mutation, the poupées were intended by the German-born artist to form a counterimage to the racially pure Aryan women of Nazi ideology. Antitheses to National Socialist thinking and the crude biological ideals that the Nazis worshipped, the poupées were furthermore designed to remind their audiences of repressed instincts and sexual drives that permeated human behavior, forces whose existence were denied by traditional bourgeois, Christian, and even National Socialist worldviews.[70]

In *Linus Meets Donald Duck* (1965), Heinecken presents characters from two different cartoon worlds staring blankly at one another across a tiny dollhouse bed, next to which a vase and a toilet have been positioned (Plate 1.9). There is a mismatch between the sizes of the various objects, and the tableau's action is ambiguous. Because the two characters engage with one another across a mattress, adult sexuality is perhaps implied, while at the same time, because the personae are toys modeled after well-known cartoon characters, they are associated with the childhood world. Heinecken has used contrasting lighting to further distinguish the two figures: Linus is bathed in a soft, low-level glow, while Donald's white surface blazes under a bright light that hits him from the side. Because both figures are (presumably) male, light becomes a way of indicating a form of difference that—in the context of a sexual interpretation of the image—takes the place of gender. Like Bellmer, Heinecken thus gives inanimate objects new forms of uncanny animation through pose, lighting, and assemblage. Unlike Bellmer, Heinecken makes the sexuality much less overt in his doll photographs (although it is generally present), and far less patriarchal and heterosexual as well. In Bellmer's poupée photographs, the implied point of view is consistently one of an adult male viewer regarding a younger (and presumably less powerful) girl. Thus even though they are potentially critical of straight male sexual identity—suggesting that it is violent and perverse—the poupées still maintain this subject position by rendering it fixed and consistent. In contrast, sexual identity seems to be much more ambiguous in Heinecken's photographs, gay as well as straight relations are evoked, and the implied viewer seems much less stable.

The sexual ambiguity characteristic of the doll photographs is also on display in *The Eager Bridegroom* (1965) (Plate 1.10). Here Heinecken has arranged five paper dolls in a row; in the center of the image we see the eager groom in his bathrobe, flanked by a flower girl and best man on the left, and his bride and a maid of honor on the right.[71] Framed against a black background, the figures are obviously flat—something that is emphasized by the shadows that fall on the best man and maid of honor—and they thus remind the spectator of their status as clichés or stereotypes. We are social types, they seem to suggest, paper skins that can be put on and taken off. Although the figures all come from the same set and thus are commensurate in style and scale, the bridegroom is distinguished from the other characters through his clothing. While they are dressed for the wedding, he wears a bathrobe and carries a towel, revealing a

> **PLATE 1.9.** Robert Heinecken, *Linus Meets Donald Duck* (1965). Gelatin silver print, 9 ⅝ x 14 ½ inches (24.45 x 36.83 cm). Center for Creative Photography, The University of Arizona. Robert Heinecken Archive. COPYRIGHT 2022 THE ROBERT HEINECKEN TRUST, CHICAGO.

> **PLATE 1.10.** Robert Heinecken, *The Eager Bridegroom* (1965). Gelatin silver print, 14 x 19 ½ inches (35.56 x 49.53 cm). Collection Center for Creative Photography, The University of Arizona. COPYRIGHT 2022 THE ROBERT HEINECKEN TRUST, CHICAGO.

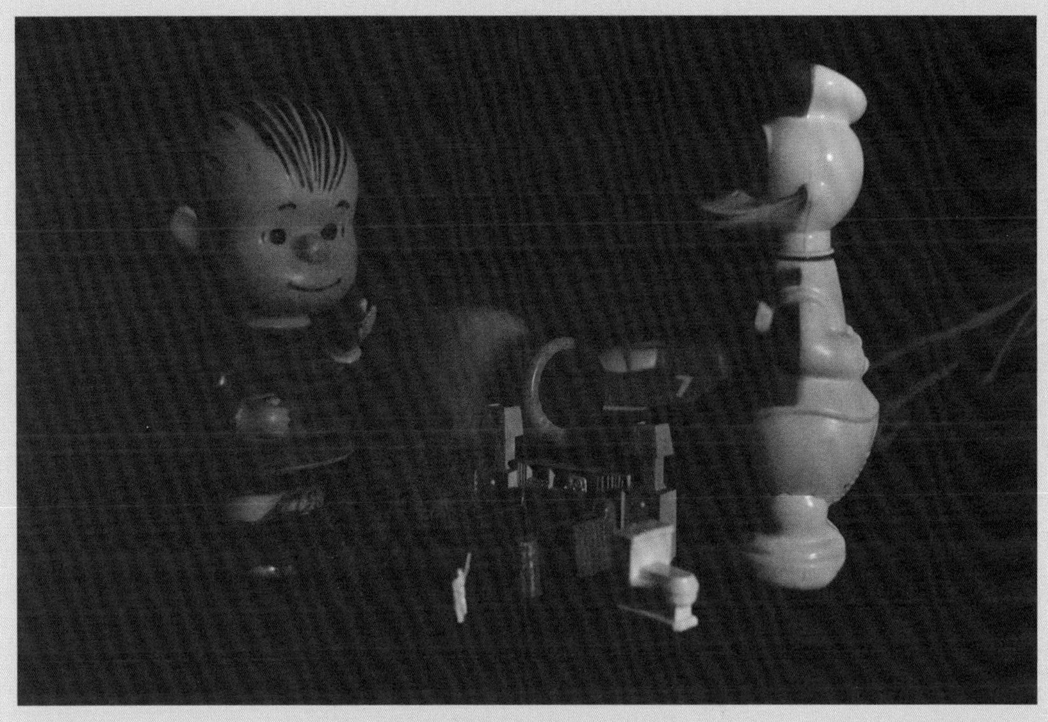

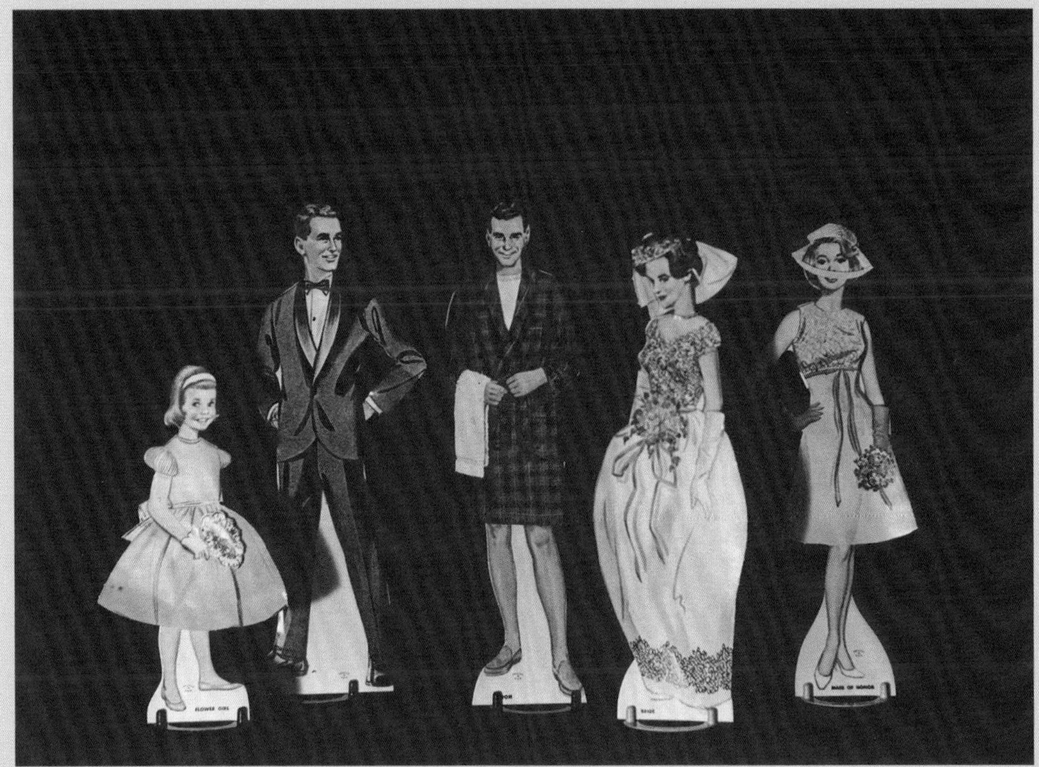

FLOWER GIRL
MAID OF HONOR

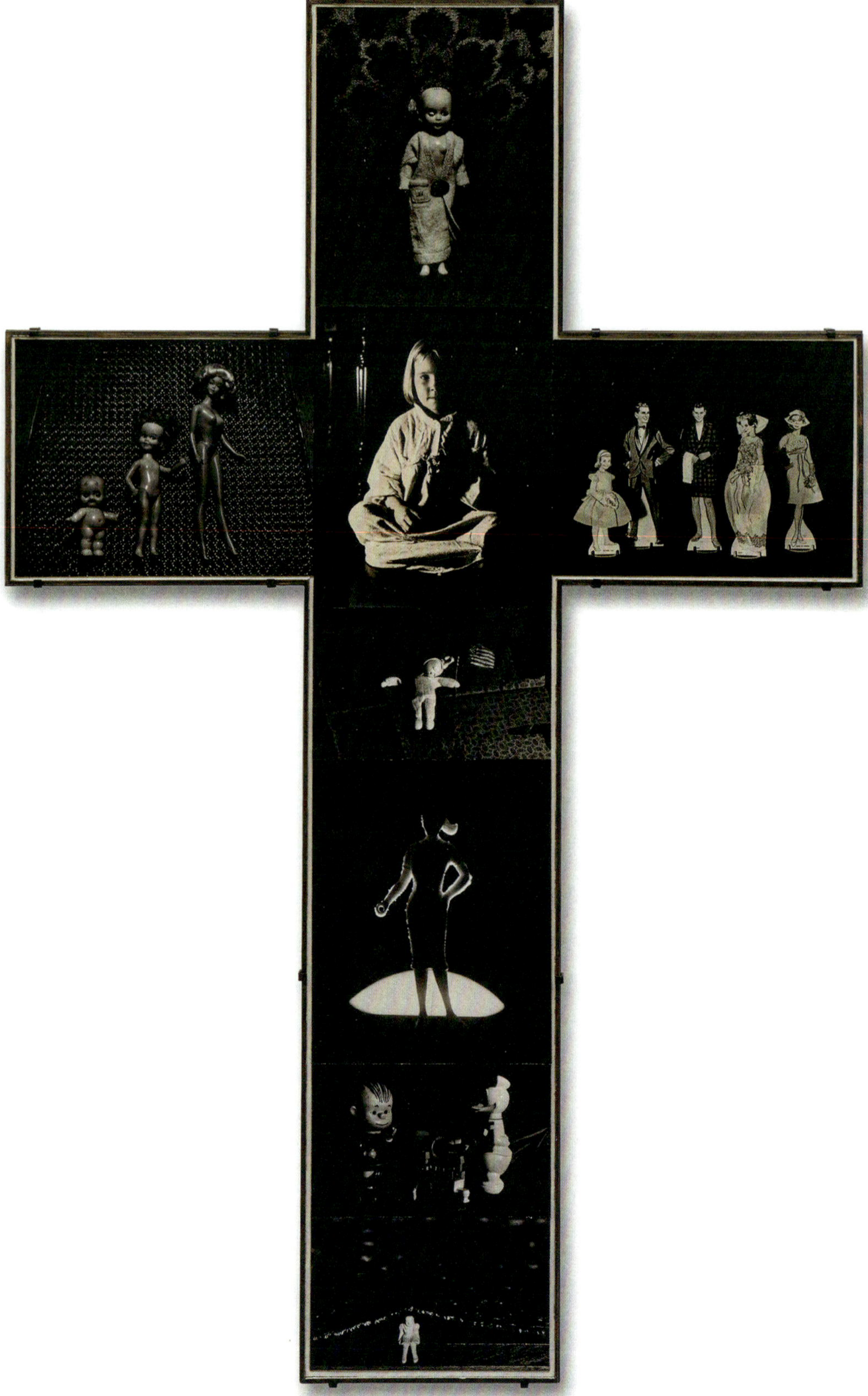

private face as opposed to a public one. This contrast between public and private—home and church—is further emphasized by the coloring and positioning of the figures, who can also be read as comprising a gay and a lesbian couple. Because of their similarly toned (dark) clothing and close proximity, the two men can be read as forming a pair. Likewise, the bride and the maid of honor, both wearing light clothing, can be read as a twosome. Despite being composed of mass-produced figures that embody patriarchal and heterosexual role models, the image exudes a polymorphous sexuality and an ambiguity about sexual identity that runs through it like a subtext.

Parodying the producers of contemporaneous advertising photography, Heinecken "sold" an image of America through an assemblage of objects. He mobilized easily grasped clichés to suggest a narrative or convey a "message." Unlike advertising photographs, which generally strove for maximum comprehensibility and popularly, Heinecken's gelatin silver prints made sure that the stereotypes did not line up in the accepted order. Instead, in his doll series popular clichés were used to represent unexpected narratives and relations, stories and affinities that would provoke questions instead of mindless acceptance and consumption.

As the series developed, Heinecken began to combine the uncanny doll photographs into more sculptural works he called "visual poems." *Visual Poem / About the Sexual Education of a Young Girl* (1965) is probably the best known and most important of these works (Plate 1.11). A cruciform assemblage of eight gelatin silver prints, it presents a seated portrait of Heinecken's six-year-old daughter Karol, surrounded by seven doll photographs, including *All American Doll, Linus Meets Donald Duck,* and *The Eager Bridegroom.* As suggested by the didactic title, Heinecken understood the doll photographs to represent images that helped form his daughter's gender, sexual identity, and the future public and private roles she would assume. By playing with different characters drawn from the world of popular culture, the work implies, she would be taught to direct her desires according to images created by consumer society.

In addition to the works already discussed, Heinecken also encircled the seated Karol with four other images that, like the doll photographs, present characters and character types against the grain, suggesting a critique of the 1950s family ideal. *Happy Doll* (1965) features a nude female doll, sitting on a board, with patterned fabric pressing down on her head; it evokes the oppression of women through sexuality and domesticity. *Toy Prostitute* (1965), on the other hand, is a frontal portrait of a winking doll posed like a geisha in a bathrobe against a floral background. Although the figure is clothed, sexuality is once again implied to be an instrument of domination and control. *Doll Growth Chart* (1965) presents three nude dolls of different ages (a baby, a girl, and a young woman) positioned against a grid formed by chair caning. The image resembles a scientific presentation in which representative samples of a certain type or species are compared. Yet despite its typological format, it undermines commonly understood distinctions between organic and industrial development. Finally, *Doll with Ready Hand* (1965) consists of a standing doll in a spotlight, viewed from behind, with one hand on her hip and the other extended. The image implicates the mass media; it is as if we are watching a singer's performance from behind the stage. The doll's empty hand, waiting for a microphone to fill it, can also be seen as making a masturbatory gesture and thus becomes a source of uncanny discomfort.

As Heinecken's visual poem suggested, the mass media allowed for the reproduction of both sameness and difference. The various characters and social types that surrounded Karol (Linus, Donald Duck, Barbie, and the bride and bridegroom) projected a normative world of the 1950s family ideal. However, when they were juxtaposed in nontraditional ways, they became host to a diverse array of alternative forms of desire and affiliation. Furthermore, because of the cruciform shape of the work as a whole, *About the Sexual Education of a Young Girl* evoked not only a world of religion hovering around its subject but also an atmosphere of mourning. The assemblage's mournful quality was reinforced by a number of its component images, for example, *All American Doll,* with its fallen soldier connotations. And by evoking mourning and the Vietnam War dead in the context of a work that purported to be about the sexual education of a young girl, it reminded its viewers that mass culture allows its subjects to identify with multiple genders, roles, and even species.

More than a decade before David Levinthal and Laurie Simmons, postmodern photographers who made heavy use of dolls and toy figures since the late 1970s, Heinecken employed uncanny doll photography to analyze the social construction of identity in an increasingly commodified and violent mid-1960s America. As the 1960s progressed, parents and children were becoming more and more conscious of a "generation gap," a distinct difference in interests and values between the people who became parents in the late 1940s and 1950s—the silent generation—and their offspring, who were known as the baby boom generation. Heinecken's doll photographs seem to grapple with this perception not in a didactic way but by raising questions about whether there was a mismatch between the dominant ideals of the American culture in which he had been raised and the values that his children needed in order to best live their lives. And while Heinecken's practice of doll photography lasted only a year, it revealed the artist to be a master of assemblage and social criticism. After visual poems like *About the Sexual Education of a Young Girl,* which mixed a representation of a living person with images of arranged objects, Heinecken stopped photographing dolls. Instead, he focused more on the strategies of appropriation that he began to use with "The American Image Ideal," developing them to a Dada-like level of simplicity and power. The resulting series, *Are You Rea*, became one of his best-known works.

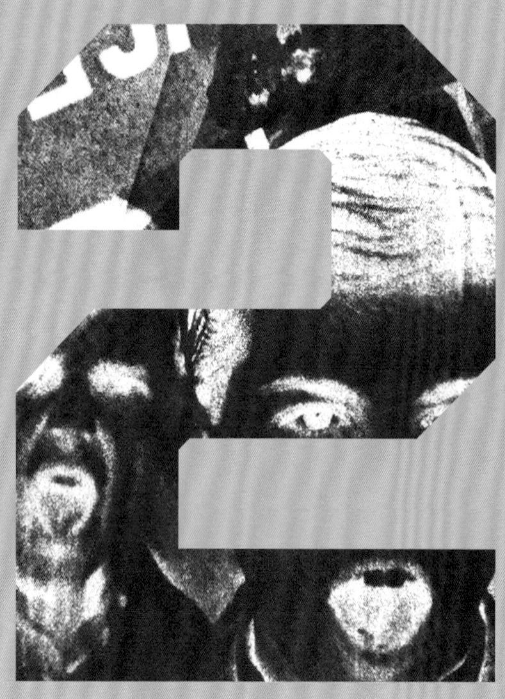

2

Appropriation
and the Photogram
in the 1960s

IN 1968, Robert Heinecken released one of the signal works of his career, *Are You Rea,* a portfolio of twenty-five lithographs of grainy, ghostly, tonally reversed photograms taken from the pages of popular magazines. Disclosing the artist's debt to surrealist theory, the introductory text professes interest in "the multiplicity of meanings inherent in aleatory ideas and images" and declares that "these pictures do not represent first hand experiences, but are related to the perhaps more socially important manufactured experiences which are being created daily by the mass media."[1] André Breton is then quoted at length. One could hardly ask for a more concise articulation of the genealogy linking Dada and surrealism, the assemblage and montage practices of West Coast artists such as Wallace Berman, Edward Kienholz, and John Baldessari, and the strategies of postmodern photography associated with Richard Prince, Barbara Kruger, Cindy Sherman, and others.

Yet rather than viewing Heinecken through the lens of postmodernism, it is best to understand the artist first and foremost in his own paradoxical terms—namely, as a "documentarian" of "manufactured experience." Like contemporaneous pop artists on both coasts, Heinecken kept his eyes fixed on the commodification of everyday life, and he described experience not as given or spontaneous but as preconditioned and fabricated. To live in American society in the 1960s was to participate as never before in an unending process of consumption; it was thus impossible to criticize consumer ideology from without.[2] Acknowledging his own entanglement within the systems that subtended U.S. consumerism, he frequently incorporated his own particular obsessions and biography into his art. In this respect, his photograms, lithographs, transfer drawings, transparencies, collages, and photographic sculpture from the second half of the 1960s were not only in dialogue with pop but resemble the new documentary photography of the time—that of Diane Arbus, Lee Friedlander, and Gary Winogrand, among others—in that they assemble an individualistic selection of motifs and details, presenting a social statement from an unabashedly subjective point of view. But Heinecken took the implications of such photographic subjectivity considerably further than the new documentarians did, laying bare his personal tastes and predilections in a shocking and unflinching way.

As Heinecken became more and more successful over the course of the 1960s, his creative output burgeoned. Between 1964 and 1974, he presented seventeen one-person shows and appeared in approximately eighty-five group exhibitions.[3] Important solo venues during this time included the Long Beach Museum of Art (1965), the Pasadena Art Museum (1972), and the California State University Art Gallery, Long Beach (1973), as well as three commercial galleries—the Focus Gallery (1968) in San

Francisco, and the Witkin Gallery (1970) and Light Gallery (1973) in New York—all of which helped to expose his art to an ever-growing audience. His group exhibitions, moreover, which spanned the photography and the art worlds, included such prestigious venues as the Museum of Modern Art (1967, 1968, and 1970), the George Eastman House (three times in 1967 and once in 1969), the Library of Congress (1971), the Philadelphia Museum of Art (1972), the San Francisco Museum of Art (1973), the Fogg Art Museum (1974), and the Whitney Museum of American Art (1974).[4] During this time, his work was increasingly written about by critics and poets (including A. D. Coleman, Charles Hagan, and Marvin Bell); influential curators, such as Nathan Lyons and Peter Bunnell, began to champion his photographic practices.

Heinecken's career as an important and influential educator also grew considerably. At UCLA, he received tenure during the 1966–67 academic year (while on sabbatical in Germany), and the series of photography courses that he developed at the university's extension program only a few years before became a degree program within UCLA's newly reconfigured College of Fine Arts.[5] Offered at both the graduate and undergraduate levels, Heinecken's program was the first in the University of California system to grant a degree in photography.[6] Heinecken also participated vigorously in the Society for Photographic Education (where he served as chair in 1971 and 1972), developing a network of colleagues and associates that helped him to advance his vision of photography and photographic education in general and to disseminate it further in the public realm. He additionally began to publish his views on photography and education, and he encouraged UCLA to both collect and exhibit contemporary photography, sometimes curating the shows himself.[7]

At the same time as he was achieving this increased success and recognition as an artist and professor of photography, Heinecken also embarked on a series of artistic interrogations that would turn out to have profound significance for the development of contemporary photography. In the mid-to-late 1960s, these included transfer drawings, sculptural photography, and work with transparencies and collage—all practices designed to undermine dominant standards of photography, explore the role of photo-reproductive media in relation to the body and society, and engage with issues raised by the expanding U.S. counterculture. Perhaps Heinecken's most important "para-photographical" project during this time period, however, was his exploration of the photogram technique between 1964 and 1968 conducted under the title *Are You Rea*. Like his work in other media, Heinecken's photograms were documentary in that they were engaged with social and political debates then affecting American society: questions having to do with sexual mores, consumer society, social and political unrest, the power of youth, and the role of the United States as a national and international power. These debates, fueled by the burgeoning counterculture, helped to undermine the family and corporate values of the 1950s, replacing them with more individualistic and heterogeneous ideals and allegiances.[8] In addition, however, they also raised questions similar to those being posed by pop artists like Robert Rauschenberg and Andy Warhol, questions having to do with the nature of art and its role in contemporary life, the tension between art and politics, and the relationship between handmade and mass-produced images. But because they explored these issues from the point of view of photography and not painting or sculpture as did most of the pop artists, Heinecken's works of this era revealed aspects of U.S. consumer culture that the better-known artists did not investigate.

Are You Rea

When Heinecken began to contact-print magazine and newspaper pages onto photographic paper in 1964, he was well aware of the photogram's long history as both document and art.[9] A photogram is commonly considered to be a unique image made without a camera or lens. There is no mediating negative; objects are simply arranged on the surface of a sheet of chemically prepared photographic paper, exposed, and then developed, the resulting image supposedly bearing direct traces of its worldly referents. Inspired by surrealism's use of the cameraless photograph as a means of chance and automatism, the artist proofed some two thousand pages over four years, removing leaves from *Time, Newsweek, Women's Day*, the *New York Times*, and other publications and contact-printing them on gelatin silver paper.[10] The photogram process captured both the front and back of each page, superimposing one image on the other. Over the four years he worked on the *Are You Rea* project, Heinecken created approximately thirty-five different gelatin silver photograms, which he printed in editions ranging from three to nine iterations. Then in 1968, Heinecken produced the *Are You Rea* portfolio, consisting of twenty-five lithographic prints made from the original photograms.

In the *Are You Rea* series as a whole, the mid-1960s American world appears as a conflicted space of burgeoning youth, sexuality, spectacle, consumption, and violence. In some images, grainy figures seem to move and interact with others as if caught in successive freeze-frames of an image sequence. In other works, ghostly X-ray copies interact with text and commodities. Words, when readable, often seem to fight the juxtaposed actors. Playing between legibility and nonsense, the *Are You Rea* photograms and lithographs focus attention on the media's tactical use of constant repetition, on the power of its labels and definitions, and on the fact that we respond to its cues in a disjointed, distracted, and physical way. In addition, they document chance encounters in the national press, combinations of spectacular elements that represent clashes between specific identities and ideologies defined in terms of race, gender, class, nationality, and subculture.

To assemble his portfolio in 1968, Heinecken redacted the mass of images he created over the years by devising thematic groupings— lesbianism, cosmetics, women and children, marriage triangles, and social issues. Picking five images in each of the five categories, he then sequenced and collated them into an evocative quasi-narrative, with passages of three to four images repeating the same typology and another image or two amplifying, augmenting, or transforming the theme.[11] As a close reading suggests, *Are You Rea* shows Heinecken wrestling with the countercultural concerns of his time: sexuality, consumerism, social and political unrest, the power of youth, new types of celebrity, lifestyle, and fashion, and the individual's relationship to the state.

When read in its original order, the portfolio interpolates its viewers, addressing them as critics and consumers. It begins with two introductions. The first is a signed and numbered title page with a three-paragraph text that explains Heinecken's process—a technique that organically combines photogram and montage practices and links the resulting pictures to both the mass media and the documentary tradition. The second introductory text is a long quote from *Les Vases Communicants* (1932) by André Breton that praises the poetry of a chance encounter between disparate things. Breton asserts that everything "is an image and . . . the least object which has no symbolic role assigned to it is capable of standing for absolutely anything." The highest task of poetry, he argues, is to generate forms of montage: "to compare two objects as far distant from one another as possible, or, a quite different method, to confront them brusquely and strikingly."

The viewer is then presented with a second title page, the portfolio's first picture. The text at the top of what looks like the cover of a woman's fashion magazine demands "ARE YOU REA," the truncated question evoking a materialistic culture in which readers "find" themselves in idealized images and ad copy (Plate 2.1). Our eyes are first drawn to the tonally reversed figure of a young woman that occupies the center space, who wears large sunglasses and removes her shirt to reveal her bra; dark, spectral, and assertive, her form is both alluring and aggressive. Slowly other forms emerge both in front and behind her: two mod boutique chairs, a vitrine with ladies' shoes, and a second woman curled in the chair closest to the picture plane.[12] Lines and grids interconnect the

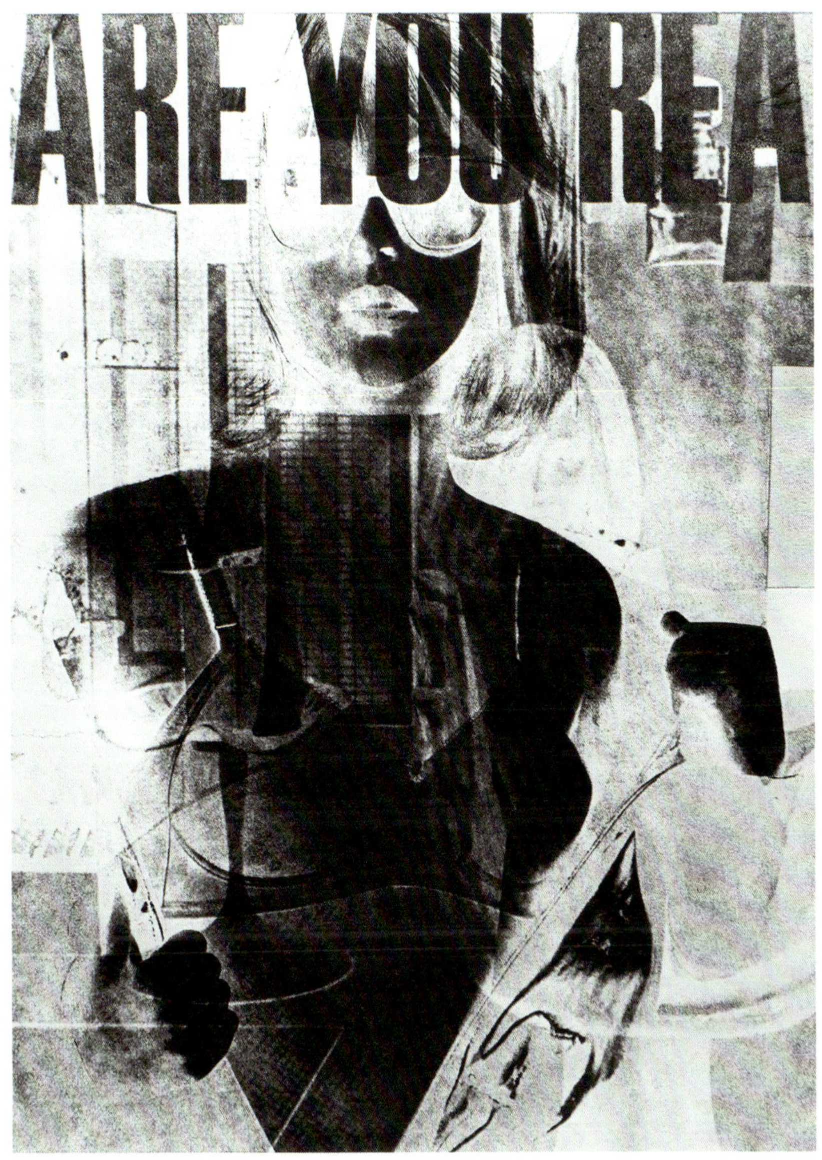

PLATE 2.1. Robert Heinecken, *Are You Rea, 1964–1968* (1968). Photolithographic print based on a gelatin silver print photogram from a magazine page, 10 $\frac{13}{16}$ x 7 $\frac{7}{8}$ inches (27.4 x 20 cm). 90/500, Plate 1. Private collection. COPYRIGHT 2022 THE ROBERT HEINECKEN TRUST, CHICAGO.

figures and objects, embedding them in a half-photographic, half-cubist space in which everything seems fluid and interrelated.

Within this vertiginous spatial context depicted on the portfolio's "cover," image and text combine in ambiguous ways. First, despite its legibility and apparent simplicity, the text is confusing; slightly truncated at the top, it suggests that it might be missing letters as well. It thus implies that it may not be asking the beholder if we are "rea" (presumably either the woman in the picture or someone she is addressing) but, rather, if we are "real" or "ready." The three letters are also an anagram for the Equal Rights Amendment (ERA) and, depending on how we pronounce them, a nod to one of Heinecken's artistic ancestors, Man Ray. Second, the text's radical ambiguity is mirrored by the visual structure of the image. Despite the fact that the photogram betrays its origins in the world of women's fashion magazines, designed to appeal to a youthful and consumer-oriented demographic, the figures it presents do not fit into clear categories of race or gendered behavior. The primary figure is ethnically ambiguous; although she is most probably white, her facial features and inverted skin tones do not allow the viewer to be certain.[13] In addition, she bares her bra, a gesture that is simultaneously inviting and—because it recalls chest-baring figures like the Marianne symbol of revolutionary France (depicted, for example, in Eugène Delacroix's *Liberty Leading the People*, 1830)—slightly threatening. Indeed, although the lithograph was released months before the famous feminist protest of the Miss America Contest in Atlantic City, New Jersey, on September 7, 1968, organized by the New York Radical Women, which associated feminists (falsely, it turns out) with bra burning, the brassiere, as Heinecken's image suggests, was a motif that could embody feminist as well as consumerist and sexual connotations.

After the cover page (1), Heinecken shifts the orientation of the image to a landscape format (2) before immediately switching back to the more conventional portrait format of the mass-market commercial magazine in the next image (3).[14] Over three pages (2–4), we are presented with a series of close-ups and medium shots of attractive (sometimes seminude) fashion models who are all in some way merged with one another: a Picassoid double face made up of two similarly sized visages; a standing woman synthesized from two models draped with sumptuous patterned fabrics; and a crouching figure in lingerie with two enormous eyes emerging from her side and flank. In all of these images, signifiers of race, bodily integrity, and "normality" are destabilized, and the constant pairing of the women introduces the theme of lesbianism. No additional text appears in the sequence until the final image (5): a scene in which a dress model, her hands bound and facing the viewer on her knees, merges with an another model, turned away from the reader, displaying her underwear.

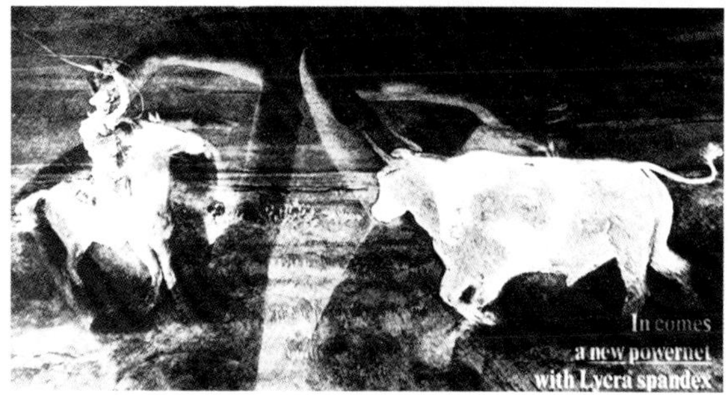

A fragment of advertising copy, "of Eve . . . ," floats next to the head of the kneeling figure. Two inward-turning figures, united at the arm and cheek, they combine with the text to suggest a subjective space of female encounter, absent of all men. And in this way, Heinecken emphasizes a lesbian subtext running beneath the heterosexual ideology promoted by mid-1960s clothing and fashion advertisements.

The next image (6) flips the orientation of the picture field back to landscape mode, suggesting the end of one sequence or the beginning of another (Plate 2.2). It depicts a horse-riding cowboy about to lasso a steer—imagery that Richard Prince would make famous a decade and a half later to allegorize the construction of American identity through cigarette advertisements.[15] White and spectral, the horse, rider, and bull confront one another against a darker mass, which consideration reveals to be two lingerie models, shot from below, looking upwards and shielding their eyes. A Western plain appears in the distance, and floating in the bottom right corner is copy reading, "In comes a new powernet with Lycra spandex." Once again, figures merge with one another, the cowboy and his horse fusing with the head and shoulders of the model on the left, and the bull amalgamating with the head and chest of the woman on the right. As human mixes with animal, vision (enacted by the women) is contrasted with action (shown by the cowpoke roping the steer). Furthermore, although the theme of lesbianism continues, a man has appeared in the portfolio for the first time.

After the cowboy and lingerie models, we are presented with multiple close-ups of women's faces interspersed with young feminine bodies and snippets of language that address a female consumer: texts reading "You don't have to be an angel . . . just look like one!" (7), "no-cal" (8), and "The make-up that's Barely There" (9) adorn different images. The theme that emerges in this section is that of women and cosmetics—or, to disclose its underlying implications, the remaking of human bodies into aestheticized images that incarnate social and commercial coding. For the most part, the page montages make the sensually posed fashion models seem hybrid and monstrous, creatures with extra eyes, limbs, heads, and other growths. Their effect seems both violent and conventionally erotic at the same time. In the final image of the sequence (10), a clothing model in a sequined halter dress faces the viewer, hands on her hips; within her body a second head grows, illuminated as if by an X-ray machine or television screen (Plate 2.3). A third head, also framed by a screen, floats to the side of the model's face. Like the visage in her chest, it depicts the president's

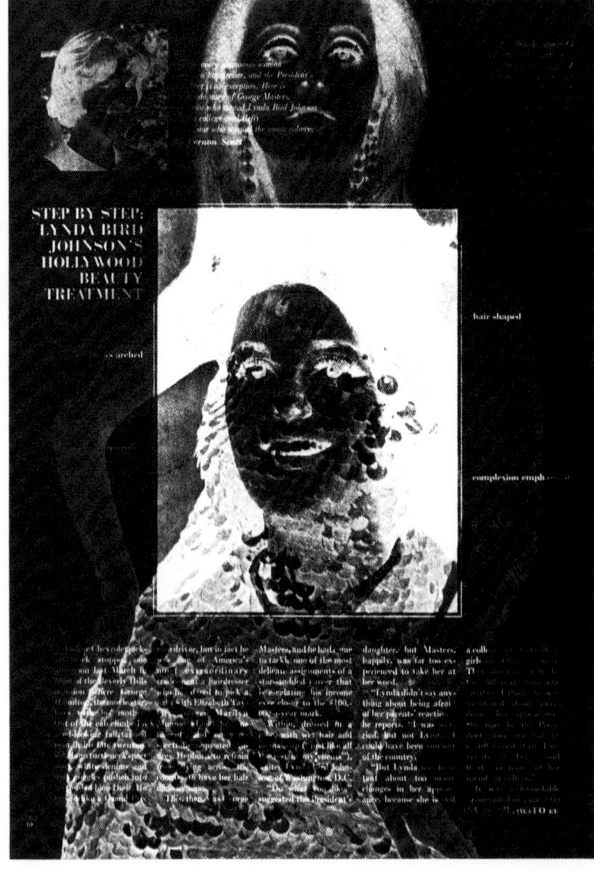

PLATE 2.3. Robert Heinecken, *Are You Rea, 1964–1968* (1968). Photolithographic print based on a gelatin silver print photogram from a magazine page, 10 13/16 x 7 7/8 inches (27.4 x 20 cm). 90/500, Plate 10. Private collection. COPYRIGHT 2022 THE ROBERT HEINECKEN TRUST, CHICAGO.

eldest daughter, Lynda Bird Johnson, and promises, "step by step: lynda bird johnson's hollywood beauty treatment." Framed against a dark background, the figure's pose and direct gaze make it seem slightly confrontational; more disturbingly, its assemblage of different visages evokes a process of replication in which each copy is slightly different from the one that came before it. A bricolage of images and texts, the lithograph emphasizes the surface of the body and how even minor celebrity—in the mid-1960s, Lynda had achieved press notice for dating actor George Hamilton—demands a new and more manufactured presentation of self.

The next sequence (11–15) focuses on maternal bonds: relationships between women and children. Bodies are morphed together in unnatural and disconcerting ways; in addition to being merged with one another, the women and children are also synthesized with everyday objects and the environment. The suturing together of mother and child connotes pregnancy and growth, but the often-frightening chimeras suggest mutations and abortions as much as they do new life. In one picture, a woman in a black-and-white bikini is cut in half by a fork and spoon knifing into a bowl of spaghetti; the headline reads, "The proud Italian sauce. It changed 17 million minds about packaged spaghetti dinners." The body, the photogram suggests, is consumable, something that can be packaged, devoured, and then eliminated. In another image, mother and child create a squat hybrid offspring, crouching on one knee, in what looks like a position of great tension. An amalgam of an underwear model measuring the circumference of her thighs with a tape and a toddler posing in a one-piece jumper, its disturbing condition perhaps "from unnecessary pressure on the thighs." Fashion, the figure implies, can often affect people like a disease, a source of pain and malformation. In yet another image, a young woman, framed in what is simultaneously a door and a window, gazes down at the ground; a toddler in underwear appears within her body and a second toddler floats in the bottom left corner. The multiplying children once again suggest a process that merges biological with industrial production. The title, "the fortunate, fashionable rescue," prompts questions such as, Who is being rescued and from what? Once again, the 1950s family ideal—focused on home, family, and clear gender differences—is called radically into question.

After the mothers and children sequence, the viewer is presented with two images of women juxtaposed with prominent texts: a bent-over yoga model staring at the viewer from between her legs with a caption that says "Ad man do it justice;" and two couture models in pantsuits stretched in yoga-like poses superimposed with the title "The Considerate Console," and the caption, "Compare carefully." In contrast to the earlier images, which seemed to address a female spectator through a focus on clothing, makeup, and offspring, these images appear to embody a more stereotypically heterosexual male point of view: the women are objectified through their poses as well as the language that surrounds and suffuses them. In this sequence (16–20), which Heinecken selected to suggest "marriage triangles," images of male figures return to the aleatory and surreal quasi-narrative. Men's bodies morph into those of the women in ways that suggest both heterosexual and homosexual scenarios; a prominent narrative motif, which emerges in three images, is that of an onlooker observing a romantic encounter. Evoking a condition in which the relationships between men and women double and multiply, this sequence also suggests that sexuality in the 1960s was becoming more and more overt—a subject of representation that was designed to be consumed. (In particular, because implied spectators appear to watch romantic interludes, these lithographs can be interpreted as referencing the tremendous growth in pornographic imagery in the 1960s, a result of a series of court cases that decriminalized obscene materials.) In this sequence, Heinecken also reflected on the position of his project in the field of contemporary art: in one incredible image a photograph of pop art collectors Robert C. and Ethel Scull is combined with their sculptural double portrait, George Segal's *Portrait of Robert and Ethel Scull* (1965) (Plate 2.4). Although truncated and edited, Ethel's image remains relatively singular: a photographic head resting on crossed sculptural legs. Robert, on the other hand, is split; he appears on both the left and right sides of his wife, and his sculptural form becomes his photograph's own shadowy doppelgänger. An allegory of the fragmenting self, this appropriative montage prompts the spectator to consider the relationship between Heinecken's photographic practice and the more mainstream—and commercially successful—manifestations of American pop art.

In the last five images (21–25), which comprise the social issues sequence, men predominate, and the texts address a more gender-neutral or "universal" reader. John F. Kennedy's portrait appears as a fragment of an enlarged magazine reproduction of a canceled five-cent commemorative stamp above what seems to be two women writhing in either love or hate, agony or ecstasy. (The two figures are actually a single seated young woman, lit to cast a strong shadow on the carpet that she is modeling.) Evoking a context in which questions circulate about who killed the young president and the effect that his assassination was having on the United States and the rest of the world, the image suggests an explosion of psychosexual energy in everyday American life in the wake of its leader's death. The next picture juxtaposes a photograph of a dark bride situated in a Bell telephone ad, hovering over a posed group of male and female protesters (Plate 2.5). Printed in black, the bride's ad copy—"When

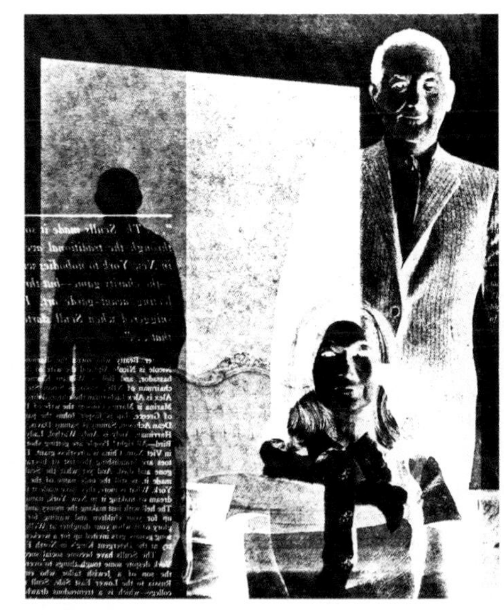

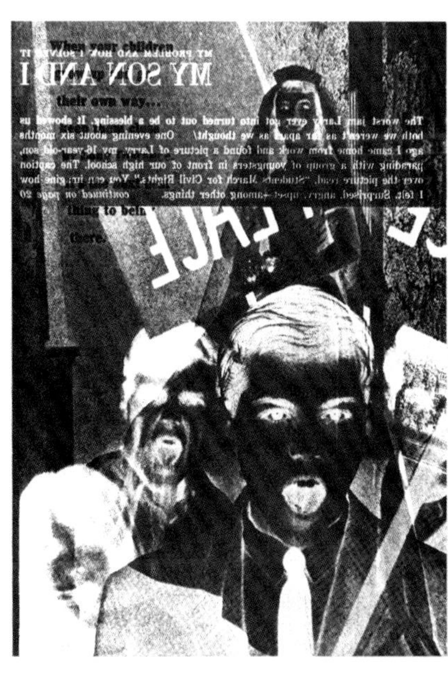

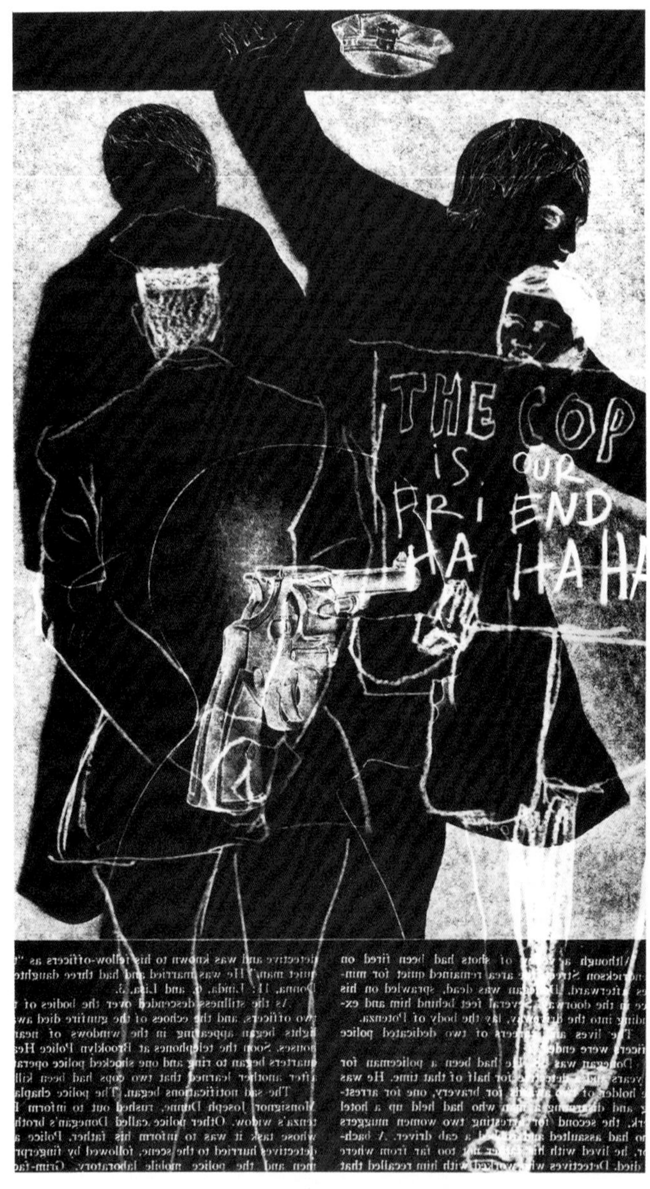

PLATE 2.6. Robert Heinecken, *Are You Rea, 1964–1968* (1968). Photolithographic print based on a gelatin silver print photogram from a magazine page, 10 ¹³⁄₁₆ x 7 ⅞ inches (27.4 x 20 cm). 90/500, Plate 25. Private collection.

your children grow up and go their own way . . . keep them close with Long Distance. It's the next best thing to being there"—is legible but just barely; it is partially obscured by the protesters' reversed peace signs and the first paragraph of an article printed in white, which discusses a mother's reaction to finding her sixteen-year-old son marching for civil rights outside his high school. Significantly, both the normal and the reversed copy synergize with one another, reminding us of how magazines carefully coordinate content with advertising in order to intensify their readers' desire to consume. The next picture presents a portrait of Maharishi Mahesh Yogi, the Beatles' famous guru and father of Transcendental Meditation, merging with a cigarette ad that promotes Lark's new special filters: "More than a million people like what Lark does." It is a trenchant document demonstrating the conflation of spirituality, celebrity, and consumption in the late 1960s.

In the second-to-last picture of the social issue sequence, we are presented with an obscure and radically disjointed image that juxtaposes President Lyndon Johnson speaking to soldiers in Vietnam with an advertisement that depicts a newly engaged young woman who asserts that "a diamond is forever," the famous De Beers advertising slogan, coined by Frances Gerety in 1947.[16] Made from the top half of a *Life* magazine cover, it presents an uncanny tableau in which Johnson seems to bless two kneeling supplicants, a couple who are illogically merged with both one another and a floral wreath. The human forms are only barely distinct; as a whole they appear like an explosion of morphing yet still interrelated elements. The text, "the president's trip," also evokes Kennedy's journey to Dallas, lending another set of associations to the assemblage of figures and objects. The ensemble thus seems to challenge the military ideal that had previously meant so much to Heinecken: the United States in Vietnam is juxtaposed with Dutch colonial exploitation, and the U.S. president is linked to an explosion of body parts. In the final picture we see a police officer with a gun behind his back, pointing it at a man holding a sign that reads, "The cop is our friend. Ha, ha, ha" (Plate 2.6). Two slightly larger men, viewed from behind, flail in the background; a light silhouette of a man's head encircles the cop's gun, and a policeman's hat floats overhead. Once again the protagonists in the lithograph are racially ambiguous, although here a contrast between white and Black ethnicities is suggested through the tonal differences between the heads of the different antagonistic figures.[17] Evoking urban violence, racial conflict, and the repressive actions of the U.S. police in relation to African Americans as well as young antiwar protesters, the portfolio ends on an apocalyptic note.

As suggested by *Are You Rea,* Heinecken's art of the 1960s anticipated postmodernism through its concentration on "manufactured experiences" and its recourse to strategies of appropriation and montage. Like postmodernists such as Barbara Kruger and Richard Prince, Heinecken employed these strategies to both record and destabilize what he felt were the manufactured identity positions promulgated by the contemporaneous mass media. In addition, like many of the postmodernists, Heinecken made use of iconography evoking a variety of different subjectivities, ones that included both male and female points of view.[18] Making its audience simultaneously viewers and readers, *Are You Rea* thus documents different variants of the male and female gaze, from the maternal to the emulating to the eroticizing to the macho, aggressive, and even sadistic. By moving from montages of ideal female identities constructed through fashion and lifestyle magazines to powerful and violent male identities as portrayed by the news media, Heinecken's portfolio critically explores a range of American gender stereotypes that were promulgated in the 1960s. (If Man Ray is evoked at the outset, James Earl Ray is suggested by the conclusion.) The strategies of appropriation and montage are here combined to criticize ideology, to make implicit values explicit, and to encourage their reevaluation by juxtaposing them in new and provocative ways.

With its references to debates around gender, sexuality, race, and spirituality, as well as its allusions to the growth of the mass media, generational conflict, new forms of art, military involvement in Vietnam, urban violence, and political assassinations, *Are You Rea* is a document of its time, but one that uses artistic strategies to defamiliarize the everyday world presented by the culture industries in order to provoke a socially critical audience response. The mid-to-late 1960s, it suggests, was a time marked by the ascendance of countercultural values, a moment when the individual and collective paradigms that dominated the 1950s lost their power to unite an overwhelming majority of Americans, and when the new archetypes and forms of social life that were emerging were not only more varied than ever before but also more riven by conflict and difference.[19] To make sense of this situation, *Are You Rea* suggested, Americans would have to adapt—become more adept at negotiating differences and more able to adopt fresh habits and novel modes of being.

Pop Art

As suggested by the plate depicting Robert and Ethel Scull in the *Are You Rea* series, in addition to West Coast assemblage, Heinecken consciously engaged with pop art through his exploration of the photogram technique. There were distinct differences between West and East Coast pop, and Heinecken navigated between both trajectories. As Cécile Whiting has argued, pop art in LA consisted of "a variety of styles that evoke and redefine the urban vernacular."[20] Encompassing artists as diverse as Ed Ruscha, David Hockney, Vija Celmins, Billy Al Bengston, Llyn Foulkes, and even Judy Chicago, Noah Purifoy, and Simon Rodia, LA pop was not constrained to a particular look or medium. Instead, it was focused on its environment as a new form of (postmodern) city that was neither urban nor suburban but instead possessed multiple centers connected by a web of freeways. Playing between representation and abstraction, pop art in Los Angeles during the 1960s thus explored a range of imagery, including signage and advertising, facades and commercial building typologies, and the California consumer lifestyle (through an iconography of human figures, cars, food, leisure products, city- and landscapes). In addition, pop art in LA also often evoked a fragmented and mobile gaze, much like that of a driver in an automobile, a point of view that seemed suspended between criticizing and valorizing the new West Coast urban condition.

Heinecken was highly aware of the LA art scene as it developed in the 1960s and 1970s, and he shared a number of the pop LA obsessions, including an interest in signage, advertising, ideal male and female types, and images of consumption. In addition, like "art studs" Ruscha and Bengston, Heinecken cultivated a look and persona, and he advertised himself through ironic performances at schools and conferences as well as through the media. As Whiting notes, "Ruscha and other young L.A. artists exploited advertising culture—placing outrageous photographs in the art press—to promote their identity as studs as much as their art."[21] Emphasizing their embrace of a self-involved male mode of existence built around cars, motorcycles, sex, surfboards, consumption, and pleasure, these artists—many of whom showed at the Ferus Gallery—portrayed themselves as "a new type of creator: young, handsome, heterosexual, and inspired by a hedonistic California lifestyle."[22] In contrast to these LA pop artists, Heinecken did not focus on Los Angeles as a city very much in his art, and his public presentation of self, although macho and "cool," was even more tongue-in-cheek and self-undermining than those of the Ferus artists. Developing a Western persona, which he signified through long hair, beard, blue jeans, and denim clothing, Heinecken would simultaneously emphasize and undermine his sexuality. A good example of this is revealed by Jo Ann Callis's portrait of the artist, *Valentino Heinecken* (1974), in which he appears barefoot in a turban with pink sunglasses and red toenails.[23]

Although he engaged with pop art in LA, in many ways Heinecken was more clearly in dialogue with pop art in New York, particularly with issues raised by Robert Rauschenberg and Andy Warhol. In Manhattan in the late 1950s and early 1960s, the focus of pop art was primarily on painting, with artists intentionally undermining the qualities most prized by the New York School of the 1940s and 1950s, such as originality, expression, composition, formal presence, inventiveness, the handmade, and gesture. Inspired by the composer John Cage, Rauschenberg took on the history of modernist painting, destabilizing the values of the previous generation of American abstract painters through the incorporation of photographic representation and the stuff of everyday life into his paintings, which were also partially created with more traditional materials like oil and acrylic paints. At the same time, he continued the pictorial tradition of abstract expressionism and color field painting by emphasizing gesture and facture and by using appropriated mass media images and everyday objects compositionally as formal elements within larger pictorial formations.

Warhol went even further than Rauschenberg in the project of negating Western painting by purging qualities that Rauschenberg still retained. He thus eliminated gesture, implemented serial composition and monochrome color schemes, and employed an iconography and rhetoric that celebrated the most ubiquitous forms of consumer culture: mass-produced products like Coca-Cola and Campbell's Soup; celebrities like Marilyn Monroe, Liz Taylor, and Jacqueline Kennedy; and news images like car crashes and suicides that depicted anonymous deaths and violence. However, like Rauschenberg, Warhol never fully renounced painting, and as a result for many critics and art historians he came to represent a fundamental break or rupture in the history of modernist art: the turning point between modernism and postmodernism.

In the mid-1960s, Heinecken briefly explored the process of ink transfer drawing, using it to investigate imagery taken from the mass media—a technique that Rauschenberg had been using since 1958 for similar ends.[24] Created by soaking magazine fragments in solvents like turpentine, acetone, or lighter fluid and then contact printing them on paper by rubbing their backs with a pen nib or other implement to transfer a reversed image of one side of a magazine page, transfer drawings were mechanical, painterly, and graphic all at the same time.

As suggested by works such as *Sleeper/Muscleman* (1967) and *Comic Strip for Teenagers* (1967), Heinecken used this technique to mix typology with narrative.[25] On the one hand, these works display distinct archetypes—idealized young men and women who exhibit opposing characteristics: hardness, consciousness, and action in the case of the former, and softness, unconsciousness, and passivity in the case of the latter. The grid structures reinforce this sense of a comparative typology illustrating clear gender differences. On the other hand, the figure types seem to interact and merge—a function of the film- or television-like structure of the formal composition (a series of similarly sized frames), the figures' multiple poses, and Heinecken's disturbing superimpositions of their corporeal forms. Through this process of movement, the transfer drawing creates an ambiguous quasi-narrative in which different characters display their bodies in conformity with traditional gender stereotypes and simultaneously seem to act so as to undermine them. Unlike Rauschenberg's transfer drawings of the 1960s, in which the juxtaposed magazine images were more disparate as well as associated in a more aleatory manner, Heinecken's ink transfer drawing montages seem almost didactic, sociological lessons about gender difference.[26] But under their didacticism run uncanny and disruptive chains of meaningful association: a sense of clear gender stereotypes breaking down and of sexuality in a state of flux.

Rauschenberg used the transfer drawing technique as a means of bringing mass-reproduced imagery into the practice of abstract gestural painting as defined by the abstract expressionists and color field painters. As such, these montages, which often also incorporated marks made in gouache, watercolor, or colored pencils, related to both Rauschenberg's three-dimensional "combine" paintings of the 1950s and early 1960s—uniting actual objects with abstract painterly fields and gestures—and his silkscreens of the 1960s, which used images drawn from the mass media but in a smoother, less handmade way.[27] Although Rauschenberg's transfer drawings perhaps tended to pull the spectator's focus to the content of their imagery more than his other works, they remain tied to modernist ideas and compositional practices developed in the field of postwar abstract painting in the United States. Heinecken, on the other hand, used the transfer drawing technique for different ends. He was not interested in disrupting the painterly tradition. In addition, Heinecken's interests seem more content driven as well as uniquely focused on the paradoxical nature of the photographic medium as an avenue of representation that produced images that were simultaneously real and artificial.

Heinecken's achievements in relation to pop art become clearest, however, when we compare him to Warhol. Because of their radical and complex engagement with their respective media—painting and sculpture in Warhol's case, and photography and printing in the case of Heinecken—both artists raised radical philosophical questions in relation to the nature of art and representation. In 1962, after a brief period of "hand-painted pop," Warhol began to use the silkscreen process, which removed all traces of his hand from the canvas. Working with assistants, who often did the actual painting, the New York artist simplified his subjects through cropping and intensifying the graphic contrast of his appropriated photographic sources, frequently reducing them to a single, central, almost schematic image that was then repeated and organized within grid formats. Focusing on celebrities, commodities, and everyday death or disaster, Warhol's pop paintings between 1962 and 1966 have since grown in status to become some of the fundamental landmarks in the history of twentieth century art. For many contemporary critics, historians, and philosophers, Warhol radically changed the essential nature of modern art by merging fine art with mass culture and everyday life in a radically new way. Although he kept them in certain ways distinct—Warhol remade the image and the object rather than just appropriating them as readymades—he seemed to eradicate the distinction between high and low in a more trenchant manner than any other artist before him.

For Arthur Danto, Warhol represented a "new era of art," a condition of postmodernism, in which artworks could no longer be distinguished from real things.[28] As the philosopher argued:

> most of the philosophy written about art before Warhol was of scant value in dealing with his work: philosophical writings could not have been written with art like his in mind, as such work simply did not exist before he created it. Warhol demonstrated by means of his Brillo Box the possibility that two things may appear outwardly the same and yet be not only different but momentously different. Its significance for the philosophy of art was that we can be in the presence of art without realizing it, wrongly expecting that its being art must make some immense visual difference.[29]

Warhol's Brillo Boxes were fundamental extensions of one of the controlling ideas that motivated his silkscreen paintings of the early 1960s, most notably his Campbell's Soup Cans. One of their central innovations was to upend the distinction between the fine arts and consumer culture. But because of their philosophical radicality, they also shared an attribute with "certain religious objects, which we expect to look momentously different from ordinary things but which are disguised, one might say, by their ordinariness."[30] Furthermore, at the same time as they undermined what philosophical aesthetics said art was, Warhol's paintings and sculptures also seemed to define the social and cultural moment in which they arose through the deadpan representations they appropriated.[31] In particular, they appeared to represent the era's distinct desires and fears as they pertained to human subjects, namely celebrity, commodification, and death.[32]

Benjamin Buchloh concurs with Danto about Warhol's fundamentally transformative impact on modern art—his position as an avatar of postmodernism—when he argues that Warhol was "singularly prepared to perform the historically necessary transformation of the artist's role in the American post–World War II context, the transformation of an aesthetic practice of transcendental negation to one of tautological affirmation."[33] As this formulation suggests, however, Buchloh is more critical than Danto about Warhol's ultimate impact on the development of contemporary art. As Buchloh sees it, Warhol used mass cultural iconography, deadpan ironic commentary, mechanized production procedures, and nontraditional modes of distribution and display to mimetically internalize and repeat the violence of the changing social and artistic conditions of the 1960s—a time marked by tremendous growth in the mass media and a corresponding loss of power held by the sphere of fine or advanced art:

> Warhol's "scandalous" assaults on the status and the "substance" of pictorial representation were motivated by the rapidly dwindling options of credible artistic production, a fact that had become more and more apparent as the conventions of modernism and avant-garde practice had finally been rediscovered, but even more so by the increasing pressure and destruction that the accelerated development of the culture industry exerted now on the traditionally exempt spaces of marginal artistic deviance.[34]

Evoking and negating central modernist strategies like seriality, monochromy, light reflectivity, and gridded composition, as well as the participatory aesthetics of Rauschenberg and Alan Kaprow, Warhol engaged with Western painting in order to represent the evacuation of all existential and metaphysical meaning from modern art; through this gesture, he marked his time as separate from what came before. Moreover, by means of his popular iconography, his post-abstract representations, Warhol developed a new vision of the American subject, a construct of the mass media, who simultaneously contemplates "the Other (in endless envy at fame and fortune as much as in sadistic secrecy at catastrophe) and the perpetually vanishing Self (in futile tokens and substitutes)."[35]

Because of the power of his art and its ability to seemingly affirm all ideologies and subject positions, Warhol ultimately undermined the criticality of fine art for Buchloh—its ability to counteract the growth of consumer culture:

> Warhol has unified within his constructs the views of both the victors and victims of the late twentieth century: the entrepreneurial world view, its ruthless diffidence and strategically calculated air of detachment that allows it to continue its operations without ever being challenged in terms of its sociopolitical or ecological responsibility; and the phlegmatic vision of the victims of that world view, the consumers, the "all-round reduced personality," who can celebrate in Warhol's work their proper status of having been erased as subjects. Reduced to being constituted in the eternally repetitive gestures of alienated production and alienated consumption, they lack the slightest opening toward a dimension of critical resistance.[36]

Embodying a kind of flattening of humanity and emptying of self-awareness in the 1960s, Warhol's art portended the ever-greater insufficiency in art's critical power that was to come.

Like Danto and Buchloh, Thomas Crow notes the characteristic way in which Warhol both celebrated and evacuated American "subjects," the manner in which he represented them while also rendering them empty of life and meaning. Crow finds this central enigma in Warhol's art in the (democratic) ubiquity or "impersonality of the images [Warhol] chose and their presentation, his passivity in the face of a media-saturated reality, and the suspension in his work of any clear authorial voice."[37] More than the other critics, however, Crow emphasizes the powerful social conflicts and anxieties that Warhol staged in his art. For Crow, Warhol's significance lay in how he dramatized the breakdown of the commodity exchange in American society, the moments when consumer goods could no longer satisfy—and even destroyed—their possessors. His art also disclosed the disturbing effects that the mass media was having on the American psyche and its processes of mourning. In his images of tragic celebrities like Monroe, Taylor, and Kennedy, Warhol revealed instances in which "the mass-produced image as the bearer of desires was exposed in its inadequacy by the reality of suffering and death."[38] Such celebrity images uncovered a new sense of loss, "the absence of a richly imagined presence that was never really there."[39] And in his subtle handling of the quasi-mechanized silkscreen medium, "Warhol found room for a dramatization of feeling and even a kind of history painting."[40] Likewise, in his images of disasters, deaths of anonymous people who through their destruction were given their fifteen minutes of fame, Warhol managed to convincingly represent tragedy in the contemporary moment. As Crow puts it, "We cannot penetrate beneath the image to touch the true pain and grief, but their reality is sufficiently indicated in the photographs to force attention to one's limited ability to find an appropriate response."[41] The works in the disaster series thus "have in common with the celebrity portraits and product labels . . . a fascination with moments where the brutal fact of death and suffering cancels the possibility of passive and complacent consumption."[42] As a result, while both acting out and representing through painting and sculpture the destruction of the centered American subject in the 1960s, Warhol also inspired conviction about his representation of his contemporary moment; his was a convincing "peinture noire" or "a stark, disabused, pessimistic vision of American life."[43] In contrast to Buchloh, Crow is much more optimistic about the social-critical impact of Warhol's art, and thus that the rise of postmodernism did not entail American art losing nearly all critical autonomy and being subsumed within the sphere of mindless entertainment.

Just as Warhol did during the first half of the 1960s, Heinecken appropriated material from newspapers, magazines, and advertising to expose unlikely combinations of sex and violence discoverable in the U.S. mass media. And like Warhol, he mixed representations of celebrities with those of ordinary people, which in works like *Are You Rea* he structured into dark visions of contemporary American life, while at the same time referring to and undermining established conventions of art photography through appropriation and montage. Unlike Warhol, Heinecken did not develop a longstanding interest in the practice of portraiture, nor did he achieve the considerable success and recognition that Warhol had received since the 1960s, something that had to do with his choice of a different medium, photography, in which to produce his art.

As Danto, Buchloh, and Crow argue, Warhol's significance related to his engagement with the history of modern and modernist painting and sculpture, a record of development that he contested through the choice of a particular type of (anonymous, everyday) imagery as well as by introducing certain photographic practices into the more traditional and elevated medium of art-making. It was the media of painting and sculpture that served as the focus of his attack—and for Crow, the formal handling of the silkscreen process—that gave Warhol's art its power and particular resonance. Heinecken, on the other hand, engaged with the history of photography, which he contested through a similar type of commonplace American iconography, as well as by consistently focusing on previously photographed and mass-reproduced imagery. The power and resonance of Heinecken's art, in other words, were tied to his engagement with the photographic medium, which he defamiliarized through appropriation, the mixing of temporally distinct photographic practices, and the combination of photography with other media (lithography, for example, in the case of *Are You Rea,* or as we shall see, television in other works). Although Heinecken, like Warhol, powerfully and complexly represented the various crises of identity that Americans were experiencing in the 1960s, he did this through a channel that was still considered to be uncritical and solely contributing to these crises.

Photography, as the comparison between Warhol and Heinecken suggests, was in many ways still the antithesis of painting and sculpture in the 1960s; and it was only the latter mediums that could provide a space for autonomy and truth—or so artists and critics believed. As a result, Heinecken's achievement—the use of photographic appropriation and montage to explore the social and psychological effects of the mass media understood as a system designed to construct identity while inciting mass consumption—could be easily overlooked. Heinecken did not enact contemporary art's crisis as did Warhol (through the latter's performance of the modernist painter's loss of autonomy). Instead, Heinecken dramatized the role of the photographer as a mass consumer of images. This figure, as his oeuvre suggests, was both voyeuristic and objectifying, but also surveilled and constructed in turn. And though less recognized during the course of Heinecken's life, it nonetheless presents important implications for the understanding of contemporary art and photography in the 1960s and 1970s.

The primacy of painting and sculpture during the pop revolution was based on a false, but (then) rarely criticized assumption: namely, that photography could not in itself function as a critical and self-reflexive medium in which to explore the dissolution of credible art and integral subjectivity in the mid-twentieth century. That this was of course incorrect is proven by *Are You Rea* as well as another series of troubling works created by Heinecken at this time, his early Kodalith transparencies. These works remind the spectator of a different aspect of Warhol's art, one that was singled out by Danto most strongly: namely, Warhol's ability to undermine the distinction between art and nonart in such a disturbing and profound way.

Heinecken made his transparencies with Kodalith film, a reproductive technology used in print production to prepare images and text for mass reproduction. Kodalith transparencies were used in the preparation of halftone plates for newspaper and magazine production as well as in lithography, standing as intermediaries between the original, more detailed photographs and the printing plates used to make the final mass-produced product. Creating a high-contrast image that lacked gray areas, this medium tended to make its subjects more abstract as well as to foreground the process of publishing photographs, that is, integrating them with texts and translating them onto the printed page. In Heinecken's hands, the Kodalith transparency was used to create seemingly exact images of magazines and newspapers that longer contemplation revealed to be both truthful and misleading in a significant way. On the surface they seemed radically nonartistic, literal reproductions of everyday disposable culture, but with close reading and study they transformed, producing chains of disturbing associations, like carefully constructed artworks.

As Long As You're Up (1965) reproduces two facing pages taken from the March 1965 issue of *Esquire* magazine (Plate 2.7). A few pieces of the original page and a little text along the interior fold have been roughly torn away, and the image has been blown up slightly; in addition, the overall contrast of the black-and-white spread has been increased. Otherwise, the two pages have been left unaltered.[44] On the right we see the largest image: a reclining man on a sofa, looking up to the left, a caption above his head commanding, "As long as you're up get me a Grant's." On the left, a young girl appears; she stands with bare feet. The caption next to her reads, "Let her love you . . . ," and a donation form below implores the reader to give to the Foster Parents' Plan, Inc., an international children's relief organization that Jacqueline Kennedy had promoted in 1962. From one perspective, the transparency looks like an unaltered transcription of a double-page spread: typography, image quality, and layout seem to match between the two pages. From another perspective, the contrasts and connections between the pages seem too humorous and shocking to be nonintentional. The two figures appear to interact, the man calling to the little girl as if she were his wife. Likewise, the captions contrast in a striking and comical way: the man addresses the viewer, while the little girl is spoken about—something that gives the man more subjectivity and agency. Highlighting the stereotypical gender roles promulgated by the mass media, the spread suggests that even the sight of deprivation did not get in the way of the pleasure of consumption. In addition, the text situated between the two advertisements concerns JFK's assassination and the 889-page government report about it that was released in 1964. An excerpt from "A Critique of the Warren Report," by Dwight Macdonald, *Esquire*'s left-wing film critic, it examines the controversies that surrounded Kennedy's death. On the one hand, the transparency seems completely nonartistic; its subject, a torn double-page spread, is mundane, and its literal representation of the subject seems redundant and unoriginal. On the other hand, its subtle focus on national tragedy in the context of a critique of the media suggests both a self-reflexive awareness of the ideologies promulgated through U.S. advertising and consumption

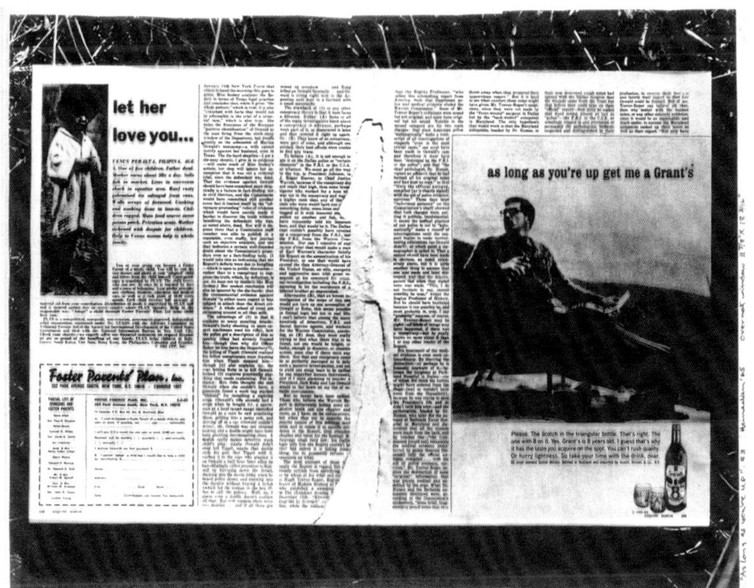

PLATE 2.7. Robert Heinecken, *As Long As You're Up* (1965). Black-and-white film transparency, 15 ½ x 19 ⅝ inches (39.4 x 49.8 cm). The Robert Heinecken Trust, Chicago. COPYRIGHT 2022 THE ROBERT HEINECKEN TRUST, CHICAGO.

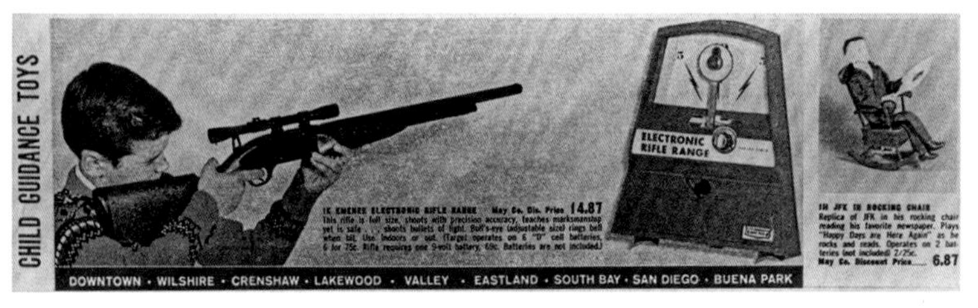

PLATE 2.8. Robert Heinecken, *Child Guidance Toys* (1965). Black-and-white film transparency, 5 x 18 ⅟₁₆ inches (12.7 x 45.8 cm). The Art Institute of Chicago. Gift of Boardroom, Inc.

as well as a mournful desire to come to terms with collective loss. Even more than Warhol's early silkscreens and sculptures, the transparency seems both radically nonartistic and richly significant at the same time, representative of the profound tensions that wracked the mid-1960s.

Still more resonant is Heinecken's most famous transparency of the 1960s, *Child Guidance Toys* (1965), a slightly blown-up montage of two fragments of the same page of an advertising supplement published by the *Los Angeles Times* on November 24, 1963, two days after JFK's tragic death (Plate 2.8).[45] Here a young boy sights down the scope of his toy rifle at an electronic target behind which President Kennedy sits in a rocking chair. Originally the Kennedy image was placed in a line of five toys above the target; Heinecken's appropriation of the image, however, eliminates the other playthings and moves the president down into the line of fire. When he first saw the conjunction of the two toys, Heinecken must have been shocked by the juxtaposition, as it seems to exemplify a common fear of the time that mass media and mass consumption could promote violence, an apprehension that has only gotten more pronounced since the 1960s. To emphasize this collective anxiety, Heinecken shifted the president into alignment with the shooter and target, while at the same time using the characteristics of the Kodalith transparency to suggest a nonartistic, antiauthorial type of work. Toys, the image suggests, can be used to train budding assassins, and the messages our newspapers transmit can sometimes be deadly.

Mansmag

The comparison with Warhol reveals important aspects of Heinecken's achievement: he is significant because of his introduction of New York pop concerns—appropriation, readymade imagery, a focus on stereotypes promulgated by the mass media, and an obsession with sexuality and death—into the development of photography over the course of the 1960s, interests that later became celebrated as signature characteristics of photographic postmodernism. As we have seen, Heinecken's magazine photograms and transparencies were radical gestures within the history of photography—designed to undermine all traditional ideas about authorship, invention, and the distinction between high and low culture. In addition, in their most radical forms, they caused their spectators to question the distinction between art and nonart. At the same time as they questioned this distinction, they were also profound documents of the crises that wracked 1960s American society: war, racism, gender inequality, and the growing power of youth. And finally, they revealed their context as a moment in which the mass media had come to permeate everyday life to such an extent that it had created a second order of reality—a world of *simulacra,* to use the postmodern term, in which manufactured experiences were beginning to be taken as the things themselves. Like the contemporaneous media theory of Daniel Boorstin and Marshall McLuhan, Heinecken's art suggested that the world had been transformed through the new communication technologies that were making it a "global village," a densely interconnected network where information—in the form of sounds, images, and texts—traveled more quickly and more widely than ever before.

Because they so trenchantly fulfilled these multiple functions, Heinecken's photograms, lithographs, and transparencies of the 1960s are, in their own subterranean ways, comparable to Warhol's achievements in painting and sculpture, although they have received much less acclaim since their creation. This is the case, I argue, because of their position in the photography world of the 1960s rather than the world of art then. In photography at this time, where the most important trajectories seemed to be either formalist–modernist or subjective documentary, the central focus in Heinecken's practice on the photographer as a conflicted consumer of mass media images was not appreciated—or even fully grasped. His performative renunciation of the idea of the photographer as a creator of new images was not understood, and his critique of manufactured experience was seen as something odd, peripheral, and not really definitive of the moment. In addition, as suggested by *Are You Rea,* the photograms were only fully realized when Heinecken brought them together into sequences, creating quasi–magazine-like forms. Photography, this seems to suggest, finds its full realization not in single images but in the creation of larger assemblages of representation. *Are You Rea* remains a powerful document of 1960s society and the ways in which the most important social issues of the time were intertwined with the media and with a consumer lifestyle. Like Warhol, but through very different means, Heinecken focused on new forms of American identity that were developing in the 1960s, ones that were enmeshed in the culture industry as both subjects and objects—as consumers identifying with particular celebrities and events, and as potential news stories, just waiting for their fifteen minutes. This can be seen even more clearly in Heinecken's second sequenced photogram publication, which was based on a more prurient type of publication.

In *Mansmag* (1969), Heinecken employed lithography again, in order to print photograms of appropriated pages from a soft-core porn publication on top of one another in vivid four-color inks (Plate 2.9). An edition of 120 "variants," as he called them, each with a unique combination of colors, the magazine was a conceptual intervention into a visual genre that was decidedly nonart: a network of forms and themes that seemed totally lowbrow, prurient, and beneath serious consideration for the time. Over the successive pages of Heinecken's magazine, cartoons and "real" bodies fuse and pull apart, their almost flickering forms morphing into one another from various angles. Bodies repeat both across and between pages, and the visual field defined by the magazine's borders is often geometrically bifurcated, a segmentation that can suggest successive frames in a film (Plate 2.10). Denying the indexical clarity desired by the pornographic gaze, Heinecken's monstrous bodies produce bafflement and disquiet as well as pleasure, a sense of uncanniness that keeps the spectator suspended between desire, humor, and horror.

One reference in the journal's subtitle was to its source material: *Cavalcade*, formerly *Man's Cavalcade*, an American men's adventure magazine that began publishing in 1957 and that by the mid-1960s had rebranded itself as an adult magazine in the model of *Playboy*. *Cavalcade* was perhaps chosen as the source for Heinecken's photograms because of the way in which it evolved from a publication that focused on male adventure to one that concentrated on heterosexual male desire and the female body. Masculinity, as expressed through sex, sport, humor, leisure, and travel, was both a powerful and dynamic force in the American psyche. The subtitle's other reference, more obscure, was to Hendrik Nicolaas Werkman, the avant-garde Dutch artist, printmaker, and typographer who was murdered by Nazis in 1945, just days before Dutch liberation. A little-known avant-garde artist and publisher who expanded the possibilities of print media through his layout, typography, and a wide variety of different printing, inking, and collage strategies between the 1920s and 1940s, Werkman was an underground martyr for Heinecken, an idiosyncratic creator who was executed for his formally subversive art. Once again there is an uneasy conflation of sex and violence in Heinecken's sources and references, an evocation of processes of mass reproduction and mass destruction taking place simultaneously.

As we have seen, Heinecken's photograms, lithographs, and transparencies of the 1960s focused on sexuality, consumption, power, and violence: deep-seated psychic drives that were addressed by the mass media as well. In addition, the artist was obsessed with combat and

> **PLATE 2.9.** Robert Heinecken, *Mansmag: Homage to Werkman and Cavalcade* (1969). Offset lithography on bound paper, comprising twenty-four four-color lithographs (including covers recto and verso), 8 ¾ x 6 ⅝ inches (22.2 x 16.8 cm). Edition of 120, back and front covers. Private collection. COPYRIGHT 2022 THE ROBERT HEINECKEN TRUST, CHICAGO.

> **PLATE 2.10.** Robert Heinecken, *Mansmag: Homage to Werkman and Cavalcade* (1969). Offset lithography on bound paper, comprising twenty-four four-color lithographs (including covers recto and verso), 8 ¾ x 6 ⅝ inches (22.2 x 16.8 cm). Edition of 120, pages 5–6. Private collection. COPYRIGHT 2022 THE ROBERT HEINECKEN TRUST, CHICAGO.

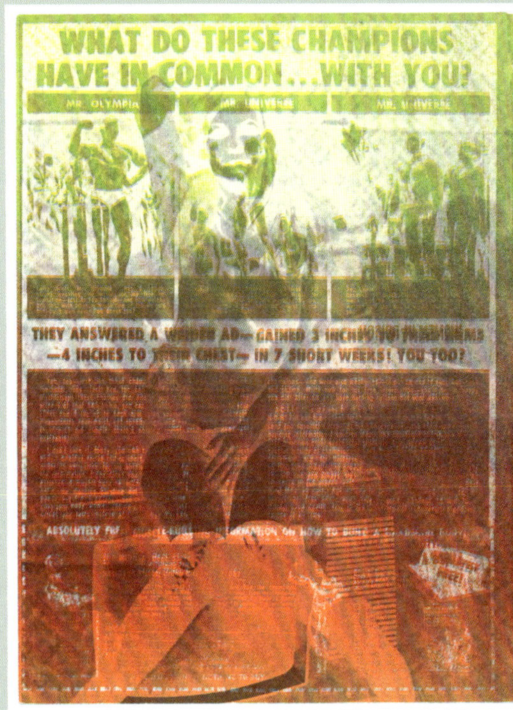
WHAT DO THESE CHAMPIONS
HAVE IN COMMON...WITH YOU?
MR. OLYMPIA   MR. UNIVERSE   MR. UNIVERSE
THEY ANSWERED A WEIRD AD—GAINED 3 INCHES TO THEIR ARMS
—4 INCHES TO THEIR CHEST— IN 7 SHORT WEEKS! YOU TOO?

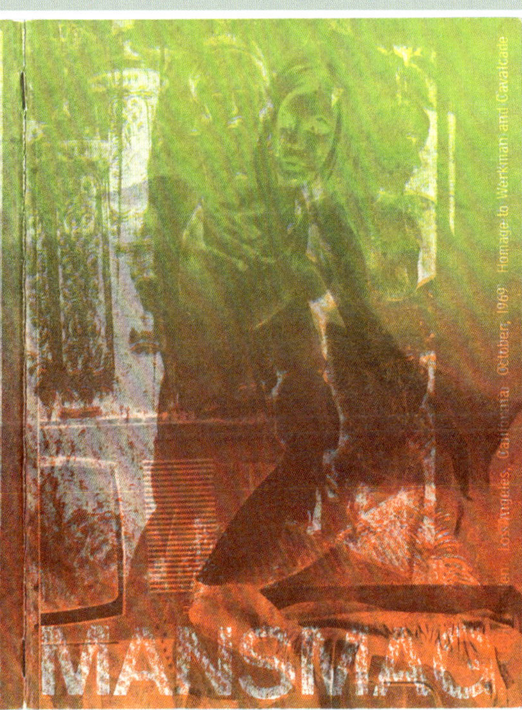
MANSMAG

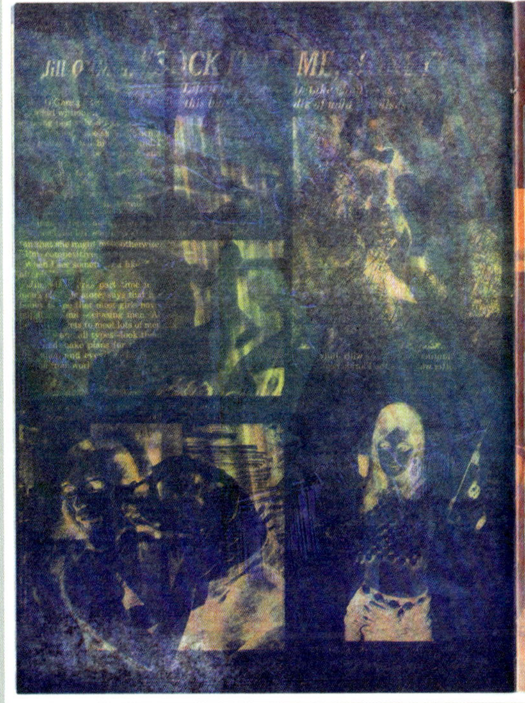

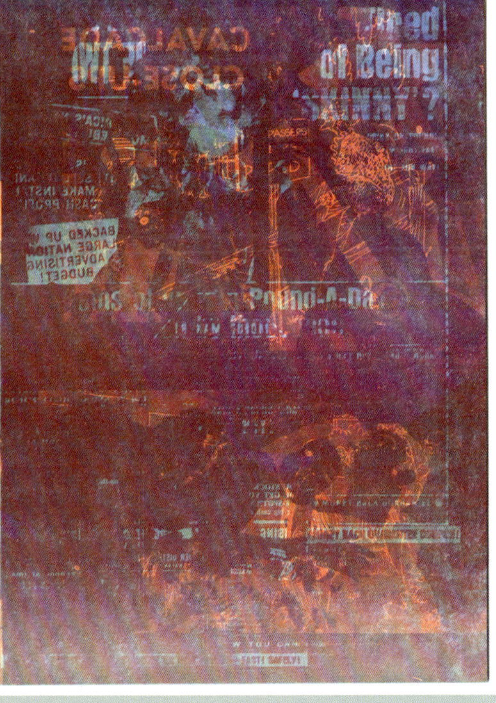
CAVALCADE
CLOSE-UP
Tired
of Being
'SKINNY'?
BACKED UP
BY A
LARGE NATIONAL
ADVERTISING
BUDGET!

destruction—in part the result of his ten-year career in the military—
something that linked him to the general fascination with warfare and
representation in 1960s art in LA, a tendency that can be seen in the
work of Vija Celmins, Llyn Foulkes, and the so-called War Babies, among
others.[46] This concentration on instinctual energy was a result of Heinecken's interest in the construction of identity through the mass media. It
is by investing images and objects with psychic urges that we begin to
construct ourselves through the representations and commodities that
we consume. As Warhol realized as well, certain types of imagery call out
to individuals more than other types of images do; by using the pictures
that most affected him on a physical level, Heinecken could explore how
the world produced by the mass media helped him construct a specific
model or understanding of himself. Heinecken appropriated images of
objectification because it was through these motifs that American consumer ideologies could be most clearly portrayed. But objectification cut
both ways: in the photography world he would become identified with his
imagery and labeled a misogynist in the 1970s, because his iconography
could become a shorthand for his gaze, thus obscuring the complexity of
his defamiliarizing strategies and gestures. We will return to these ideas
in the next chapter, which examines the artist's merging of photography
with sculpture in the late 1960s and early 1970s.

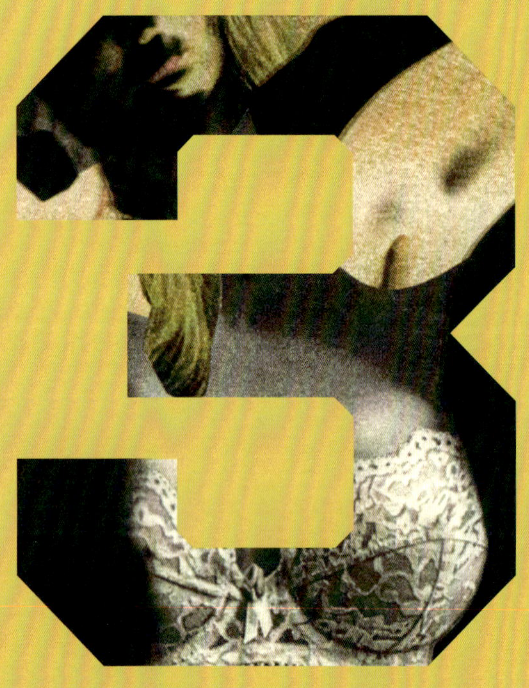

THE PHOTOGRAPHIC OBJECT

Heinecken's Materialism

THE MID-1960S were a watershed moment for Heinecken: a time period during which he began numerous important media-based explorations. Although less well known than the photograms, Heinecken's sculptural photographs between 1965 and 1970 were in certain ways equally significant. These works reveal his commitment to processes of printing and materially engaged making as opposed to techniques of shooting or taking images. They comprise flat, nonresolving puzzles consisting of photographic body parts; geometric cubes and rectangles in which corporeal forms were suspended and mixed; and boxes containing photographic transparencies of human and organic subjects layered in between plexiglass. Exploring how photography could pull back from the real in order to represent subjective concerns, collective concepts, and a heightened awareness of the technological apparatus, Heinecken's photographic objects were consciously conceived as counters to prevailing ideas that photographs were simply transparent documents of things that existed in the world.

As Heinecken put it around 1964 in a talk at a Society for Photographic Education meeting that was published a few years later:

> We constantly tend to misuse or misunderstand the term reality in reference to photographs. The photograph itself is the only thing that is real, that exists. The elements in the print are simply referents of various kinds which operate on various levels. Obviously, no picture, photographic or otherwise, can hope to come close in duplicating or even simulating reality.

In opposition to photographs that merely—or primarily—tried to reproduce reality, Heinecken proposed more experimental forms: representational objects that emphasized their materiality and were also clearly constructed.[1] As he insisted, "Many pictures turn out to be limp translations of the known world instead of vital objects which create an intrinsic world of their own. (There is a vast difference between taking a picture and making a photograph.)"[2]

To make a photograph, for Heinecken, was to manipulate it, to transform it back into an object—not a reproduction of an original, now absent set of persons and/or things, but rather a new assembly of material forms that represented something more intersubjective or collective. "Once you open the shutter of a camera you have made the first manipulative step away from the real," he noted. "Any step you take beyond that is really only a relative position on a sequential continuum of possible alteration. The end of this sequence is complete obliteration of the image."[3] Although Heinecken's photographic objects never demolished their subjects completely, they did change them radically, providing insight into how photography affects human beings on physical, conceptual, and social levels. As Heinecken put it in a talk published in 1965, a discourse on the kind of photographic practice that he exemplified in his own work and that he tried to impart to his students at UCLA: "The photograph in this context is not a picture of something but is an object about something. It seeks to trigger response, not simply to identify subjects or situations."[4] As was the case with Heinecken's manipulative photography in general, photographic objects were intended to create richer and more multivalent meanings—to pull the representation away from (simple) indexical reference and toward the complexity of artistic signification.

The importance of Heinecken's sculptural photographs lay in their direct attack on the modernist value of medium purity that was central to straight photography, still the prevailing aesthetic on the West Coast. Photographs, according to the common understanding of them, reduce the three-dimensional world to a two-dimensional surface, and this capability has always been part of their basic nature or essence. For this reason, Heinecken's attempt to turn photography back toward the third dimension in the late 1960s did more than simply muddy photographic reference, make it less indexical and more allegorically complex. In addition, Heinecken's photographic objects seemed radically offensive to the prevailing modernist conventions of contemporary art across all media: ungainly attempts to deny a fundamental property of their medium. Their seemingly formal ungainliness and inappropriateness was further emphasized by Heinecken's conventional, almost kitschy photographic subjects—nudes, trees, and the like—subject matter that seemed both banal and traditional. To some critics, they seemed like dead ends. As Hilton Kramer put it in a review of Peter Bunnell's landmark show *Photography into Sculpture* at MoMA in 1970, in which Heinecken and a number of his graduate students took part, the photo-objects on display there were "facile tricks and vulgar distortions" that leave "photography and sculpture pretty much where [they] found them—separate artistic entities."[5] Yet it was this disruptive and disturbing effrontery, as we shall see, that allowed these hybrid works to raise new questions about the photographic medium.

Blocks and Stacks

Heinecken's earliest photographic sculptures were either his figure puzzles or his three-dimensional cubes and rectangles that included images of body parts on either four or six faces. Because they abstract, fragment, and reduce the human figure in various ways, Heinecken's corporeal "blocks and stacks," as he called these latter works, can be seen as exploring the ways in which the photograph can begin a process whereby the continuous values of the real world are ultimately rendered discrete and thus subject to reproduction, manipulation, and commodification.[6] For this reason, although Heinecken never used computers, these works seem to anticipate what we would now recognize as the digitization of vision, the ways in which analog or continuous visual experience is sampled and quantified—reduced to binary code—in order to be reproduced, reworked, transmitted, and exchanged.

Figure Cube (1965), one of Heinecken's earliest blocks, is among his most disturbing photo-objects (Plate. 3.1).[7] Here Heinecken recycled six separate squares cut from an earlier photograph, a nude figure study he shot circa 1963, pasting them over Masonite to produce a stark and symmetrical geometric hybrid, an artwork that alternates between image and object. The cube's rigid shape seems to compress and mutilate the fragments of the female body that it contains; simultaneously, by breaking up the original photograph's single-point perspective, it creates what appears to be a destabilizing play of different points of view. Suturing together a combination of disjointed fragments that evoke a violent and incomprehensible world in which the natural order has been suspended, *Figure Cube* thus presents the human body as the ultimate commodity, as if butchered and ready for shipment. Thereby, like Warhol's Brillo boxes but in a different manner, it suggests a dystopian vision of the modern world in which human beings lose power and originality as they submit to the dictates of technology and machines.

Other photo stacks, like *Figure in Six Sections* (1965) and *Transitional Figure Sculpture* (1965), present the body with slightly less violence.[8] Here Heinecken recycled earlier figure studies, but by leaving his models whole, he projected a marginally more harmonious vision of humanity in the clutches of geometry and measurement. The works' combination of positive and negative imagery suggests that a person's anatomy can be seen in multiple ways; there is much less of a sense—as there is with *Figure Cube*—that the human form has been harmed through the mere fact of its photographic replication. *Fractured Figure Sections* (1967), however, breaks the figure down again, mixing its parts in less than logical orders,[9] once again suggesting Heinecken's concerns about the deleterious effects of the photographic apparatus and technology and instrumental thinking in general (Plate 3.2).

The stacks also project more positive associations; all three cut human form into discrete units that can be manipulated by turning them around the work's vertical axis. The confluence of photography and sculpture, they suggest, makes the flesh more open to transformation. As the various slabs of the stacks are turned, moreover, the figure moves in and out of focus, resolving and dissolving depending on the relative positions

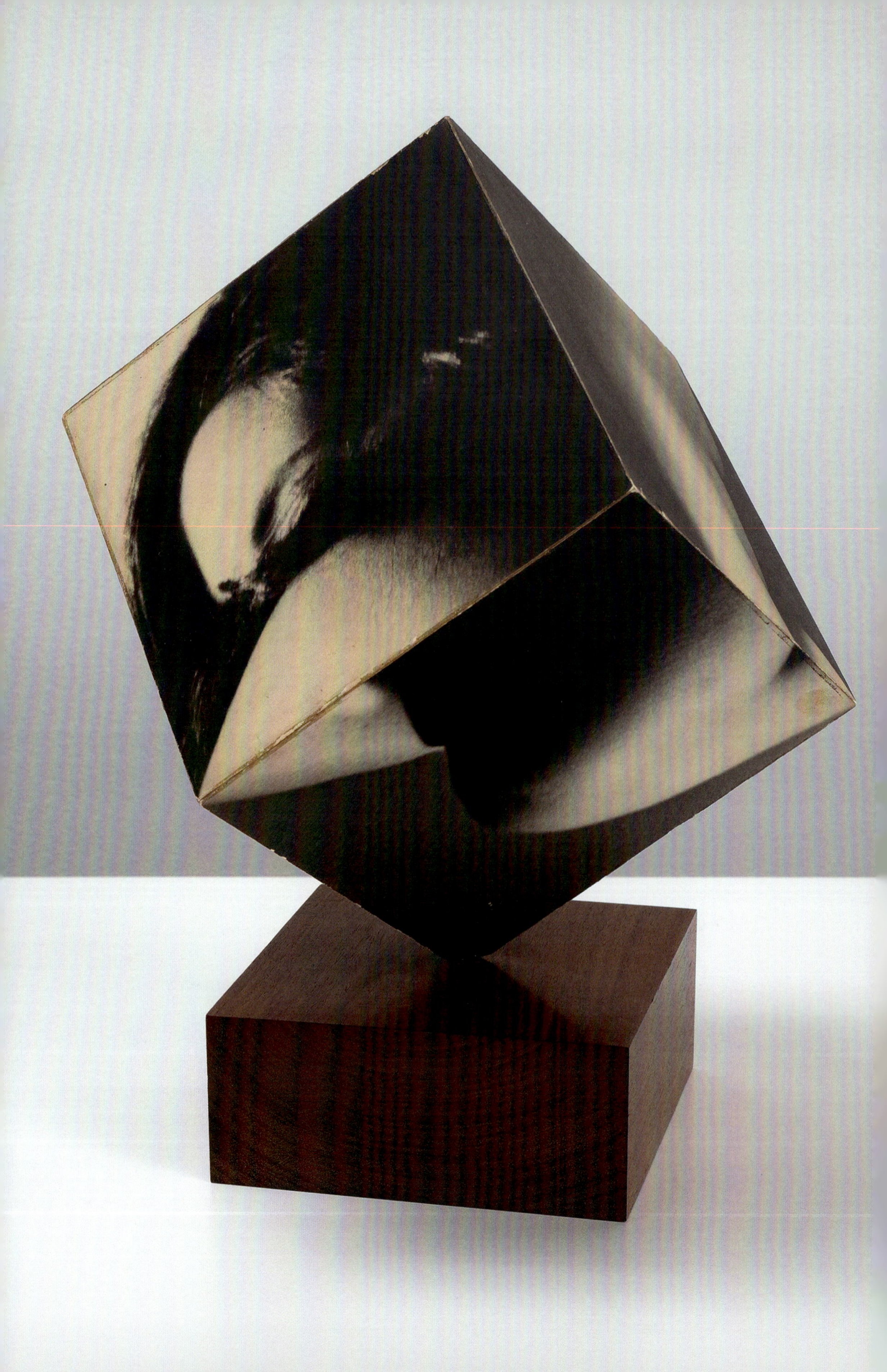

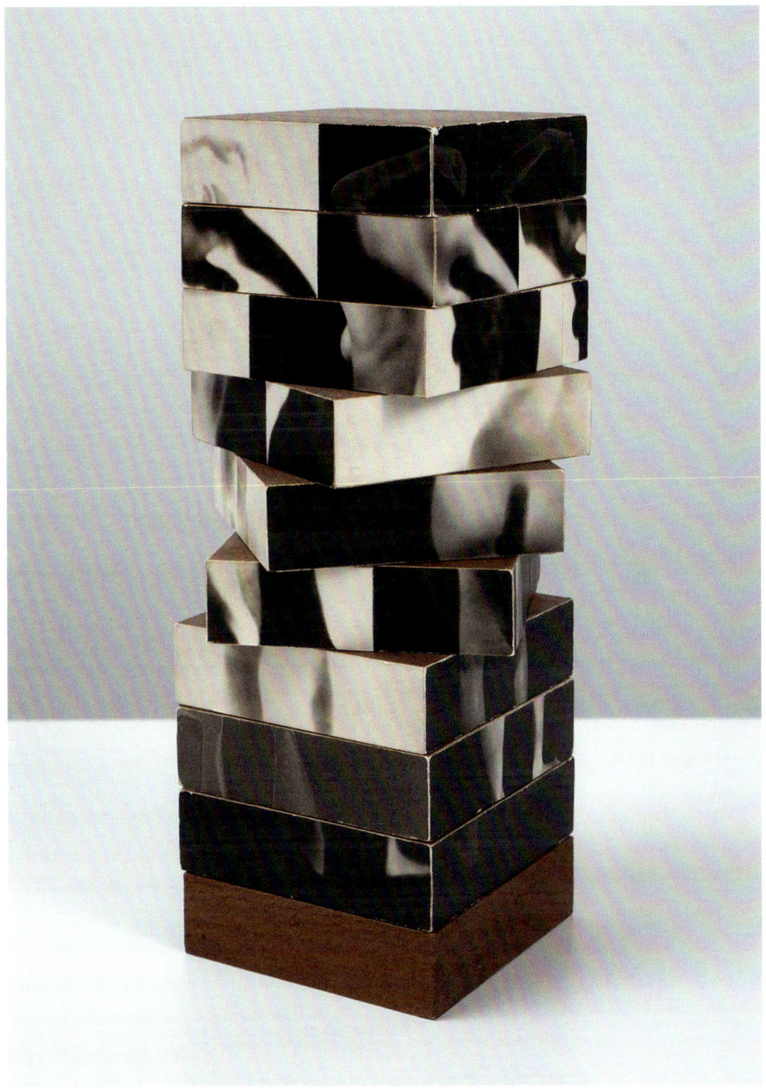

of the individual elements. It is as if the body has taken on capabilities that we normally attribute to the camera's focus ring. All the stacks also combine positive and negative images, a characteristic that serves to draw the viewer's attention away from violence done to the human figure and toward more reflexive concerns about the properties of the photographic medium and the nature of vision. Created with an awareness of both John Cage and Dada, the stacks have participatory elements: they encourage the viewer to manipulate them, and thus they surrender a certain amount of artistic control, inviting chance, contingency, and change into the works themselves. These photo-sculptures, in other words, have no fixed or "final" forms; they remain open, incorporating viewer response into their material structures.

Despite their innovative nature, however, the blocks and stacks seem deficient in scale. As Eva Respini points out, in addition to engaging with happenings and participatory art (through their creation of an active viewer who manipulates them), the works also have a relationship to minimalist sculpture in that they elicit phenomenological interpretations similar to those made by Michael Fried responding to the works of Robert Morris, Donald Judd, and Carl Andre, among others.[10] In other words, because they contain representations of human figures, and because they call on us to manipulate them, they potentially encourage us to experience them in relation to our own bodies and the environments in which they are contained. Due to their small sizes, however, Heinecken's blocks and stacks seem more like models than full-scale minimalist artworks. They have much less "theatrical" presence than three-dimensional minimalist sculptures; the fact that they were not blown up to (human) scale reveals an important trajectory that Heinecken left undeveloped.

Through their sectioning of the human body, moreover, Heinecken's blocks and stacks also evoke a historical reference. As Heinecken noted in 1971, they stand in a lineage of works that include the pioneering photo-sculptures of François Willème, created in the 1860s.[11] Willème's process involved photographing a subject in a custom-designed, circular studio, simultaneously taking multiple exposures from equidistant positions surrounding the sitter. Intended as a means of copying preexisting sculptures as well as a technique to create original full-figure portraits, reliefs, and portrait busts, Willème's process was used to create three-dimensional representations of celebrities and political figures—such as actors from the Comédie-Française, the king and queen of Spain, and Ulysses S. Grant. The process was briefly popular before 1870, during which time it spread to both England and the United States. An attempt to democratize the production of sculptural portraits in a manner corresponding to the popularization of two-dimensional likenesses during the first few decades of photography, Willème's photo-sculptural technique seemed to fulfill the medium's promise to develop toward ever-greater realism and permeation of everyday life. After the invention of the stereoscope process in the 1850s, which, through the combination of two slightly different photographs in a specially designed viewer, produced an illusion of three-dimensional representation, photo-sculpture seemed a natural—if marvelous—advance.

As Robert Sobieszek has argued, the guiding idea behind Willème's process—that a fully formed sculpture could arise through the combination of a set of two-dimensional profiles—grew in influence in the decades following 1860, impacting the work of August Rodin, among others.[12] And this principle, that photography could "section" the world and then be used to build it up anew, reveals a new sensibility engendered by the photographic medium: a belief that by breaking down reality into discrete outlines or slices of information, photography can help us not only to accurately replicate the world but more and more to change it. Once one begins to build a new three-dimensional form out of two-dimensional samples, it becomes much easier to add new elements that deviate from the original person or object but appear to possess the same truth or reality as all the other component parts on display.

Through their references to the history of photographic sculpture, their intermixing of positive and negative images, and their sectioning of photographic and sculptural forms, Heinecken's blocks and stacks engender new questions about the development of photography and how it affects real bodies in space. In the first place, by evoking the specter of Willème, they remind the viewer of the longstanding trajectory in photography that sought ever-greater realism and verisimilitude. One tendency in photography, in other words, has always been focused on constructing the perfect simulacrum, a copy that could not be distinguished from its original; and many of photography's various key developments—for example, stereoscopy, photo-sculpture, color, and chronophotography—can be understood as milestones in this quest for perfect illusionism. Second, through the division of bodies into positive and negative forms, the blocks and stacks evoke the idea of binary code, an awareness that continuous values of visual experience can be reduced to discrete ones, units of information that allow for the manipulation and mass reproduction of the visible world. Finally, by evoking a process of sectioning, the blocks and stacks emphasize the role that the photograph plays in creating a cross-section or partial view of the real, a contour that can be used to build it up anew. Although a product of a predigital view of the world, these works thus anticipate the ideas that undergird today's effects-based digital languages with their assumption that reality—when sampled and quantified—becomes a stepping-stone for new forms.

Figure Puzzles

Unlike the corporeal blocks and stacks, Heinecken's figure puzzles employ their small scale in a powerful way. Geometric fragments cut from the photographer's earlier figure studies once again provided the source material for these new works. Consisting of multiple square or triangular components, they all present human form as a board game to be played on either a square or a circular surface. Significantly, none of the figure puzzles possesses a solution in the sense that their components can never be arranged in a configuration that depicts a complete human being.[13] In

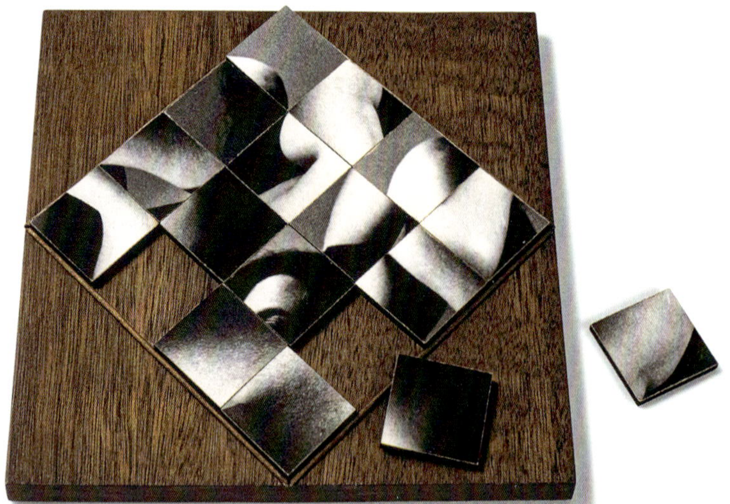

some of these works, all the fragmentary body parts glued to the game pieces are different, while in others, the same set of body parts repeats multiple times. In a few Heinecken has varied the vertical height of the playing pieces as well—their elevation off the horizontal surface. Early works, like *Refractive Hexagon* (1965),[14] *Kaleidoscopic Hexagon* (1965),[15] the various *Multiple Solution Puzzles* (1965),[16] and *24 Figure Blocks* (1966),[17] evoke games like chess and checkers as well as kaleidoscopes and other optical devices (Plate 3.3). Like the stacks and blocks, they represent impossible bodies, amalgams of fleshy protuberances and orifices, sometimes punctuated with tiny details such as nipples or hair.

As Heinecken developed his photo-sculptural idea of the body as game, he hybridized the figure more and more, something that can be seen in his *Breast Bomb* and *Figure Flower* series from 1967 and 1968. Works with these themes were made in a variety of media, and they include assemblages of gelatin silver prints, groupings of transparences, and clusters of photographic emulsion canvases stretched over wood. To make these sculptural photographs, Heinecken once again recycled nudes he had shot a few years earlier, selecting regions of their bodies and cutting out a set of shapes. The appropriated fragments were printed on a range of different substances including paper, film, and linen. In general, the participatory element was eliminated in the *Breast Bombs* and *Figure Flowers*. Nothing was left to chance; the image was fixed in a particular configuration as if the game was over. Even more than the early figure puzzles, however, these works evoked the distorted surrealist nudes of André Kertész, Bill Brandt, and others. Like the surrealist images before them, they were metaphors for human bodies existing in times of war and rapid technological change. In addition, and perhaps most important, the human images Heinecken created are also radically hermaphroditic: their shapes were neither conventionally masculine nor conventionally feminine but, rather, a radical intermingling of both. Thus although they were created from images designed to satisfy a straight male gaze, the identities and sexualities these photographs convey were neither conventional nor binary.

Breast/Bomb #6 (1967), for example, consists of nine square canvases mounted on wood and printed with photographic fragments that originally depicted parts of a female body (Plate 3.4).[18] In their new arrangement, the components suggest an organism that is both phallic and feminine at the same time. Although *Breast/Bomb #6* is largely flat, the squares in some of the other works in this series were made of different thicknesses, and their dissimilar levels of projection from the surface emphasized the cuts in the human form depicted by the photographic imagery. For

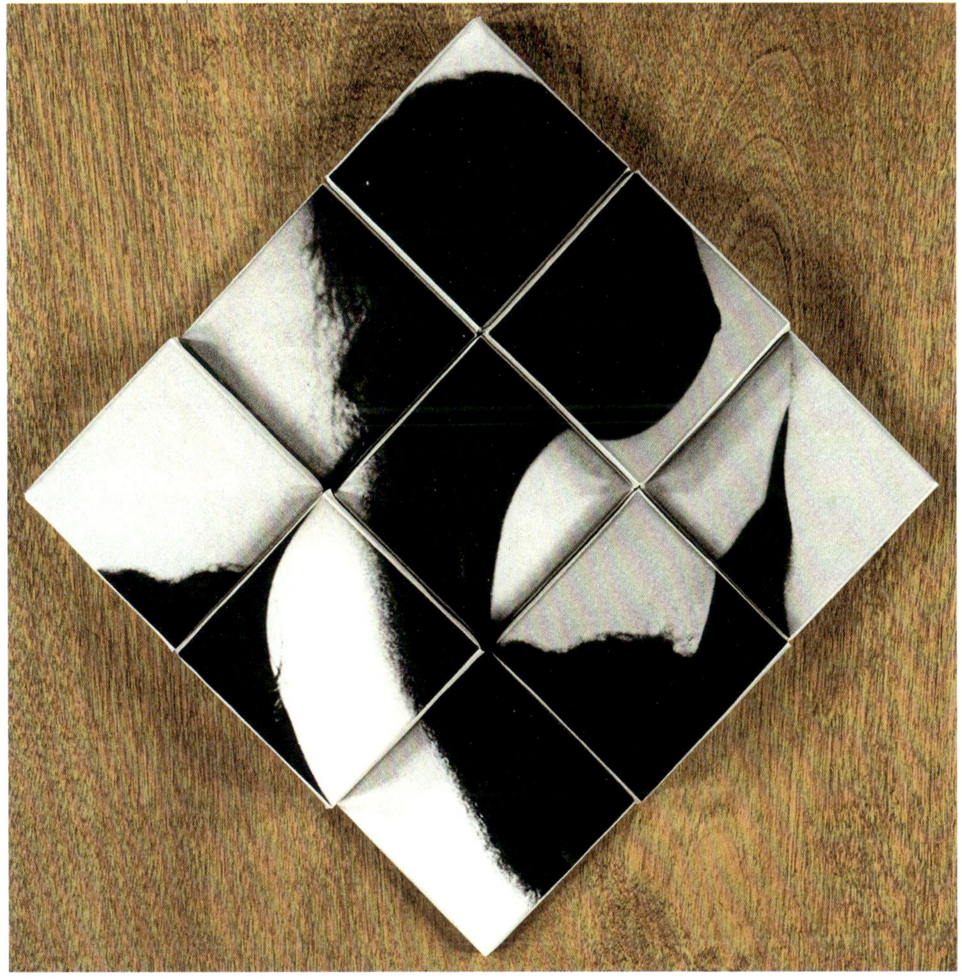

Heinecken, the *Breast/Bombs* could be displayed either horizontally or vertically. When they were exhibited horizontally in game orientation, the variation in the depth of the panels in some of the works made them more landscape-like. In this configuration, these *Breast/Bombs* recall the innovative game-like sculptures that Alberto Giacometti made between 1930 and 1933 such as *Circuit* and *No More Play,* where the verticality of sculpture was shifted horizontally, and the work itself was simply and directly conceived of as a base, as Rosalind Krauss has argued.[19]

For Krauss, the shift from the vertical to the horizontal marked Giacometti's most significant contribution to the development of modern sculpture, a transformation that undermined sculpture's representational functions and connected it again with the presymbolic, prerepresentational world of actuality.[20] Inspired by the base materialist theories of the dissident surrealist Georges Bataille, Giocometti's game-board sculptures suspended sculptural representation, causing it to alternate "between the symbolic [dimension] and the real decay of matter."[21] As a result, the process of three-dimensional representation was connected to what it was not: a play of (base) material and psychic forces out of which all (higher) form and meaning emerge. Thereby a space was created within which to rethink the formal concerns of sculpture, as well as the nature and significance of what it meant to be human.[22]

In contrast, Heinecken's hybrid *Breast/Bombs* seem to shift between the horizontal and the vertical, at home in either orientation. They are not so much critiques of the traditional forms of sculpture as they are articulations of central photographic concerns pertaining to the play between object and image and the interchange between two and three dimensions. As photography transforms the human body, they seem to suggest, we both gain and lose attributes, characteristics that signify different aspects of what it is to be human. Yet like Giacometti's horizontal sculptures, Heinecken's *Breast/Bombs* also project a base materialism, in that they mix meaning (photographic realism) with nonsense (destabilizing montage juxtapositions), and they embody profound attacks on traditional notions of what it means to be a person. Representations that dismantle and reassemble human anatomy in service of an expanded and more critical conception of humankind, they project a sense of people in which our highest and most evolved characteristics are inseparably bound to our lowest and most primitive qualities.

As suggested by works in the *Breast/Bomb* series, in addition to the desire to undermine the male gaze and evoke nonbinary sexuality, Heinecken's dimensional images also express a strong drive to connect eroticism and violence. The breast, an erogenous zone as well as a primary symbol of motherhood, is here reconfigured to suggest both a non–gender-binary body and a mushroom cloud. Because of the bombing motif, the Vietnam War was a real but distant sort of reference, evoking the growing presence of armed conflict in American life during the second half of the 1960s. In the later years of the decade, images of bombing, the wounded, and the dead began to circulate more frequently in the news—a result of the devastating U.S. bombing campaign that began in early 1965.[23] *Life* magazine, for example, depicted wounded GIs on its cover on February 11, 1966, and a wounded marine on the October 28 cover. On February 25, 1966, its cover depicted jet fighters flying against a dawn sky over South Vietnam.[24] Corresponding to the escalation of the American involvement in Vietnam, as well as the rising body count among U.S. troops, the proliferation of this increasingly disturbing war imagery also signaled a growing popular discontent about the nation's involvement in the Southeast Asian conflict.

Beyond their evocation of Vietnam, Heinecken's *Breast/Bombs* also pointed to the radical fissuring of American identities that was taking place in the second half of the 1960s—a psychic dismantling to which Heinecken sought to contribute. To a certain extent, a more homogenous sense of U.S. identity—as white, heterosexual, patriarchal, corporate, consumerist, and politically conservative—held sway in the 1950s. In the subsequent decade, however, the civil rights movement and rise of the counterculture radically questioned this ideology, a critique that was furthered by the rapid growth of feminism, the ecological movement, and various forms of identity politics—for example, the Chicano, Native American, and gay rights movements—by the end of the decade. New ideas about what it was to be an American and what it meant to lead a fulfilling life began to take root; young people in particular began to reject the older social roles of their parents' generation. Strongly criticizing traditional forms of American identity, they embraced new ideals, particularly around more progressive concepts of race, sexuality, occupation, drug use, and lifestyle.

This transformation had a number of different effects. On the one hand, the older patriarchal ideals became viewed as dangerous, repressive, and inhumane—an ideology that supported racism, sexism, colonial aggression, and the destruction of the environment. On the other hand, the counterculture's rejection of 1950s moral values and their embrace of more tolerant ideas about sexuality, drugs, racial mixing, and lifestyle created a backlash—a sense on the part of older and more conservative Americans that all morality was breaking down and that the latest generation of U.S. citizens was rapidly destroying the country. Both sides could point to phenomena that proved their points. The escalation of the Vietnam War and the wave of political assassinations that struck progressive leaders confirmed the bankruptcy of the old order in the eyes of young progressives and radicals. For the other side, the increase in drug use, sex outside of marriage, and the growth of dropout culture suggested a lack of values affecting the youth who were to create the nation's future. And with their conflation of sexuality and violence, as well as their focus on the human body in a state of radical transformation and change, Heinecken's *Breast/Bombs* pointed to the generational forces that were dividing Americans in the second half of the 1960s, as well as to the new roles and identities that were beginning to emerge.[25]

Layered Images

As discussed earlier, Heinecken employed Kodalith transparencies to create seemingly exact reproductions of magazines and newspapers.[26] On the surface these works appeared radically nonartistic and literal, but upon close reading and contemplation they transformed, emerging as sharp allegories for fundamental conflicts inherent in 1960s U.S. culture. Although the medium was not inherently sculptural, Heinecken often used the Kodalith process in sculptural ways. His preferred way to display the approximately twenty-five transparencies that he made in the mid-1960s was to mount them in plexiglass box frames hung vertically out three to five feet from the wall. Through this form of presentation, he hoped to create a maze-like gallery environment in which each transparency framed a view of the space that included spectators and other works. He also wanted the transparencies to be lit in such a manner as to cast shadows on the floors and walls.[27] No doubt inspired by installation photographs of Duchamp's *Large Glass* framing both spectators and glimpses of the gallery behind it (or firsthand experience of the same), Heinecken understood his transparencies to be devices through which the spectator gazed: temporary frames for an active and mobile experience of the world.[28] Heinecken's transparencies, one could thus say, emerged out of the artist's desire to change the standard ways of viewing and understanding photographs as well as his proclivity for a kind of double vision, a seeing of images through other images. Both these concerns would have a lasting impact on his art.

Between 1966 and 1969, Heinecken further explored the possibilities of the positive Kodalith transparency by combining it with collages taken from newspapers and magazines. Including works such as *Figure Parts/ Hair* (1966),[29] *Costumes of a Woman* (1966),[30] *Camouflage Suit for October* (1966), *Costume for Feb. 1968* (1968),[31] *V.N. Pin Up* (1968),[32] and *U.C.B. Pin Up* (1969),[33] these transparency collages explored questions of gender, sexuality, the performance of social roles, and the politics of the Vietnam

War. To create these hybrid works, Heinecken recycled earlier nudes, but not ones that he had taken himself. Instead, he purchased images from a mail-order supplier, The Latent Image (TLI), a company that was owned and operated by the photographer Larry Caye, which sold pinups and erotic images between the mid-1960s and the mid-1990s.[34] Although TLI later sold color prints and slides, at the time that Heinecken patronized it the company only offered undeveloped black-and-white negatives to customers.[35] Using this strategy to circumvent prevailing laws against mailing sexually explicit images across state lines, TLI marketed itself as "the perfect answer for the photographer who doesn't have the opportunity to shoot live models."[36] Each undeveloped roll contained twelve exposures of an attractive young model enacting a series of poses; it thus had sequential and temporal qualities in addition to its erotic ones; for the amateur photographers who purchased these negatives, it no doubt helped to engender a fantasy that they were photographing the models themselves. Heinecken developed the negatives and then selected one pose, which he blew up, printing it on Kodalith sheet film. He subsequently placed the Kodalith on top of a series of collaged magazine and newspaper images, which it partially masked.

Early transparency collages, like *Figure Parts/Hair* (1966) and *Costumes of a Woman* (1966), explored the body as a container of remixed body parts combined with other natural and manufactured products. Although not three-dimensional, they have sculptural qualities because the Kodalith film appears as a clear layer affixed to the top surface of a collage. Particularly in comparison to Heinecken's gelatin silver prints and lithographs, these works evoke a process of looking from one space into another. This heightened sense of spectatorship is reinforced by the material contrast between the Kodalith film, a medium associated with the process of print production, and the printed, mass-reproduced pages beneath, the products of the publishing industry. A kind of before-and-after dichotomy (a distinction between a manufacturing process and its product) is thereby set up. In terms of subject matter, these works suggest that the human body is culturally constructed, an assemblage of stereotypical qualities or a costume that one puts on and takes off. As such, they perhaps evoke the sociological insight—developed by Erving Goffman in the late 1950s—that human beings present themselves in everyday life by playing roles like actors on a stage.[37]

In the transparency collages of 1968 and 1969, the mood becomes much darker. The theatrical presentation of self in everyday life is connected to the Vietnam War, and the pinup format reveals its important links to the militarized body. *V.N. Pin Up* (1968) presents a figure study, her body cut off below her hips, her arms raised above her shoulders, and

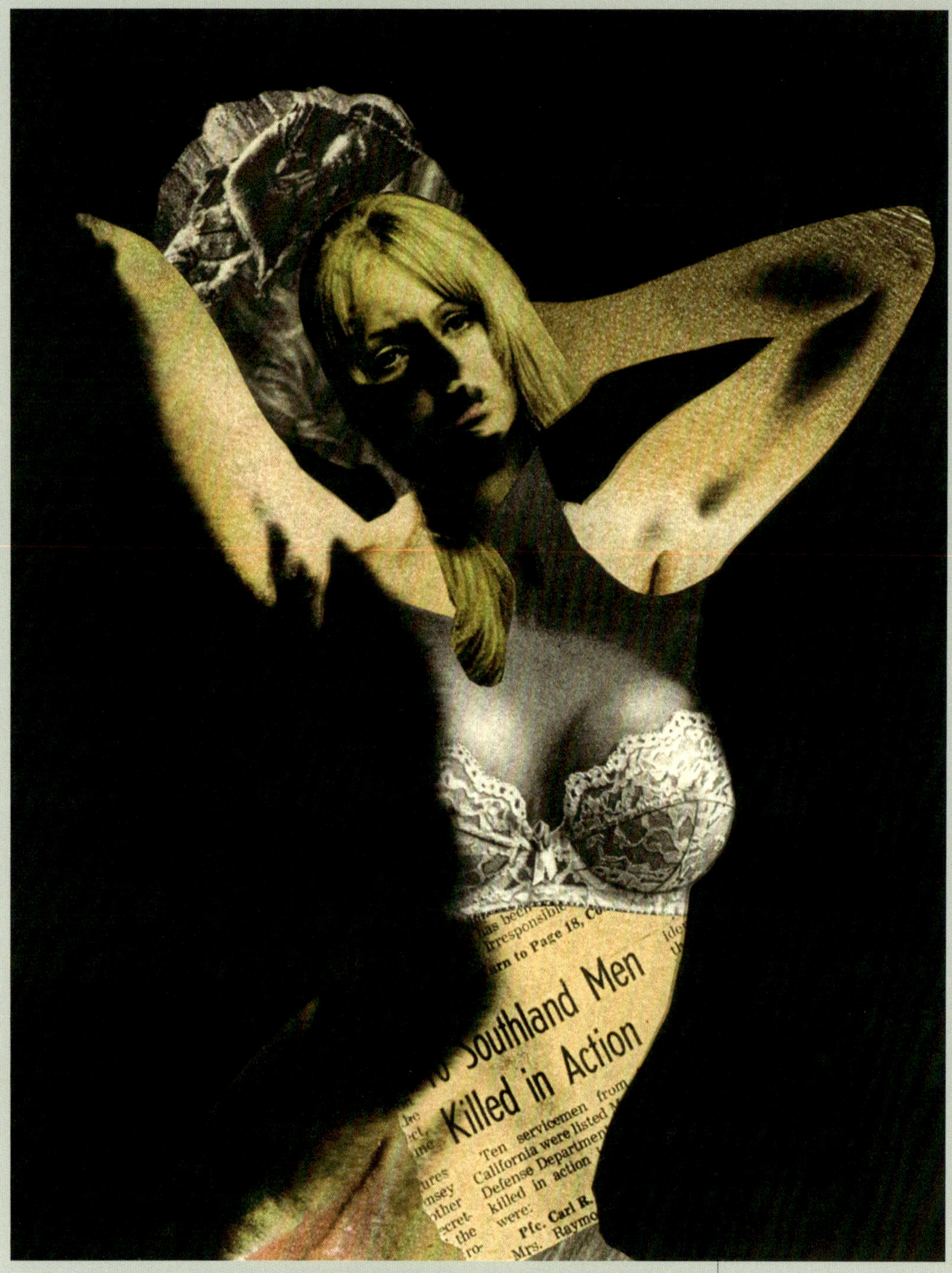

PLATE 3.5. Robert Heinecken, *V.N. Pin Up* (1968). Black-and-white film transparency over magazine-page collage, 9 x 7 inches (22.9 x 17.8 cm). Museum of Contemporary Art, Chicago. Gift of Daryl Gerber Stokols. COPYRIGHT 2022 THE ROBERT HEINECKEN TRUST, CHICAGO.

her hands cupping the back of her head (Plate 3.5). The subject's head and torso are superimposed with collage fragments, including the head of a second woman, a lace brassiere, and a fragment of a newspaper article reporting that ten LA-area men had been killed in action. Finally, a Kodalith overlay of a figure striking a similar pose is placed on top of the collaged woman. Through the title—*V.N.* suggests Vietnam—and appropriated newspaper text, the image is specifically connected to the Vietnam War, as well as the casualties it was inflicting on southern California in particular. Evoking the pinups that servicemen consumed as temporary decorations in their wartime barracks, the hybrid figure evokes the horror of war and longing for home at the same time.

By the time Heinecken got around to appropriating the format, the pinup possessed a long and varied history. As it is commonly understood, a pinup is an idealized image of a sexually attractive person—generally a woman—in a state of partial or total nudity.[38] Intended as a domestic decoration to be attached to a wall or another flat surface, it is a mass-produced picture, generated from either drawn, painted, or photographic source material, and almost universally considered to be a lowbrow form of art. To a lesser extent, *pinup* can also refer to the subject of this type of representation.

As a genre, the pinup underwent a long development, emerging in the late nineteenth century when burlesque performers would use cartes de visite, cabinet cards, and postcards as souvenirs and advertisements to promote themselves. Since that time, pinups have been featured on a variety of different mass-produced items, including but not limited to calendars, magazine covers, "art cards," and promotional images produced by movie studios, not to mention the foldout pages designed to be removed from the centers of magazines, which are commonly known as "gatefolds" or "centerfolds." Erotic in nature, pinups have for the most part possessed an unstable relationship to pornography. In many cases, particularly since the 1950s and the rise of photo-illustrated men's magazines like *Playboy* and later, in the 1960s, *Penthouse,* they have been considered quasi-pornographic. In many other cases, particularly before 1949, they were thought to be more innocent, held distinct from pornography and accepted in contexts where obscene images would not be.

Pinups were also profoundly ideological. Although mass produced, they cultivated an intimate or one-on-one relationship with their spectators, through open or inviting poses, a straightforward gaze that suggested candid eye contact with the viewer, and text that addressed the spectator directly or implied a private conversation that was being surreptitiously overheard. Often connected to print advertising for a wide variety of consumer products (from Coca-Cola beverages and Kodak cameras to

General Motors cars and Coppertone suntan lotions), pinups were used to incite consumer desire for a commodity, give it allure, and generate connotations of affluence and pleasure. Although not exclusively a creation of the United States, pinups were strongly associated with America. Around the turn of the twentieth century, early pinup figures like the Gibson Girl and the Christy Girl were thought to represent ideals of American fashion, breeding, education, and comportment (while at the same time implicitly valorizing specific ethnic and class hierarchies). In the 1930s and 1940s, Petty and Vargas Girls helped to promulgate a new type of American beauty in the pages of *Esquire* magazine, a youthful girl-next-door, in whom eroticism was combined with innocence and playfulness. During the Second World War, this simultaneously sexual and chaste figure became mainstream—a symbol of America and the values for which its servicemen were fighting. In addition to the pinups produced by painters and illustrators, movie star pinups—particularly of Betty Grable and Rita Hayworth—were also mobilized to support armed endeavors.

Given to soldiers as images that would boost morale and arouse their fighting spirits, the World War II pinup conflated sex and violence, channeling libidinous energies of young men into aggressive military actions. Removed from the pages of *Esquire*, which issued a special military edition during the war, and *Yank, the Army Weekly*, among other publications, these militarized pinups distracted their consumers from the horrors of combat and motivated them to keep fighting. As Bob Hope supposedly said, "Our American troops are ready to fight at the drop of an *Esquire*."[39] World War II pinups served a number of additional ideological functions as well, including directing male desire in heterosexual directions (particularly important in contexts like the military that were primarily homosocial), as well as promoting American body types in overseas locations. The nice yet sexually attractive girl-next-door became an image representing the country for which U.S. servicemen were willing to kill and be killed. In addition, as a number of commentators have noted, the military pinup also accustomed its consumers to see the body as something that could be easily combined with new technologies and processes of mass reproduction.[40] It is thus not surprising that pinup figures were painted on the nose cones of airplanes and on the sides of bombs. Right after the war, Rita Hayworth even received the dubious distinction of decorating the surface of Able, the first nuclear weapon detonated at Bikini Atoll on July 1, 1946.

Vietnam

In his transparency collage pinups, Heinecken drew on the pinup genre's diverse meanings and iterations, combining them with historical references created through the works' titles and appropriated image fragments. On the one hand, these transparency collages made reference to the new, more pornographic uses to which the pinup had been applied since the 1950s with the advent of mainstream men's magazines like *Playboy*. Both a sign and an agent of the mainstreaming of pornography—the growing acceptance of obscene images in American life—this type of pinup helped to legitimize objectifying and potentially violent forms of the heterosexual male gaze. As a result, the historical events that Heinecken cited through the collage fragments located within the clear areas of the transparencies were implicitly linked to a patriarchal point of view. On the other hand, given the referenced war imagery, Heinecken also mined the meanings of the genre that accrued to it in the context of the Second World War; in particular, the pinup's role as a signifier of American values, its ability to conflate sexuality and violence, and its uncanny undermining of distinctions between humans and machines. Consequently, historical events and occurrences specific to the late 1960s were connected to the World War II era, a moment that in retrospect seemed to possess a more innocent, heroic, and forthright masculine ideal.[41] If the sexual attitudes attributed to American servicemen during World War II appeared somewhat naïve and even chaste from a standpoint more than two decades later, then, as Heinecken's contemporary pinups implied, the association of sex and violence in the Vietnam era seemed to carry much more sinister associations. The female body was not simply a national symbol for which U.S. soldiers fought and laid down their lives; it defined a battleground as well, an acknowledgment of the fact that, in addition to enemy soldiers, American warfare targeted (noncombatant) women and children.

Costume for Feb. '68 (1968) presents four women who pose with their arms above their heads (Plate 3.6). Like *V.N. Pin Up*, they are collages of fragmentary images appropriated from magazine pages, overlaid with a Kodalith transparency that sets them off against a dark background and suggests that we are peering through a partially opaque screen at forms that we can only incompletely make out. Posed in a three-quarters view, the figures turn toward the viewer, while at the same time mirroring one other. In contrast to *Costumes of a Woman*, they do not appear to be the same form repeated multiple times; their outlines, however, are similar, with the outer two figures and the inner two figures echoing one another very closely. Collaged with car parts, grass, the heads and arms of women and children, and groupings of tiny soldiers in helmets and battle gear, they appear as monstrously hybrid creatures, assemblages of natural and technological elements. Because of the repeated pose, the four women perhaps resemble fashion manikins, designed to display clothing; in addition, due to the repetition of their forms as well as the reduction of their

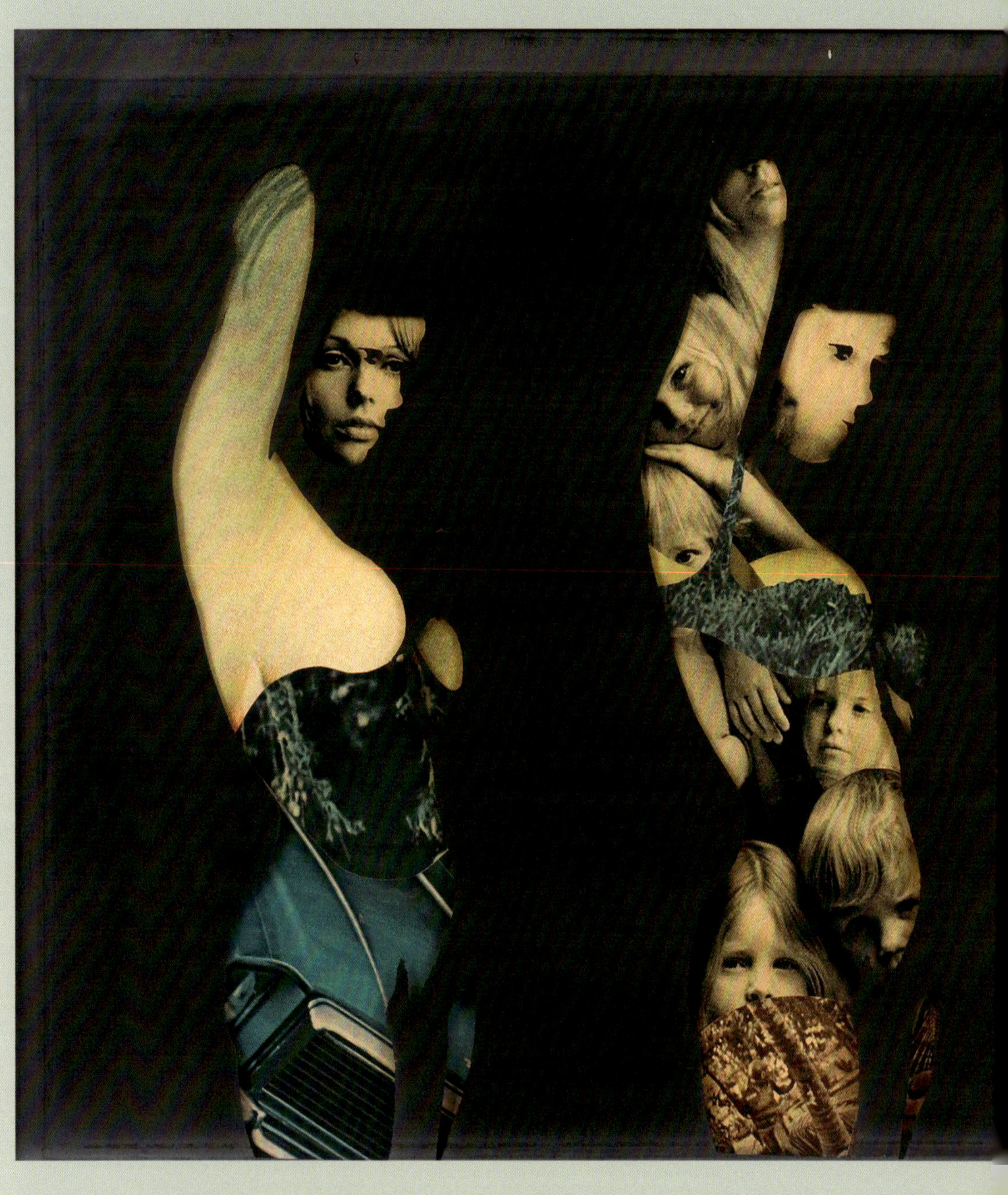

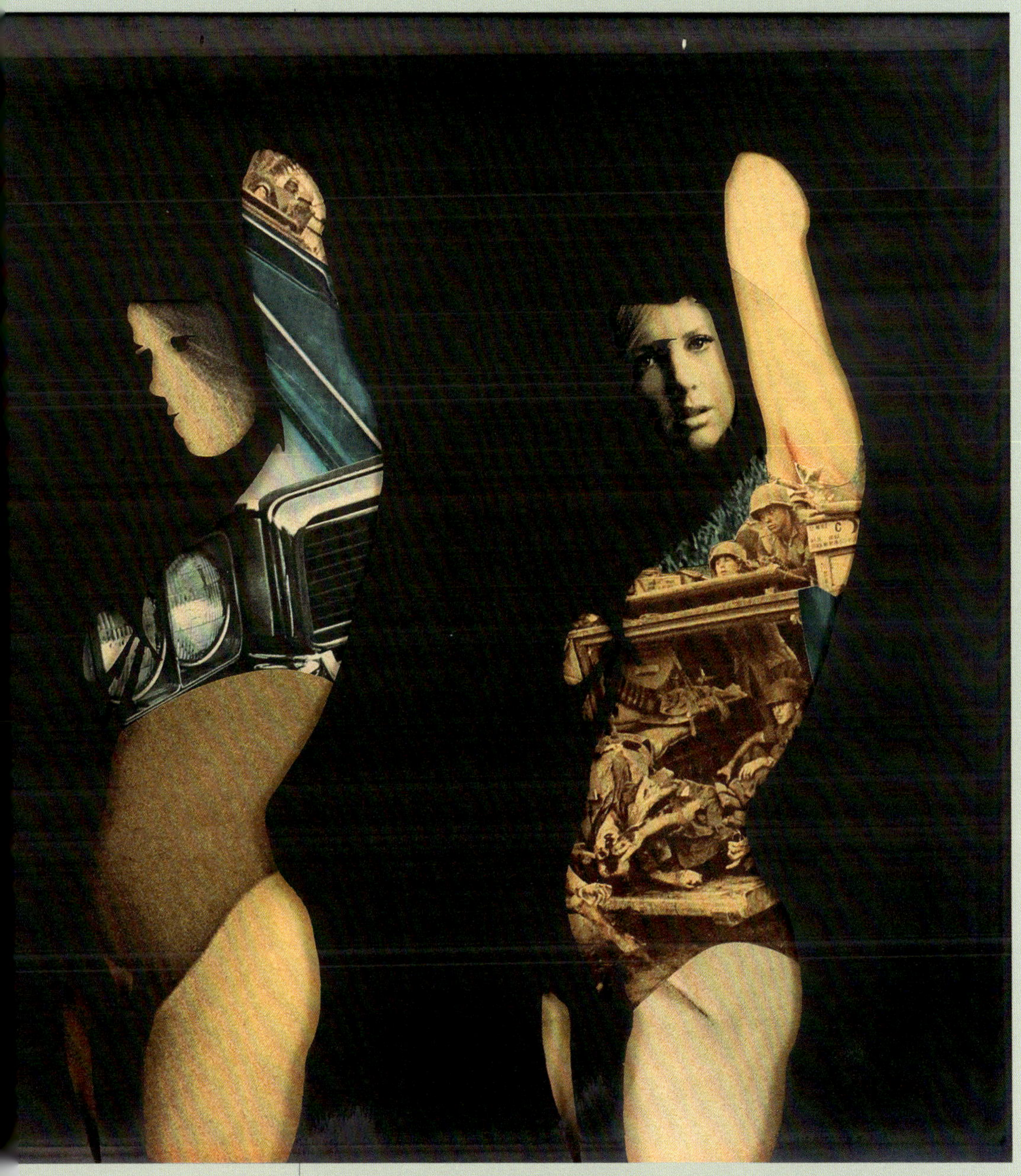

PLATE 3.6. Robert Heinecken, *Costume for Feb. '68* (1968). Black-and-white film transparency over magazine-page collage, 10 x 19 inches (25.4 x 48.26 cm). Private collection. COPYRIGHT 2022 THE ROBERT HEINECKEN TRUST, CHICAGO.

bodies to essentially a head and torso, they seem a little like targets hung up in a shooting range.

The title of the collage alludes to a month that witnessed the Tet Offensive, a wave of surprise attacks on South Vietnamese and U.S. troops and their allies that began on January 30, 1968, during a cease-fire held in celebration of the Vietnamese New Year. As historians now commonly understand it, the offensive—a massive military action carried out by the North Vietnamese People's Army and their guerrilla allies, the southern National Liberation Front, or Vietcong—marked a turning point in the war.[42] A coordinated series of approximately 150 assaults on key military and civilian centers across the whole of South Vietnam, including five of the country's six major cities, most provincial and numerous district capitals, and many hamlets, it was one of the largest military campaigns of the war, an operation that led to unforeseen consequences for both sides. Although the North Vietnamese and the Vietcong initially achieved shocking victories—including a surprise attack on the U.S. embassy and the South Vietnamese presidential palace in Saigon (now Ho Chi Minh City)—they were quickly beaten back, losing all their territorial gains in a time period ranging from a few hours to a few weeks. As a direct result, the Communists sustained devastating human and material losses, and their primary strategic objective—to inspire the civilian population of South Vietnam to rise up against their government—was never achieved.

Despite the military defeats, however, the offensive proved to be a political victory for the North and the Vietcong, since it dramatically changed public and political opinion in the United States about the long-term prospects of the war and whether the country's Cold War aims of stopping the spread of Communism in Southeast Asia were achievable. Although public sentiment against U.S. involvement in the war had been growing since 1965, when President Johnson committed ground troops in substantial numbers, the majority of Americans and most U.S. politicians and news outlets remained on the president's side through the end of 1967, believing that the war was being won. The initial Communist successes during the Tet Offensive, however, proved that—despite the U.S. government's previous assertions to the contrary (including a successful public relations campaign initiated by the White House in 1967 to shore up support)—the Communists continued to possess the ability to wage large-scale warfare on the South. Once it became apparent that the conflict was far from over, a much-discussed credibility gap began to plague the administration, a sense that Johnson and his generals had not been honest with the American people about the true nature of the conflict.

As a result of this gap, public opinion increasingly turned against the war, and major news outlets, like *Time, Newsweek,* and the *New York Times,* began to publish more critical editorials about U.S. involvement in Vietnam. Even the big three television networks, ABC, CBS, and NBC, whose reports had generally been very supportive of the war, became more critical in terms of their broadcasters' commentary as well as the types of imagery that they became willing to show. Responding to the change in public sentiment, Johnson refused his generals' requests for additional troops, stopped the U.S. bombing campaign, and began to actively seek peace negotiations with the North. Combined with the economic drain that the war was having on the country—the president had refused to raise taxes to pay for the conflict, something that contributed to spiraling inflation, a growing deficit, and the threat of a worldwide financial crisis—the war helped to divide the Democratic Party, creating opposition to Johnson's reelection from both the right and the left. Ultimately, Johnson decided not to run for a second term, and although American troops did not fully pull out of Vietnam until the end of 1973, the U.S. goal was no longer victory but, as the next president, Richard Nixon, would put it, "peace with honor."

In light of the Tet Offensive, its political fallout, and the new distrust of the U.S. government that was created, *Costume for Feb. '68* seems a trenchant articulation of the charged and highly mass-mediated situation in which Americans suddenly found themselves. The pinup form evoked U.S. soldiers' desires for domesticity and pleasure during wartime, while at the same time suggesting—by means of the figures' target-like forms— that the women and children depicted in the image might be the victims of military aggression as well. That this was not a far-fetched conjecture was widely confirmed in November 1969, when the events of the Mỹ Lai massacre of March 16, 1968, became publicly known: an estimated five hundred unarmed South Vietnamese villagers, including many women and children, were killed by U.S. Army soldiers. Although Heinecken's artwork predates the large-scale public exposure of this horrific act of wanton murder, it appears to directly confront the fears circulating at the time that U.S. soldiers in Vietnam were less honorable than their counterparts during World War II.

Furthermore, because it mixes printed image fragments with a photographic transparency, a technology used in print production, *Costume for Feb. '68* also suggests that the mass media had become a lens through which the public saw everything from the most political to the most personal of events. It thus seems to allegorize the growing awareness at the time that U.S. conduct of the Vietnam War was dramatically influenced by the media—newspapers, magazines, radio, and television—industries that exerted a huge effect on public opinion. Indeed, as Chester J. Pach Jr. and other media historians of this war have argued, the Tet Offensive created important changes in broadcast wartime coverage.[43] Before the offensive, the American television viewer generally saw a distanced overview of a disjointed conflict, one that was presented without much commentary or analysis. Behind-the-lines interviews and human-interest stories predominated, and the representation of military operations in the field did not generally show actual fighting or its effects in a close-up or graphic manner. Once the Tet Offensive started, however, things changed, and television viewers at home began to experience incidents of war in a much more direct and explicit manner.

The new broadcast situation, as Pach argued, was more graphic, disturbing, and visceral:

> No longer was the war in the background; instead, the fighting intruded into film reports in frightening and uncontrollable ways. Within a week, viewers saw two members of television crews suffer wounds while covering battle. During the fighting near the presidential palace, ABC's Piers Anderton and his camera operator recorded the anguish of an injured South Vietnamese soldier moaning in the street, while NBC's Douglas Kiker described the agony of Ban Me Thuot, as the film showed a city of rubble and refugees. . . .
>
> The most sensational story during Tet was the cold-blooded execution of a Vietcong officer in the streets of Saigon. The shooting followed a street battle between the Vietcong and South Vietnamese marines. An NBC crew recorded the fighting and the assassination in its entirety; an ABC camera operator stopped filming at the moment of death. Both reports aired on the nightly newscasts on 2 February; both contained commentary that was extraordinarily restrained. As the victim was led to his death, NBC's Howard Tuckner explained, "Government troops had captured the commander of the Viet Cong commando unit. He was roughed up badly but refused to talk. A South Vietnamese officer held the pistol taken from the enemy officer. The chief of South Vietnam's national police, Brigadier General Nguyen Ngoc Loan, was waiting for him." Neither Tuckner nor Roger Peterson, who narrated the ABC film, suggested that the shooting was an atrocity or a measure of the authoritarianism of the South Vietnamese regime. For Robert Northshield, the executive producer of the "Huntley-Brinkley Report," the film was newsworthy not because of its political implications but on account of its stunning images of death. Northshield, though, considered some of the scenes too "rough" for the television audience, and so he trimmed footage of blood spurting from the shattered skull of the victim. Perhaps as many as 20 million people watched the execution film on NBC; many more saw a photograph of the moment of death, published in almost every major newspaper.[44]

The photograph was *Saigon Execution* (1968), by Eddie Adams, an image that Heinecken cited as having an important effect on his thinking about

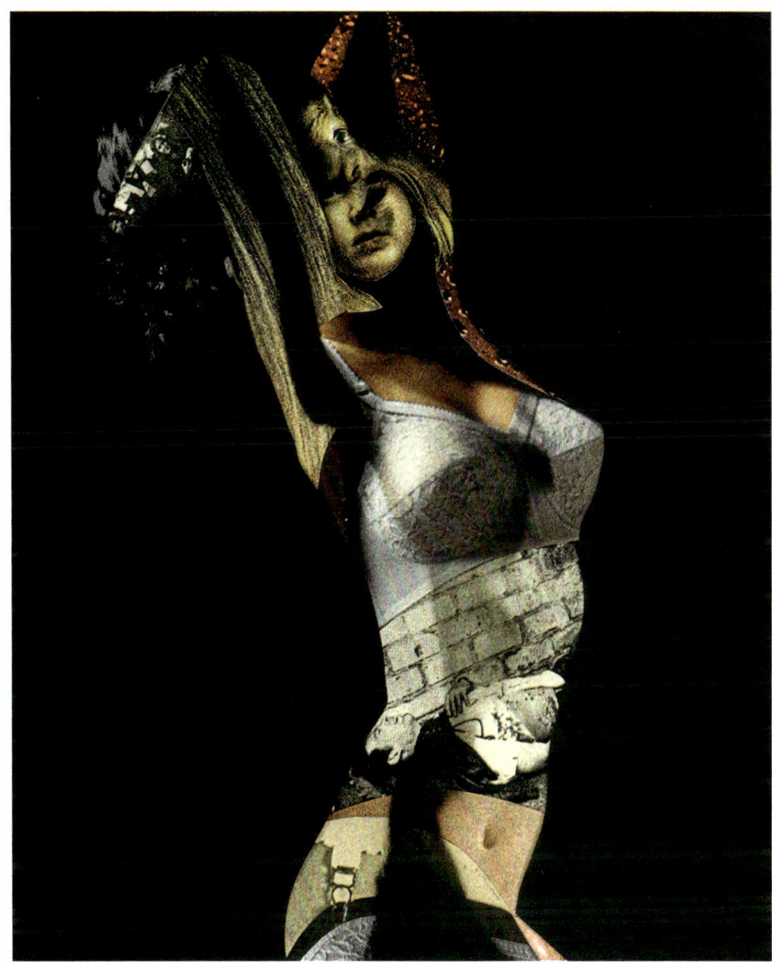

photography at the time.[45] By suggesting that the "costume" for February 1968 was an amalgam of sex, commodities, and graphic violence, Heinecken's mixed-media collage evoked this new stage of military reporting by the mainstream television stations and press, while also implying that support for the overseas conflict was going out of fashion.

The War at Home

In contrast to *Costume for Feb. '68*, *U.C.B. Pin Up* (1969) focuses more directly on the home front (Plate 3.7). It presents a figure that is very similar to *V.N. Pin Up:* a three-quarters view of a young woman in a classic pinup pose with her elbows above her head, her arms framing her hair. A mixture of black-and-white and color images cut from magazines, she wears a bra and panties with garters. Superimposed on her midsection is an image of a bullet-riddled corpse lying next to a brick wall with his shirt hiked up above his stomach; a hippie crowd scene, possibly of antiwar protesters, is applied to her right forearm, and a second face is merged with her regular one. A transparency of a Kodalith pinup, roughly mirroring her pose, is layered on top of the image, tying it together, and suggesting a dark vertiginous field in which different layers of representation mix and overlap with one another.

The title of the collage refers to the University of California at Berkeley, and in conjunction with the image of a civilian corpse lying on a city street it suggests the shocking events—given much play in the national press in the spring and summer of 1969—around the creation and violent suppression of People's Park, a community-controlled, user-developed public commons a block east of Telegraph Avenue and adjacent to the Berkeley campus.[46] People's Park was created by a coalition of different groups—in particular hippies, protoenvironmentalists, and student radicals from the antiwar and free-speech movements—in a vacant lot owned by the university in April and May 1969. Slated by the administration to eventually become the site of new student housing, the three-acre dirt lot, which had been seized by eminent domain and cleared of houses the year before, had become a dumping ground for trash and an occasional parking lot after the university temporarily ran out of funds for the completion of the building project. Reclaiming the empty land as a public space for free speech, recreation, community gardens, and musical events, a core group of local activists inspired approximately one thousand local volunteers to build the park in three and a half weeks.

Although there was widespread support for the new park from the citizens of Berkeley, local merchants, and students and faculty of UC Berkeley, the university administration ultimately refused to relinquish its original plans for developing the lot. On May 15, a day that would become known as Bloody Thursday, the university evicted local supporters camping in the park overnight and erected a fence around the property, backed up by the Berkeley police, the Alameda County Sheriff's Department, California Highway Patrol officers, and other law enforcement groups. In response, a group of two thousand to three thousand protesters, who were attending a noontime peace rally at Berkeley, left the event and marched on the park, where they clashed with police. As the afternoon wore on, the crowds of protesters grew, destroying property and allegedly throwing rocks and debris at the police, who responded with nightsticks, tear gas, and eventually shotguns filled with birdshot and buckshot. A bystander, James Rector, was shot in the lower torso while observing the altercations from a nearby rooftop and later died from his wounds; another man, Alan Blanchard, was permanently blinded. Numerous protestors were hurt and hospitalized, many from gunshot wounds.

On May 16, Ronald Reagan, then governor of California, declared a state of emergency and sent 2,700 National Guard troops to the area to restore order; a 10 p.m. curfew was established, and all forms of public assembly outlawed. Despite this, protests continued; subsequent demonstrations—some joined by Berkeley faculty—were met with more violence and tear gas, until Reagan rescinded the curfew and the prohibition on public assembly on May 25 and finally withdrew the National Guard on June 2, in the wake of huge public outcry, with marches sometimes growing to somewhere between twenty thousand and thirty thousand participants. In response to the tragedy, the university announced its willingness to reconsider the possibility of a public park to be leased by the city and used by the community, moving toward the idea of a common resource that would be jointly run by the university and the local community. Reagan and the UC Board of Regents, however, rejected any compromise solution. After the protests ended, the land formerly occupied by People's Park remained fenced in; it was kept fallow until late 1972, when after much public outcry the area was finally leased to the city and became a dedicated public park once again.

In light of the history of People's Park through June 1969—a record that includes incidents like one that occurred on May 20, when Governor Reagan authorized National Guard helicopters to drop tear gas on thousands of demonstrators at a protest on Berkeley's Sproul Plaza, one of the largest aerial deployments of tear gas on American soil until that time—*U.C.B. Pin Up* appears to be a commentary on the tumultuous events in Berkeley.[47] Through its title and fragmentary images, in other words, it evokes the story of the park's construction, destruction, and the subsequent demonstrations and battles between the State of California and its citizens over the area's eventual fate; it uses the pinup format to once again suggest an ideological framework that supports both militarism and a patriarchal vision of society. In particular, the bullet-riddled corpse, with his shirt hiked up to its chest, recalls James Rector, shot in the torso, who remains the most prominent martyr associated with these events.

More broadly, like Heinecken's other pinups, *U.C.B. Pin Up* evokes the idea of a dense interchange between reality and the media—a fitting association for a story about a park whose origins can in part be traced to an open call for volunteers in the *Berkeley Barb* on April 18, 1969. Significantly, as the transparency collage suggests, the violence of war had come home to roost. Echoing the viciousness of the attacks on civil rights protesters earlier in the decade, the events at Berkeley reminded all Americans that their country—a nation that was waging war in Southeast Asia to stop the spread of Communism—was also willing to deploy helicopters and bullets against its own citizens at the first signs of dissent. Like Heinecken's other pinups, it juxtaposed appropriated images with a generic form of popular culture to comment on contemporary historical events. And although it was more two-dimensional than sculptural, its construction of a layered image—a representation in which things are seen through a frame that contextualizes them—is protosculptural and points to Heinecken's final form of photo-object, which was featured prominently in *Photography into Sculpture,* the show at the Museum of Modern Art in 1970 that exposed the sculptural photography movement to a larger, national audience.

MoMA 1970

In 1970, the Museum of Modern Art in New York presented two exhibitions that helped to define photography's place in the art museum. The first, *Photography into Sculpture,* displayed photo-based works as hybrid and expressive forms of art—objects whose characteristics contradicted then-dominant ideas of modernism in the photographic art world but that were nonetheless intended to signify photographers' subjective responses, ideas, or interpretations about the world.[48] The second show, *Information,* introduced conceptual, land, and systems art to a broader audience. In it, photographs were frequently employed as components of larger works and, in a few instances, as stand-alone pieces.[49] They were not, however, used for their intrinsic formal characteristics but, rather, like more traditional news or scientific photographs, for the ways in which they documented processes, actions, events, objects, or ideas.

While *Information* would go on to have an immediate and intensifying effect in the years after 1970, *Photography into Sculpture* would make much less of an impact until the second decade of the twenty-first century—although, as Darryl Curran noted, it seemed to have an "underground" influence in the years after it toured the United States in the early 1970s.[50] Both exhibitions, however, as well as their subsequent histories, illuminate much about the relationship between art and photography at the beginning of the 1970s, and for this reason, they help us to understand the significance of Heinecken's photographic sculpture in the second half of the 1960s.

Curated by Kynaston McShine of MoMA's department of painting and sculpture, *Information* took place between July 2 and September 20, 1970. The show presented more than 150 artists from fifteen countries; it was, as McShine wrote, a presentation of "the strongest international art movement or 'style' of the moment which is 'conceptual art,' 'art povera,' 'earthworks,' 'systems,' 'process art,' etc. in its broadest definition."[51] In some ways a hodgepodge of recent trajectories in contemporary art, the exhibition focused on the move away from traditional art mediums that was gaining steam in the art of the United States, Western Europe, and Latin America during the second half of the decade, a tendency that critics Lucy R. Lippard, a contributor to *Information,* and John Chandler had termed the "dematerialization of art" in 1968.[52] The exhibition also included more than forty experimental films as well as documentation of conceptual architectural projects. Its only "common denominator," as McShine noted, was that all the artists were "trying to extend the idea of art beyond traditional categories."[53]

The artworks presented in *Information* were notable for their heterogeneity as well as their difference from traditional fine art media like painting and sculpture. Some of the artworks in *Information* by figures like Hans Haacke, Group Frontera, Hélio Oiticica, and Adrian Piper were participatory in nature, inviting their audiences to contribute to a larger systemic whole that integrated artist, spectator, and work. Among the most famous of these were *MoMA Poll* (1970) by Hans Haacke, an installation that offered visitors the opportunity to take part in a survey, complete with ballot boxes and a photoelectric counter, answering yes or no to the query, "Would the fact that Governor Rockefeller has not denounced President Nixon's Indochina policy be a reason for you not to vote for him in November?"[54] Also participatory but in radically different ways were the "nests" of Hélio Oiticica's *Barracao Experiment 2* (1970), twelve-foot-high cellular structures made of wood, mattresses, pillows, and netted curtains in which audience members were invited to lie down. Inspired by the informal architecture of Brazil's favelas, they attempted to define a new type of social space in which public and private experience merged in unexpected ways.[55] Other works, including contributions by Vito Acconci, Richard Long, Joseph Beuys, Robert Smithson, and Hans Hollein, were simple actions or processes that were performed by the artist. Still other contributions, by John Baldessari and Yoko Ono, among others, were proposals or instructions for artworks that anyone could perform. Yet other artworks were temporary installations realized by assistants, for example, those of conceptual artists Sol LeWitt and Lawrence Weiner. A number of other works included in *Information* were purely textual, including those of Carl Andre, Stanley Brouwn, and Christine Kozlov, or printed books or other publications, as for example in the case of Art and Language, Michelangelo Pistoletto, Jeff Wall, and Ed Ruscha.

Although photographs were prominently displayed in *Information,* they were generally used as parts of larger (intermedial) works, and they were primarily employed as "evidence," as was noted in another press release for the event.[56] They were definitely not presented as artworks in themselves. A few photographic works, it could be argued, went beyond the evidentiary function. *Anonymous Sculpture, Cooling Towers* (1961–70), by the German photographers Bernd and Hilla Becher, consisted of a roughly square grid of thirty photographs (five photographs high by six photographs wide), flanked by one photograph of a drawing and one text panel.[57] A typology presenting a specific kind or category of industrial architecture, it fit with the exhibition's conceptual theme by focusing viewers' attention on the general form that subtended the various particular iterations of cooling towers that were depicted. At the same time, the careful formal composition characteristic of the photographs, as well as the detail and contrast range produced by the Bechers' large-format cameras and careful printing techniques, also placed the work within the tradition of modernist art photography.

For the most part, even the works in *Information* that were primarily photographic deemphasized the artistic aspects of the photograph in favor of its documentary or evidentiary functions, its ability to refer to the apparatuses of communication and the nature of signification, or photography's capacity to dematerialize art by indicating an idea, performance, or process. Thus, for example, *One and Three Chairs* (1965), by the conceptual artist Joseph Kosuth, presented a chair, a photograph of the chair, and a blown-up photographic reproduction of its dictionary definition, provoking the MoMA audience to think about the nature of the object in relation to its visual and linguistic representations.[58] And by making the connections between the three different aspects of the work tautological—that is, equivalent, corresponding to the linguistic form of an analytical proposition, signifying "a chair is a chair is a chair"—Kosuth hoped that his viewers would contemplate the idea of art as opposed to considering the chair as something factual or in the world.[59] Likewise, Jan Dibbets's *Shadow Piece (The shadows in my studio as they were at 27-7-69 from 8:40–14:10 photographed every 10 minutes)* (1969) consisted of a six-by-six grid of thirty-four photographs, with two text panels and a wall label.[60] As the title suggests, the work encouraged its viewers to focus not on the photographs but on the idea of the passage of time or the camera as an instrument that records temporal development. For the artists included in *Information,* the photograph became an unambiguous means indicating something beyond it. It was, in short, a transparent index, a medium of evidence, or a channel for information.

In contrast to *Information, Photography into Sculpture* continued to focus on photography as an artistic practice—in part by emphasizing he photograph as something that is crafted. Comprising fifty-two works by twenty-three artists, the exhibition opened at MoMA on April 8, 1970, and ran until July 5; it then traveled to eight additional cities, before closing at the Otis Art Institute in LA on March 5, 1972.[61] Challenging the prevailing conventions of modernist photography—most particularly, straight photography's emphasis on medium specificity—as well as many of the traditional ideas surrounding the nature of the photograph, the show was devoted, according to Peter Bunnell, its curator, to highlighting a new trajectory in the medium emerging in the work of select young photographers in the late 1960s.[62] This trajectory, which appeared primarily on the West Coast of the United States and in Canada, embraced a three-dimensional turn in what was traditionally assumed to be a two-dimensional form of representation. Committed to questioning the nature of the photograph as a physical object, the show was also intended to reveal the recent introduction of new qualities and materials into the medium, among them "topographic structure, image participation, tactile materiality, procedural time, and the technology of plastics, liquid emulsions, fabrics, dyes, film transparencies, and emitted light."[63] Significantly, photo-sculpture, at least as it was presented by the exhibition, transformed the role of the photographer from a documentarian who recorded the world—albeit from a particular point of view and through a particular sensibility—into someone who remade it in a new, much more subjective and conceptual way.

Bunnell considered Heinecken the main figure behind the new photo-sculptural work that was being produced, and as he developed the roster for *Photography into Sculpture,* Bunnell consulted with the LA photographer, who pointed him in the direction of a number of the artists.[64] These included some of Heinecken's own graduate students, such as Ellen Brooks and Michael Stone, who ultimately became part of the show.[65] Heinecken contributed six works exhibiting the full range of his photo-sculptural practice: blocks and stacks, figure puzzles, and a new form of transparency collage consisting of film and plexiglass. These works from 1968 and 1969 were small, open-ended wooden boxes containing layers of film and plexiglass, photo-objects that were very different from the blocks, stacks, and puzzles. In works such as *Venus Mirrored #6* (1968), *Transparent Figure/Foliage #1* (1969), and *Transparent Figure/Foliage #2* (1969), all included in *Photography into Sculpture,* Heinecken combined transparencies of nude figures, adding branches and foliage, to create kaleidoscopic images that blurred the boundaries between human and nonhuman.[66] *Venus Mirrored #6* is typical of these works in that the different layers of imagery seem to merge with one another (Plate 3.8). In this photo-sculpture, at least two differently sized, tonally reversed nudes, their arms clasped above their heads, are copied, flipped vertically, and juxtaposed, creating a symmetrical hybrid composed of a multitude of only semidistinct figures that seems to rotate on a vertical axis. Recalling *Tomorrow* (1924), Man Ray's famous composite image that echoes and overlays multiple nudes, *Venus Mirrored* presents a vision of the human

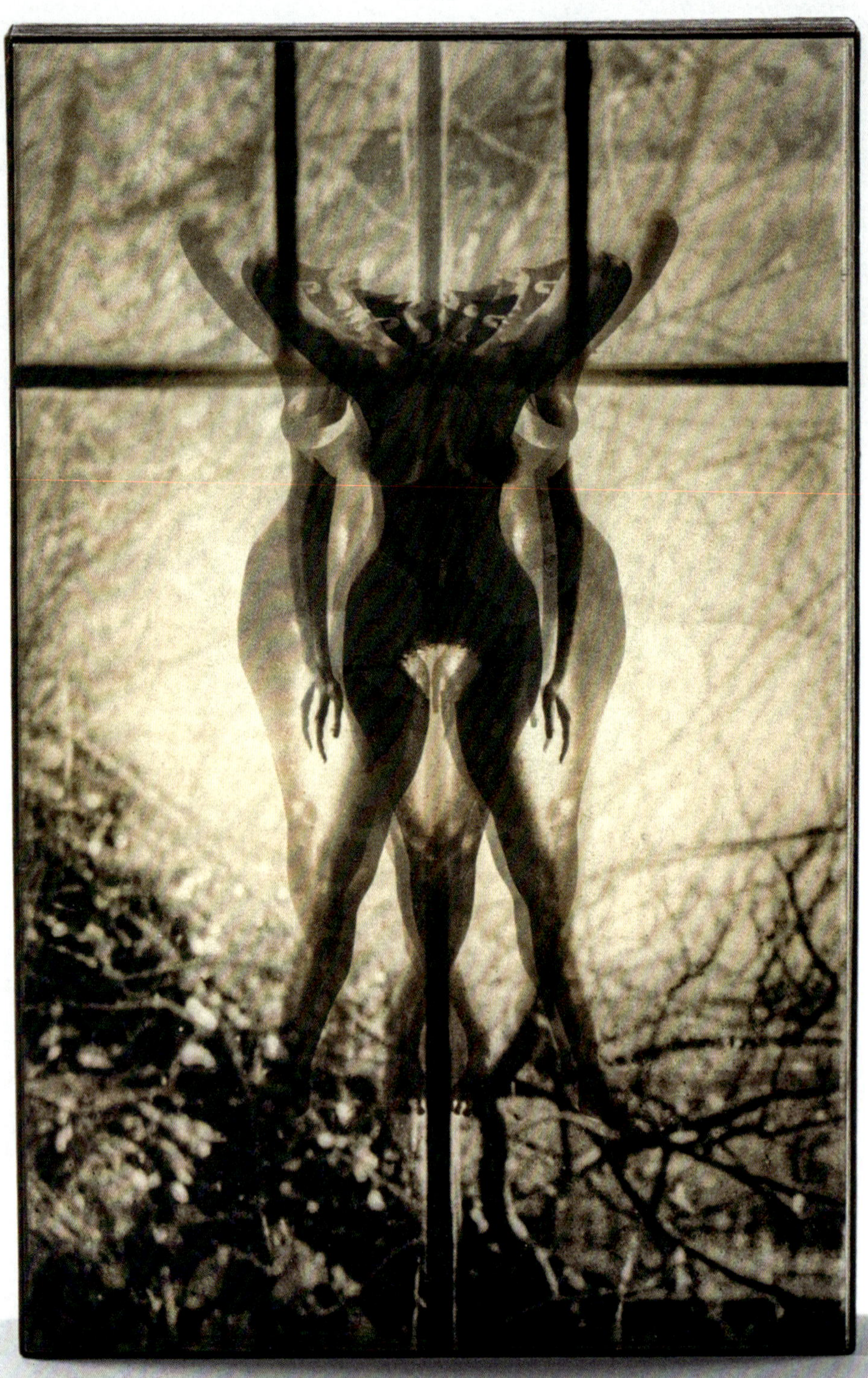

body that suggests its transformation through movement and the technologies of modern vision.

Unlike May Ray's *Tomorrow,* which does not present its figures as negatives or contain additional imagery (and thus appears somewhat more legible than Heinecken's later composite), *Venus Mirrored* also overlays a network of branches at the top and bottom of the image, thereby suspending the distorted human form within a framework of horizontal and vertical linear elements that seem to support the body as if it were a scientific specimen impaled on some kind of scaffolding. In this way, Heinecken's artwork further emphasizes the idea of scientific visualization techniques evoked by the negative transparencies and geometric elements, since the latticework of branches also suggests veins or nerves revealed through medical imaging. (The *Figure/Foliages,* which render the human body and the natural imagery even more abstract, further emphasize the impression of scientific imaging: they evoke both X-rays and representations made in a microscope.)

Douglas Prince also presented film and plexiglass boxes in the show, developing other aspects of this form of photo-sculpture. Like Heinecken's boxed images, Prince's works were intimate in scale and—like nineteenth-century cased images such as daguerreotypes and ambrotypes—they invited their viewers to pick them up and examine the image from different angles.[67] Also like Heinecken, who later noted how much he admired Prince's photo-boxes, Prince printed images on separate layers of film that he then combined into open-ended assemblages, separating each layer with plexiglass and uniting all elements by means of a surrounding wooden frame. Unlike Heinecken, Prince restricted himself to positive transparencies, and he carefully orchestrated the different image layers to create a heightened sense of three-dimensional illusion, with the different layers that defined foreground, middle ground, and background working together to create a coherent, if slightly surreal, representation of the physical world.[68] In contrast, Heinecken's cased images were much more antinaturalistic: it was hard to tell what exactly was depicted and—because of the conflation of different scales—the viewpoint from which the image was taken.

Heinecken's art possessed numerous affinities with the "conceptual" art included in *Information.* Like the *Information* artists, Heinecken was focused on tautology (in his case, the literalness of the nude) and system (geometry and references to the photographic apparatus); he also sought to dehierarchize art (blur the distinction between viewers and makers by encouraging audience participation); and he was concerned with the media and different forms of mass communication. In contrast to the *Information* artworks, however, Heinecken's photo-objects were decidedly more corporeal and impure, more pop, and more idiosyncratic. They seemed to undermine their conceptual nature through their recourse to the genre of photographic nudes and pinups, which made them seem less serious than the social, political, and philosophically minded works of the *Information* exhibition.

If Heinecken's photo-objects were not accepted as important art in the 1970s, this was not due to a lack of significance. Instead, it had to do with different assumptions that governed the still-separate worlds of contemporary art and contemporary photography. Contemporary artists turned to photography in the 1960s and 1970s with the assumption that it was indexical and not artistic—that it was an objective medium and not a channel of subjective expression. They saw photography as a transparent channel of communication. Heinecken, on the other hand, explored photography as a manipulative medium that targeted his body, an avenue of representation that appealed to his deepest instincts and drives. Through photography's address to the consumer, he perceived, the medium became an avenue of social construction, a mechanism that modeled and molded behavior through the production of popular consumer images.

Heinecken's artistic exploration of photography as a medium of social construction often tended to link the collective with the personal through the medium of performance. Heinecken also consistently connected photography to other media like illustrated newspapers and magazines as well as to television, an acknowledgment of the important systems of production in which photography played a role. Heinecken used his medium throughout the 1970s to explore different photographic genres such as news and specialty magazines, pornography, and instantaneous photography. Although he continued to command a significant presence in the photography world, his conceptual use of photography did not break through to the contemporary art world, despite its similarities and close proximities. His imagery could be dismissed as kitschy or sexist; and the material qualities of Heinecken's photo-sculptures were confounding to artists and audiences alike, in short anyone who assumed that photography generally functioned as a clear and transparent channel. It would take until the 1980s for photography to be taken seriously by the artworld as a medium through which personal and collective identities were constructed. And the artists to demonstrate this were not Heinecken and the *Photography into Sculpture* photographers but, rather, a different group altogether.

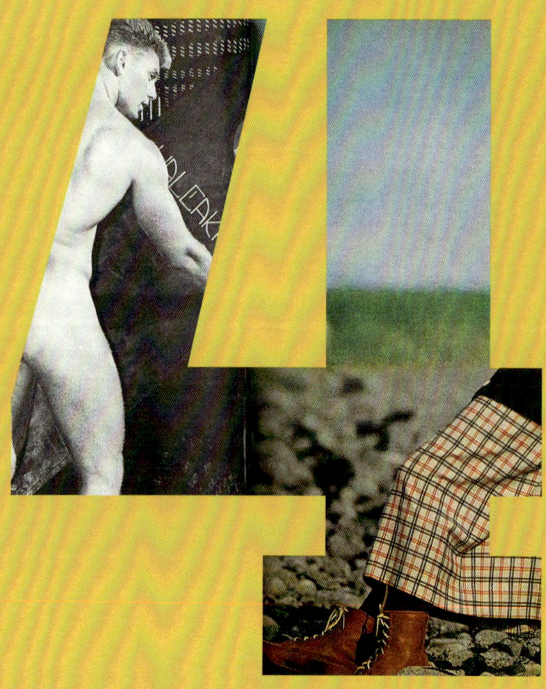

MAGAZINE WORK

American Disaster
and Identity

BETWEEN 1969 AND 1974, Heinecken created a series of magazines that radically questioned the status of art as well as the nature of everyday life in the United States. Produced during a time of growing disillusionment with the social and political changes that had wracked the country in the 1960s, these magazines pointed to an expanding social malaise that would become characteristic of the 1970s. More than a decade later, in the late 1980s and early 1990s, Heinecken returned to his altered magazine strategy to reflect on photography and celebrity at a time when broadcast and print media were about to become subsumed into digital networks. These later works, which emphasize physical cutting and incising, now read like odes to an analog world that was ending as well as anticipations of viral environments to come.[1]

Like his photograms and lithographs, Heinecken's altered magazines of the 1970s and 1990s were extremely self-reflexive and aware of the history of photography as well as the other mass-reproductive media with which photography was combined. They seem to acknowledge and respond to the evolution of the American magazine and to the important shifts in the nature and makeup of popular periodicals that took place between the 1960s and 1990s. As was the case with his other output, Heinecken's magazine work was motivated by his longstanding desire to document and explore the impact of the mass media on American life. Through a variety of different strategies, he combined an investigation of the ways in which images and texts addressed the mass consumer with an analysis of the specific desiring bodies to which capitalist appeals were made.

The 1970s, the time of the "failed" presidencies of Nixon and Carter, and the Reagan–Bush era, of course, were very different cultural moments; and Heinecken's respective bodies of magazine work responded to their differences. The 1970s are generally understood to be a "lost decade," one rocked by political and economic crisis, in which America's power waned internationally, while its population seemed to grow more self-focused and narcissistic. In the 1980s and 1990s, on the other hand, the United States appeared to itself as much more powerful; after the collapse of the Soviet Union during the Bush presidency, the United States emerged again as the predominant superpower, supported not only by its military but also by the growing might of its technology and financial industries.

In the late 1960s and early 1970s, Heinecken's magazine work engaged with American disasters—the Vietnam War, social and economic injustice, and political corruption—individual and collective traumas that he linked to crises in traditional forms of identity. Like contemporaneous cultural critics Tom Wolfe and Christopher Lasch, Heinecken homed in on what he saw to be the decade's most dominant personality traits, which the artist depicted through images that blended consumer products with

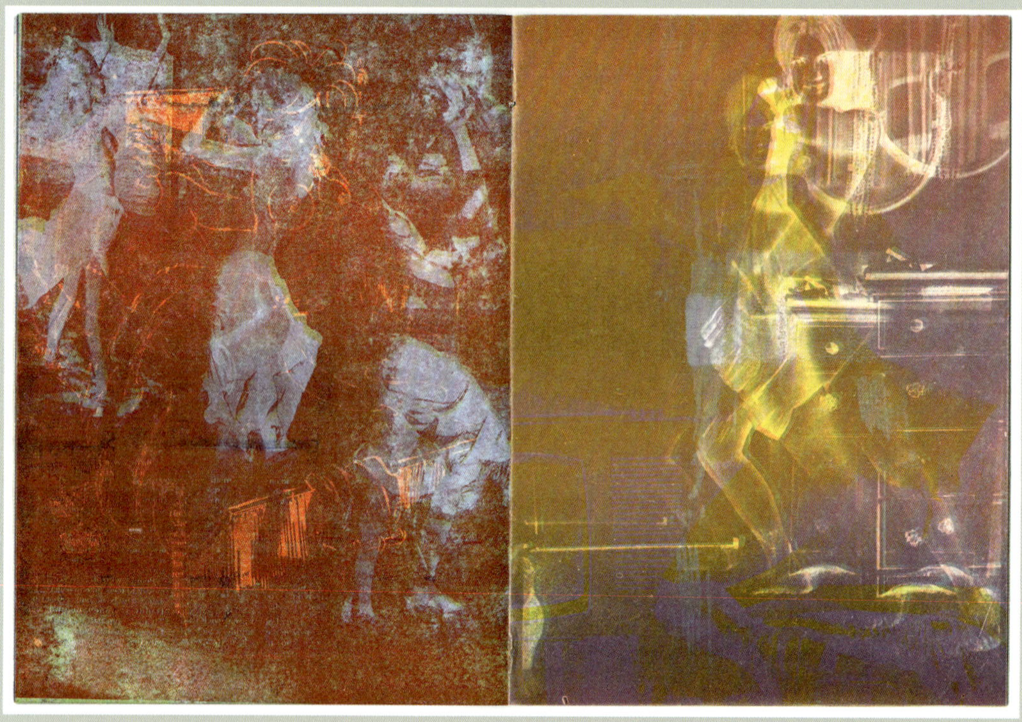

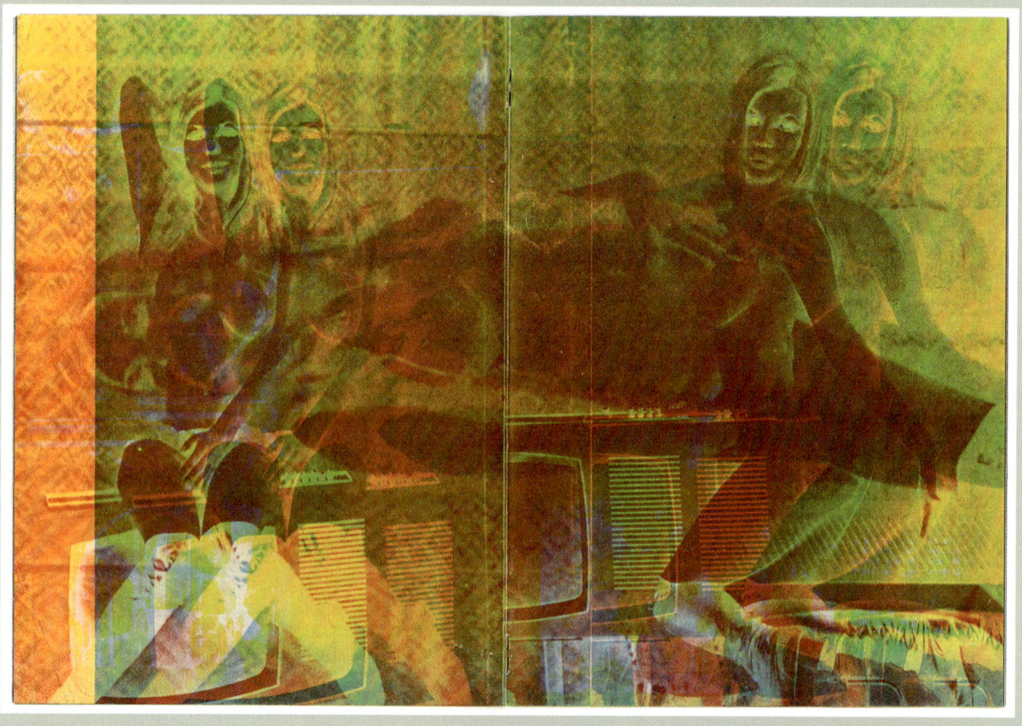

sexuality and violence.[2] More than Wolfe or Lasch, however, Heinecken unmasked the racism and sexism inherent in American capitalism and individualism in the 1970s. Associating consumption with sexual exploitation, war, and colonialism, his magazine work pointed to a contradictory male gaze, one that asserted its predominant and "universal" nature at the same time that it undermined itself from within.

Mansmag

Heinecken's first full-length magazine was the *Mansmag: Homage to Werkman and Cavalcade,* which he published in an edition of 120 in October 1969 (Plates 2.9, 2.10, 4.1, and 4.2). As noted in chapter 2, *Mansmag* used the same process as *Are You Rea*: photograms derived from magazine pages that were then transferred onto lithographic plates and finally printed, on an offset press, as an edition of connected prints. Unlike his famous portfolio, however, Heinecken impressed the plates of *Mansmag* using four different colors, mixing two colors on each side of the page. Instead of making a single pass with the same printing plate, as he did with *Are You Rea,* he ran each magazine page through the press a total of four times—twice per side—in order to create a two-sided periodical that was folded down the middle and stapled at its center. As a result, the images published in *Mansmag* were in general denser and less legible than in the earlier portfolio and also much more sensual and evocative. In addition, in comparison with *Are You Rea,* which still presented itself like a traditional artwork, *Mansmag* evoked a much more vernacular form: a mass-market magazine.

Mansmag also had a more specific conceptual focus than *Are You Rea.* Heinecken created his periodical by appropriating all the pages from a single issue of *Cavalcade,* recomposing the overprinted results into a new periodical consisting of matte front and back covers printed on heavy stock with twenty pages (ten folded sheets) of thinner glossy stock inside.[3] Because of the different colors used to double-print the same plates, each variant of *Mansmag* was unique; not only are the hues different, but their specific combinations reveal and obscure each plate's imagery differently. Yet despite its variety and the mysterious nature of its images, the magazine was also a document: a sample instance of a mainstream men's magazine addressed to—and thus helping to socially construct— the heterosexual male consumer subject of the emerging Me decade. As opposed to *Are You Rea,* which seemed to address a more general mix of male and female readers, *Mansmag* presented itself as a defamiliarization of a particular magazine genre as well as the specific forms of desire and subjectivity in which that genre trafficked. It concentrated on a particular demographic, men wishing to view stimulating content; its text and imagery evoked the specific subject position of a heterosexual man seeking erotic gratification and fantasy. This subject position, it suggested, was in crisis, divided from within by contradictory impulses and beliefs.

When examined more closely, the iconography of *Mansmag* reveals itself to consist of posing cheesecake figures interspersed with story and ad copy. The cover presents overlaid images of a seminude model, wearing go-go boots and panties, posing with a television set. Throughout the magazine, women appear both singly and in groups, and the multiple overlays—the original photogram juxtapositions of both sides of the page, and then the double printings in different colors—make the images appear to move like colored X-rays. Full-page shots of models are mixed with pages that contain tinier pictures presenting multiple poses and blocks of text suggesting sequences and actions. In general, an impression is created of a moving mass of ominous hybrid figures, who may or may not be part of the same group or story, and who are represented from a multitude of different viewpoints. In some pages, photographic and cartoon figures merge, creating uncanny hybrid personages that perhaps evoke the earlier cartoon tintypes or comic foregrounds patented by Cassius Marcellus Coolidge in 1874.[4] Other spreads present uncanny groups of doppelgängers created by the off-register printing of the same photogram image in two separate colors, a strategy that also produces a sense of 3-D prints meant to be viewed through red-and-green-colored glasses.

The language that punctuates the flow of images unequivocally addresses a straight male subject. Amid story titles like "Sex Is an Airline Stewardess" and "I Never Met a Man I Didn't Like," the reader is asked, "Why pay more?" "What do these champions have in common with you?" And more than once, "Tired of being skinny?" The title "The Bodyshop" —possibly the name of one of *Cavalcade*'s recurring departments—is also repeated; it is a found fragment of copy that makes explicit the commodification of the corporeal form produced by the pornography industry. In addition, ads for model slides and photos crowd the inside cover and first page, evoking self-reflexive associations and referencing the erotic photo service The Latent Image, which Heinecken found fascinating in part for its attack on photographic authorship.[5] A deconstruction of the mainstream men's magazine genre, Heinecken's parodic publication suggested that men who read these types of magazines liked to fantasize about themselves in the role of photographers. Erotic pleasure and vision, *Mansmag* suggested, were irrevocably linked in late-1960s America, but sometimes in unstable or contradictory ways.

A document of the end of the 1960s, *Mansmag* enacted a crisis of male subjectivity by mixing up and transforming the objects of its desire.

Emphasizing the commodification of masculine identity, the radical magazine juxtaposed images that incited male desire with text that repeatedly evoked its inadequacy and failure. In addition, the erotic images are fragmented and recombined, their gender thereby rendered fluid. In this way, *Mansmag* critically undermined the fixity of gender identity on which the heterosexual male voyeur depended. Instead, it attributed a fundamental bisexuality to the straight male gaze. If sexual gratification is linked to the power of an objectifying and commodifying mode of seeing the world, the work suggested, then it ultimately does not matter if the object of the gaze is male or female or someone in between. "Straight" male desire could be stimulated by just about anything.

Time (1st Group) and *Periodical #1*

Quickly, Heinecken turned from manipulating and reprinting magazine pages as he did with *Mansmag* to working with them directly and transforming them much less. *Time (1st Group)* (1969), for example, consisted of pages cut from the famous newsmagazine, overlaid with lithographs of a cheesecake model posed with a television set—images once again appropriated from *Cavalcade*—and then reassembled (Plates 4.3 and 4.4). With its iconic Raquel Welch portrait cover, this edition of sixteen volumes, or variants, utilized the repetition of seemingly lowbrow or vulgar figures to mix the human body with text and consumer products, thus serving a similar purpose to Heinecken's earlier photogram strategy but with simpler and more legible means. In spreads that focus on war and politics, leisure and consumption, the quasi-pornographic, self-reflexive images remind the viewer of how money and society objectify, manipulate, and

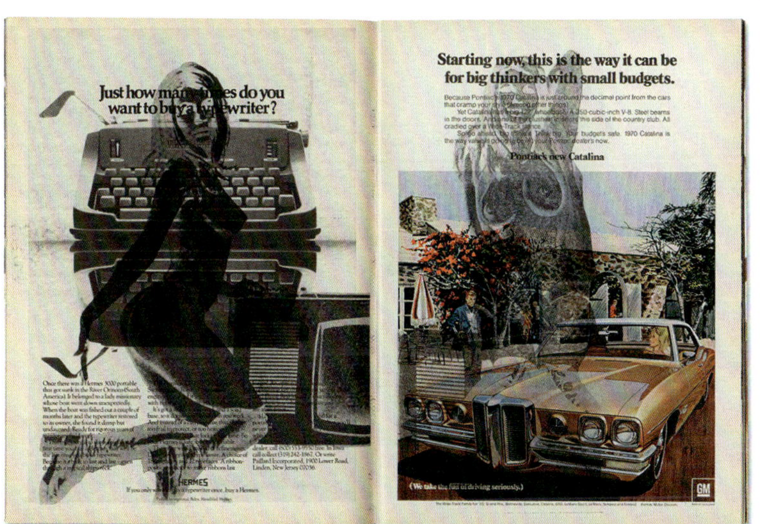

PLATE 4.3. Robert Heinecken, *Time (1st Group)* (1969). Found bound magazine recollated with offset lithography, 10 ¾ x 8 ⅛ inches (27.31 x 20.64 cm). 3 of 16. Private collection. COPYRIGHT 2022 THE ROBERT HEINECKEN TRUST, CHICAGO.

One Republican's Ordeal

The Haynsworth fight was rough on all Senators, but it was particularly painful to those Republicans who had doubts about the judge's fitness for the high court. Typical of these troubled Senators was Maryland's Charles McC. Mathias Jr., 47, a former Congressman serving his first term in the Senate. He talked about the agony of his decision to vote against Haynsworth to TIME Correspondent Neil MacNeil.

I went to the President's aides very early in the game, when the smoke began to rise, and conveyed my serious doubts about the nomination," says Mathias. "They asked me to keep an open mind to the end. So I did not put myself in the position of an irreversible commitment." But Mathias could not shake his doubts about Haynsworth. "There is a crying need for the Supreme Court to be lifted above controversy and suspicion. I also wondered what effect a condonation of Judge Haynsworth's actions would have on the judiciary at large. I could only conclude that it would lower standards at a time when the expectation is that they will be raised."

Mathias began to get pointed mail and telephone calls from his home state. "It's not so much what they say as the way they say [it], how extreme their d[is]appointment will be. You get the p[etty] functionaries who threaten party [retaliation]. You get the man who does b[usiness] with the Government—and it [may] be that he was instigated by [someone] in the Administration to ca[ll] . . . [The im]plication is that the man's [business] might be taken away if Math[ias voted] negatively. "A Maryland [applicant] for a [po]sition in the Admin[istration] was [told] that there was no [ques]tion about [his] qualifications and th[at] the question was whether a Senator'[s v]ote could be [de]livered for Haynsw[orth]—which the job seeker promptly ca[me] to me with."

The Administration handled Mathias tactfully. President [Ni]xon talked to him about the nomination twice. "He never put any personal pressure on me," says Mathias, and he thinks he knows why he was handled so gingerly: because he would blow the whistle on any undue arm twisting. "I know what the Senate floor is for."

When he finally announced his opposition in the Senate, one Republican Senator snarled at him: "Wait until I get in front of that committee and start question[ing] some of those Maryland judges and ask how [...] the [federal] Four appointment[s] to the federal bench in Maryland are, in fact, opening up.

Mathias brushed off hints that he might [lose] patronage power if he went against the party. He thinks that most Administration jobs now require technical competence, and that patronage is not as much of a lever as it once was.

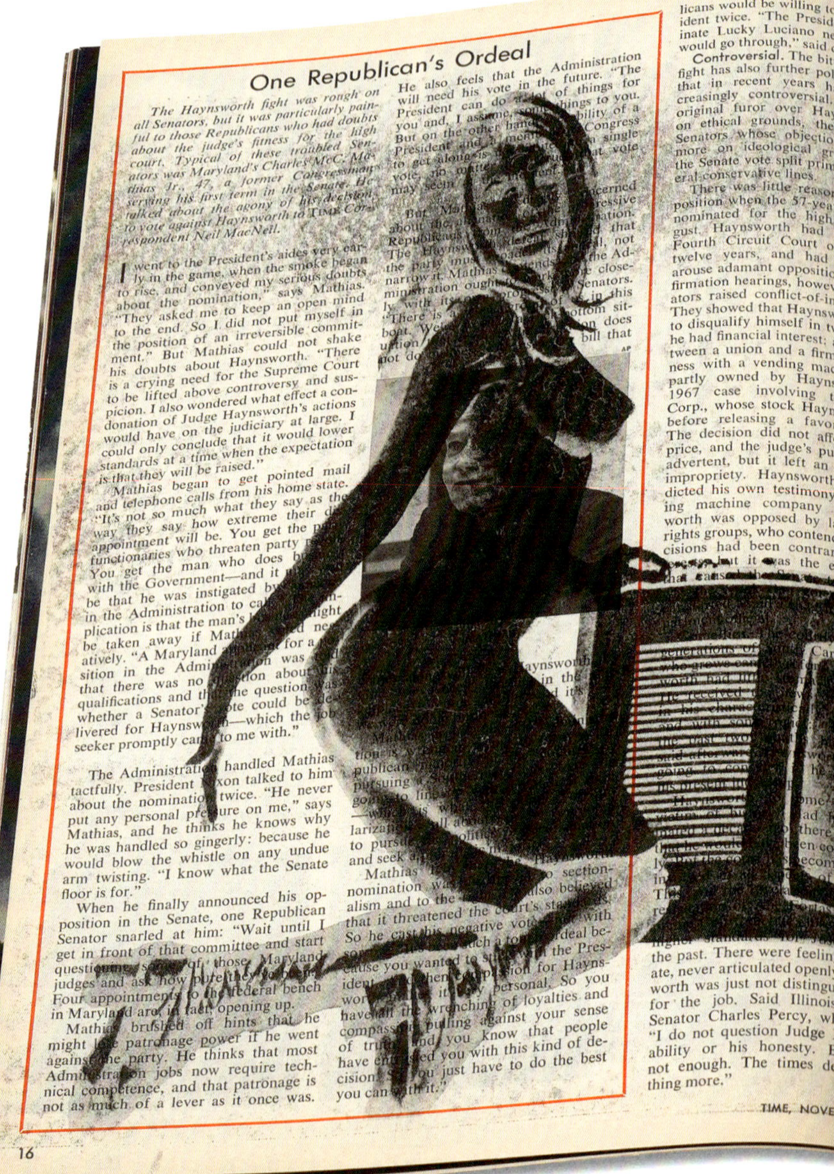

He also feels that the Administration will need his vote in the future. "The President can do a lot of things for you and, I assume, some[thing of the in]ability of a [...] But on the other hand [...] Congress President and a member [...] a single vote [...] to get along [...] vote no matter [...] may seem [...]

But Mathias [...] concerned about the [narrowness...] gressive Republicans [...] The Haynsworth [...] that the party must broaden its [app]eal, not narrow it. Mathias [...] the close-ministration ought [...] Senators. [...] "There is a [...] of us in this boat. We [...] bottom sit-uation does [...] bill that [...]

[...] tion is [...] publican [...] pursuing [...] going to line [...] —which is [...] larization [...] all about [...] to pursue [...] politics [...] and seek a [...]

Mathias [...] Haynsworth nomination was [...] also believed [...] alism and to the [...] section-alism [...] that it threatened the court's standards. So he cast his negative vote [...] with such a tough ordeal be-cause you wanted to stick with the President [...] compassion for Hayns-[worth] when it [...] personal. So you [...] have all the wrenching of loyalties and [...] ruling against your sense of trust [...] you know that people have en[trusted] you with this kind of de-cision [...] you just have to do the best you can with it.

[...] licans would be willing to bu[...] ident twice. "The President [...] inate Lucky Luciano next [...] would go through," said one.

Controversial. The bitter fight has also further politic[ized ...] that in recent years has [become in]creasingly controversial. A[fter the] original furor over Hayns[worth] on ethical grounds, there [were] Senators whose objections [rested] more on ideological grou[nds ...] the Senate vote split primari[ly along lib]eral-conservative lines.

There was little reason t[o ex]position when the 57-year-o[ld judge was] nominated for the high c[ourt last Au]gust. Haynsworth had ser[ved on the] Fourth Circuit Court of [Appeals for] twelve years, and had do[ne little to] arouse adamant opposition. [At the con]firmation hearings, however, [Sen]ators raised conflict-of-inte[rest issues]. They showed that Haynswor[th failed] to disqualify himself in two [cases where] he had financial interest: a l[awsuit be]tween a union and a firm th[at did busi]ness with a vending machi[ne company] partly owned by Haynsw[orth, and a] 1967 case involving the [...] Corp., whose stock Haynsw[orth bought] before releasing a favorab[le decision]. The decision did not affect [the stock] price, and the judge's purc[hase was in]advertent, but it left an ap[pearance of] impropriety. Haynsworth [also contra]dicted his own testimony o[n the vend]ing machine company aff[air. Hayns]worth was opposed by lab[or and civil] rights groups, who contende[d that his de]cisions had been contrary [...] but it was the eth[ical question] that caus[ed ...]

[...] higher standards [...] the past. There were feelings [...] ate, never articulated openly, [that Hayns]worth was just not distinguis[hed enough] for the job. Said Illinois [Republican] Senator Charles Percy, who [...]: "I do not question Judge H[aynsworth's] ability or his honesty. Bu[t that is] not enough. The times dep[...] thing more."

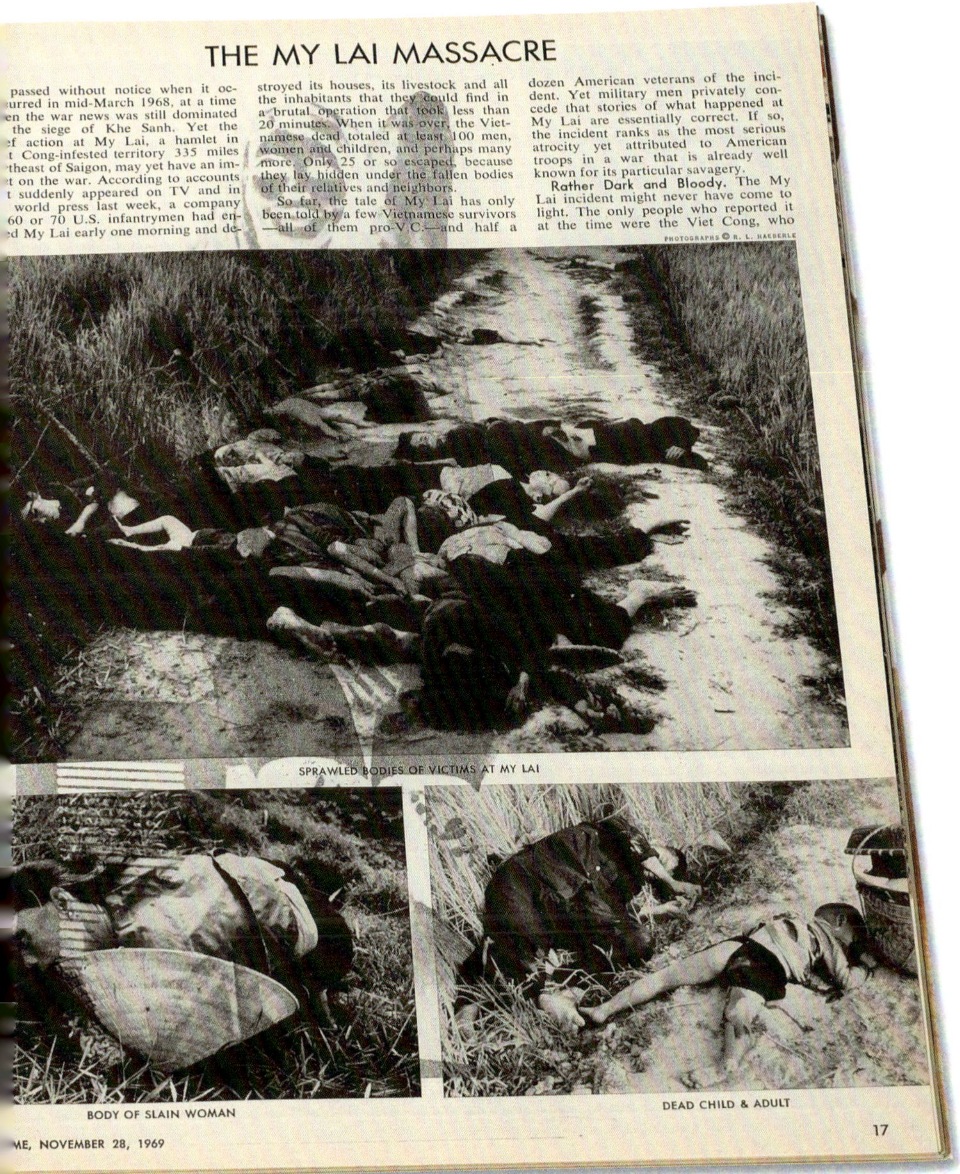

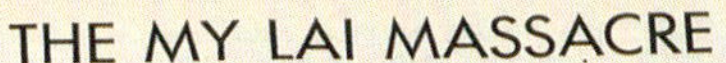

THE MY LAI MASSACRE

...passed without notice when it oc- ...curred in mid-March 1968, at a time ...en the war news was still dominated ...the siege of Khe Sanh. Yet the ...ef action at My Lai, a hamlet in ...t Cong-infested territory 335 miles ...theast of Saigon, may yet have an im- ...t on the war. According to accounts ...t suddenly appeared on TV and in ... world press last week, a company ...60 or 70 U.S. infantrymen had en- ...ed My Lai early one morning and de- stroyed its houses, its livestock and all the inhabitants that they could find in a brutal operation that took less than 20 minutes. When it was over, the Viet-namese dead totaled at least 100 men, women and children, and perhaps many more. Only 25 or so escaped, because they lay hidden under the fallen bodies of their relatives and neighbors.

So far, the tale of My Lai has only been told by a few Vietnamese survivors —all of them pro-V.C.—and half a dozen American veterans of the incident. Yet military men privately concede that stories of what happened at My Lai are essentially correct. If so, the incident ranks as the most serious atrocity yet attributed to American troops in a war that is already well known for its particular savagery.

Rather Dark and Bloody. The My Lai incident might never have come to light. The only people who reported it at the time were the Viet Cong, who

PHOTOGRAPHS © R. L. HAEBERLE

SPRAWLED BODIES OF VICTIMS AT MY LAI

BODY OF SLAIN WOMAN

DEAD CHILD & ADULT

TIME, NOVEMBER 28, 1969

17

PLATE 4.4. Robert Heinecken, *Time (1st Group)* (1969). Found bound magazine recollated with offset lithography, 10 ¾ x 8 ⅛ inches (27.31 x 20.64 cm). 3 of 16. Private collection. COPYRIGHT 2022 THE ROBERT HEINECKEN TRUST, CHICAGO.

destroy the human body. Once again—but now in the context of a weekly news digest—identity is revealed to be in crisis: its fixity is weakened, and outside threats appear on all sides. In particular, a gap between the male spectator and a more general mix of reader opens up, the former indicated by the *Cavalcade* imagery and the latter by the text, images, and layout of *Time*.

Like all of Heinecken's appropriations, the selection of *Time* was strategic. As Sammya Johnson and Patricia Prijatel note about the development of the American mass-market magazine:

> Probably the most dramatic change in content came in the 1920s. Three magazines—*Time, Reader's Digest,* and *The New Yorker*—were created in response to shifts and attitudes towards work and leisure time following World War I. Each periodical offered new approaches to reading in a fast-paced society. While other magazines were publishing long pieces about immigration or labor strife, along with serialized romances, westerns, and mysteries, *Time* and *Reader's Digest* chose to focus on brevity and the need to know.[6]

Time addressed a general mix of readers with a broad range of interests. It purported to give you the world—a digest of the most important actors and events—and despite a preponderance of "masculine" subjects, its copy and images were addressed to both genders.

In the early 1970s, when Heinecken appropriated images from it, *Time* reigned as the leading U.S. newsmagazine: the company had engineered the formula of giving a concise weekly roundup of the most substantial news.

> Henry Luce and Britain Hadden founded *Time* in 1923 because they believed busy Americans were poorly informed. Newspapers, they said, were unorganized and random in their content, making it difficult for people to understand what was happening in the world around them. *Time*'s content was driven by four key concepts, which continue to be followed today: (1) the week's news would be organized logically in short departments; (2) while both sides of a story would be told, *Time* would be evaluative and interpret what the news meant; (3) writing would be crisp, curt, and complete; and (4) emphasis would be on the personalities who made the news. The weekly news magazine was a new animal, grounded in a group journalism approach where field correspondents gathered data that would be organized and rewritten by editors in New York. Articles in *Time* seldom had bylines, but they did have perspective—Luce's particular ideas on politics, government, economics, and philosophy shaped each issue for many years.[7]

Addressed to a general reader and assuming what it affirmed to be an "objective" view of the world, it was a perfect foil for men's magazine imagery, since it presented itself as nongendered and nonclassed (or, rather, inclusive of all common identities or subject positions).[8] In combination with the appropriated cheesecake images in Heinecken's destabilizing *Time* variants, however, *Time*'s objective viewpoint broke down, and both the general mix of readers and the male spectator were called into question.

As a magazine *Time* changed over the years; eventually, for example, bylines began to appear regularly and Luce's influence waned by the end of the 1960s. *Time*'s framing mission, however—to produce a concise, balanced, accurate, and somehow general and objective summary of the news—remained consistent. And the magazine's model of comprehensive coverage and personality-driven content must have appealed to Heinecken precisely because it was there—with *Time*'s specific mix of hard news, celebrities, and popular culture—that he could most compellingly use strategies of defamiliarization and estrangement to subvert a supposedly objective representation of the historical record. By playing a male spectator off of a purportedly more general mix of readers, his *Time* variants destabilized both positions while constructing analogies among capitalism, sexuality, and (because of the Vietnam content) Western colonialism.

If the *Time* variants seemed to focus more on contemporary news and the dialectic between a general readership and a male viewer in crisis, then the *Periodical* series—each issue of which comprised multiple variants—seemed more specialized and specific, exploring a multiplicity of different genres and subject positions that American magazines reflected and also helped to produce. Like the *Time* variants, however, Heinecken's periodicals sought to juxtapose and transform various modes of identity through the manipulation of images and texts that addressed different types of viewers and readers, often of a more subcultural type. To make *Periodical 1* (1969), for example, Heinecken simply cut up and reconfigured a group of twenty-six magazines ranging from *Glamour, Good Housekeeping, Woman's Day*, and *Tiger Beat* to *Sports Illustrated, Field and Stream, Playboy, True Detective*, and *Guns and Ammo*, without adding any overlays. The end product was a set of nineteen twenty-six-page variants, each containing a single leaf from each magazine, with facing pages often pointedly juxtaposed.

A close reading of one example demonstrates the importance and radical nature of Heinecken's appropriated magazine strategy. As we page through the seventeenth variant of *Periodical #1*, we experience a cacophony of voices: not only different forms of advertising-address, but also a series of fragmentary stories on a variety of subjects that shift in tense and gender. The magazine begins with a photocopy of a handwritten list of the magazines and stories used, a conceptual opening that articulates the

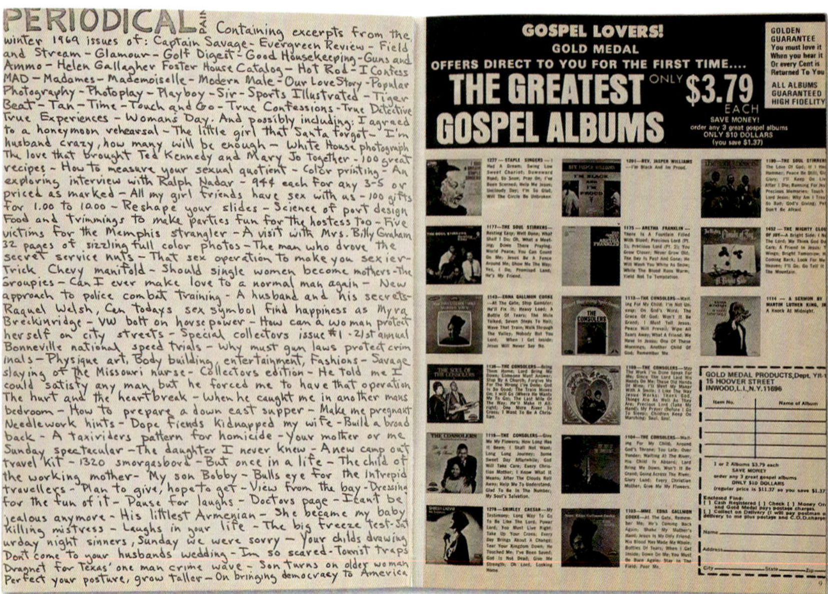

system by which the work was generated (Plate 4.5). Heinecken's enigmatic introduction is coupled with an ad for mail-order gospel albums, a contrast that suggests the ubiquitous nature of advertising and how it was increasingly permeating American consciousness. The reader then begins a series of stories: a profile from a music magazine that is mixed with a story about teenage delinquency and sex; an account of a woman's drinking problem connected to a sensuous scotch ad directed at men; and a narrative about bad marriages juxtaposed with a gay physique pictorial. Although the voices are fragmentary and start and stop in random places, the various accounts blend in the reading experience, creating a surreal narrative in which conflict reigns and stereotypical plot fragments intermix without clear logic.

In addition to presenting a set of ever-changing melodramas and editorials, Heinecken's double-page spreads also break or stop the reading experience, provoking the spectator to examine broader conceptual relationships between image and text across divergent genres. In one double-page spread, a nude male model, viewed from behind, seems to converse with a clothed fashion model, who shades her eyes, perhaps in an attempt to peer beneath the surfboard he coyly clutches to hide his genitals (Plate 4.6). By aligning gay porn with a fashionable woman's gaze in this way, the montage evokes multiple subject positions while raising questions about the fixity of gender identities. At another juncture, a page from a magazine comic, a snippet of heterosexual male pornography, and

PLATE 4.5. Robert Heinecken, *Periodical #1* (December 1969). Various papers, reassembled magazine, side-stapled and taped-in, plain heavy stock cover, 10 ¾ x 8 ½ inches (27.31 x 21.59 cm). 1 of 19. Private collection. COPYRIGHT 2022 THE ROBERT HEINECKEN TRUST, CHICAGO.

an image of an array of household kitsch cut from a home shopping magazine collide with one another, revealing disturbing areas of overlap in humor, sexuality, and commodification.

There is a highly charged atmosphere in Heinecken's magazine, a sense of the contemporary world as overly permeated with sex, adolescent humor, and violence. In many places, images highlighting the consumer's concern for external appearances are selected. In others, ravaged human bodies are depicted, forms that are exploited—and thus victimized a second time—through their photographic representation in the entertainment media. Our bodies are both idealized and destroyed, the magazine implies, by a popular culture that reproduces, augments, and ultimately replaces us. In one double-page spread, a violent image of a man's bullet-ridden corpse is combined with an advertisement for a shotgun that encourages the reader to buy the weapon for their unborn grandson (Plate 4.7). Mixing two different types of magazine (crime and gun collector), Heinecken here constructs a chain of cause and effect that undermines our traditional concepts of space, time, and influence. In another spread, a football player faces off against a father holding a crying toddler. Here the violence is incipient, and once again the connections between actors undermine traditional gender stereotypes.

The other eighteen variants of *Periodical #1* produce a similar effect. Paging through them, we experience a mingling of tongues: not only various forms of advertising-address geared toward a variety of education levels and tastes, but also a variety of subjects and voices, some first-person confessionals, some omniscient and ostensibly ungendered news stories. If advertising and consumer culture often work by defining subjects in terms of a clear set of properties—something that occurs through the targeting of a specific demographic audience—then the *Periodical #1* variants might be said to unmoor identity by addressing a reader who is always changing. In this way, the *Periodical #1* images differentiated themselves from the *Time* series, which through the cheesecake overlays contrast the objective presentation of newsworthy events with a heterosexual male perspective, albeit one that was in the process of quickly falling apart. The *Periodical #1* series, on the other hand, mixes perspectives even more insistently; the adult straight male voyeur is only one form of spectator constructed by the montages of images and text, and many other identities or subject positions are also consistently evoked.

Periodical #2–#10

Heinecken created nine more issues in the *Periodical* series between 1971 and 1972, using the appropriative and documentary strategies that were

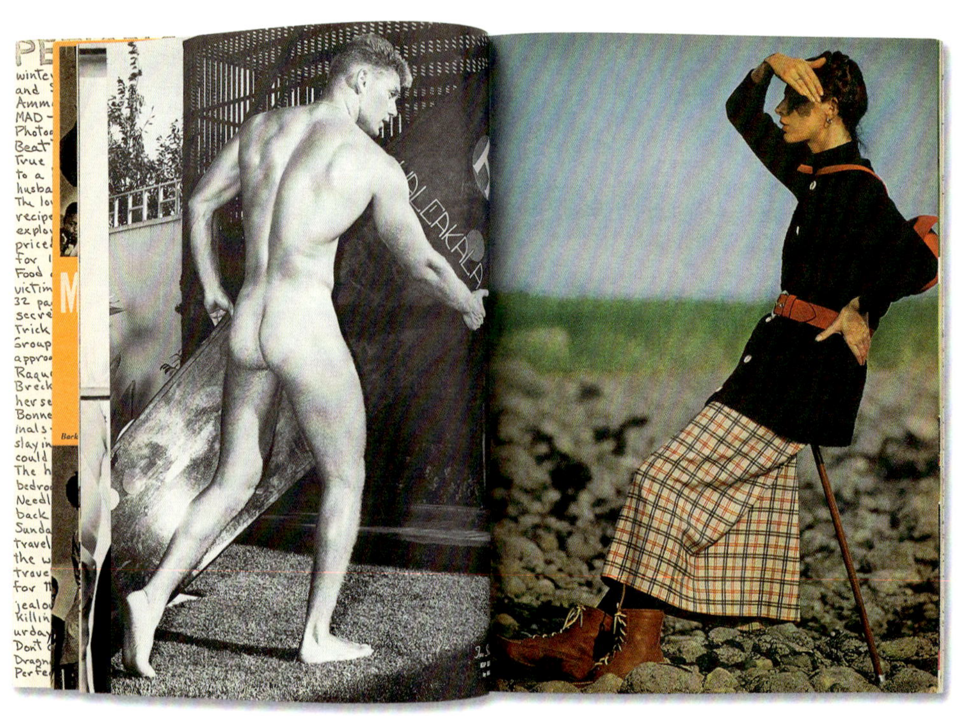

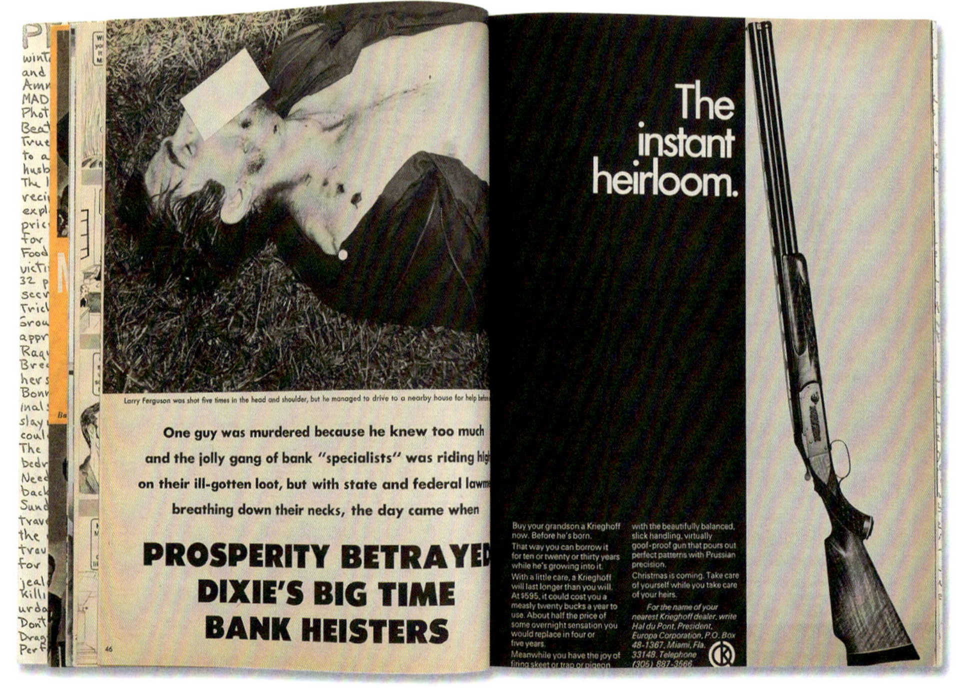
Larry Ferguson was shot five times in the head and shoulder, but he managed to drive to a nearby house for help before

One guy was murdered because he knew too much
and the jolly gang of bank "specialists" was riding high
on their ill-gotten loot, but with state and federal lawmen
breathing down their necks, the day came when

PROSPERITY BETRAYED
DIXIE'S BIG TIME
BANK HEISTERS

46

The
instant
heirloom.

Buy your grandson a Krieghoff
now. Before he's born.
That way you can borrow it
for ten or twenty or thirty years
while he's growing into it.
With a little care, a Krieghoff
will last longer than you will.
At $595, it could cost you a
measly twenty bucks a year to
use. About half the price of
some overnight sensation you
would replace in four or
five years.
Meanwhile you have the joy of
firing skeet or trap or pigeon

with the beautifully balanced,
slick handling, virtually
goof-proof gun that pours out
perfect patterns with Prussian
precision.
Christmas is coming. Take care
of yourself while you take care
of your heirs.

For the name of your
nearest Krieghoff dealer, write
Hal du Pont, President,
Europa Corporation, P.O. Box
48-1367, Miami, Fla.
33148. Telephone
(305) 887-3566

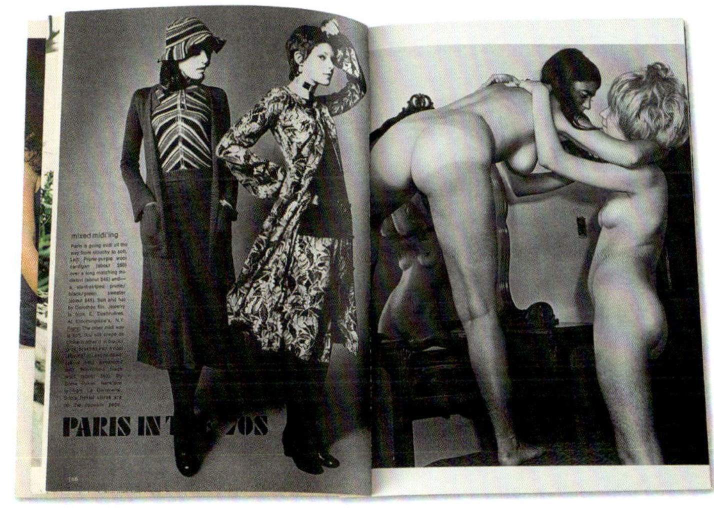

becoming his stock-in-trade. The altered magazines were made in varying edition sizes ranging from three to nineteen. And although they were created from extremely mundane materials, each variant was unique, producing its own specific—and highly charged—reading experience. Throughout the *Periodical* series, Heinecken would alternate montage techniques, switching between lithographic overlays, simple disassembly and recombination, and a kind of photo-collage wherein he cut out shapes on a magazine page to let the images on adjacent pages show through. In *Periodical #2, Periodical #3,* and *Periodical #4,* Heinecken continued the *Periodical #1* montage strategy—simple disassembly and recombination— but introduced more graphic imagery into the mix, reflecting the changing standards of mass-market men's periodicals (Plate 4.8). In these magazines, more graphic 1970s-style pornography (somewhere between cheesecake and what today would be called hard-core) and fashion imagery appear in combination again and again: cosmetics ads and nude photos are juxtaposed to suggest the merging of products and flesh; fashion models and centerfolds meet in faux lesbian encounters that embody but also exceed a male gaze. Marlboros and Virginia Slims, whiskey and TV dinners jostle one another in high-keyed color. The natural and the manufactured are consistently combined.

The typological impulse that connects Heinecken's work to that of Bernd and Hilla Becher and, closer to home, the conceptual photography of Dan Graham, Ed Ruscha, among others, is most in evidence in *Periodical #3* (1970). Here Heinecken balances the groupings of figures so that the same number of models appears on both sides of the spread.[9] There are, however, some significant differences. If his conceptualist cohorts

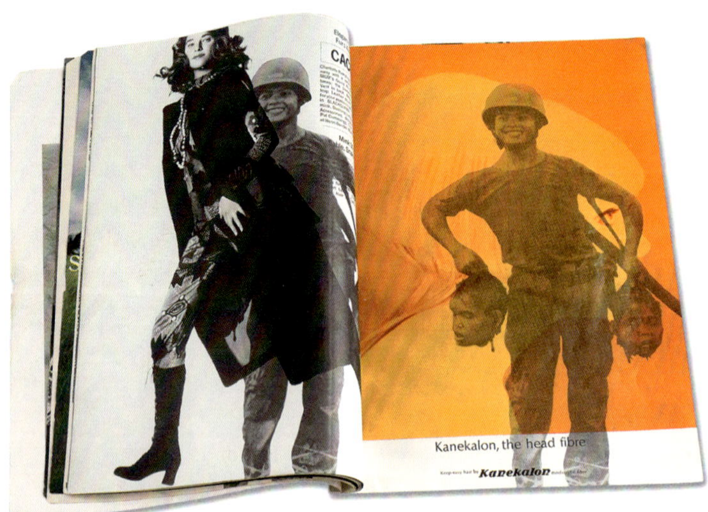

PLATE 4.9. Robert Heinecken, *Periodical #5* (February 1971). Offset lithography on found printed magazine, side-stapled and taped-in, repurposed magazine cover, 12 ¼ x 9 inches (31.12 x 22.86 cm). 6 of 6. Private collection. COPYRIGHT 2022 THE ROBERT HEINECKEN TRUST, CHICAGO.

saw potential in the tropes of banality—gas stations, prefab homes—Heinecken was the opposite. The quotidian experience that manifests itself in much conceptual photography of the time is of much less interest to him. Instead, he went right to experiences that surpassed the banal—a visceral stew of sex and violence that evoked social and political concerns.

In addition to an increasingly graphic sexuality, imagery of grotesque brutality shadows the series. In *Periodical #5* (1971), a smiling and highly androgynous Southeast Asian soldier carrying two severed heads is repeatedly superimposed across the pages of different magazines including *Vogue* and *Living Now* (Plates 4.9 and 4.10).[10] Although the androgynous figure is male, its juxtaposition with different female fashion models makes it appear even more feminine and less binary. In page after page of this altered periodical—as well as the one-off pages that Heinecken also produced with this motif—the shocking and brutal image undermines the messages of the advertisements and articles. Floating above, below, and on top of a variety of different figures, objects, and texts, this gender-bending representation of male violence contrasts with affirmative advertising statements like "This is the way love is in 1970," "America. Where you can look like this and do all that," and "The glare-killers are man-killers now."[11] Although Heinecken remembered the figure as Vietnamese, the soldier is actually Cambodian, and the heads are reportedly of two North Vietnamese soldiers fighting in Cambodia in late 1970 or early 1971.[12] Shot by Dieter Ludwig and published in *Time* on February 1, 1971, the news photograph that Heinecken appropriated was a grisly document of Nixon's "secret war" in Cambodia, wherein U.S. bombers supported Cambodian and South Vietnamese forces battling the

People's Army of Vietnam and the Viet Cong.[13] As such, it infiltrates the images of fashion and home design, adding a shocking experience of violence to what is supposed to be a pleasurable contemplation of models of aspiration. The Cold War worldview that supported U.S. capitalism and consumption, *Periodical #5* suggests, mobilized signs of race and gender as a way to encourage assent and participation.[14] Through its gender-bending image of toxic masculinity, it questioned America's military ideal as well as the country's guiding familial, social, and economic principles.

But it did even more than that. Despite the fact that it exists in hundreds of unique variants, both bound issues and one-off imprints, the *Periodical #5* montage has become one of Heinecken's most iconic works, precisely because of the disturbing power of its social and political critique. Although the montage evokes both male and female spectatorship—the male reader drawn by the "hard" new stories and the female reader interpolated by the fashion and celebrity coverage—the visceral nature of the Ludwig image links it to Heinecken's earlier pornographic overlays. The *Periodical #5* montage thus seems to project an objectifying, controlling, even military perspective—a point of view that Americans traditionally associated with a masculine subject. Like pornography, the montage suggests, images of violence simultaneously objectify and simulate, somehow bypassing the spectator's rational and ethical modes of apprehension and instead appealing much more directly to their body. Yet this supposedly dominant and controlling white male gaze is created through an image of a racial Other that is both similar and different. The figure has similarities with the male gaze associated with U.S. culture in that it is engaged in an act of terrifying violence. It is different, however, in that it is feminized and thus appears desirable, like a non-Western woman in a colonialist fantasy. Confronted with an object of desire that undermines the clear distinctions that determine and regulate its operation, the still-patriarchal U.S. male gaze of the 1970s is confounded, and the objectification of race and sex is revealed to lie at the heart of the capitalist economy.

Heinecken also deployed this montage for a guerrilla action he performed a few times in 1972, when he returned altered magazines to newsstands or doctors' or dentists' offices for an unsuspecting public to discover. The artist described the process as follows:

> I simply took that image of the guy with the heads and put it into offset plates and then took magazines apart so that I had single pages of all these different magazines. Then I just ran them through the offset press so that the image of the Vietnamese soldier with the heads is imprinted on the back and front of all of these pages through a variety of magazines—news, fashion, whatever. Next I recollated them into individual magazines

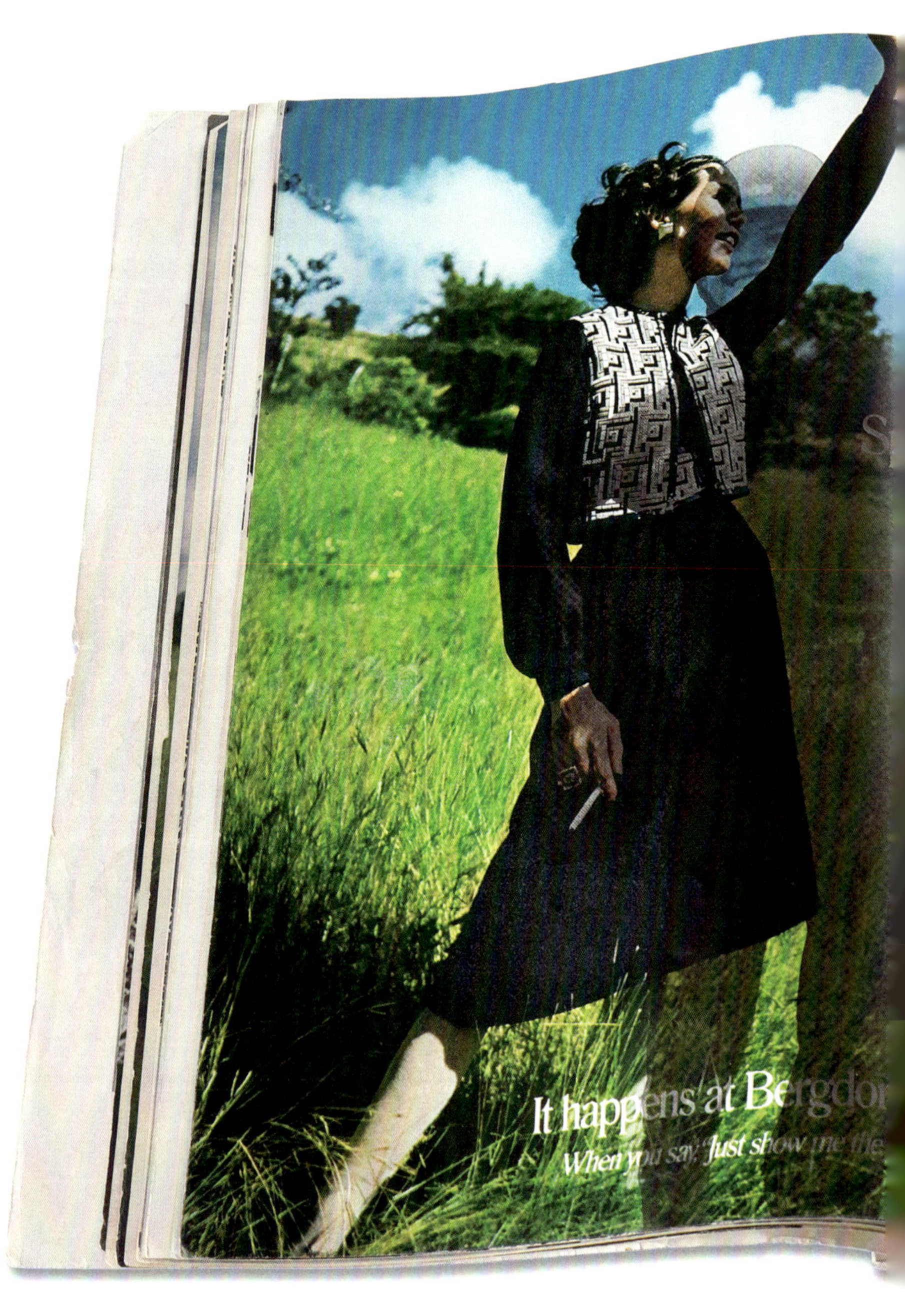

It happens at Bergdor
When you say, "Just show me the

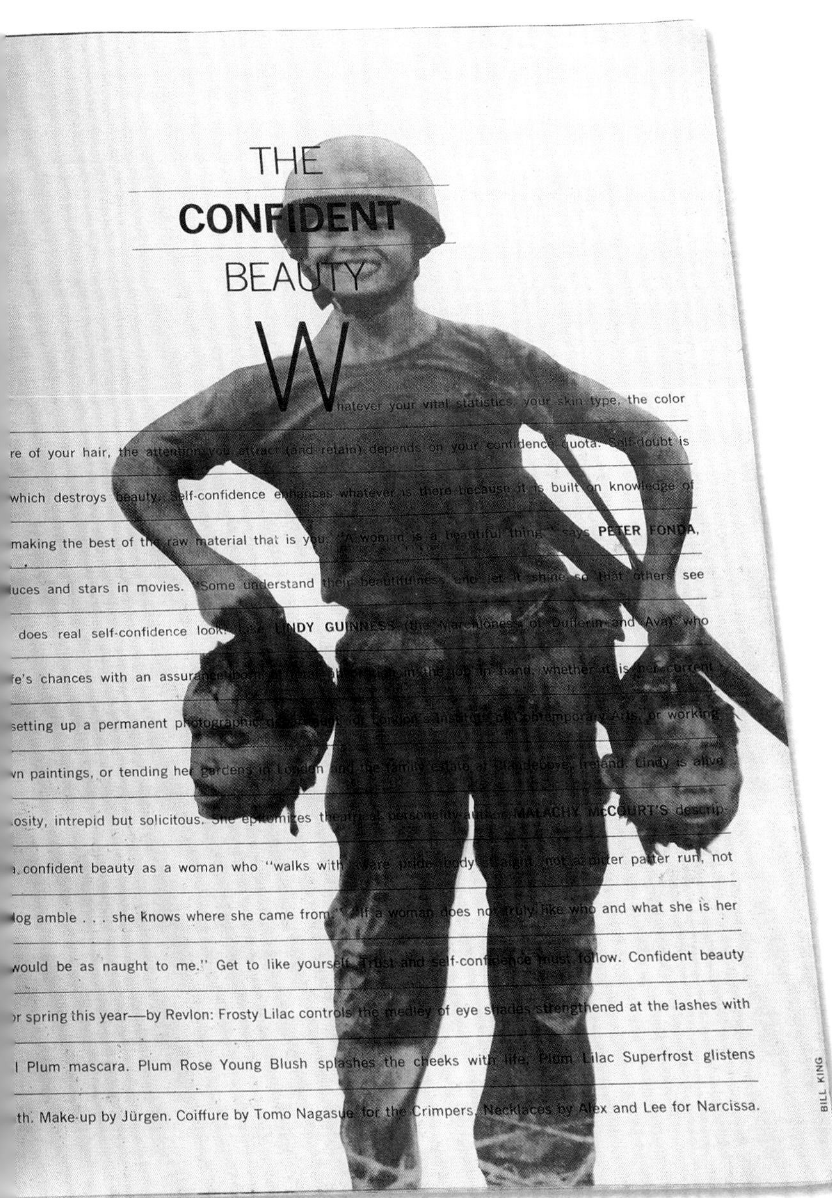

PLATE 4.10. Robert Heinecken, *Periodical #5* (February 1971). Offset lithography on found printed magazine, side-stapled and taped-in, repurposed magazine cover, 12 ¼ x 9 inches (31.12 x 22.86 cm). 6 of 6. Private collection. COPYRIGHT 2022 THE ROBERT HEINECKEN TRUST, CHICAGO.

that would have on every page this image in black ink over color, over all
kinds of different articles from the magazines. Then a certain number,
I think seven or eight of those, I snuck back onto the newsstand. I put
Time magazine covers on these things, because *Time* magazine was— At
least, in observing people at the newsstand, you might go thumb through
Playboy or *Good Housekeeping,* but *Time,* you know what it's going to be.
It's all the news that you need to know about in one week. You buy it, put
it under your arm, and get on the bus. So you're gone from the place when
you discover that you've got something screwy in your hands. Then I also
took a group of those and put them in dentists' and doctors' offices where
they have all these magazines. My dentist was in Westwood here. Those
offices are empty in the morning. Nobody cares if you're waiting or not. You
just put it in there and go. So those two places were where I fed it back into
the system, so to speak. But a distribution of seven or eight or whatever it
was in a city like Los Angeles, or another seven or eight in a doctor's office,
that's nothing. There's no effect.[15]

When asked why he did it, he simply replied:

I just liked the idea that somebody somewhere is going to open this
magazine up and going to be confused about it, is going to wonder about
it. The real energy of all of that goes into the artwork and the exhibitions.
The actual penetration of the culture on an individual level was an interesting thing to me, but the effect was not there. As a better effect,
I took maybe five hundred of these individual pages and mailed them
out to everybody that I knew, who are already, for the most part, people
who would not need this.[16]

Using his address book and the Society for Photographic Education mailing list for this task, he recirculated his intervention, inserting it into a
broader channel of communication where it would continue to have a subversive function.[17] Despite his pessimism about the effect of his guerrilla
action, the gesture was important as it speaks to Heinecken's intentions
regarding his altered magazines, namely, that he saw the mass media as
capitalist, ideological, and controlling—a tool of corporations and govern-
ments; and that he believed that his artistic project was in part to unmask
and disrupt the institutions and actors that benefited the most from the
new and growing systems of the media. In addition, the effect of Heinecken's gesture was deferred not absent; over time, it has increasingly
grown more apparent. The stereotypes in which patriarchal U.S. culture
trafficked, Heinecken demonstrated, could be reconfigured through
simple but strategic manipulations. Although powerful, the mass media,
he established, was not hegemonic; it could be sabotaged from within.
All that was necessary was a channel through which the reconfigured

products could be fed back into the system. This speaks to the strength of digital communications, which granted previously passive audiences new powers to be publishers in their own right since the 1990s. Although this avenue was not available to Heineken in the early 1970s (and, indeed, throughout his life he remained in fundamental ways an analog photographer), his appropriation and montage strategies were exceedingly effective and powerful. As we see today, all they needed to come to fruition was a digital revolution.

Periodical #6 (1971) continued the lithographic overlay technique but added a harder, more 1970s-style nude to the reassembled pages. Unlike the bodies in *Cavalcade,* or even *Playboy,* these nudes suggested the more gynecological focus of magazines like *Penthouse.* (The magazine that Heinecken appropriated is unknown, but it was definitely not mainstream, since its imagery was even more graphic and focused on genital detail than *Penthouse* was in the early 1970s.) Featuring pubic hair, labia, and fetish clothing, Heinecken's new, more hard-core aesthetic presented bodies in constant motion. Not only did the contrast between the two lithographs—the same model in two different poses—create a sense of progression and narrative, but the interpenetrations of bodies with other bodies as well as consumables such as perfume and contraceptive foam, suggest action and change. *Periodical #7* imprinted an overhead shot of a TV dinner on every page, a form that Heinecken associated with the 1960s and 1970s. They were something he purchased frequently during this time—meals that he fed his kids while his wife was away at work as a nurse in the afternoons and evenings. TV dinners were also emblematic of the way the medium was permeating everyday life more and more completely.[18] By placing a mass-produced dinner over different magazines pages, he alluded to this fact, suggesting that the consumer was beginning to be simultaneously addressed from a multitude of different, sometimes conflicting media and points of view. Heinecken also did a series of sculptural photographs of TV dinners in 1973. Here, the photograph was crumpled slightly to give the image a contradictory form of dimensionality. In addition, a knife and fork were often pictured on either side of the dinner and a partially smoked cigarette sometimes graced one of its compartments. Emphasizing the satiation of appetites on multiple levels, these sculptural photographs satirized the 1970s while standing as emblems of the decade. In this way, the sculptural photographs resembled Heinecken's altered magazines, which also presented American identity as interpellated by a world of products to be experienced or consumed.

In *Periodical #8* (1972) Heinecken returned to imprinting a 1970s-style nude over every page. This time, however, he used shots of two different models, thus adding even more narrative possibilities to the mix. And

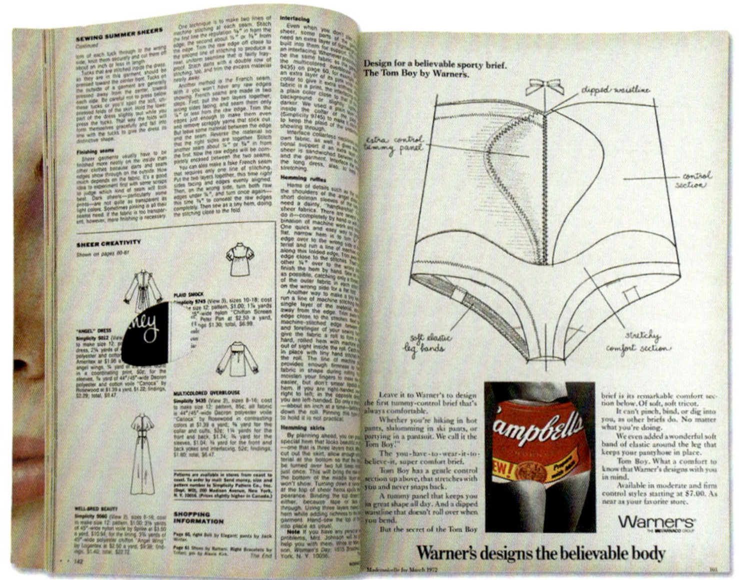

while Heinecken continued to use lithographic overprinting and full-page reassembly in this series, with *Periodical #9* (1972) he added a third technique, a new form of photomontage (Plate 4.11). Here, photomontage was not practiced in the traditional avant-garde manner—cutting up photographs or printed photo-illustrations and then collaging them together on a background. Instead, Heinecken treated the technique as an archaeological process: the excising of shapes or elements on bound pages to let the adjacent pages bleed through. It was not a simple edit, but a marvelous find, something that occurred in the world and yet spoke to the larger time as if it were shaped by an artist. The significant juxtaposition happened by chance, as Heinecken just discovered it. Carefully cutting out bras, panties, grooming products, and other merchandise, Heinecken revealed partial images beneath: a recognizable person or object glimpsed through a misshapen aperture. Heinecken's cuts also created a puzzling shape on the excised leaf's other side. Once again, the overall effect was to create a document that was both heterogeneous and iconic, a profane illumination of his contemporary moment. By constructing an assemblage of contradictory messages, appeals that stepped on one another in their attempts to get to the consumer, these archaeological magazines were both literal and magical. And in the final *Periodical #10* (1972), Heinecken returned to a modified overlay technique, now rubber-stamping censor's bars over the eyes of every figure in the volume. In this way, by suggesting that each person depicted in the public sphere needed to hide their identity, Heinecken's magazine made the mass media's power seem even more suspicious.

The American Magazine

For Heinecken, the importance of magazines lay in their role as advertising media, easily comprehensible visual materials that provoked or elicited desires to experience or consume things. As he described the type of magazine he used, the type of spectator he sought to construct was both a viewer and a reader as well as a customer:

> Basically it's an advertising device, just like television. I mean, we get to see television, but we don't get to see it without the advertising. Anytime that you use television, let's say, or printed material, people are aware of the fact that the advertising is paying for it. You're not going to get one without the other in a conventional cultural situation. The material is already sorted out for you in the sense that if you use a magazine or television, you know what it is.[19]

The contents of magazines were always recognizable, and the magazine format framed everything it contained as a commodity, something that was to be purchased and enjoyed. As Heinecken's altered periodicals suggested, one of the central characteristics that made the American magazine format successful was its consistent combination of images with texts—everything between its covers was at least titled or captioned and thus preinterpreted for the reader. Another characteristic that made the American magazine successful was its generic tendency, the fact that magazines often specialized, selecting certain repeatable subjects and avoiding others. By Heinecken's time, even before you opened your favorite magazine, you knew what to expect.

As it developed over the twentieth century, the mass-market magazine had elaborated a phantasmagoric world of iconic types and activities for every behavior and every form of possession. Heinecken was deeply aware of this world's history, and in his art he sought to make the gendered, raced, and specifically capitalist characteristics of magazine subjects and narratives more apparent.[20] Heinecken's magazine work also specifically reflected and responded to profound changes that had altered the postwar U.S. periodical industry in the 1960s—changes that had helped to promote a diversification of human identity types.

Initially a product made for elite communities, which then was disseminated to the middle class, the U.S. magazine was transformed again in the late nineteenth century into a vehicle directed at a growing mass market.[21] By the 1880s, industrial development, urbanization, rising literacy, and a countrywide postal and transportation network had set the stage for the emergence of a national consumer market and for the magazine to become the first general-interest advertising medium: a window onto a new, market-based sense of American identity, one that reflected—but also began to undermine—traditional social categories based on gender, race, class, or nationality.[22]

Early general interest magazines included *Ladies' Home Journal* and *Saturday Evening Post*, publications that presented idealized visions of American life along with advertisements for products that purported to enable readers to attain these ideals on their own bodies and within their own particular environments.[23] In the context of the appeal to a general mass audience, the combination of narrative—whether fictional or journalistic—with illustrations (and increasingly with photographs) proved to be extremely powerful. Circulation of the most popular American magazines grew to one million newsstand single-copy sales by the late nineteenth century, and into the multiple millions of sales by the early 1920s.[24] The general interest magazine was the dominant format for U.S. magazines during the first half of the twentieth century, and it gave rise to a powerful media industry that only waned as a force after the advent of the Internet in the 1990s.[25] In addition to serving as a regular and constantly updating storehouse of American types and values, the twentieth-century mass-market magazine also supported the development of modernist graphic design beginning in the late 1920s, which in turn made the general interest magazine even more powerful and appealing.[26]

The general interest mass-market magazine remained the most popular form of magazine in the fifteen years following World War II, and its advertising and editorial content reflected the communal yet market-oriented spirit of the postwar American boom.[27] Supported by the increases in wealth, education, and leisure time that characterized the postwar decades, general interest magazines both mirrored and advanced traditional middle-class values and the bourgeois vision of the good life. The uniformity of national commodities, moreover, served as a means of valorizing social conformity in the postwar decade as well as excluding alternative forms of identity.[28]

During the 1960s, however, the American consumer magazine industry changed, moving away from general interest mass-market titles like *Life, Look,* and *Saturday Evening Post* (which all closed in the 1970s) and toward more specialized or focused publications.[29] Although niche periodicals existed throughout the general interest period, they began to proliferate and their circulations increased. Earlier forms of niche periodical, like fan and outdoor magazines, became more variegated and widespread; new forms of specialized publication were born, particularly, city- or geographically focused magazines, psychology and self-improvement publications, and periodicals—like *Boating, Car and Driver, Cycle, Flying, Golf, Skiing, Stereo Review, Popular Electronics,* and *Popular*

Photography—that focused on specific leisure activities. In addition, between 1955 and 1965, the circulations of older, more specialized publications enjoyed significant growth, for example, *Boy's Life, Sports Illustrated,* and *Scientific American.* And the sales of *Playboy,* another niche product, first published in 1953, exploded.[30]

The general interest magazine, of course, did not cease to exist. *Reader's Digest* grew during the 1960s despite being a mass audience publication, as did *Time* and *Newsweek.* Rather, what occurred is that the magazine format diversified significantly, with certain titles continuing to appeal to a broad audience and a general reader and others focusing on more and more precisely defined niches. Many special interest magazines that emerged in the 1960s had a consistent structure that promoted easy comprehension of their subject. They blended images with text, and they were formally organized into an overall issue that always mixed editorial columns with news departments and in-depth features. They also culti-vated an editorial voice or persona. Adopting a tone that was enthusiastic, authoritative, accessible, and balanced, the editors and writers presented themselves as friends or advisers to the reader. Letters sections were promoted to encourage reader identification, thus personalizing the spe-cialized magazine even further.[31]

This growth in specialized interest publications was significant because it both reflected and contributed to the production of a grow-ing set of consumer identities and aspirations that helped to diversify the largely white, heterosexual, and patriarchal ideals that the mass-market magazine promulgated during much of the twentieth century.[32] Specialized magazines could deliver a highly defined audience to their advertisers, allowing manufacturers and distributors to target specific demographic sectors of the population.[33] As a result, a new industry grew up devoted to market research into lifestyles, attitudes, and behaviors; and consumers began to be more finely organized by gender, race, gener-ation, educational level, occupation, zip code, or leisure interest.[34]

With the increasing concern for individualism and self-development in the 1960s, leisure and consumption began to substitute for class as markers of identity. In the 1970s, Americans were becoming less and less grounded in traditional class milieus, or even identified with the family ideals of their more self-sacrificing and conformist parents. Instead, they began seeking themselves in relation to others in society, whom they rec-ognized, and to whom they related, through a mass consumer culture. As sociologist Daniel Bell noted already in 1970:

> Just as in the economy the growth of what economists call *discretionary income*—income above that necessary for the fulfillment of basic

needs—allowed individuals to choose many varied items to exemplify a
different consumption style (swimming pools, boats, travel), so the
expansion of higher education and the extension of a permissive social
atmosphere has widened the scope of *discretionary social behavior.* The
more idiosyncratic aspects of personal experience and life-history—
personality attributes, or somatic body-type constitution, positive or
negative experience with parents, experience with peers—become increasingly more important than patterned social attributes in shaping a lifestyle
for a person. As the traditional class structure dissolves, more and more
individuals want to be identified, not by their occupational base (in the
Marxist sense), but by their cultural tastes and lifestyles.[35]

Increasingly in the 1960s and 1970s, specialized magazines helped to
create and reinforce these new "discretionary" tastes and lifestyles that
were taking the place of more traditional forms of American identity. In
so doing, specialized magazines reshaped not only individuals but also
subcultures, enabling readers to form new communities based around
specific types of leisure activity or forms of consumption, a process that
helped to anchor an increasingly mobile American populace and satisfy
its need for group identities. The publishers of special interest magazines
even helped to identify new consumer types. Through market research,
they targeted coalescing audiences, mining areas where mass-market
consumption was increasing.[36]

As Heinecken's magazine work between 1969 and 1974 suggests,
the magazine was a powerful device for collective individuation by the
early 1970s, but one that paradoxically caused its viewer-readers to seek
selfhood through the consumption of idealized stereotypes. Americans,
it seemed, cultivated their personas in a heterogeneous and distracted
way—or so Heinecken's magazines suggested. Moreover, as his work
implied, when Americans constructed their identities, they did it through
objects, experiences, and lifestyles that incorporated a growing diversity
of sources. It is thus not surprising that Heinecken would be drawn to
Time, one of the few dominant general interest magazines that remained;
nor is it puzzling that he would use this magazine to challenge the fundamental identity categories—gender, race, class, and sexuality—that were
used to define the social, political, and economic status quo.

As Heinecken demonstrated through his various strategies of recy-
cling and transforming appropriated magazine pages—reassembly,
overprinting, and excision—the mass media helped Americans form
themselves as individuals and communities. In response, he attempted to
draw attention to this process—to reveal the print media's stereotypes as
well as to interrupt its complacent consumption. Consider again Heinecken's iconic montage, the gender-bending soldier from *Periodical #5,* who

both solicits and undermines a male gaze that is inextricably linked to both the Cold War and colonialism. This shocking image, which simultaneously inspires and interrupts consumption, suggests that many of the primary stereotypes that allowed U.S. politics and foreign policy to function were both gendered and raced. By appropriating a nonbinary representation of male violence, Heinecken thus provoked his readers to rethink their worlds from the ground up. And by mixing fashion with porn, the general with the particular, and consumption with murder, his altered magazines prompted spectators to ask questions about the viewer-reader: who—what subject—was being addressed? These concerns were central not only to Heinecken's magazine work but to the decade as a whole.

The "Me" Decade and the Culture of Narcissism

The 1970s—both at the time and in retrospect—have often been under-stood as a decade of self-absorption and political retreat. In contrast to the 1960s, with their wide-ranging political engagement and commitment to social and cultural revolution, the 1970s were characterized by a gen-eralized withdrawal into the private sphere (albeit a "private sphere" that was conceived very differently from the way it was in the 1950s).[37] It was a decade, moreover, in which people seemed to lose ground, a moment that was continuously consumed by shocks and crises, threatening distur-bances that rocked Americans both personally and as a nation—among them, the Arab oil embargo, the U.S. defeat in Vietnam, Watergate and Nix-on's resignation, as well as increasing inflation, deindustrialization, and a sinking economy.[38] As the great progressivism of the 1960s lost steam, the country seemed to lose its purpose, and Americans became more dis-satisfied both individually and collectively.

Although produced primarily during the first years of the decade, Heinecken's altered magazines emblematize the anxiety, rage, and self-obsession that many of the decade's best social critics saw as its central characteristics. During the 1970s, the antiauthoritarianism and social activism of the 1960s was directed inward; and the self, rather than soci-ety, became the main focus of reform. As Tom Wolfe observed in 1976, Americans were becoming more selfish again, rejecting the activism and focus on the common good characteristic of the social movements of the 1960s. Instead of seeking social and political change, Americans sought to better themselves through private means, concerning themselves with refining their bodies and minds through various types of therapies, occu-pations, and spiritualisms. A series of ironic profiles sketching well-known figures as well as social types, Wolfe's famous *New York* magazine essay "The 'Me' Decade and the Third Awakening" defined the 1970s as a cluster of traits and personality formations.[39] Wolfe's initial character sketch of the period described a young LA film executive who attends a weekend (Werner) Erhard Seminars Training (EST) course that she hopes will cure her hemorrhoids, parts of herself she fears mar her sexual attractiveness. Corresponding to the self-actualizing media executive, who represented one of the newest and most powerful industries in the United States, Wolfe then pointed to Jimmy Carter and Jerry Brown as the iconic politicians of the decade, both of whom were "absolutely aglow with mystical religious streaks."[40] Like the followers of new self-actualizing therapies based in encounter sessions—movements such as Scientology, Arica, the Mel Lyman movement, Synanon, Daytop Village, and primal scream therapy—these political figures sought spiritual as well earthly salvation.

As Wolfe notes, the cultivation of the self was first an aristocratic practice and later a middle-class one; in the 1970s, on the other hand, self-development became an activity of the masses. If the three decades of postwar boom had elevated all Americans to such an extent that their needs were largely met and most had discretionary income for leisure and entertainment, then the workingman's utopia dreamed of by nineteenth-century socialists like Henri de Saint-Simon, Robert Owen, Charles Fourier, and Karl Marx had finally been achieved—but with crucial and disturbing differences. Self-development, initially an elite practice, had now become common, kitschy, and plebeian. Its transformation into a mass phenomenon over thirty years had moved it even further away from its aristocratic roots, and it had lost both its credibility and its ability to inspire conviction.[41]

Although Wolfe was highly critical of the Me Decade, he saw signs of optimism as well. He connected the new spiritualism to American revivalism, and in particular to the First and Second Great Awakenings of the 1740s and the mid-1830s, respectively, the first of which included the preachers of the New Light, and the second, the Mormons and the Oneida Community:

> We are now—in the Me Decade—seeing the upward roll (and not yet the crest, by any means) of the third great religious wave in American history, one that historians will very likely term the Third Great Awakening. Like the others it has begun in a flood of ecstasy, achieved through LSD and other psychedelics, orgy, dancing (the New Sufi and the Hare Krishna), meditation, and psychic frenzy (the marathon encounter). This third wave has built up from more diverse and exotic sources than the first two, from therapeutic movements as well as overtly religious movements, from hippies and students of "psi phenomena" and Flying Saucerites as well as charismatic Christians.[42]

Although he was unsure what this third spiritual awakening would amount to, he believed that its effects would be profound.

While Wolfe's analysis was prescient, his point of view was elitist, and his analysis of the American milieu lacked social, historical, and psychological depth. Three years later, in *The Culture of Narcissism,* social critic and historian Christopher Lasch followed Wolfe's outline in some respects, while simultaneously articulating a much more profound and trenchant characterization of the decade. Integrating Frankfurt School cultural critique with psychoanalytic object relations theory, Lasch described the culture of the United States in the 1970s as one in which narcissistic personality types had come to predominate, the result of social, economic, and technological changes that had transformed the nation for more than a century. This social-psychological situation, which he saw as an intensification of the recent past and not a break from it, was in fundamental ways a result of the growing dominance of mass culture, the mass media, and advertising in the United States.[43] The burgeoning of capitalism and mass culture, which helped to weaken the family as a source of socialization for the individual, created specific traits, behaviors, beliefs, and emotional states that could be seen frequently in individuals in the 1970s as well as in the culture at large.[44]

As Lasch later recalled, *The Culture of Narcissism* grew out of his earlier book *Haven in a Heartless World,* which argued that the family's importance in American "society had been steadily declining over a period of more than a hundred years. Schools, peer groups, mass media, and the 'helping professions' had challenged parental authority and taken over many of the family's child-rearing functions."[45] In light of this central insight, *The Culture of Narcissism* attempted to model the common psychological traits that had emerged in the wake of the diminished role of the family in modern society. Shifts in cultural authority—from the nuclear family to consumer culture and the state—produced narcissism on a mass scale, Lasch argued, a system that reproduced itself but that also exploited and ultimately destroyed the individuals out of which it was composed. Because the sources of authority that caused the developing person to individuate had changed, Americans—as both individuals and as a nation—were faced with a radically new set of issues and conflicts that they had to navigate.

For Lasch, narcissism was "the typical personality structure in a society dominated by large bureaucratic organizations and mass media, in which families no longer played an important role in the transmission of culture and people accordingly had little sense of connection to the past."[46] It was also a mode of being characterized by extreme anxiety and anger, a state in which self-gratification and grandiose fantasy were employed to cope with constant frustration, a pervasive sense of crisis, and a general loss of higher purpose. Perhaps as a result, the culture of narcissism also combined rationalism with antirationalism in a new way. Like Wolfe, Lasch noted that "science has not displaced religion, as so many people once expected. Both seem to flourish side by side, often in grotesquely exaggerated form."[47] Narcissistic personalities could cling to either perspective, often in inflexible and increasingly stereotypical ways. By helping to socialize children, advertising and the mass media thus supported narcissistic traits and behaviors that enabled American capitalism: the desire to consume, a sense of inadequacy, and focus on the present instead of the past or future. But despite its ideological nature—its support for and naturalization of the Cold War economic status quo—the culture of narcissism also reflected the contradictions and crises of contemporary American society. In particular, the narcissistic personality type had to confront two new issues in the 1970s: the globalization process, as American industries and the workers they employed were greatly weakened and undermined by outsourcing and deindustrialization; and a collective sense that the nation was losing power abroad and that the post–World War II U.S. position of leadership and hegemony in the world was being called into question. Both would have important implications.

Because it was fundamentally a product of consumer culture and the mass media, the narcissistic personality structure, as Lasch understood it, was dialectical: it was both an expression of the deepest crises and anxieties of the moment, and a means through which they were controlled and channeled:

> The psychological patterns associated with pathological narcissism, which in less exaggerated form manifest themselves in so many patterns of American culture—in the fascination with fame and celebrity, the fear of competition, the inability to suspend disbelief, the shallowness and transitory quality of personal relations, the horror of death—originate in the peculiar structure of the American family, which in turn originates in changing modes of production. Industrial production takes the father out of the home and diminishes the role he plays in the conscious life of the child. The mother attempts to make up to the child for the loss of its father, but she often lacks practical experience of childrearing, feels herself at a loss to understand what the child needs, and relies so heavily on outside experts that her attentions fail to provide the child with a sense of security. Both parents seek to make the family into a refuge from outside pressures, yet the very standards by which they measure their success, and the techniques through which they attempt to bring it about, derive in large part from industrial sociology, personnel management, child psychology—in

short, from the organized apparatus of social control. The family's struggle to conform to an externally imposed ideal of family solidarity and parenthood creates an appearance of solidarity at the expense of spontaneous feeling, a ritualized "relatedness" empty of real substance.[48]

The evacuation of "real substance" in family relationships produced by the culture of narcissism, the loss of true moments of intimacy and connection, also helped further the growth of global capitalism in the 1970s, a development that led to increased stratification and conflict between social groups and classes. With the growth of a multinational economic system, unions lost ground, capital gained greater power to exploit labor, and there was more social, racial, ethnic, and political strife. Fearful that their country was disintegrating, many Americans in the 1970s believed the middle class was eroding and more people were living in poverty. As Lasch saw it:

> The poor have always had to live for the present, but now a desperate concern for personal survival, sometimes disguised as hedonism, engulfs the middle class as well. Today almost everyone lives in a dangerous world from which there is little escape. International terrorism and blackmail, bombings, and hijackings arbitrarily affect the rich and poor alike. Crime, violence, and gang wars make cities unsafe and threaten to spread to the suburbs. Racial violence on the streets and in the schools creates an atmosphere of chronic tension and threatens to erupt at any time into full-scale racial conflict. Unemployment spreads from the poor to the white-collar class, while inflation eats away the savings of those who hoped to retire in comfort. Much of what is euphemistically known as the middle class, merely because it dresses up to go to work, is now reduced to proletarian conditions of existence. Many white-collar jobs require no more skill and pay even less than blue-collar jobs, conferring little status or security. The propaganda of death and destruction, emanating ceaselessly from the mass media, adds to the prevailing atmosphere of insecurity. Far-flung famines, earthquakes in remote regions, distant wars and uprisings attract the same attention as events closer to home. The impression of arbitrariness in the reporting of disaster reinforces the arbitrary quality of experience itself, and the absence of continuity in the coverage of events, as today's crisis yields to a new and unrelated crisis tomorrow, adds to the sense of historical discontinuity—the sense of living in a world in which the past holds out no guidance to the present and the future has become completely unpredictable.[49]

Because the narcissistic personality was not focused on future or collective goals, individuals were assumed to be powerless, and there was little sense that the status quo could ever change.

Even more disturbingly, the growth of narcissism on both an individual and a collective level, for Lasch, led also to the intensification of gender inequality and oppression:

> The battle of the sexes also constitutes a social phenomenon with a history of its own. The reasons for the recent intensification of sexual combat lie in the transformation of capitalism from its paternalistic and familial form to a managerial, corporate, bureaucratic system of almost total control: more specifically, in the collapse of "chivalry"; the liberation of sex from many of its former constraints; the pursuit of sexual pleasure as an end in itself; the emotional overloading of personal relations; and most important of all, the irrational male response to the emergence of the liberated woman.[50]

The breakdown of traditional roles and values in the 1970s, in other words, led not to a decrease in male domination and sexual violence but, rather, its increase. According to Lasch, as patriarchy became more and more ideologically indefensible and groundless, men asserted "their domination more directly, in fantasies and occasionally in acts of raw violence."[51]

> The fear of women, closely associated with a fear of the consuming desires within, reveals itself not only as impotence but as a boundless rage against the female sex. This blind and impotent rage, which seems so prevalent at the present time, only superficially represents a defensive male reaction against feminism. It is only because the recent revival of feminism stirs up such deeply rooted memories that it gives rise to such primitive emotions. Men's fear of women, moreover, exceeds the actual threat to their sexual privileges. Whereas the resentment of women against men for the most part has solid roots in the discrimination and sexual danger to which women are constantly exposed, the resentment of men against women, when men still control most of the power and wealth in society yet feel themselves threatened on every hand—intimidated, emasculated— appears deeply irrational.[52]

Although the narcissistic type could be either male or female, its rise to the dominant personality form of the decade continued to serve a patriarchal status quo.[53] Instead of helping to produce a more equitable world, the culture of narcissism—a manifestation of the central contradictions of capitalist society and the liberal welfare state—created even greater increases in social and familial division, exploitation, and violence.[54]

As suggested by his altered magazines of the early 1970s, Heinecken, like Lasch, diagnosed his society as a culture of narcissism in which masculinity was in crisis and new forms of identity were being defined. It was for this reason, it seems, that the sexual and the violent crisscrossed so much in Heinecken's work of this period. The horror of Vietnam, his magazines revealed, was fundamentally connected to the forms of consumption and desire that Americans were taught to embrace through their products and entertainments. Like Lasch, Heinecken was aware of the power of nonsexual forms of instinct, drives like aggression and the desire for death, and how the narcissistic personality structure tended to be uninhibited—that it tried to gratify all its impulses, no matter how self-destructive. Heinecken's altered magazines evoke this mentality by undermining traditional forms of identity and historical continuity through an uncanny interweaving of sexual and violent imagery into the flow of commercial communication. They interrogated the decade through deceptively simple means, indicting the time for its weak individuality and its violent, divisive, solipsistic, and ultimately self-destructive consumer tendencies.

If there was one area where Lasch's social-psychological characterization of the 1970s was still problematic, that topic was race, which Lasch subordinated to class to an inadmissible degree. Although sympathetic to the plight of disenfranchised African Americans, Lasch too quickly relegated their specific situations to those of the urban and agricultural poor, and to the crisis of white male identity and the violence on which it depended:

> In some ways middle-class society has become a pale copy of the black ghetto, as the appropriation of its language would lead us to believe.
> We do not need to minimize the poverty of the ghetto or the suffering inflicted by whites on blacks in order to see that the increasingly dangerous and unpredictable conditions of middle-class life have given rise to similar strategies for survival. Indeed the attraction of black culture for disaffected whites suggests that black culture now speaks to a general condition, the most important feature of which is a widespread loss of confidence in the future.[55]

This critique cannot be leveled at Heinecken's magazines, which document Black experience in more historically specific ways. Although they are not focused on Blackness per se, they do concentrate on the intermixing of a multiplicity of cultures and ethnicities in which African Americans and people of color play an important role. Racism, sexual violence, and class division are not to be overcome by a predominantly social, psychological, and economic analysis, but rather by a fundamental reimagining of the traits and characteristics that human beings could possess and the categories by which they understand themselves.

Consider Heinecken's *Periodical #5* montage one final time. If race and gender were fundamental categories affecting Americans' understanding of their country's foreign policy, then, as this montage suggested, colonialist appropriation abroad prepared the ground for even greater capitalist exploitation at home. The disclosure of Nixon's secret bombing of Cambodia by the *New York Times* in May 1969 caused the Republican administration to attack, manipulate, and even wiretap the press—to push back strongly against the print media in an attempt to project their own versions of their conduct of the war.[56] As suggested by Heinecken's montage, which reminds viewer-readers of this situation, the press could create a counterpolitics, but not without guerrilla tactics directed at subverting the basic identity categories in which the narcissistic culture of the 1970s trafficked. We will return to Heinecken's magazine appropriations in chapter 8. Before doing so, we need to first consider other photo-based art that he created in the 1970s, difficult and surprising work that dealt with feminism and sexuality.

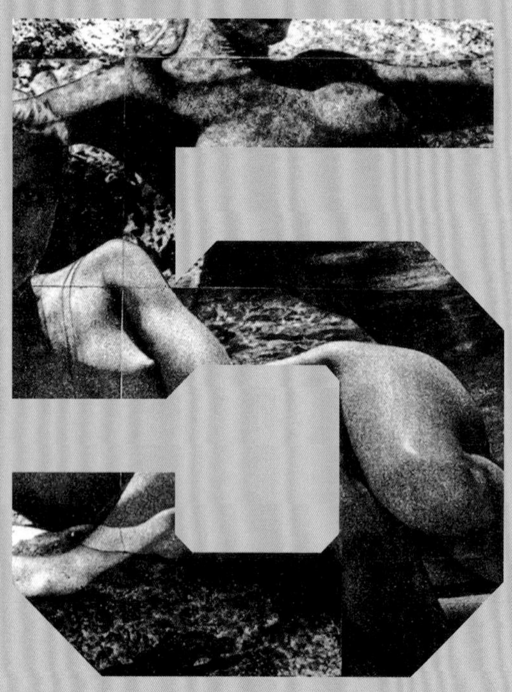

5

ART, PORNOGRAPHY, PAINTING

Heinecken's Relationship to Feminism

IN THE EARLY TO MID-1970S, parallel to his interrogation of the magazine format, Heinecken created large-scale transparencies that resembled enormous negatives or film strips as well as photo-based paintings and lithographs that dissected and recombined the human body. These latter works were accompanied by other types of experimental practice—challenging objects that ranged from multimedia installations to explorations of different types of photographic processes. Throughout this time, Heinecken also continued to produce black-and-white photograms, which often formed the basis for the larger canvases. Uniting this heterogeneity of forms and media was a common type of image: the more hard-core images of sexuality that Heinecken began to appropriate with *Periodical #2.*

Heinecken's use of pornography, and particularly of this new graphic variety that corresponds to the 1970s, is probably the most fraught issue that surrounds his oeuvre. It motivates the many accusations of sexism and misogyny that have haunted his reception, and it is the most difficult aspect of his work for his supporters to defend. Much of Heinecken's work that uses 1970s pornography, moreover, is not discussed in any sustained way, which is unfortunate, since it was central to his art at this time. As Heinecken recognized, U.S. visual culture was becoming increasingly more visceral and graphic, a tendency that had fueled its tremendous expansion during the nineteenth and twentieth centuries (and one that continues to do so today).

As the artist often pointed out, there is little consensus about the terms that we use to identify and define sexual or erotic images. Describing an exercise that he would perform with students, he noted:

> I'll take five words: sensual, erotic, sexual, pornographic, obscene. Then I'll say, "Okay, there's a range of terms that define certain kinds of pictures or activities. Now, you look at these words, and you put them in an order that you feel is from the subjective to the objective. Then you have to explain what's subjective and what's objective. Go home and do that. Think about it and come back tomorrow. We'll look at it." You can take all those rankings that they've now made—they've got five words in a line that says "objective here, subjective here"—then graph that out on the blackboard for them, show them that between these ten or twelve or fifteen people there's absolutely no consensus about what these words mean when you have to consider that there's an objective term and a subjective term. It's a very interesting exercise to do, not because I invented it necessarily, but because it just informs people that they don't know how they're going to use these terms.[1]

Sexual imagery was something that resisted clear conceptualization and that could not be precisely defined, he suggested.

Despite this ambiguity, Heinecken had his own mapping of its terms along the subjective-objective axis. The most objective terms for him were *obscene* and *pornographic*. Obscenity, as he understood it, was a legal definition, determined by "community standards," while pornography was a class of images that indicated the existence of technological, industrial, and corporate apparatuses. For there to be pornography, in other words, there had to be an infrastructure as well as willing groups of participants, that is, both producers and consumers. As he put it:

> you have to have a mechanical way of reproducing the picture—photography, film, printing of some kind. You have to have a culture of subject matter that is willing to participate in this for the money that's involved. These are our actors, basically. You have to have a distribution system, which is why you have to have a reproductive system, so you can make hundreds of thousands of these. Then you have to get them out of there. You have to make a magazine or a film. You have to get it in the mail. It has to have distribution.[2]

In addition to producers and consumers, pornography required capital and technology, as well as a functional market.

On the opposite side of the graph to *obscenity* and *pornography*, Heinecken placed visual pleasure, art, and science. First, suspended in the middle between subjective and objective were

> sensual things which have nothing to do with sex, necessarily. It can be a piece of stone or wood that's been carved in such a way that you want to touch it. You want to feel it. You want a sensed curve. You don't want angles and all that. This has nothing to do with sex. It has to do with a physical capacity to understand a feeling which doesn't arouse sexual feelings but gives you a sense of using your senses.[3]

Then, moving toward the objective pole were *erotic* and *sexual*. The erotic was "a picture or writing that's made to induce sexual feelings" but was not the pornographic, because (like a French Romantic painting or a handwritten love letter) "you can't distribute it. It's for one person to own and look at."[4] Finally, *sexual* was simply something that "depicts or talks about sexual activity. That's all it does. You can have a doctor's discussion of sex which is sexual. It's not pornographic, and it's certainly not erotic, but it has to do with subject matter that depicts sexual activity and nudity, usually."[5]

As Heinecken's mapping suggests, depictions of nudity and sexual activity were complex and fraught issues in the 1970s, a time during which both the law and sexual morality were changing. As he saw it, an appetite for pornography was a driving force behind the proliferation of multiple forms of visual representation and consumer objects in his moment; and by engaging with its products he attempted to understand the effects that pornography was having on individuals in his society.

Porn Paintings and Photograms

In 1970, Heinecken began to make paintings that explored the new, more graphic porn of the decade. Canvas panels with photographic emulsion, pastel chalk, and graphite, they presented murky tableaus in which multiple figures writhed in sexual abandon. These largely black-and-white panels were based on series of gelatin silver print photograms—which Heinecken called figure studies—that defamiliarized the new pornographic imagery and called into question the distinction between the sexual and the sensual (Plate 5.1). To create the paintings, Heinecken made 4 x 5 negatives of magazine photograms and printed different combinations of them on canvas, going over the resulting prints with lines of

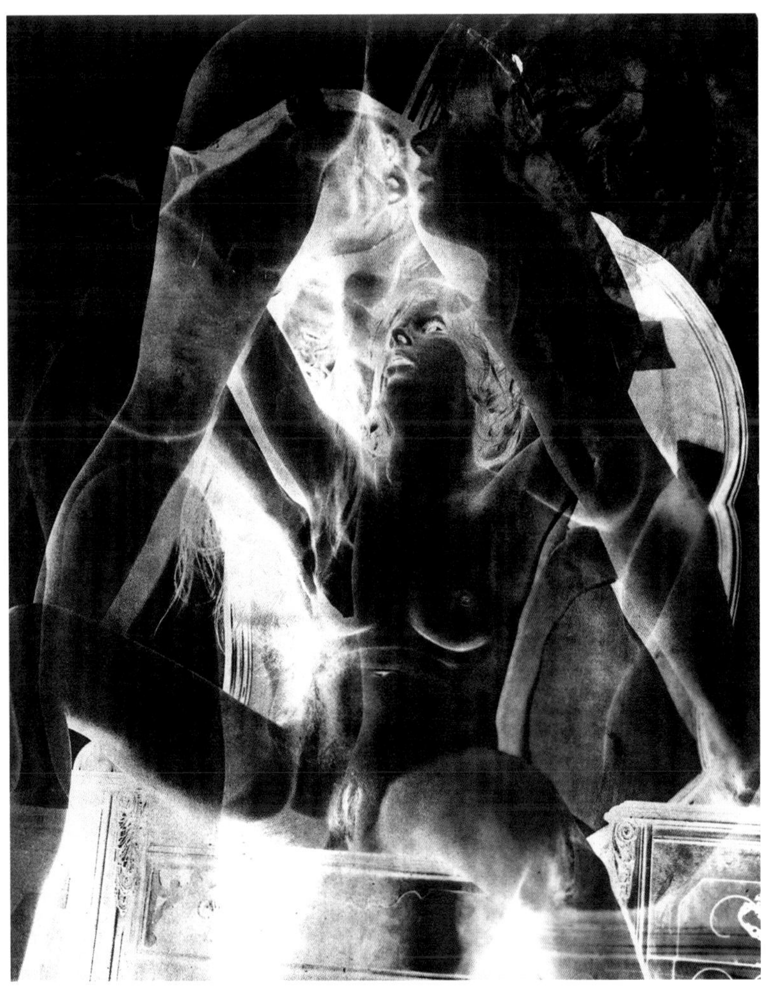

PLATE 5.1. Robert Heinecken, *Study 21* (1970). Gelatin silver print photogram, 10 x 8 inches (25.4 x 20.32 cm). Private collection. COPYRIGHT 2022 THE ROBERT HEINECKEN TRUST, CHICAGO.

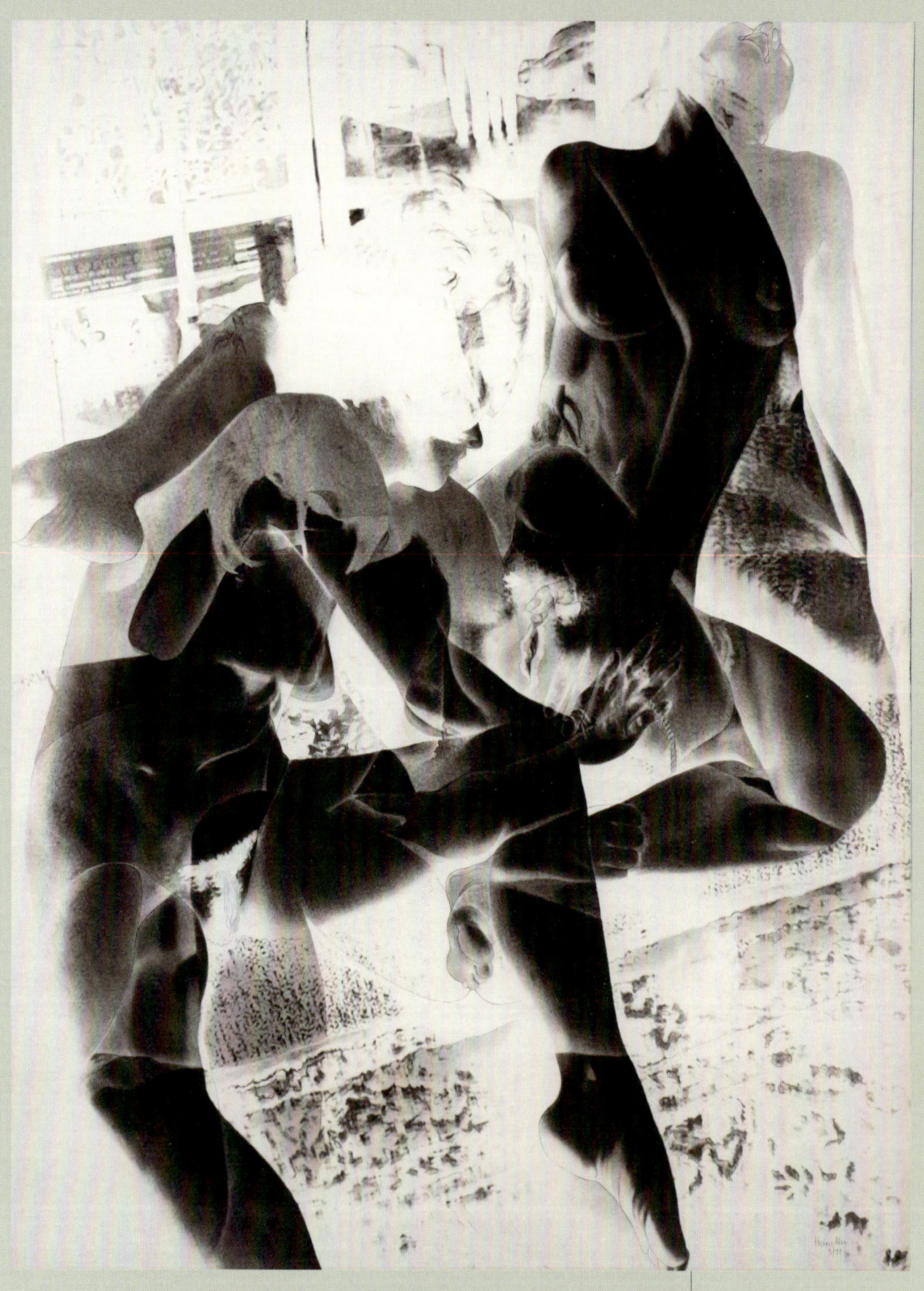

PLATE 5.2. Robert Heinecken, *Cream 6 Single* (1970). Photo emulsion on canvas with pastel in original frame made by artist with wood, black tape, staples, 40 x 30 inches (76.2 x 101.6 cm). Private collection.

chalk and often arranging the panels in rows and rectangular formats to create larger works. Although the nipples, labia, and hair depicted in the source materials continue to appear in the new images, the tonal reversals and the superimpositions of bodies make the forms and actions less clear, thus diminishing the porn's visceral effect. And by combining detail with obscurity, Heinecken seems to explore the limits of physical desire, asking the viewer to consider where corporeal response stops and abstract contemplation begins.

In canvases like *Cream 6 Single* (1970) (Plate 5.2) and *Jack Jones and the Lennon Sisters #1* (1970), the figures are abstracted still further. Once again, the tonal reversals and superimpositions render the figures almost indecipherable: it is hard to tell what they are doing or where one person ends and another begins. In addition, the figures merge with their backgrounds, the manufactured rugs and beds seeming to amalgamate with the fleshy forms that cavort on top of them. Finally, because of the increased contrast of the elements as well as the multiple interpenetrating outlines created by the superimpositions, the protagonists' bodies seem mechanized and at times almost gear-like—mechanical metaphors for the body's fate when captured through the reproductive media of photography and film. Under Heinecken's gaze, the pornographic pictorials of the 1970s seem to open up a world of mass reproduction and deindividuation, one that seems to feed on sexual instinct while simultaneously transforming human intimacy into an industrial product.

Many of these early emulsion paintings had the words *cream* or *different strokes* in their titles, an evocation in part of the masturbatory purposes for which their appropriated source materials were designed. At this time, the catchphrase "Different strokes for different folks" was also coming into vogue as an affirmation of sexual liberation and diversity, and as a reminder that human sexual response was quite varied in terms of both its objects and fantasies.[6] Thus in addition to straight male porn, *cream* or *different strokes* perhaps also evoked the contemporaneous objectification of men in the magazine and film industry.[7] Like his imagery, Heinecken's titles directed thought along multiple tracks simultaneously.

As he developed these two series, Heinecken began to combine multiple panels into larger mural-format works, and the canvases became more filmlike as well as more evocative of their origins in porn magazine pictorials: sequences of pictures of the same model or models in different positions (Plate 5.3). Describing the *Different Strokes* series, he noted, "So the first panel would be, let's say, made from a super imposition of A and B. The next one, which would be adjacent to it, would be B and C, and C and D, and so on, so that if you look at the structure of the picture it's really narrative from left to right."[8] For Heinecken, this was a film idea: "To

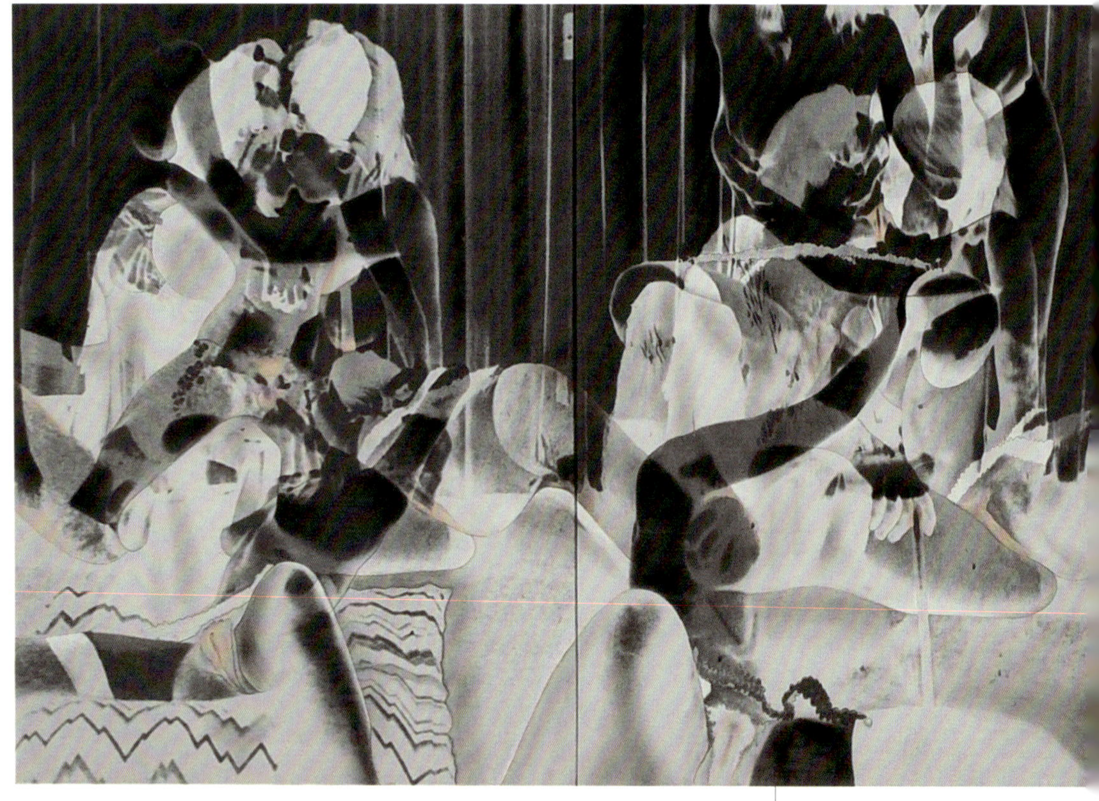

take a sequence of pictures and overlap them, or cut them I guess would be the film way, in order to make a linear time out of it."[9] As suggested by works like *Cream 6* or *Different Strokes . . .* (1970–97), to create a narrative through photography and montage did not necessarily entail naturalism. The paintings read equally as temporal sequences of images or as panoramas representing a single instant; as these multipanel paintings imply, the coupling of human forms causes space and time to break apart and recombine. In addition, when read as cinematic sequences, the grouping of human forms in the paintings gets larger and more complex as one reads from left to right, suggesting that humanity changes itself through the reproduction and consumption of porn images, becoming ever more interrelated and heterogeneous.

If superimposition and sequential development—the creating of a quasi-narrative—allowed Heinecken to abstract pornographic images and turn single figures into morphing collectives, there were nonnarrative strategies of photographic montage that could be used to achieve similar results. In 1971–72, Heinecken produced a series of works, with the titles *Figure Horizon* and *Le Voyeur/Robbe-Grillet,* that explored the pornographic body as a landscape constructed of cropped corporeal forms. In these new works, which were created as large horizontal paintings

PLATE 5.3. Robert Heinecken, *Different Strokes . . .* (1970–97). Two canvas panels with chalk and photographic emulsion, 41 ½ x 125 ¾ inches (105.41 x 319.41 cm). Private collection. COPYRIGHT 2022 THE ROBERT HEINECKEN TRUST, CHICAGO.

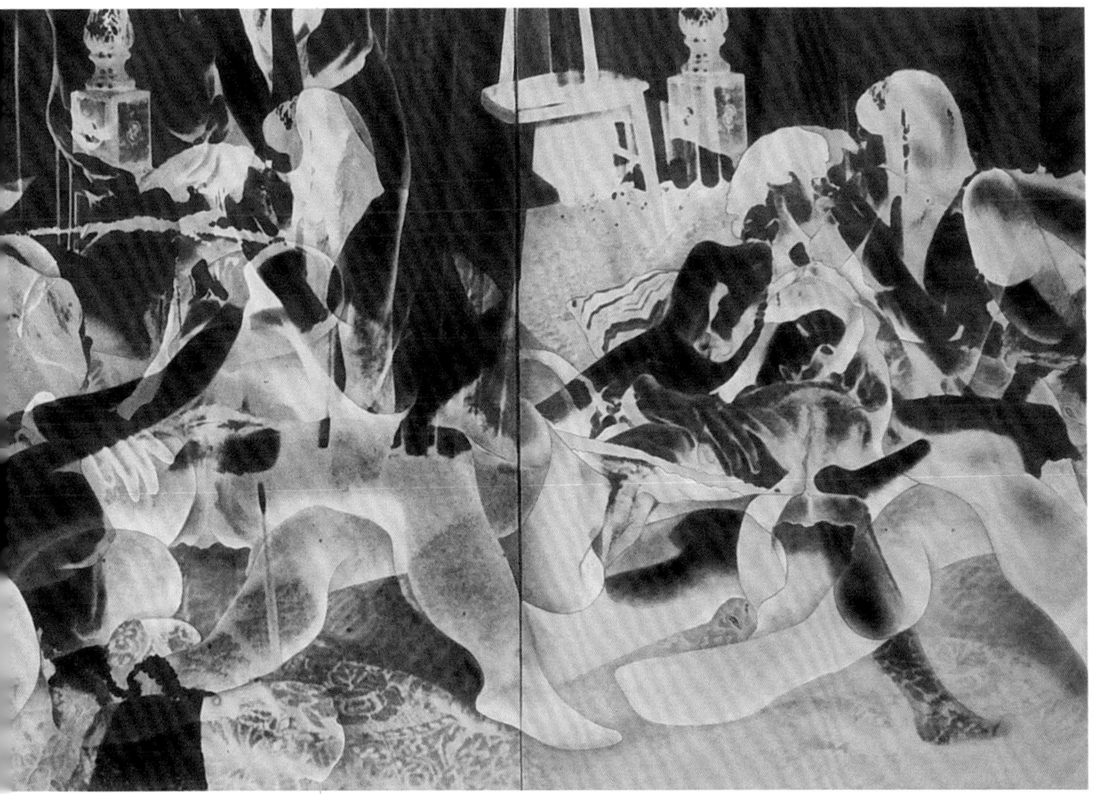

and as similarly scaled transparencies, the pornographic body seems frozen and unchanging. *Figure Horizon #1* (1971) is a ten-part emulsion-on-canvas painting that presents multiple truncated, close-up images of a naked woman (or multiple women) as an uncanny, mountainous form. Spread beyond the confines of all corporeal norms, the image evokes a sublime Western landscape in which mountains are framed against a sky.[10] It also reminds the viewer of the panoramic views of nineteenth-century Western photography, but with a monstrous body replacing what was previously nature or architecture.[11]

In some ways anticipating the surreal body photography of John Coplans by more than a decade, these paintings and transparencies work against narrative.[12] Presented as wide-screen panoramas, the various close-up body-part fragments suggest a synchronic relationship between components caught at a single instant of time. *Le Voyeur/Robbe-Grillet #2* (1972) presents a simpler version of the strategy (Plate 5.4). Once again, the figure is both human and nonhuman, individual and collective. Although the parts appear with great realism, the configuration is monstrous when taken as a whole. But instead of the active movement and proliferation that is characteristic of the *Different Strokes* and *Cream 6* series, the body seems frozen, set apart from both growth and decline.

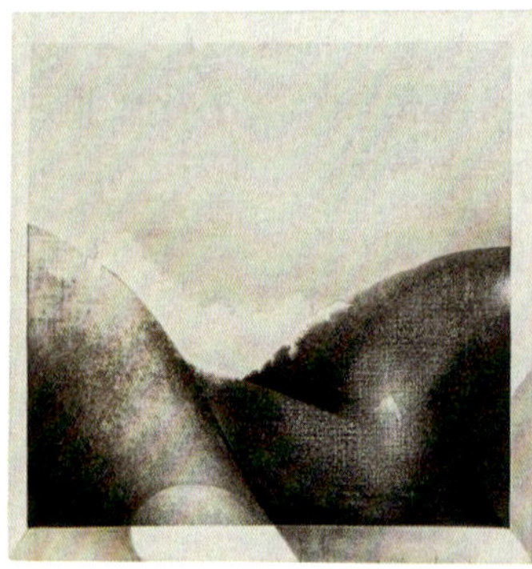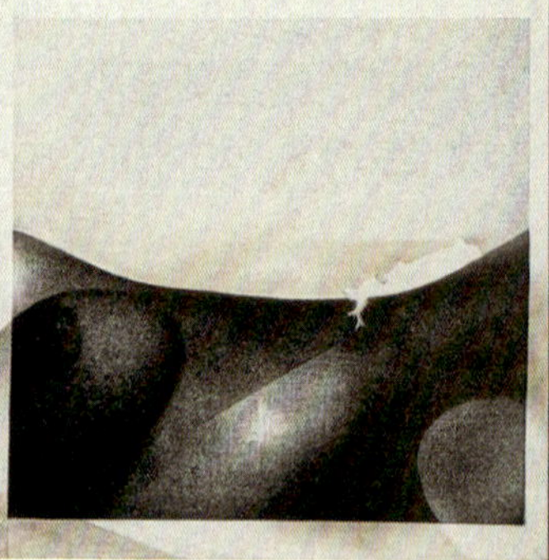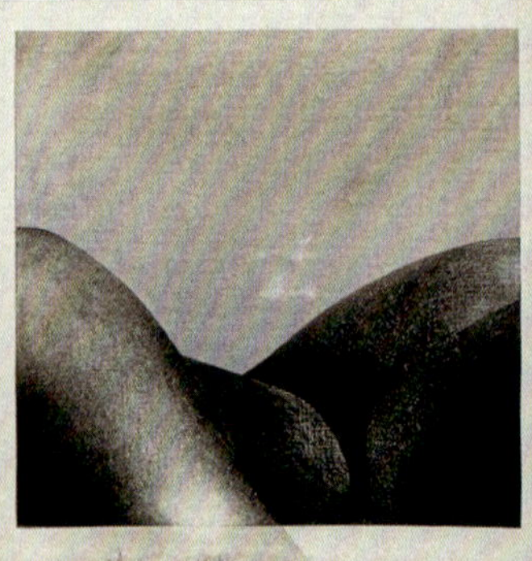

The title of this series links this paradoxical body to the act of voy-eurism, the gaining of pleasure by spying on subjects engaged in sex and other forms of intimate behavior. As the proliferation of pornography suggests, the experience of visual pleasure promotes a desire for more—for even greater excitation and gratification through multiple avenues of sensation. In addition, however, the title also serves as a reference to the New Novel (*nouveau roman*) in France, and the "objective" prose style of the writer and filmmaker Alain Robbe-Grillet. In novels like *Le Voyeur* (1955), which was translated into English in 1958, Robbe-Grillet employed a visually detailed and descriptive form of prose to narrate ambiguous stories with indistinct protagonists and events that may or may not have happened.[13] Dispensing with clear plots, chronologies, and characters, he instead focused on extensive descriptions of ordinary objects. Psychol-ogy and motivation were revealed through the enumeration of things, but even the most precise forms of portrayal, his work suggested, would not uncover truth. Instead of revealing clarity, minute observation created a disturbing slippage of meaning that lay at the heart of all experience. As Roland Barthes put it, "For Robbe-Grillet, the function of language is not a raid on the absolute, a violation of the abyss, but a progression of names over a surface, a patient unfolding that will gradually 'paint' the object, caress it, and along its whole extent deposit a patina of tentative identifications, no single term of which could stand by itself for the pre-sented object."[14] With his disjunctive story lines and repeating scenes, Robbe-Grillet's work revealed the limitations of a camera-like attention to objective detail. And as suggested by Heinecken's detailed yet nonnatural figure horizons, erotic and even pornographic photographic images could be mobilized in a similar way. Although detailed and realistic when viewed at the level of their component parts, Heinecken's paintings and transpar-encies reveal ambiguous arrays of surfaces that reject a sense of a clear or comprehensible underlying structure.

PLATE 5.4. Robert Heinecken, *Le Voyeur/ Robbe-Grillet #2* (1972). Three canvas panels with bleached photographic emulsion and pastel chalk, 14 x 40 inches (35.6 x 101.6 cm). George Eastman House, Rochester, New York. Museum purchase with National Endowment for the Arts support.

Pornography

As Heinecken's porn work suggested, Americans were confronting an ever-growing body of photographically based pornography during the 1970s, a fund of images that was exerting an increasing impact on both their bodies and their minds.[15] Photographic porn goes back to the earliest days of photography. Indeed, as Patchen Barss has argued, porn has played an important economic role in the medium's technical development and its relentless permeation of everyday life since the 1840s.[16] By the 1970s, when Heinecken began his porn work, photographic pornography was already a multi-million-dollar industry, one, moreover, that had diversified into a wide variety of related media, including mass-market magazines and, very importantly, film. Indeed, it was this diversification and mainstreaming of pornography that created the first general awareness of the extent of its proliferation throughout American culture. With the emergence and rapid growth of mainstream men's magazines like *Playboy*, which began publication in Chicago in 1953, and *Penthouse*, which started in London in 1965 and began its U.S. edition in 1969, as well as the appearance of feature-length porn films such as *Deep Throat* (1972) and *Behind the Green Door* (1972), during what is now colloquially known as "the golden age of porn," Americans could no longer deny that pornography possessed a mass appeal.[17] As Heinecken and his generation were coming to realize, pornography found a viewership at every class level, and although its consumers were predominantly men, it interested women as well. Thus in many ways porn was beginning to appear as a pressing problem in early 1970s' visual culture: a growing class of images that no one wanted to acknowledge, that seemed dangerous and exploitative, but that also possessed an uncomfortable power or seductiveness that helped it to attract an ever-larger mass audience cutting across race, class, gender, and education.

Photographic porn was thus important for Heinecken because it pointed to ambiguous and unsettling aspects of human identity and the ways in which people formed or developed themselves by means of visual codes and presentations. He seemed drawn to it because it was extremely hard to define, and because it served as an emblem of many of the new decade's most critical problems. To confront pornography, his work suggested, one had to engage with fundamental social, legal, medical, and technological concerns that placed visual culture at the heart of debates about the nature of the self, family, and society during a time of rapid social upheaval and change.

The growth of porn could be seen as emblematic of the sexual revolution of the 1970s and the desire for better knowledge about sexuality and its effects on gender and identity. The 1970s marked one of the lowest birth rates in U.S. history—a sign that the baby boom was over; Americans were marrying later, the divorce rate was increasing, and there was growing tolerance for nonnormative and nonheterosexual relationships and family structures. As spiritual practices became more diverse and more Americans characterized themselves as nonreligious, sexuality in the United States became increasingly separated from reproduction. Sex became more closely associated with intimacy, pleasure, and self-fulfillment, and there was a new openness to discussions about sexuality and its range of practices. Increasingly, photographic porn could be read as a sign of this growing openness. In addition, because photography was traditionally understood as a technology that could in certain circumstances help increase people's knowledge about the world, photographic porn was viewed by some as a medium that would reveal new insights about sex.[18]

A sign of Americans' growing focus on sexual pleasure, porn also represented some of the central dangers that photographic technologies presented to human bodies and minds. Because of its powerful indexical and iconic bonds with its subjects, photography carried (and continues to carry) strong realist associations as a medium.[19] Spectators sometimes relate to photographic representations of human bodies—and even more so to such representations in movies—as if they were the people themselves. Lens-based depictions of sex and violence were thus a special class of image, Heinecken realized; they often created moments in which the medium seemed to become transparent. Such subjects, in other words, seemed to short-circuit a person's understanding of photography as subjective and as dependent on the photographer's eye and sensibility; instead, people tended to take pornographic images as cases in which the real expressed itself without any human mediation.

Because of porn's supposed transparency, questions about the real-world effects of photographs—and the ethical relationships that their production and consumption entailed—arose frequently in discussions of pornography. Although criticisms such as these did not reach their high-point until the mid-1980s to early-1990s, when antiporn feminists such as Catharine MacKinnon and Andrea Dworkin had their greatest influence, and the conservative Meese Commission Report promoted antipornography legislation based on the genre's supposed deleterious effects, such criticisms were already raised decades earlier.[20] In the first place, antiporn advocates argued that exposure to pornography had a corrupting effect on its audience. People were thought to be desensitized by the frequent viewing of pornography and their understanding of gender and sexuality distorted or confused; in its extremest forms, this confusion could cause them to assault others. Or as radical feminist Robin Morgan said in 1974, "Pornography is the theory, and rape is the practice."[21]

Second, the pornographic subjects or actors were believed to be exploited, particularly in the case of violent pornography. And with the rise of feminism in the 1970s, Heinecken and other Americans were also becoming aware of the highly gendered nature of this exploitation: the fact that the pornography industry was largely run by men, that it catered to a mostly male audience, and that it was primarily women who were abused in its production. As a result, Americans entering the Me Decade were beginning to understand porn as a type of male-dominated or male-centered visual culture in which patriarchal gender stereotypes were formed, perpetuated, and sometimes contested; they also recognized it as a type of imagery that had real—and sometimes pernicious—effects on both individuals and societies.[22]

Because pornography was considered harmful at least to some classes of audience, it was regulated by law; and its legal history in the United States reveals porn to be intimately linked to controversies about birth control as well as freedom of expression. Since 1873, the Comstock Act had made it illegal in the United States to produce, distribute, exhibit, advertise, or possess immoral materials—defined as obscene images, texts, or other forms of representation, as well as any article or thing designed to prevent conception or procure an abortion.[23] The producers of photographically based pornography could thus be prosecuted under this Act; as a result, both photographic and cinematic pornography remained clandestine forms of entertainment in the nineteenth and early twentieth centuries, underground in terms of production, distribution, and consumption. At the same time, the growth of the magazine and film industries created an increasing appetite for depictions of heterosexual romance and human intimacy, a visual craving that was also fed by an expanding underground market in pornography. Although it is unclear which type of material—popular or obscene—stoked demand the most, both markets encouraged one another, and their popularity steadily increased across the twentieth century.

Although they would have implications for the visual during the twentieth century, the landmark legal cases concerning obscenity were primarily focused on the written word, in particular literature. In the United States, obscene writing was not a form of free speech protected by the First Amendment: the government could seize and destroy obscene materials to prevent their sale to the public as well as prosecute their makers and marketers to discourage such commerce in the future.[24] Following the British legal precedents of the Obscene Publications Act (1857) and *Regina v. Hicklin* (1868), *obscenity* was conceived in the United

States as material that could deprave or corrupt its consumers.[25] Landmark cases like *United States v. One Book Called Ulysses* (1933), on the other hand, established that not all depictions of sexuality were obscene, and that in distinguishing protected from unprotected speech one had to consider the work as a whole, its effect on the average person, and contemporary community standards.[26] On the photographic front, things were clearer: prosecutions for the production, sale, or exhibition of photographic depictions of sexuality—particularly those of the hard-core variety—did not create serious legal debate during the first half of the twentieth century. Their obscenity seemed self-evident, and as a result photographic porn was legally regulated and suppressed during this time.

The moment when Heinecken began to use photographic porn, however, was bracketed by two landmark cases—*Roth v. United States* (1957) and *Miller v. California* (1973)—which dealt with distributing (illustrated) pornographic books or advertising circulars through the mail.[27] In each case the defendant was found guilty, and the state's right to regulate pornographic text and images was upheld. But both cases also served to constrain the definition of *obscenity*, by making it conform to a set of specific criteria. In the language of *Miller*, *obscenity* consisted of "works which, taken as a whole, appeal to the prurient interest in sex, which portray sexual conduct in a patently offensive way, and which, taken as a whole, do not have serious literary, artistic, political, or scientific value." And such characteristics, moreover, were to be determined by "the average person, applying contemporary community standards."[28] As a result, even certain photographic depictions of human sexuality—for example, in the cases of scientific or artistic works—were recognized as valuable and protected under the First Amendment. The representation of genitals or sex was not in itself obscene. In representations that served either knowledge or art, even graphic depictions of sex could be tolerated.

Miller v. California came two years after the release of the Report of the National Commission on Obscenity and Pornography, chaired by William B. Lockhart, in 1970.[29] Although the Johnson administration politicians who commissioned the report intended it to serve as a way of reining in the distribution of pornography, the Lockhart commission instead found that exposure to obscene and pornographic materials did not cause harm to its consumers or encourage antisocial behavior. And since the visual representation of sex was not in itself considered harmful according to *Miller v. California*, the case helped to carve out a space in the United States for more explicit representations to be produced and distributed. In its wake, as Edward de Grazia, notes "millions of Americans became free to create, possess, disseminate, receive, sell, buy, look at, and read sexually explicit books, magazines, pictures, and movies."[30] Heinecken's porn work reflected this moment of significant change in the laws surrounding the production and distribution of sexually explicit visual images, raising questions about the nature of "obscenity" and its effects on individual and collective identity.

The Film Strips

Like the *Cream 6* and *Different Strokes* paintings, Heinecken's film strip transparencies of the 1970s used linkages between photography and cinema to explore the dividing line between art and obscenity, protected and unprotected expressions. In comparison to his transparencies of the 1960s, Heinecken's film strips were much larger, and because of the sprocket holes that framed their sides, more cinematic and self-reflexive. Early film strips like *Kodak Safety Film/Figure Horizon* (1971) are formally related to Heinecken's *Le Voyeur/Robbe-Grillet* canvases; like the paintings, they explore the nude body as a landscape and often suggest a frozen moment of time. In addition, they simultaneously resemble two different types of film—35mm photographic negative film as well as (positive) strips of celluloid motion picture film—thereby emphasizing that the mass media comprise a multitude of different technologies. The film strips from 1972, on the other hand, more fully embrace the cinematic through their vertical orientation, and the temporal development and movement in their sequences. *Film Strip #4* (1972) is a multiframe vertical strip, measuring 54 x 17 inches, that consists of composite images wherein different shots of an artistic nude commingle with stills representing tree branches (Plate 5.5). Beginning and ending with partial frames, the combinations of shots evoke developments between dark and light as well as from near and far. The artistic—as opposed to pornographic—character of the nude is emphasized by the figure's contrapposto pose, radical cropping, and association with nature (through the overlay of branches). But the flickering and movement created by the different still images along with the vertical orientation of the transparency as a whole—which evokes the cinematic as opposed to the (merely) photographic—makes the female subject more real, living, and sexual than a traditional fine art nude.

Porno Film Strip #2 (1972), on the other hand, embraces graphic sexuality much more closely and objectifies its subject to a far greater degree. It consists of a multiframe strip of composited but still discernibly explicit pornographic images taken from a contemporaneous skin magazine of the kind sold in adult bookstores or through the mail. (Although the source is unknown, its imagery is more hard-core than the type being published in either *Playboy* or *Penthouse* at the time, let alone *Cavalcade.*) In each frame of the sequence, a blonde model displays herself, exposing her genitals, while staring directly into the camera so as to meet the viewer's gaze. The shots are overlaid with foliage and branches, which partially obscure the graphic character of the woman's pose, and she is captured from both the front and behind. Although she repeats a similar pose in three of the images, each shot is different, and the changes in her position and state of nudity imply action and evoke narrative. The positive nature of the transparency and its vertical orientation encourage the viewer to see the work as a film strip and to read it temporally with the upper images in the sequence being understood as the figure's latest position and the lower images representing its previous configurations. At the same time, the numbers and letters on the strip's right edge are markings associated with 35mm photographic negative film (specifically, Kodak Plus-X Pan Film).[31]

By constructing a series of oppositions—between positive and negative, still photography and motion pictures, visceral document and multivalent art—*Porno Film Strip #2* and the other transparencies in this group provoked their audiences to consider the history of pornographic film, which had much to inform them about the development of human sexuality in the twentieth century. Cinematic porn began to be produced very soon after the birth of the medium in the last decade of the nineteenth century. Stag films, the earliest form of dirty movies, were primitive films offering explicit, hard-core representations of sexual acts.[32] Short (less than fifteen minutes), black-and-white, silent, and often lacking narrative coherence, they appeared toward the end of the first decade of the twentieth century, shown in brothels and underground venues to exclusively male spectators. Since they were illegal under the Comstock Act, stag films were seized and destroyed when they were discovered; because of their underground nature, their overall popularity is largely unknown. It seems safe to say, however, that their audience grew during the first half of the twentieth century, particularly during times of increased permissiveness, such as the 1920s. Communally consumed by a homosocial audience, stag films depicted a variety of sexual acts but concentrated on straight intercourse and fellatio. As Linda Williams has convincingly argued, they constituted a form of knowledge about sex, a show of genital parts (close-ups) and events (actions) through which men learned about sexuality and developed their concepts of gender. Stressing sexual difference, stag films tended to present their male subjects as active and voyeuristic, and their female subjects as passive and exhibitionistic, thereby reinforcing very traditional patriarchal stereotypes about differences between the sexes.[33] At the same time, they also revealed contradictions or weaknesses in the patriarchal models of human gender and sexuality that they projected.

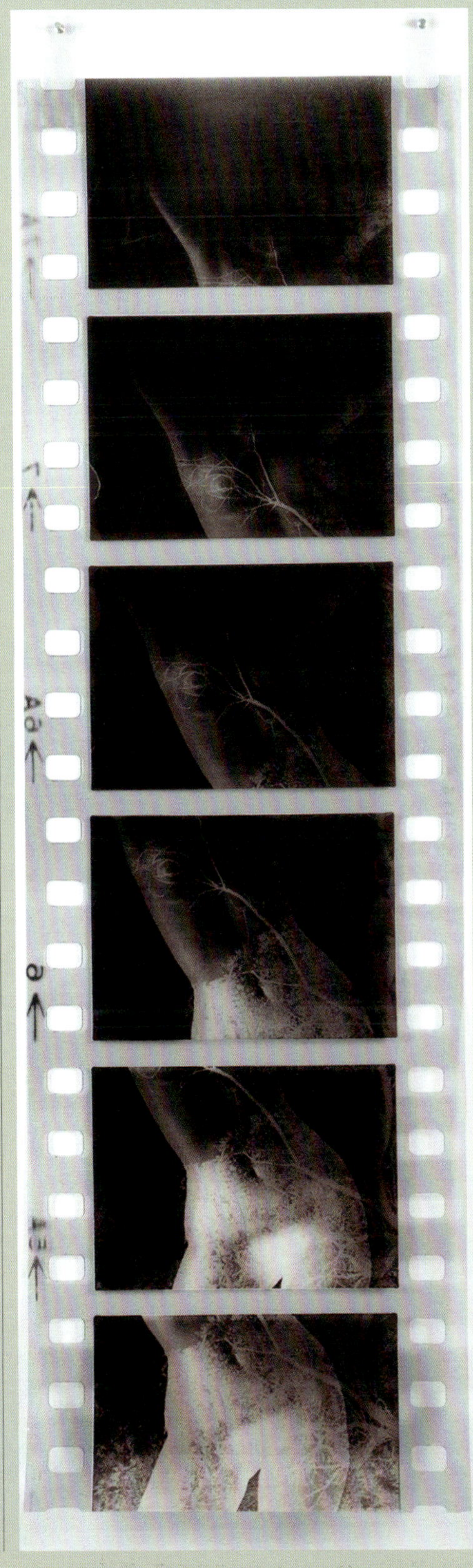

PLATE 5.5. Robert Heinecken, *Film Strip #4* (1972). Transparent lithographic film, 57 x 17 ⅜ inches (144.78 x 44.13 cm). Private collection. COPYRIGHT 2022 THE ROBERT HEINECKEN TRUST, CHICAGO.

Notably, the depictions of sexuality in the stag films—although explicit—were often discontinuous, focused on movement for its own sake, and missing narrative structural elements like rising action, climax, and denouement. (The "cum" or "money" shot, for example, was often absent.) Thus although stag films used cause-and-effect narration during the sequences that framed their depictions of sexuality (to set the scene, advance action, etc.), once sexual activity commenced, the depictions became a kind of primitive display of much more random shots (close-ups of genitals as well as "meat shots," or images of penetration). This discontinuous, nonnarrative montage was something that expelled the viewer from identification with the "eye" of the camera and toward a greater awareness of himself as a member of an audience.

As a result of the oscillation between narrative and nonnarrative presentation, stag films produced a divided spectator. As Williams puts it:

> The visual pleasure of the stag film might thus be characterized as a prolonged oscillation between two poles of pleasure. The first is inherited from, but more extensive than, the striptease: it is the pleasure of the collective male group expressing its heterosexual desire for the bodies of women on display. In this pleasure the woman's body mediates the achievement of masculine identity. The second pole of pleasure consists in moving toward, but never fully achieving, identification with a male protagonist who performs sexual acts with the female body that shows itself to the viewer. In the mode of reception characteristic of stag film, this full-fledged identification with sexual actors is impeded by apparently more pressing needs to identify with the other men in the audience.[34]

And the divided male spectator loses some of his power, because his identity appears to him unstable, and he becomes aware that he risks objectifying himself through his own gaze.

By dividing the spectator, moreover, stag films revealed anxieties inherent in the male view of sex and gender during the first half of the twentieth century. They demonstrated a desire for knowledge about sexuality on the part of male audiences as well as a concern that full knowledge could never be achieved. The American understanding of sex was evolving during this time, developing itself through multiple—moral, scientific, medical, and legal—discourses that defined it in radically different ways. And as the stag films made abundantly clear, sex could be treated equally as an object of pleasure or as an object of knowledge.[35] At the same time, unlike the feature-length porn films that were to emerge in the 1970s, stag films did not yet explicitly treat sex or sexual pleasure as a problem. Significantly, according to Williams, "the question of the woman's or man's sexual satisfaction almost never came up in these films: to insert a penis into any orifice was automatically presumed to be satisfying to both."[36] But, as Williams continues, "with the improved ability at each stage of development to see the female body 'more and better,' a new form of resistance to a hegemonic yet always vulnerable male pleasure is also introduced. In other words, at each new stage of visual intensification the previous institution of pleasure is questioned."[37] And as objectification increases, the spectator's self-image progressively declines.

By the time Heinecken created his *Porno Film Strips,* the era of the stag film was over, but not Americans' taste for porn. In the 1960s, there was greater tolerance for hard-core pornography in the wake of the earlier literature and obscenity trials; books and magazines with graphic representations of sexuality could be acquired at adult bookstores in major metropolitan centers (for example, New York or Los Angeles), businesses that were permitted to exist by civil authorities. As prosecutions for the sale of photographically based pornography dropped, these establishments acquired peep show booths, which allowed customers to view short hard-core sex movies in private. (Stag films thus enjoyed a second life as 8mm and 16mm film loops.) In addition, adult movie theaters also proliferated in this climate of increased tolerance, burgeoning from about twenty in 1960 to more than 750 by 1970.[38] But hard-core cinema in the 1970s was no longer defined by the short, episodic stag film. Instead, the feature-length porn film emerged: a sixty-to-ninety-minute color movie, made with a much bigger budget, and possessing synchronized sound, background music, and a narrative or story that contextualized the sexual "numbers" and presented a statement or viewpoint about sexuality. Perhaps most important, this new product was aimed at a mixed audience who would view the film together in the theater. Women were thereby admitted into the circle of porn viewers, and the problem of female pleasure became an even more pressing issue.

As suggested by the history of hard-core motion pictures, since the very beginnings of the twentieth century visual expressions of human sexuality were continuously being transformed into objects of mass consumption. Heinecken's porn work attempted to reflect on this phenomenon, reconfiguring straight male pornography to undermine its straightness and emphasize the polymorphousness of its desires. In the emulsion paintings and film strips, the preciousness of the art object was also subverted: by flirting with pornography in the former; and in the latter, employing a radically nonartistic medium, the blown-up Kodalith transparency. We can thus see Heinecken as performing an ironic mea culpa in the 1970s, reconfiguring what could possibly have been a personal porn obsession into ambiguous self-critique. As an artist, Heineken thus rendered himself vulnerable to criticism, because one could always

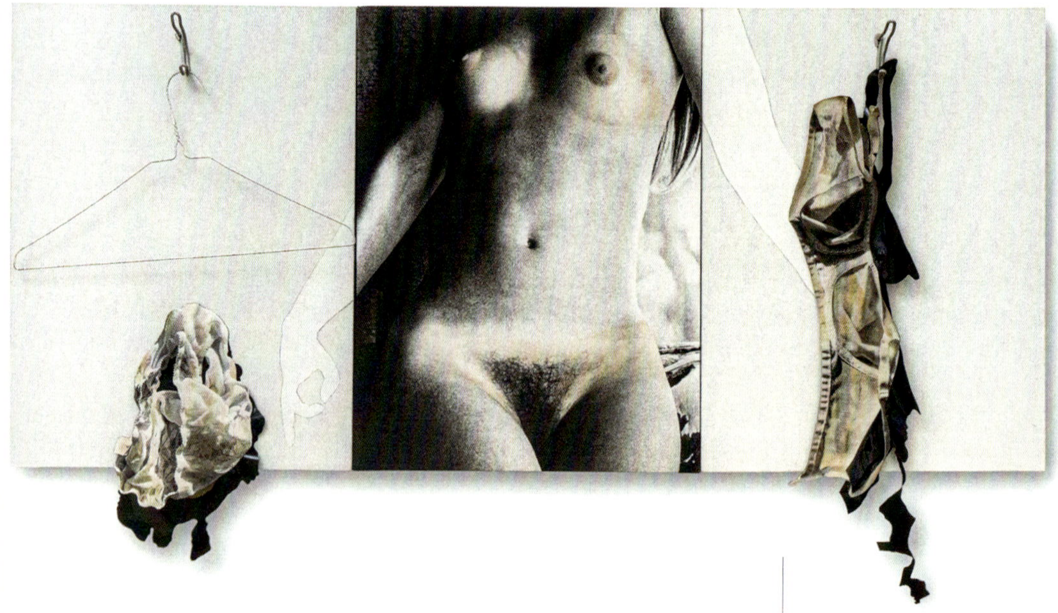

argue that his visual deconstructions of the pornographic gaze didn't cut deep enough, and he was simply reinforcing the patriarchal mode of spectatorship that he claimed to critique. As a result, the question of Heinecken's audience becomes central to the meaning of his porn work, as well as how he responded to spectators who sought to engage with this issue in his art.

Feminist Suntans and Sexual Clichés

Between 1973 and 1974, Heinecken worked on two series of porn paintings that undermined the heterosexual male gaze through a number of different strategies. The first, *Lingerie for a Feminist Suntan*, was a series of at least five multipanel works consisting of acrylic, photographic emulsion, pastel, and charcoal on canvas with wire hanger, metal hooks, and additional canvas elements (Plate 5.6). Existing in both vertical and horizontal orientations, each of the paintings depicts a solitary nude, sometimes cropped at the shoulders and thighs, surrounded by three-dimensional photographic replicas of a bra and panties, which hung on actual hooks and clothes hangers attached to the surfaces of the paintings. In all of them, photographic representation is juxtaposed with line drawing, fabricated sculptural objects, and real objects (readymades) to create a flat, quasi-banal image that raises questions about the nature of representation.

As suggested by its title, the *Lingerie for a Feminist Suntan* series conflates formal, social, and sexual issues. Although the paintings first seem

PLATE 5.6. Robert Heinecken, *Lingerie for a Feminist Suntan #4* (1973). Three canvas panels with photographic emulsion, chalk, and wire hangers, 21 x 48 x 4 inches (53.3 x 121.9 x 10.2 cm). Collection Susan and Eugene Spiritus, Newport Coast, California. COPYRIGHT 2022 THE ROBERT HEINECKEN TRUST, CHICAGO.

banal, their traditional subject and illustrative handling making them seem almost artless, longer contemplation reveals uncanny conflicts and disturbing aporias. In conjunction with the nude body and depictions of underwear, *feminist suntan* suggests the removal of clothing and the exposure of skin. Bra burning became an emblem of women's liberation in the late 1960s, a sign that women would no longer be constrained by traditional social roles.[39] Juxtaposed with the graphic nudity, however, the works suggest that such an action was double-edged: potentially liberating but also potentially objectifying. In conjunction with the photographic elements in the paintings as well as the various forms of (depicted and real) shadows, the title also promotes reflection on the nature of the photographic medium. Like a suntan, a photograph is caused by the action of light on a photosensitive surface. And as suggested by the coloration of the woman's skin where her (now removed) underwear would fit, solar rays affect the body's surface and leave traces of their presence—an inference also promoted by conceptual artist Dennis Oppenheim's ironic and disturbing photographic documentation of a performance, *Reading Position for Second Degree Burn* (1970), of which Heinecken was no doubt aware. In this performance, the American conceptual artist created a sunburn on his body that outlined the shape of a military book, *Tactics: Cavalry and Artillery,* on his chest. The documentation of the piece consisted of a textual description of the five-hour action and two truncated self-portraits: before and after photographs of Oppenheim's exposed head and chest as he lay in the sand on Jones Beach in New York.[40]

In Heinecken's photographic painting series, on the other hand, the nude seems bleached rather than burned by the sun—and thus the painting reveals photography to be a medium that can both reveal and conceal. The idea of the photographic process both disclosing and obfuscating the body is emphasized by the nude's arms, which have been reduced to outlines of different tones, as well as by the fake shadows beneath the underwear, which, because they were made from unexposed photographic paper, slowly darkened over time. Playing between different levels of representation as well as legibility and obscurity, the painting series reminds its viewers of the fundamental ambiguity of photographic representation—the fact that photography, which seems to uncover the real, also dresses its surfaces in representations that obscure its truths. Finally, the literalness and quasi-banality of the image challenge the spectator to question the painting's status as art. As depicted, the nude seems very traditional and generic; its pose seems stereotypical; and the treatment of the image seems plain and uninspired. And by flirting with the banal, Heinecken's painting seems even less artistic than Oppenheim's conceptual documentary photographs.

Through a superimposition of formal, social, and sexual associations, the *Lingerie for a Feminist Suntan* series undermines the female nude's target audience—the heterosexual male viewer. The works' critique of authorial vision combines with reflexivity to provoke the engaged spectator to consider the mass media's effects on human sexuality, and whether the increased flow of information about sex in the mid-1970s improved or harmed Americans' intimacy. As the series suggested, clothing—in this case lingerie—could be used to excite traditional forms of male desire as well as to counter them by being reconfigured into symbols of resistance. Like photography, clothing could be an instrument of liberation as well as one of control. Revealing vision to be a medium through which desire and libido are excited and regulated, Heinecken's series also suggested that the male gaze was easily led. There is something transparent and over-clear about the paintings that makes them seem easily graspable (and thus dismissible). But this dismissibility, too, is an illusion. Although the paintings initially seem objectifying, they depict the female subject as if caught in the act of disappearing from the scene, of withdrawing from the male gaze. Going against the idea of sexual consummation, they raise doubts. And as such, they use mainstream porn stereotypes to make palpable the straight male fear of female pleasure—the man's doubts about whether he can sexually satisfy a figure that resists definition and seems to actively elude him.

Like the *Lingerie* series, the *Cliché Vary* series seems trite at first but soon reveals uncanny contradictions that relate to gender and sexuality. And like the earlier series, it juxtaposes formal, social, and artistic issues. *Cliché Vary* began in 1974, with three large multipanel paintings, and continued over the course of the 1970s with a succession of lithographs. The title was a pun on *cliché verre,* the French term for the early photographic process, first used in the 1850s, of coating a glass plate with an opaque substance, scratching a drawing on it, and then printing the handmade negative on photosensitive paper. As suggested by Heinecken's pun, photographic reproduction was intimately connected to the circulation, and variation, of clichés or stereotypes. The subject of the *Cliché Vary* series was once again the female nude, appropriated from a men's magazine and shot in different positions and from different angles. As was the case with his *Figure Horizons,* the body in this series is made monstrous through cropping, juxtaposition, montage, and repetition.

The three large paintings that Heinecken created in 1974 were subtitled *Autoeroticism, Fetishism,* and *Lesbianism,* respectively. Multipanel works comprising between eleven and sixteen (square or rectangular) modules, they consist of photographic emulsion on canvas with pastel chalk (Plate 5.7). In each, appropriated elements from a porn pictorial were combined to create a monstrous multipart figure that hovered

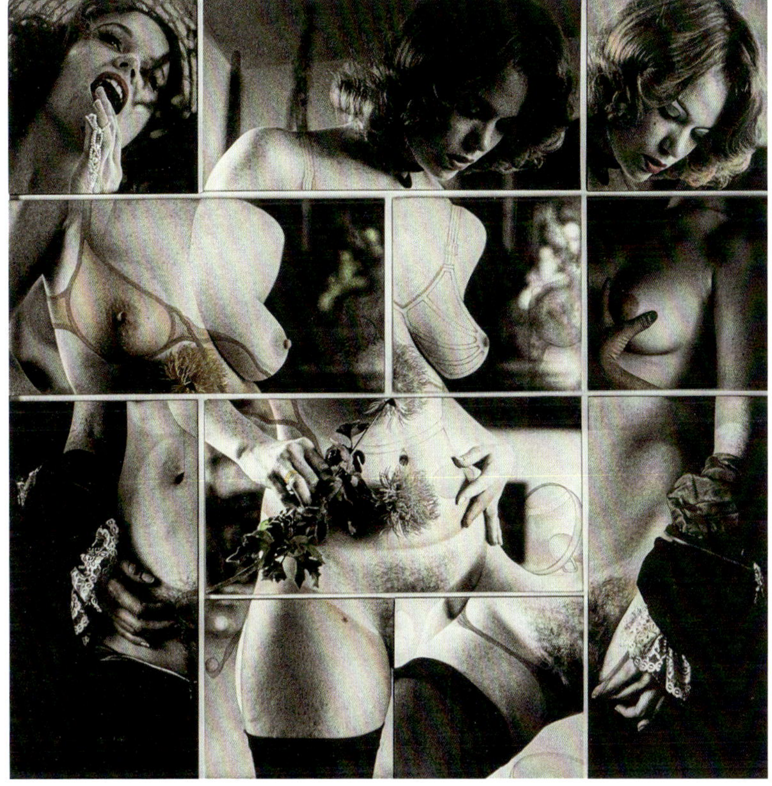

between unity and multiplicity. Some panels combine photographs with drawings while others overlay photographs with other photographs. And while the figure's form seems to continue across the various panels, it is impossible to discern where her body ends and the environment or other figures begin. Likewise, while the nude's different poses and angles imply narrative, motion, and time, the overall grid structure evokes stasis and a realm outside of time. Areas of color, produced by pastel overlays, add to the heterogeneous nature of the paintings—part drawn, part photographed, clearly cut up and reassembled.

In addition to their pornographic nature—their graphic detail that reveals nipples, pubic hair, and labia, as well as their subtitles, which suggest different modes of erotic satisfaction—what is striking about these paintings is the way that they challenge conventional notions of art. In comparison to much figuration in pop art, Heinecken's paintings seem more like standard kitsch. Their detail, poses, and overlays make them seem lowbrow, in other words, unsophisticated and in poor taste. It is significant that Heinecken never used actual hard-core pornography in his paintings—that is, imagery that showed sexual acts like penetration or ejaculation. Such images, his work seems to admit, could not be transformed to the extent that their sexual provocation would not be their primary attribute. But if not hard-core (and thus obscene), Heinecken's *Cliché Vary* series was offensive—like a bad attempt at art, locked within an earlier ideal of beauty.

Like *Lingerie for a Feminist Suntan,* the *Cliché Vary* series attacked the stereotypes that supported straight male vision, and in particular the fixity that it ascribed to sexual desire. For the straight male gaze, as traditionally conceived, desire is always for the opposite sex, and gender (as well as other) distinctions are generally strongly reinforced. In *Cliché Vary*, on the other hand, the straight male gaze is undermined from within. A clear vision of the model's genitals is constantly frustrated, often by the interruption of a frame. Thereby, the focus of male desire is fragmented, disrupted by the emergence of something undefined and unexpected. In addition, longer contemplation reveals that the model has multiple phallic appendages, a characteristic that makes her more masculine and communicates that she does not need the male body to achieve sexual satisfaction. Finally, the figure is multiplied: it appears as part of a group, and as such it seems completely focused on its various doppelgängers instead of the male spectator. Using elements entirely drawn from pornographic products that were marketed to a straight male audience, *Cliché Vary* thus introduces same-sex desire as well as other forms of sexuality into images that supposedly defined the straight male gaze.

Space/Time Metamorphosis

In 1975 and 1976, Heinecken produced two medium-sized paintings consisting of gelatin silver emulsion on canvas with chalk. This series, which featured attractive nude models, a man and a woman, seemed even more literal and photographically based than the *Cliché Vary* series. In *Space/Time Metamorphosis #1,* an alert woman, striking an athletic recumbent pose, peers directly into the camera, while in the air and rocks around her multiple doppelgängers appear, holding postures that evoke both active and passive states (Plate 5.8). Earth, air, ground, and rock merge into one another, and a square linear grid both divides the space and further unifies it. The photographic canvas of the male figure is slightly clearer, as is the rectangular grid that measures its forms and spaces. The figure is repeated four or five times, with four of the poses being very similar: a frontal shot of the young man's body taken from a low-angle viewpoint. (A reclining figure in the background may be a woman, but the features are obscured, and like the central man's, the background figure's posture emphasizes passivity and submission.) Like the earlier canvas, the multiplying figure merges with air and rock: space and time, as the series title suggests, are in a state of alteration.

When comparing the two paintings of the series, what is striking is how active and dominant the woman is in comparison to the man. Whereas her figure is often tense and coiled, evoking incipient action, his is largely passive: supine and exposing his genitals as if he were a woman in a men's magazine. This female side of the male model is emphasized by his long hair, full lips, and sleepy eyes, as well as the fact that Heinecken has used montage to give the central male figure breasts in two of its iterations. Even though the man plays with his penis—which multiplies, appearing in various stages of tumescence and limpness—his posture is largely one of display, inviting spectators to imbibe pleasure from their gaze, and perhaps to take charge in their fantasies. Like the other porn works, the two *Space/Time Metamorphosis* paintings undermine traditional gender distinctions on which the straight male gaze depends.

The source images for the two paintings were life models taken at the Ansel Adams Workshop in Yosemite National Park, where Heinecken taught during the summer in the mid-1970s.[41] He combined negatives that he had made himself, as well as negatives created by other photographers (such as Joanne Callis and Virgil Mirano), and the central figures were not mass-media stereotypes but, rather, individuals he knew.[42] As a result, these works bring up questions of ethics and consent more directly than other works by Heinecken; they show the artist to be exploring objectification in person as a photographer in front of a model he presumably directs. Significantly, the female model was Twinka Thiebaud, who would shortly have a large impact on the course of Heinecken's life.

Between the 1950s and the 1970s, Heinecken seems to have developed a less family-oriented and more narcissistic mode of being. When he married his first wife, Janet, in 1955, he immediately began raising children with her, emulating the family ideal of the 1950s. Marine training had given him discipline; and art education had set him on an academic career that would provide him with a livelihood and sustain an artistic career in the context of the California State University system. But despite his organizational ties, Heinecken increasingly hewed to a countercultural ideal over the course of the 1960s, seeing the academic system as a context where he could make art and pursue a bohemian lifestyle. For Heinecken, the exploration of alternative states of consciousness through nicotine and alcohol use were part of this countercultural ideal, as was the exploration of sexuality outside of marriage.[43]

In the mid-1960s, he began having affairs with other women, although he continued to live with Janet and their children until 1975. As he put it:

> At some point, I'd say about 1965, things sort of began to go wrong with us. I start screwing around. I think she did a little bit, too. It never bothered—I

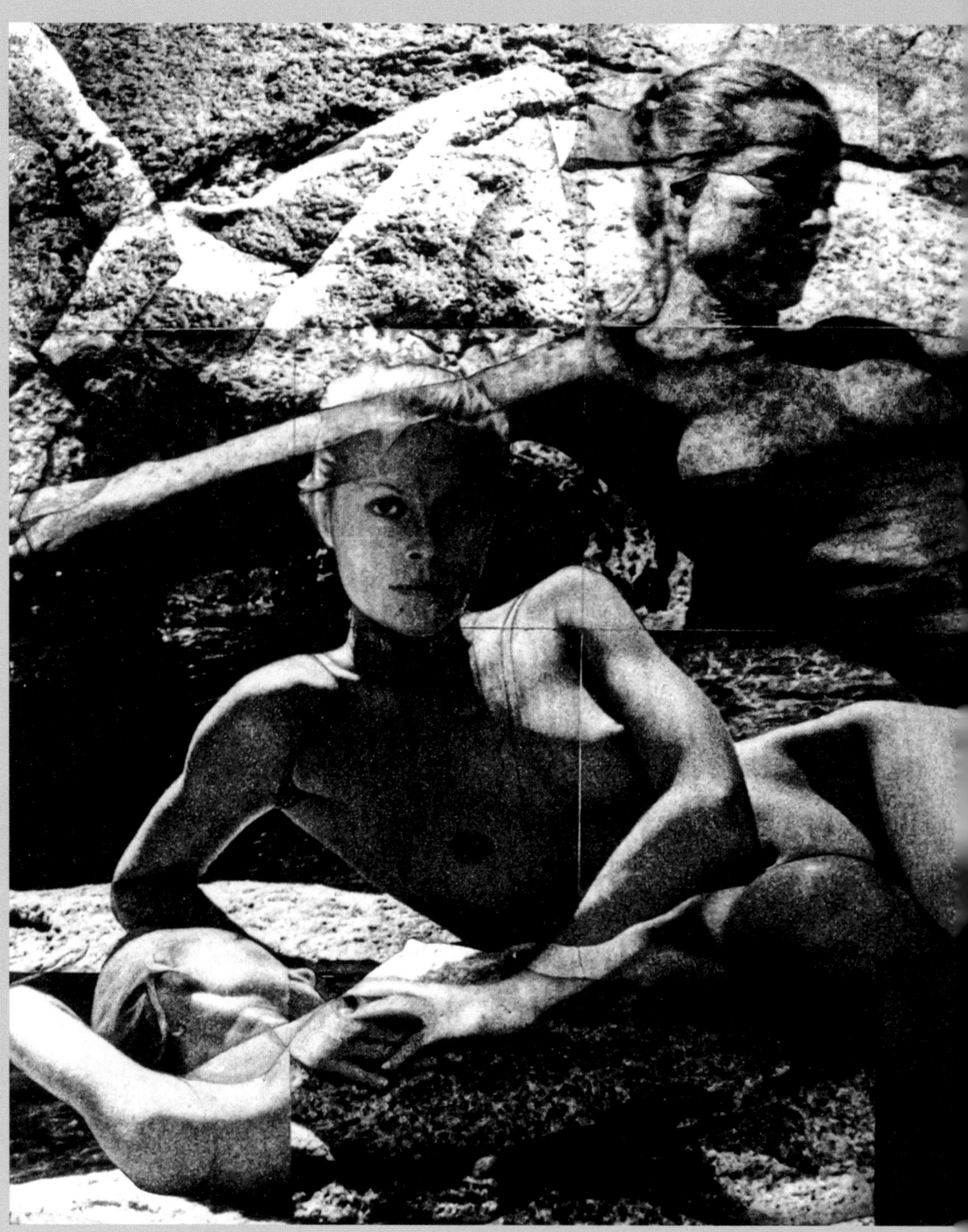

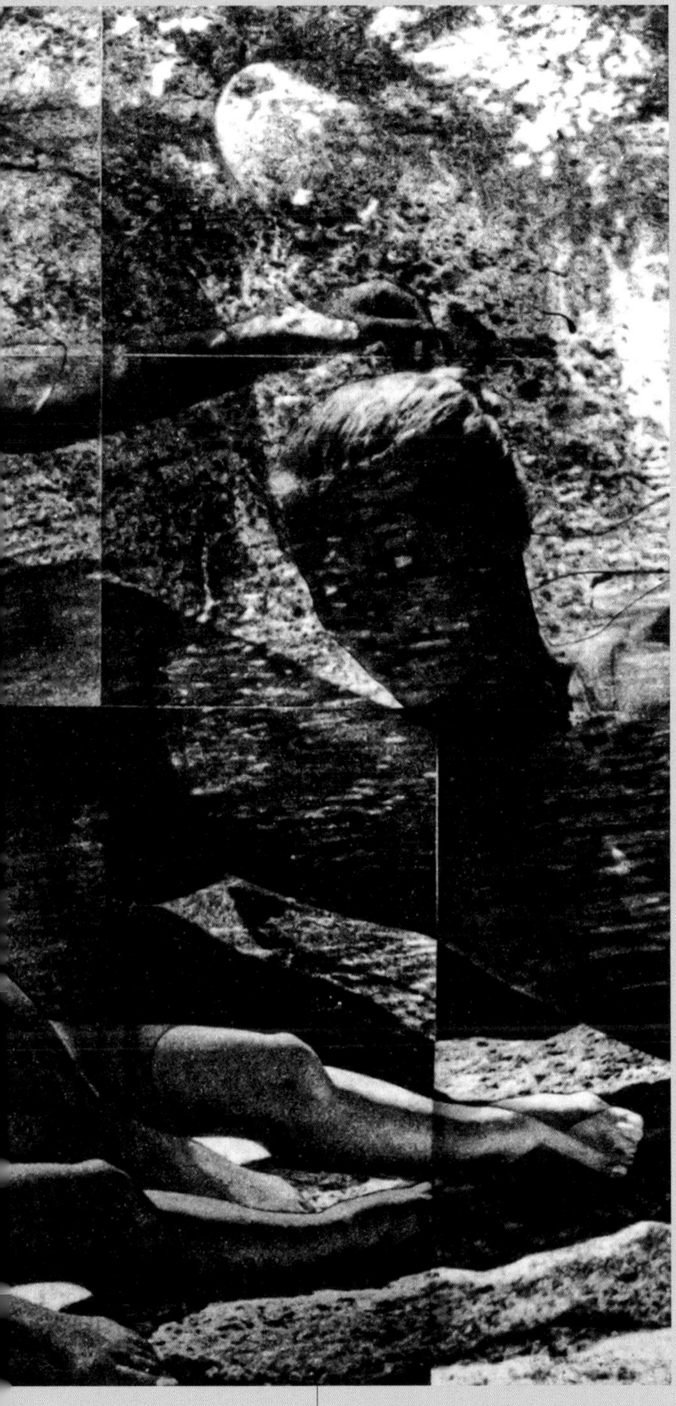

PLATE 5.8. Robert Heinecken, *Space/Time Metamorphosis #1* (1975). Gelatin silver emulsion on fabric with drawing, 42 x 62 inches (106.7 x 157.5 cm). Museum of Fine Arts Houston. COPYRIGHT 2022 THE ROBERT HEINECKEN TRUST, CHICAGO.

mean, it never came up. But it was always that I was married and at home or whatever. Again, the time period is such that this was not an uncommon situation. It may still not be uncommon. It was part of this whole attitude about individuality, I guess.[44]

In the summer and fall of 1975, however, Heinecken had a six-month affair with Twinka Thiebaud, whom he had met the year before at the same workshop. The daughter of Wayne Thiebaud, the pop painter, Twinka was a model and aspiring actress.[45] Heinecken fell in love with Thiebaud and left his family for good as well as his house on Viretta Lane where his studio was situated.[46]

Through Thiebaud, Heinecken was introduced to Henry Miller, then in his eighties, with whom Twinka was living at the time as his cook and caretaker. Heinecken recalled:

> She had this small apartment within the house itself. I lived in a place in Venice on Bay Street, which was just this one-room situation, but I spent most of the time with her in his house, because there was enough room for both people. I would just go back and forth like that. That was a very exciting time period for me romantically, sexually, whatever. Because, as I said, she was probably the most obvious model for all these different people like Jack [W.] Welpott and Judith Dater and other people. People just knew her.[47]

In part, Heinecken's desire for Thiebaud seemed to stem from the fact that she was a known photographic subject, a figure who at that time was being used to generate iconic photographic images.

Heinecken's infatuation with Thiebaud ran aground when he had to confront her polyamorous lifestyle. Their affair ended because Heinecken couldn't bear her infidelity:

> While we were together, two things happened for whatever reason, prob-ably due to my psychic state or whatever. I started drinking more than I should have, which was a problem off and on anyway. And she began to get into situations where the phone would ring in the middle of the night, and her agent or some guy that was helping her said, "Love, so-and-so is in town. He needs some companionship," and she would have to go no matter what, because that was what a person in that situation— You do that. I mean, anything you can do that's going to put you into the professional circuit is necessary. And I couldn't take it. I was just that conventional, in a sense, that I thought— Well, what's perverse about it is that I expected Janet to accept my behavior, but I wasn't ready to give this woman the same freedom that Janet had given me, and I was troubled. I don't know exactly what happened, but I couldn't handle this lifestyle. Also, I had no

studio, and I'm either living in this room or I'm at Henry Miller's. So I'm not doing anything really except trying to collect my thoughts. It wasn't a time that I accomplished very much.[48]

When Heinecken and Thiebaud split up, instead of returning to Janet and his family's home, he moved into a studio on Venice Boulevard in Culver City at the end of 1975.[49] Although he couldn't handle the complete sexual liberation of Twinka's lifestyle, Heinecken was also rethinking his commitment to his marriage and the family ideal.

Pornography as a Feminist Issue

By addressing feminism directly in some of his titles, Heinecken seemed interested in drawing an audience who would not necessarily see his porn work favorably and who would be looking for signs of misogyny in his practice. His motives for addressing feminism in his porn work were obscure, but it is not inconceivable that he wanted a response that would critically engage with the contradictions his work brought up. Over the course of the 1980s, a discourse grew up around Heineken's use of pornography and his stance on feminism that affected his growing status in the fields of contemporary photography and art. Plainly put, this discourse saw Heinecken as a misogynist, a male photographer who objectified women and was critical of feminism—attitudes that critics ultimately ascribed to his art as a whole. In the context of the culture of narcissism, Heinecken's art could be viewed as a defensive attack on women—the reaction of a fearful male ego confronted by women's rising power in the contemporary moment. And a number of artists, critics, and educators chose to interpret his art that way, often mounting articulate and powerful attacks against his appropriative practices, while at the same time forms of appropriation similar to Heinecken's were being used by photographers who were loosely united by the concept of postmodernism.

As Eva Respini and others have noted, Heinecken's work was criticized strongly during the 1980s (and beyond) for supposedly having conservative and misogynist tendencies:

> The critique of Heinecken's use of sexually explicit images coincided with the writing of feminist theory, specifically theories about the "male gaze" as a defining force in culture and the lens through which much of art history is read. Women in the arts were increasingly aware of gender-driven imbalances, and they organized accordingly. A Women's Caucus of the SPE was formed in the early 1980s; there, Heinecken's work was the subject of much debate. In 1982 he participated in a symposium about pornography

and art at New York's International Center of Photography, alongside Susan Sontag, Hollis Frampton, and Joyce Neimanas; a review of the event noted that Heineken left "all conclusions about the obscenity or sensuousness of his pictures up to the audience. . . . Granting that some people might interpret these pictures as sexist propaganda, he merely stated, 'I tend not to see it that way.'" Heinecken's muted response to the feminist critique seemed characteristic. In 1992 the SPE named him an "Honored Educator," and a journalist reporting on the disappointment of the Women's Caucus at Heinecken's selection referred to him as a "misogynist photographer." When questioned later, the artist replied that he did not know "whether to be more insulted at being called a 'misogynist' or a 'photographer.'"[50]

When attacked, Heinecken always seemed to defer or dissemble; he never attacked his critics back.[51]

The critiques by rising radical photographers were just as withering. Photographer and theorist Martha Rosler, whose contemporaneous work shares many interesting parallels with Heinecken's, called his art "pussy porn" in 1979, while also recognizing its similarities to the theory-inspired "structural" approach of the postmodern photographers who were beginning to gain attention in New York.[52] In the late 1980s, Allan Sekula criticized some of Heinecken's television work for similar reasons. The photographer-theorist took umbrage at a James R. Hugunin article on Heinecken in *Spot,* which very favorably discussed *1984,* a book by Heinecken, in part by using Sekula's theorizations of the body and the archive in relation to photography.[53] In response, Sekula wrote a letter to the journal disputing Hugunin's characterization of Heinecken as a left-wing guerrilla artist.[54] Sekula's two-page letter focused on Heinecken as a social critic, and how his form of media critique was deficient, more in sympathy with the concerns of the right than those of the left. As Sekula argued, in his art "Heinecken is deploying 'smartness' to cover for intellectual laziness and ignorance. Heinecken is never in complete control of the always delicate devices of parody, and his 'ironic' distance keeps collapsing into a rather naked and awkwardly worded wish-fulfillment fantasy."[55] As a result, Heinecken's art embodied the stereotypes that Hugunin argued Heinecken's art deconstructed. Instead of subverting the status quo, Heinecken's photographically based appropriations affirmed normative constraints, particularly when it came to race and gender.[56]

Although Sekula focused on a different body of work, he also applied it to the appropriations of porn discussed here, as well as Heinecken's oeuvre as a whole. In addition, because the letter clearly outlines Rosler and Sekula's basic reading of Heinecken, a reading that others have subsequently followed, it is important to note it, as it speaks to some of Heinecken's central artistic concerns and the misunderstandings that have emerged around his art. For Heinecken's critics, his irony devolved into an affirmation of subject positions that he only pretended to criticize. He didn't parody the sexism and racism of the media: he embodied it.

Throughout this book I have consistently argued against this reading. Instead, as has been demonstrated, Heinecken continually challenged traditional views of race, gender, class, and sexuality in his art throughout his career, blending this practice with a sophisticated analysis of photography and the broader mass media. Even his most hard-core work—the pornographic work of the 1970s—suggests that instead of reinforcing a defensive male ego, Heinecken's art further undermined it. Thereby, it destabilized the straight male gaze and acknowledged the important impact that feminism was beginning to have on art and society. Pornography might not equate with exploitation and rape, as radical feminists like Morgan, McKinnon, and Dworkin argued, but it was having a profound effect on sexual and gender identities, an influence that Heineken's guerrilla artworks were attempting to make palpable.

Why did Heinecken's detractors see him as the symbol of misogyny in photography instead of its critic? The answer, I think, is Heinecken's positionality. Heinecken never completely rejected his own subject position, his own tastes, attitudes, and points of view, which he continued to refer to as part of a broader mix. On some level, Heinecken's critics responded to their perception that Heinecken was aroused by his subject matter, that he was drawn to such pornographic representations of women's bodies, even if he used them to criticize his own viewpoint and desires. Sometimes, as we shall see in the next chapter, Heinecken's positionality emerges as a kind of hedonistic "maleness," a raunchy attitude akin to the writing of David Mamet or *National Lampoon* magazine. At other times, as was the case with Heinecken's work on pornography, his own subject position came out through an embrace of visual materials that most directly embodied a straight male gaze. Positionality in his art, however, did not mean affirmative support of the status quo; instead, it meant that the destabilization of the values and concepts that supported straight male subjectivity were largely carried out from a position that acknowledged its privilege and entwinement with traditional family and social structures of regulation and control. What Heinecken's critics failed to recognize was that even in his most explicit artworks, he remained deeply critical, connecting visual forms with social practices in powerful and destabilizing ways. Indeed, although continuing references to his own subject position were detrimental to Heinecken's career in the 1980s and 1990s, in retrospect it seems like an important characteristic of his art. It also makes his position seem closer to feminist thought in that it seems to stress that no artist or theorist should divorce themselves from their specific histories or the positions in their societies that their histories traverse. Like certain feminist photographers today, Heinecken engaged with porn because he recognized that it exerted a profound social and psychological effect on both himself and others—a pervasive influence that needed to be confronted and understood.[57]

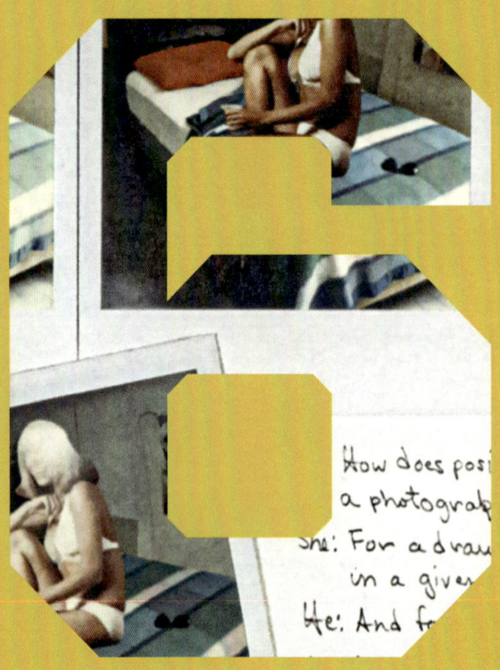

6

THE POLAROID EXPERIENCE

Instantaneous Photography and the Performance of Identity

BEGINNING IN THE MID-1970S, Heinecken turned his attention to Polaroid photography, a popular alternative form of photographic practice, which he explored intensively for the next decade, using it to examine the ever-growing commodification of American life. During this time, Heinecken investigated Polaroid photography through a variety of different technologies, including SX-70 photographs and large-format Polaroid images, as well as by creating handmade and printed books that utilized the distinctive SX-70 square-format look. His most extensive body of work connected to the family of processes created by the Polaroid Company was the *He:/She:* series, which was produced in a number of different formats but focused on the Polaroid SX-70 print. Reflecting on dating, self-fashioning, and consumption in the 1970s, *He:/She:* revealed how the combination of word and image could both produce and contest the commodification of everyday life. A second, also extensive body of work emerged out of the dating material in the early 1980s: *Lessons in Posing Subjects,* montages of Instamatic photographs presenting typologies of human poses, pseudosociological analyses of commercial types and behaviors. Thus, although Heinecken began by using Polaroid processes to document his own body and everyday life, he soon repurposed them for appropriation, rephotographing images of models in clothing catalogues and appending to them humorous and personal dialogues.

Heinecken's engagement with Polaroid photography centers on the social production and performance of identity. Sourcing material from clothing catalogues, television news broadcasts, and his own personal life, he constructed a quasi-sociological investigation into the nature of American selfhood during the increasingly narcissistic 1970s and early 1980s.

By the time Heinecken took up Polaroid photography in 1976, the company that bore the name was already in its third decade of existence. Synonymous with the instantaneous process, the first truly popular alternative to the Kodak Company's bestselling photographic system, the Polaroid Company, led by the visionary inventor Edwin H. Land, produced its first instant camera and film packet in 1948.[1] Over the fifty years prior to the founding of Polaroid, Kodak had already progressively popularized photography by making it simple for amateurs to make—"You Press the Button, We Do the Rest," as the company first advertised in 1888. But by creating the first truly amateur photographer, one who did not need know how to expose, let alone develop or print photographic images, Kodak also introduced a greater time lag into the practice of photography. Exposed film had to be sent to a lab to be developed and printed, thus creating a significant gap between the instant the photograph was taken and the moment the photographer could see it again. Although nineteenth- and early-twentieth-century photographers also had to wait before seeing the developed photograph, they often printed them themselves, and the connection between the original exposure and the finished representation was generally closer and more intimate.

One of Polaroid's many major innovations over the years was to combine Kodak's simplification and automation of the shooting process—through reflex mirrors, automatic exposure, integrated flash units, and split-image focusing, among others—with a novel film packet that contained all the chemicals needed to develop and print an image. Once the film was exposed, the film packet was removed from the camera, and the photograph separated from the negative, which was discarded. A unique image that appeared within minutes of its taking, the Polaroid print became associated with a new kind of intimacy and immediacy. Although it could never rival Kodak's hegemony, Polaroid photography was embraced by consumers, and the company was highly profitable from nearly its beginning until the end of the 1980s. One key to its success was the fact that Polaroid was constantly innovating; it added color film in 1963, and in 1972, it introduced the SX-70 Land Camera, the form of Polaroid photography through which Heinecken initially became involved with the process. Another central aspect of its popularity was the way it increased the integration of photography with everyday life. After the introduction of SX-70 instant photography, Americans became much more aware and knowledgeable about the interrelated processes of photographing, viewing, and posing, practices they found pleasurable. And as these complex activities grew in popularity as leisure activities, Americans were trained to participate in their own self-objectification. In certain ways, the selfie era had begun.

The SX-70 produced square-format photographs that were embraced by both artists and the public at large. Although the format evolved slightly over the years, in its original form the SX-70 image was 3.1 x 3.1 inches surrounded by a slightly larger white border. Glossy and rich in color, it was prone to fading, but when kept out of direct light the photograph preserved a seduction and an impact born of the abstracting power of the Polaroid flash and color system. Artists and photographers alike were drawn to the format during the 1970s and 1980s, including Andy Warhol, Lucas Samaras, Robert Mapplethorpe, David Hockney, Les Krims, Edward Weston, and André Kertész. It had sensuous, painterly qualities, including rich colors, flattened forms, and dramatic tonal contrasts. Moreover, the SX-70 print possessed a private and magical character: a unique image, it appeared in front of the photographer in less than a minute. And because it bypassed the developer, the Polaroid was intimate and vernacular—one could do anything in this type of photograph, it seemed, since it evaded the scrutiny of outsiders. Questions of obscenity and censorship no longer appeared to apply to this sort of representation. It was also a format that encouraged its own manipulation: immediately after development, its soft surface was receptive to manual manipulation with a burin or other marking instrument (a technique employed by Krims and Samaras), and its square format encouraged the formation of larger collages of prints (as seen, for example, in the work of Hockney or Joyce Neimanas, who introduced Heinecken to the process).

Heinecken's engagement with the SX-70 format began in the mid-1970s, during a period in which his artistic practice was severely disrupted by a series of events that included the breakup of his marriage and the destruction of his studio. Although brief, his passionate affair with Twinka Thiebaud changed him radically, causing him to question his role as a family man and to explain himself to the loved ones whom he hurt. As he later recalled, he didn't complete much new art between the summer of 1975 and the spring of 1977. Instead, he started writing intensely, externalizing his feelings and thoughts about his marriage and other relationships.[2]

While living with Twinka at Henry Miller's house, he also played with his own name. Miller took to calling him Raoul.[3] Before meeting the writer, Heinecken generally went by the name Bob, but after knowing Miller, he called himself Robert, a symbolic name change that he later memorialized in one of his *He:/She:* conversations.[4]

Significantly, when the artist realized that he was too jealous to stay in a relationship with the free-spirited Thiebaud, he did not return to Janet and his children. Instead, Heinecken moved into a Culver City studio at the end of 1975, separating from Janet after twenty years of marriage.[5] In the spring of 1976, Heinecken traveled to Chicago to do a photography workshop, becoming reacquainted with the photographer Joyce Neimanas, an assistant professor at the School of the Art Institute of Chicago (whom he would marry in 1984).[6] During the trip he and Joyce became involved, and that summer she joined him in Los Angeles, beginning a relationship that would last until his death in 2006.[7] Joy was recently divorced, in part because she wanted to focus on her creative practice instead of immediately having children.[8] Within a few years, Heinecken and Neimanas leveraged their academic positions to create a two-city living situation, working alternate years and living in the other's city when not teaching, eventually turning this arrangement turned into a two years on, two years off system.[9] Joy, Heinecken recalled, opened up new vistas for him; through her he got to know gay people better, specifically Robert Loescher, a pre-Columbian art historian at AIC.[10] And his love for her drew him back toward monogamy; as he recalled, the couple got married in order to symbolize that they were not going to sleep with other people anymore.[11]

Another set of circumstances that severely impacted Heinecken's ability to make his art revolved around his studio. Since he worked at home before his separation, he lost his main studio when he went to Yosemite in the summer of 1975.[12] Although he eventually rented a space in Culver City, where he continued to work on his porn paintings and lithographs, Heinecken's studio was destroyed by a freak explosion in the summer of 1976 while he and Joy were living there. The explosion occurred on June 16, when an excavation machine on a street-widening project struck a gasoline pipe buried under the median strip on Venice Boulevard near the studio. Pressurized gasoline shot up, vaporized, and then exploded, demolishing nearly all the buildings on the block. Homes, stores, cars, and people were all lost in a conflagration that the *Los Angeles Times* dubbed the "West LA Holocaust." Robert and Joy escaped death because they had fortuitously gone to Darryl and Doris Curran's apartment to feed their cats while the Currans were away on a trip and had ended up staying the night there. Had they not made this impromptu decision, they most likely would have been killed.[13]

Heineken had spent the year 1976 working on lithographs from his *Cliché Vary* series, and they were all gone. As he recalled later:

> I was absolutely despondent, because I had just come off of a Guggenheim [Fellowship] on a sabbatical leave. I had the whole studio laid out with all these prints. I had just finished printing a whole edition of these *Cliché Vary* prints. I had a lot of other materials stored there that were all gone, which was very devastating. We just got in the car and drove for maybe a week or two. We went up north and tried to forget the whole thing.[14]

Like the breakup of his family, the Culver City studio explosion affected both his psyche and his art and perhaps prompted him to set out in a radically new direction in his work.

He:/She:

The SX-70 process offered Heinecken more than a new means to help instigate a shift of direction within his art; it also allowed him to combine images directly with his handwritten dialogues. Heinecken successfully defended a master's thesis on graphic design in 1960, and he continued to write throughout his life. Writing was always important to his art—as an element within the artworks themselves as well as through a supplementary field of notebooks, brochures, articles, pamphlets, and grant applications. In the mid-1970s, however, writing preoccupied Heinecken to an even greater degree. After the losses of his home and studios, it became a convenient way to explore his artistic concerns while living a nomadic lifestyle; in addition, it helped him achieve a new, more auto-biographical focus. Turning an ironic sociological gaze on the changes going on in his own life, he examined his conversations around dating and sex for clues about himself as well as the character of his contemporary media-saturated society.

Sometime in the early 1970s, Heinecken began to work up snatches of dialogue between unnamed male and female characters. Inspired by Yukio Mishima's updated Noh plays, they were based on things he had said or heard but then sometimes rewrote to emphasize their allegorical qual-ities.[15] Between 1977 and 1979, he produced more than fifty text-image collages, pairing one to six SX-70 photographs with a dialogue, a series that he titled *He:/She:*.[16] Like David Mamet, whose landmark play *Sexual Perversity in Chicago* (1974) also criticized U.S. society by representing an up-to-the-minute "battle between the sexes," the *He:/She:* series pre-sented a stark view of gender relations during a post–sexual revolution, pre-AIDS era: a permissive and narcissistic time in which relationships between men and women seemed to be getting more aggressive and antagonistic.

Heinecken's inclination in this series was to put word and image at odds with each other; although the texts and photographs related to one another, it was rarely in an unambiguous way. For example, in *She: I sup-pose some dumb thing I say . . .* (1976–78), Heinecken presents an array of self-portraits as a horizontal grid. In each he poses with what appears to be a different woman, although in the central image the person's face is too obscured by shadows to tell (Plate 6.1).[17] Below these double portraits, the handwritten dialogue suggests that at least some of the transcribed conversation is fictionalized. "She: I suppose some dumb thing I say will end up in these writings. He: It's possible. She: You'd twist it around, wouldn't you? He: Probably, but I don't identify anyone personally anyway. She: I know, and that's what's wrong with it."[18] In addition to casting doubt on its own veracity, the conversation also makes the images more enig-matic. Although it is plain that it is Heinecken in each photograph, it is not clear if the women are all the same person (as the dialogue implies), or two or three different people. The Polaroid SX-70 photograph, a type of image that connoted privacy and intimacy, is here rendered less personal, less individuated. The female speaker is decentered, while her words are clearly critical of Heinecken as both a subject and an author.

This sardonic, somewhat despairing battle between the sexes contin-ues in other works of the series, like *She: I am beginning to feel uncomfortable with you sometimes* (1975–78). Another SX-70/text montage, *She: You prob-ably don't even know my last name* (1974–78), pairs an oddly cropped female nude standing against a wall in a motel room with an improvised bar on a

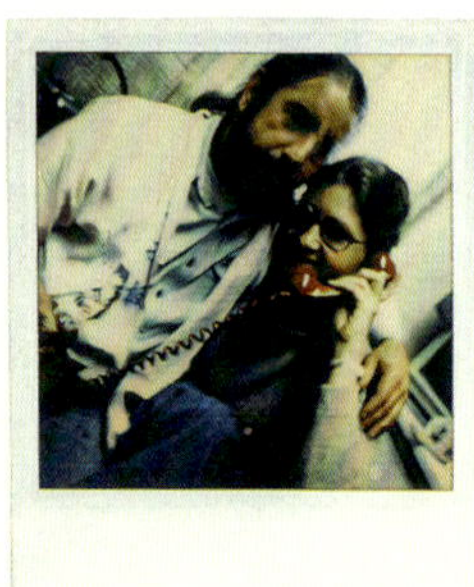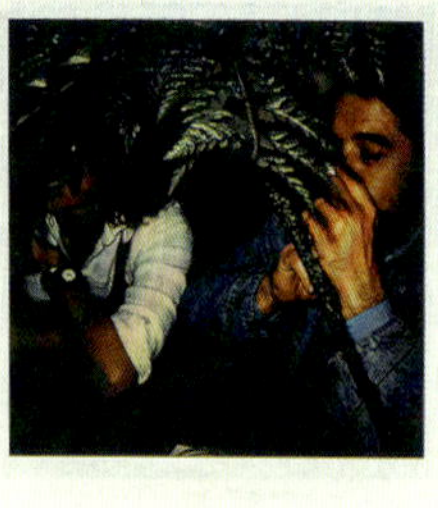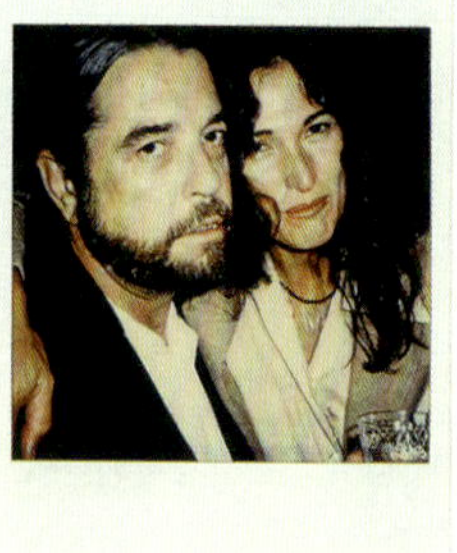

PLATE 6.1. Robert Heinecken, *She: I suppose some dumb thing I say . . .* (1976–78). Three internal dye-diffusion transfer prints (SX-70 Polaroid) and text on board, 11 x 14 inches (27.9 x 35.6 cm). Private collection. COPYRIGHT 2022 THE ROBERT HEINECKEN TRUST, CHICAGO.

table in the same space; between these two images, an exterior shot of a motel appears, a flamingo decorating its railing.[19] Below the three SX-70 prints, which connote a sexual encounter outside of the home, a dialogue suggests anonymous sex and postcoital misunderstanding. Once again, the view of gender relations seems laced with despair. "She: You probably don't even know my last name. He: No, I don't, but I know your body. She: It's Clover. He: Is it yours or your husband's? She: My name, or my body?" Proper names are made ambiguous, and marriage is compared to slavery. The dialogues in other montages like *He: I like the pool for its geometry* (1975–78) and *He: that's a very nice place for a mole* (1977) seem less antagonistic and despairing, but they still evoke the sparring wordplay that was a mainstay of couples on television for many decades. This repartee was generally presented as a battle of both intellects and values: for excellent examples of this sparring, see Lucy and Ricky in *I Love Lucy* (1951–57); Edith and Archie in *All in the Family* (1971–79); and Maddie and David in *Moonlighting* (1985–89). And as is also the case with these television comedies, Heinecken's artworks suggest that the struggle between the sexes never resolves.

Joyce Neimanas introduced Heinecken to the SX-70 as a tool of artistic practice, and thus it is not surprising that a number of the *He:/She:* collages represent intimate encounters between the two of them.[20] The couple called the SX-70 "the bedroom camera," acknowledging its early role in the development of the amateur pornography genre.[21] *He: Lying here—the sun is directly in my eyes* (1976–78) presents alternating close-ups of Joyce's vagina and left eye. The dialogue is a jokey and obscure series of one-liners, only loosely related to one another through repeated words and metaphors. "His" lines are written under the images of her genitals, which appear clinical or even scientific in terms of their realism and matter-of-factness; "her" voice, on the other hand, appears beneath glimpses of her face, which are granted more subjectivity and autonomy because the eye takes on different expressions. Words and images analogize and amplify one another, but they do not resolve. Through the dialogue, a surreal scenario unfolds in which Robert seems to be giving Joy oral sex and she seems to get less and less interested in the activity as time progresses. On the dialogue's allegorical level, gender relations are discussed through metaphors of blinding and burning, while processes relating to eyes, ears, mouths, and genitals are intermixed with one another.

As Mark Alice Durant, one of Heinecken's most informed and incisive interpreters, noted in 2003, dialogues like those in the *He:/She:* series are in certain ways "anachronistic" and "embarrassing."[22] Speaking from a later and more socially conscious perspective, Durant argued: "It's simply that these male/female exchanges, far from being revealing, instead betray a limited and highly circumscribed vision of the machinations of heterosexual power dynamics."[23] While it is true that Heinecken is once again focused on male heterosexuality in this series, his artworks do not reinforce or amplify it. Rather, he consistently presents a vision of male heterosexuality that undermines or disrupts itself. The destabilizing attack on heterosexuality can be seen in the undermining of corporeal distinctions that occur in the text, a dismantling that is amplified by the photographs with which the handwriting is paired. By juxtaposing four pairs of eye/vagina combinations, Heinecken stresses their formal similarities, as well as their different but related erotic charges, while simultaneously differences between body parts are broken down. By alternating subject positions, the work further subverts gender distinctions. Although Heinecken maintains his status as the author, his pronouncements are taken to pieces at every turn. Thus although *He: Lying here . . .* evokes the objectification of women through the straight male gaze, it also disrupts the process, by simultaneously invoking female spectatorship, and by presenting a narrative in which senses become confused and Joy ultimately rejects Robert's desires.

Heinecken's destabilization of heterosexuality can also be seen in a number of works that include close-ups of his own penis. In *He: You look pensive* (1975–78), Heinecken juxtaposes an image of his erect member thrusting out of a pair of woman's panties with one of his left hand grasping a pink toy gun in a white holster.[24] These photographs are framed by two more: on the right, a couple, probably Robert and Joyce, in amorous repose on a bedspread or carpeted floor, and on the left the same striped, hotel-like space now devoid of human presence. The connotations of the images are obvious: Heinecken both feminizes and infantilizes his own sexuality and makes it seem furtive as well. The dialogue, which criticizes his actions, also gives the woman the final word: "He: You look pensive. She: I'm wondering if all of this is related to the male menopause. He: Perhaps it's more like a late puberty. She: Both have the same transparency."

In another work, *Ostensibly the Autocross, Used Shoe, Red Word, Valentine Joy, Phone Fetish, Polaroid Puzzle* (1977), Heinecken presents five shots of his penis in various stages of tumescence in contact with a red shoe; in the sixth, rightmost print of the photomontage, the shoe has been replaced by a red phone.[25] The dialogue consists of a creepy exchange between a male telephone caller who seeks to scam a woman into letting him into her home through an offer of a free pair of shoes. As is the case with *He: You look pensive, Ostensibly the Autocross* disrupts heterosexual male sexuality, here by evoking fetishism, obscene phone calls, and violence directed at men's genitals—through the blood-red objects positioned at Heinecken's crotch. And in *She: You have a beautiful cock . . .* (1977), Heinecken presents six close-ups of his penis gradually becoming more erect; once again he is wearing panties. Like the panties, which feminize Heinecken's member, the dialogue undermines the heterosexual male equation of penis size with masculinity.

> she: You have a beautiful cock.
>
> he: Thank you, I . . .
>
> she: Not too big, not too small, just right.
>
> he: I sometimes think about . . .
>
> she: Just remember this—Every woman would much rather be fucked twice by a 5 inch cock than once by a 10 inch one.
>
> he: And 3 times by a 3 ⅓ inch cock, and four times by a . . .
>
> she: Yes. It's always a matter of frequency—and density.[26]

Although by no means entirely negative, Heinecken's representation of heterosexual male desire takes on a dialectical and critical light. And while the dialogue begins with a compliment, throughout the exchange He is constantly being interrupted by She, and the last four lines evoke the idea of a rapidly shrinking penis.

As the *He:/She:* montages developed over the late 1970s, they exhibited a profound change—moving from depictions of Heinecken and people in his own environment to appropriated imagery much more disconnected from the artist's physical presence and everyday life. As a result, Heinecken became more distanced as both author of his art and as agent within its quasi-narratives. This was the case because in the earlier Polaroid-text montages Heinecken was much more clearly identified with the He, in particular because of his use of self-portraits in relation to the handwritten dialogue. Likewise, the presentation of unique Polaroids suggested that the works were transcriptions from the artist's life. At the same time, however, throughout the *He:/She:* series, Heinecken also clearly signaled that he was transforming his life into a work of fiction, thus disrupting the intimate and "real" character of the Polaroid instantaneous prints. He did this through the aphoristic and allegorical dialogues, as well as by posing or staging the figures/objects and embedding them in fragments of narrative. As the series developed in the 1970s and early 1980s, these nonautobiographical aspects became more prominent. Photographic staging continued a process whereby real life became a series of stereotypes, clichés whose reproduction and dissemination changed both consciousness and behavior.

He: How does posing for a drawing differ from a photograph? #4 (1977) marks the transition from a fund of images that seem autobiographical to a collection that appears appropriated (Plate 6.2). The last of four different variants, which juxtapose the same images with different texts, it presents four SX-70 photographs of a life-sized photographic cut-out depicting a blonde woman in a bikini perched on a single bed in what looks like a young man's dorm or bedroom (a pinup hangs on the wall behind the model). The top grid of three SX-70s vary only slightly. Although each shot is unique and has slightly different framing, the only alteration between the prints is the exposure, which runs from light on the right to dark on the left. The fourth SX-70 print, which is tilted and presented below the other three, shows the effect of the camera's flash on the cardboard figure. The dialogue overlays reflexive and psychological concerns.[27] It makes the viewer aware of the photographic apparatus in relation to other forms of artistic representation while it signals the role that pinups and other forms of mass-media images of women play in the formation of heterosexual male sexuality. As a result, in contrast to the earlier quasi-autobiographical montages, *He: How does posing . . .* raises the question much more directly about how media images embodied and reinforced the traditional roles, behaviors, and characteristics of American men and women of the time.

Photographic reflexivity was also central to another early SX-70/text montage that did not fit directly into the *He:/She:* series. *One Double Pack* (1977) presents twenty SX-70 prints depicting a Polaroid Model 2 camera arranged in a grid of five rows and four columns.[28] While the photograph at the top left of the grid depicts the actual camera, each succeeding print is a photograph of the photograph immediately preceding it. As a result, reading from left to right and top to bottom, the camera becomes more and more obscured by darkness and lack of detail. Beneath the photographs

is handwritten text reflecting the how-to jargon of photography specialists and instructors. It states that what we see with our own eyes is not
the same as what the camera sees. This reflexivity characteristic of *One
Double Pack* was initially buried in the *He:/She:* series but it reappears in
the later works that use appropriation. Among the *He:/She:* works that use
rephotography are *She: What's the matter kid?* (1977–79), which contains
three images of bedrooms taken from furniture catalogs, and *He: You have
very exquisite taste in lingerie* (1979), which uses five prints of the same
clothing model in different underwear.[29] As Heinecken's imagery became
less autobiographical and more about the images he consumed, this
reflexivity extended beyond the medium of Polaroid photography and into
the related media of illustrated books and magazines, media that incorporated the Polaroid (as well as all other forms of photographic technology)
as a component in a larger network of intermedial signification.

The *He:/She:* series culminated with a sixty-six-page spiral-bound
book, which reproduced fifty-six dialogues and interspersed them with
ten reproductions of SX-70 prints, all depicting generic couples reshot
from 1970s clothing catalogues (Plates 6.3, 6.4, and 6.5).[30] Unlike the
earlier photographic montages, a more developed He and She emerge—

PLATE 6.2. Robert Heinecken, *He: How does posing for a drawing differ from a photograph? # 4 (of 3)* (1977). Four internal dye-diffusion transfer prints (SX-70 Polaroid) and text on board, 11 x 14 inches (27.9 x 35.6 cm). Collection Center for Creative Photography, The University of Arizona. COPYRIGHT 2022 THE ROBERT HEINECKEN TRUST, CHICAGO.

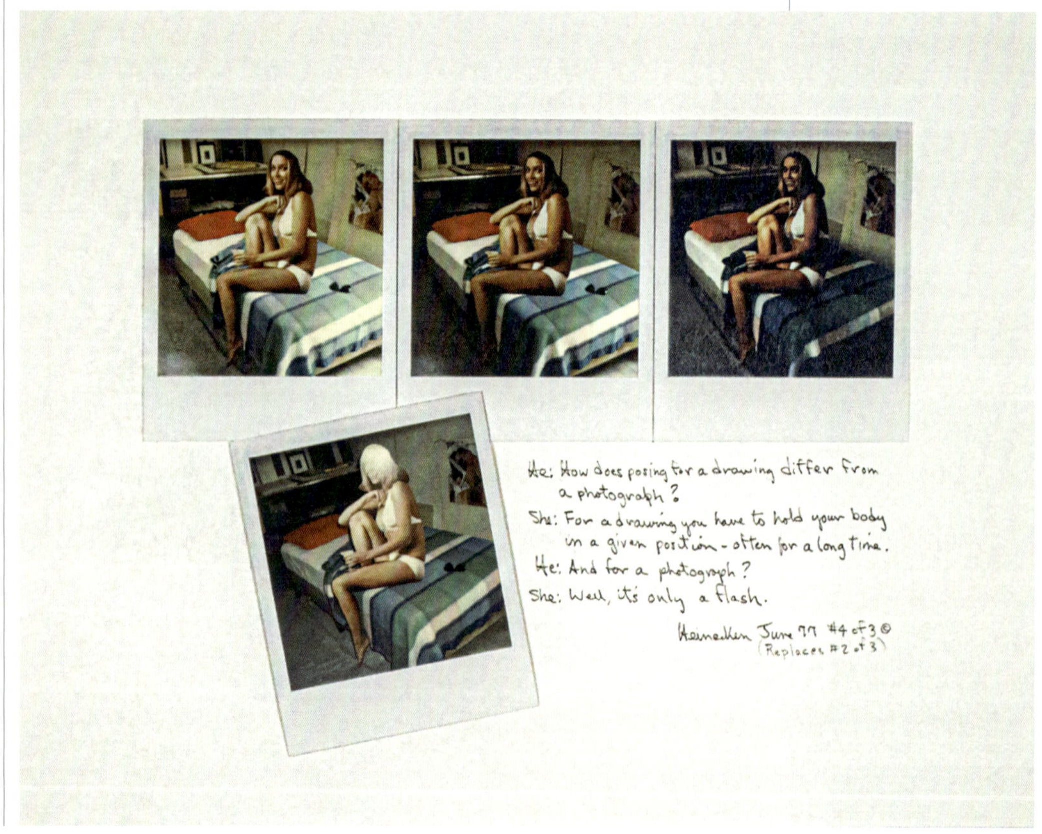

loose characters created by the accumulation of multiple written scenes, although She remains very fragmented and multiple. (While all the photographs are new, a number of the dialogues are reprised from the earlier collage works; here in their new context, which is shaped to resemble a reporter's notebook, they seem to cohere more closely and present partially continuing characters.) As *He:/She:* unfolds, the reader becomes aware that all the conversations seem to be taking place in the context of a dating situation. In comparison to She, He occupies a more stable subject position. He is separated from his wife and family; he is an artist and a teacher; his name may be Robert; he was a fighter pilot in the Marines; and he is generally older than she. She, on the other hand, appears to be one of a changing set of women. This is suggested by the tone and subjects of the dialogues, which depict conversations between people who have just met or who have met each other fairly recently. These shifts of subject position characteristic of She were in part inspired by the writing of Alain Robbe-Grillet, in whom Heinecken remained very interested.

Handwritten on lined pages as if they were transcriptions in a reporter's notebook, the dialogues are short, amusing, and aphoristic. Sex is their primary topic, but they also touch quite frequently on other subjects, such as art, life, the body, eating, drinking, traveling, relationships, sleeping, teaching, objects, vision, names, and popular culture. Taken as a whole, they read as fragments of a larger conversation, clusters of dialogue that speak to a broader condition. Through these conversations, Heinecken paints a picture of a neurotic and intellectual consumer lifestyle, where the script rarely goes as planned: "He: Do you come here often? She: Yes, I suppose so. He: Do you live here? She: Right across the street. He: There are no buildings there. She: In my car. I live in my car."[31] While most of the dialogues are clear, a few are written in a much more disjunctive and ambiguous manner: "He: Maybe tonight we could make love? She: I think that would be an appropriate size relationship. He: I beg your pudding? She: Bunilla."[32] A sense pervades the text that male-female relationships are intimately connected with consumption, and while the man's desires are sometimes frustrated, there is an unequal power relationship in most of the scenes that works to his advantage.

The sexism that emerges in Heinecken's dialogues is disturbing, and even though it is presented in a socially and formally critical way, it is easy to see why critics would want to dismiss or ignore this work. "She: Ideally, what do you want in a woman? He: My cock. She: I'm serious. He: One who picks me out—over 30—has been married—has already done drugs—likes to cook and travel—short enough to see over—tolerates cigarettes—working in a creative field—likes to drink in bars—has had children—is independent—a little zany—likes sex. . . . She: Jesus! What

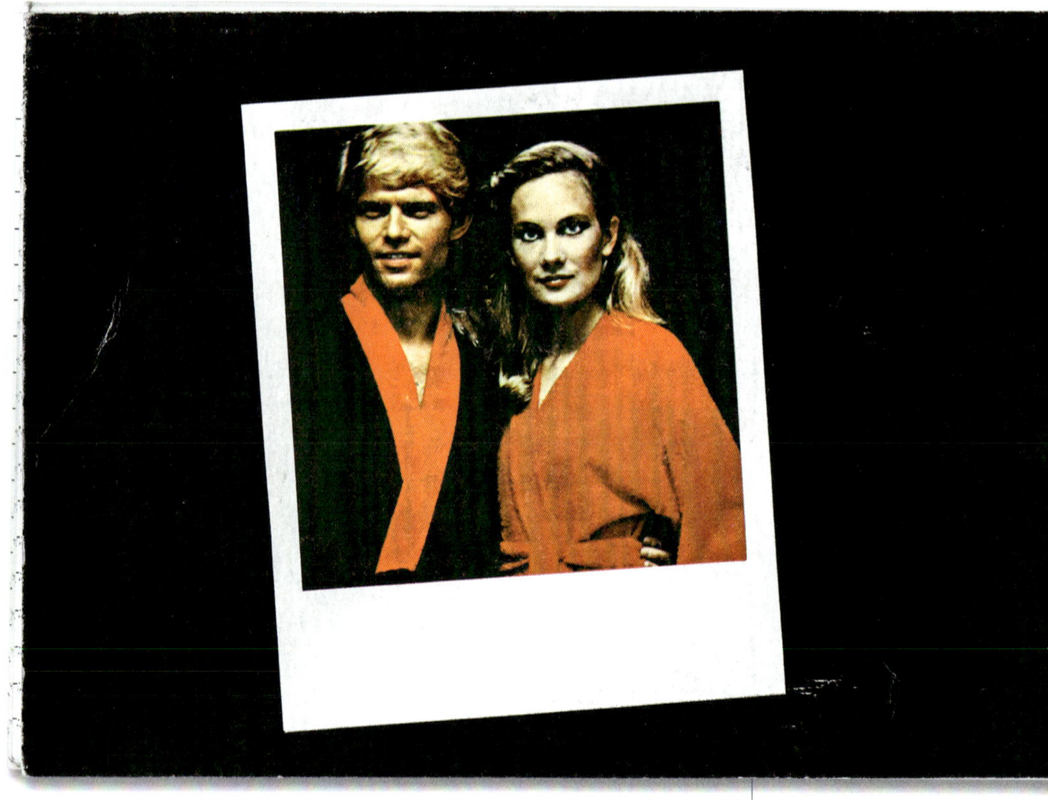

would you settle for? He: Usually any 3 or 4. She: What about now, tonight? He: One who picks me out."[33]

Like the porn paintings and transparencies, the *He:/She:* notebook refuses to disconnect itself from a patriarchal male point of view. Without the illustrations, it might even have been possible to dismiss Heinecken's book as adolescent, sexist, and uncritical of the situations he describes. However, with the Polaroid prints the work signifies differently, transforming into an acute critique of the lifestyle it depicts as well as a trenchant formal investigation into the medium of photography. As in Heinecken's work as a whole, ideology is criticized from within—for him, there was no outside to the dominant value system from which to mount an external or "objective" critique. But he could render the sexist aspects of his own gaze impotent. To create each of the ten images that illustrate *He:/She:* Heinecken began by using the SX-70 camera to rephotograph staged, costumed, and artificially lit images of fashion models posing in clothing catalogues. Using a new and popular photographic process against the grain to provoke reflection on the relationships among photography, the body, and stereotypes of identity, he made his handwritten dialogues even stranger and more uncanny, thus rendering their underlying values and power relations much more apparent and susceptible to attack.

PLATE 6.3. Robert Heinecken, *He:/She:* (Chicago: A Chicago Book, 1980). Spiral-bound book with offset lithography, 6 ½ x 9 ¼ inches (16.5 x 23.5 cm), n.p. (72 pages), eight color illustrations, back and front covers. COPYRIGHT 2022 THE ROBERT HEINECKEN TRUST, CHICAGO.

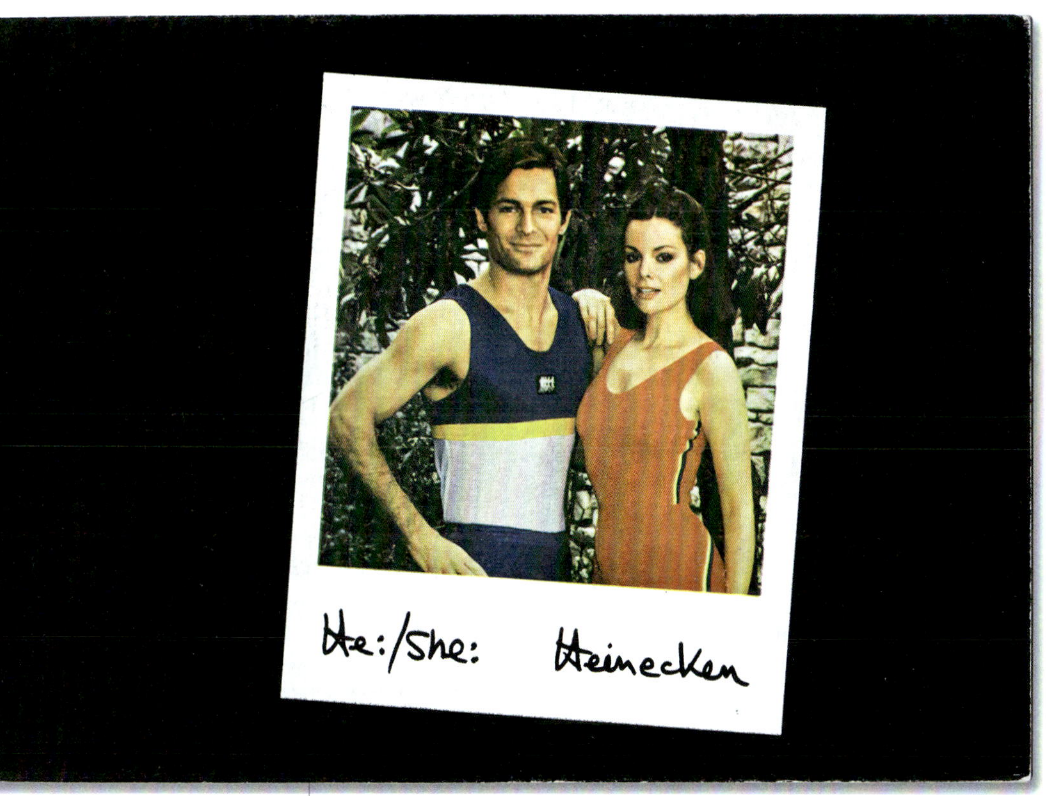

A unique print, the SX-70 photograph was strongly associated with everyday life and the self-documentation of amateur photographers during this time. Because of these associations, the image's indexical qualities were heightened, and the viewer was encouraged to read such photographs as direct and unmediated transcriptions of human lives and activities. By rephotographing staged images of ideal couples in *He:/She:* Heinecken thus associated the indexicality of the Polaroid with the airbrushed clichés of 1970s and 1980s swingers' clothing, thereby bringing a weird uncanniness into everyday life. As we read through the text, the successive images of different couples call the unified identities of both speakers into question. Although the fragmentation of the language renders the female subject unstable, it is through the photographic reproductions that He becomes most strongly divorced from Heinecken's own persona and autobiography. And by suggesting that the various dialogues are the expressions of a shifting cast of different people, the photographs separate the text from the specific life of their original author, thereby transforming the conversations into more general allegories of consumer culture.

The uncanniness and destabilizing character of the reproduced Polaroids come from their obviously staged character: the different couples all seem carefully posed and airbrushed. Despite the indexical and

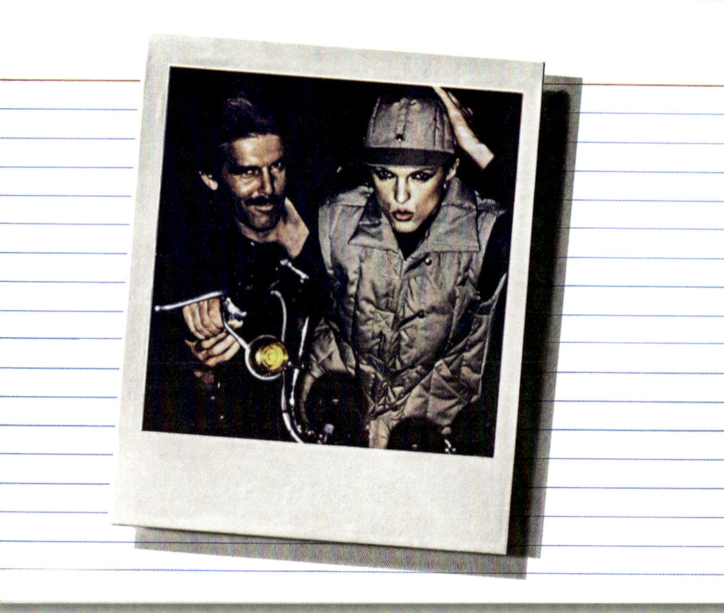

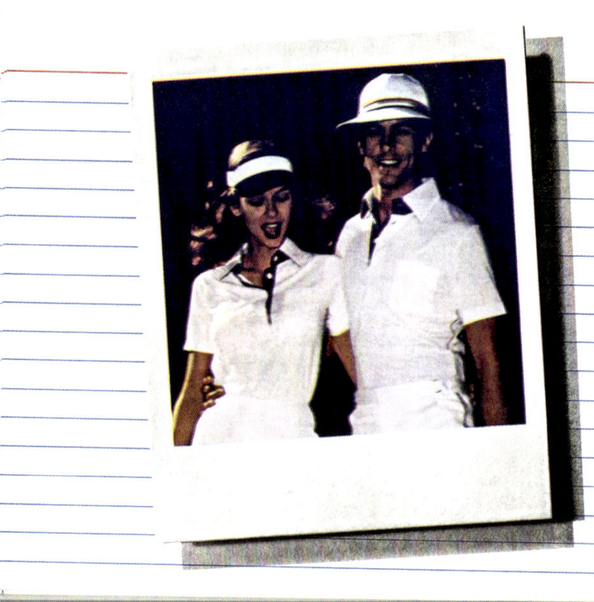

 Robert Heinecken, *He:/She:* (Chicago: A Chicago Book, 1980). Spiral-bound book with offset lithography, 6 ½ x 9 ¼ inches (16.5 x 23.5 cm), n.p. (72 pages), eight color illustrations. COPYRIGHT 2022 THE ROBERT HEINECKEN TRUST, CHICAGO.

She: It's very nice of you to offer to drive me
all the way back to Big Sur.
He: I mean it.
She: Unless of course, you have ulterior motives.
He: All motives are ulterior.
She: That's cynical.
He: Compared to motives, all desires are expressed.

He: I don't think I've seen you around here before.
She: I've been up north for awhile, but this still is
one of my favorite beaches. My name is Beth.
He: What are you looking at there?
She: Just these grains of wet sand. They're so beautiful.
He: Here, look at them through my magnifying glass.
She: Oh, wow! This is even better. Thanks.
He: Everything becomes exquisitely abstracted
and exists beyond literal context. A
separate, private visual world surfaces.
She: I think I'd like to use this glass
to look at the head of your cock.

▼ **PLATE 6.5.** Robert Heinecken, *He:/She:* (Chicago:
A Chicago Book, 1980). Spiral-bound book with offset
lithography, 6 ½ x 9 ¼ inches (16.5 x 23.5 cm), n.p.
(72 pages), eight color illustrations. COPYRIGHT 2022
THE ROBERT HEINECKEN TRUST, CHICAGO.

documentary character suggested by the Instamatic format, in other words, the couples appear generic or stereotypical: ideal types in a consumer culture pantheon representing the early 1980s. And by selecting staged and acted photographs and rephotographing them so that they initially appear to be intimate, the Polaroids in *He:/She:* make plain the forms through which lived experience starts to become fictional, a series of mass-media clichés. Through clothing, consumption, and desire, these images suggest, the consumer is sold a lifestyle in the forms of ideal domestic and leisure situations that seem to make life—and work—worthwhile. As Heinecken's book reveals, it is by encouraging us to dress up and pose that the photographic medium makes us more open and susceptible to media's constant bombardment. And in combination with alcohol, cigarettes, and sex, consciousness becomes a disjunctive collective product, a stream of personal and scripted elements. No mere critique of the straight male gaze, *He:/She:* is a subversively startling work: a book that illuminates the tools and strategies through which the Me Decade extended itself into the 1980s.

Lessons in Posing Subjects

Between 1981 and 1982, Heinecken created approximately forty-one text/SX-70 montages that he called *Lessons in Posing Subjects.* Each work compiled between four and fifteen prints arranged in regular rows or grids along with a typewritten text. Like the later *He:/She:* images, the photographs were copies of advertising illustrations taken from mail-order clothing and underwear catalogues—reproductions that were generally published at about 2 x 3 inches in size.[34] Unlike the *He:/She:* images, however, the SX-70s were not used to illustrate a personal narrative, no matter how allegorical. Instead, these slightly enlarged appropriations were employed to explicate a fantastic and satirical text purporting to tell advertising companies and clients how to best pose models: what to do, what to avoid, and what the meanings of some of the gestures and clothing patterns were.

Lessons in Posing Subjects/Lingerie (Two and Three Subjects) (1981) presents a good example of Heinecken's ironic, pseudosociological approach (Plate 6.6). Two grids of four SX-70s are separated by a three-paragraph text elucidating how to pose lingerie models so as to avoid suggesting lesbianism. Each image in the top row contains a double portrait, while the bottom row presents arrangements of three, a principle of selection that gives the montage a strong typological character. As we scan the images, we think we perceive a more fundamental structure, a gendered performance (women standing next to one another in a configuration that suggests either friendship or sexual attraction) that

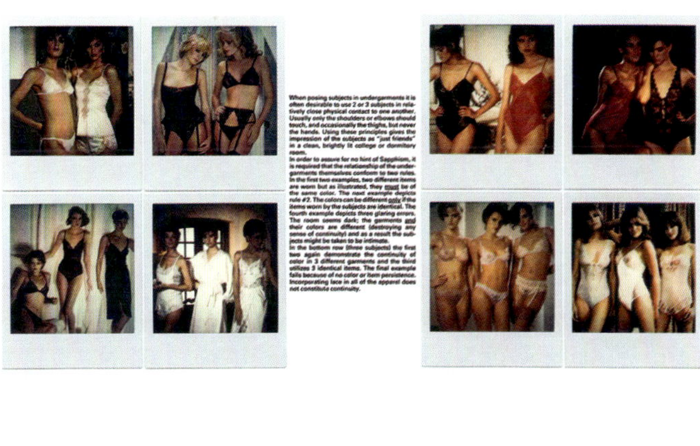

the text explains. At the same time, although the implications of the text seem true—that clothing advertisers employ sexually charged scenarios to inspire viewers to purchase their products—the details of the analysis seem in places a little far-fetched. And because of Heinecken's phrasing and word choices, the analyses frequently seem ironic or absurd. Thus the idealizations carried by the visuals are called into question by the texts, and the more we regard the double and triple portraits, the more their limited nature becomes manifest. Because of the sameness of the models, the spectator becomes aware of a diversity of appearances that do not materialize.

Many of the montages in the series—for example, *Lessons in Posing Subjects/Lingerie (Garters)* (1981) and *Lessons in Posing Subjects/Lingerie (Full Length Nightgowns)* (1981)—purport to help their advertisers avoid making their images too explicitly sexual; like *Lessons in Posing Subjects/Lingerie (Two and Three Subjects),* they end up reminding the spectator about how companies use sex to sell products, and how limited the range of ideals circulated by the mass media truly is. Others like *Lessons in Posing Subjects/(Beds)* (1981) and *Lessons in Posing Subjects/Lingerie/Subject Suitability* (1981) show how the environment changes our perception of the subject (Plate 6.7). In these latter montages, the inadequacies of typologies are no longer the focus but, rather, the contextual nature of visual signification. While most of the montages focus on female models, a few, like *Lessons in Posing Subjects/Matching Facial Expressions* (1981), *Lessons in Posing Subjects/Distancing* (1981), and *Lessons in Posing Subjects/Maintaining Facial Expressions* (1981), employ male models as well (Plate 6.8). In these male or mixed-gender montages, either the ideality of the admired male characteristics is contested or we are prompted to explore the contextual nature of gendered body language, how physical relationships between figures affect and guide the meanings we attribute to them.

Later works in the series—for example, *Lessons in Posing Subjects/ Standard Pose #4 (Fingers/Neck)* (1982) and *Lessons in Posing Subjects/ Standard Pose #7 (Hands Touching)* (1982)—are the most deadpan (Plate 6.9). Heinecken's focus here is on female poses and the significations that they convey. Because of the repetition of gestures between the rows and grids of photographs, they stress the highly learned and conventional nature of body language and gesture; they seem the least undermining of the typological frameworks on which they seem to rely. Finally, in a few montages like *Lessons in Posing Subjects/Hair Style Transformation* (1982) or *Lessons in Posing Subjects/Maintaining Facial Expressions (Female, Blond)* (1981), Heinecken selects the same model sporting multiple attires and hairstyles. In these works, the viewer is made aware of how personality seems to change based on clothes, grooming, lighting, and mise-en-scène or context.

Heinecken's *Lessons in Posing Subjects* series anticipates the "gangs" works of Richard Prince of the mid-1980s and 1990s.[35] Like Prince's postmodernist appropriations, Heinecken's gridded multiples undermined concepts of originality and authorship, while at the same time presenting themselves as unmasking ideologies promulgated by the magazine industry. Despite these similarities, *Lessons* are less deadpan and more self-mocking than Prince's montaged appropriations; they also differentiate themselves from Prince's work through their greater textual emphasis, which ascribes greater culpability to the spectator who is also very much a reader and a capitalist: we are addressed as clothing manufacturers endeavoring to maximize the sales of our products.[36] The *Lessons in Posing Subjects* series also seems highly aware of the quasi-scientific use of photographs in conceptual art of the 1970s, although once again Heinecken's works distinguish themselves by seeming to ridicule their own premises in a much more sarcastic, quasi-juvenile way. But more than postmodernism and conceptualism, Heinecken's series must be understood in terms of the conceptual framework with which he was engaging, specifically that of the sociologist Erving Goffman, whose concept of selfhood as performative and culturally constructed had a powerful impact on American sociology between the mid-1950s and late 1970s.

Goffman's *Gender Advertisements*

As curators and scholars have noted, Heinecken's *Lessons* series was directly inspired by Goffman's *Gender Advertisements*, a sociological

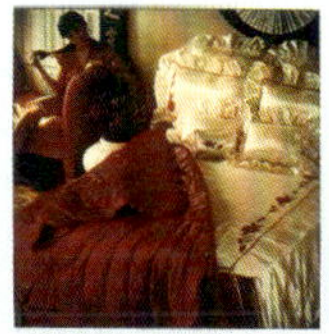 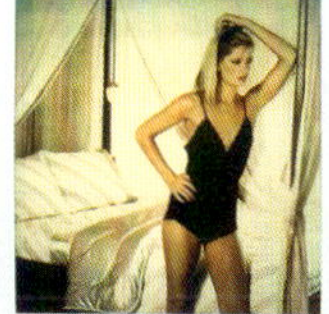 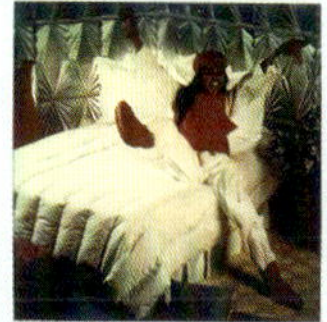 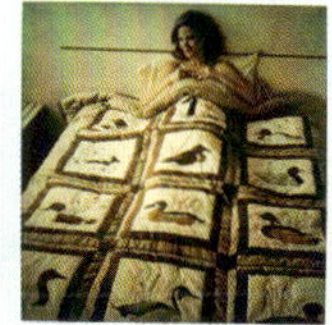

Combining the subject with a bed is a rather complex pose. The prevailing mores of the culture require certain applications. The top row depicts four acceptable approaches which mitigate the problem. a. The subject contemplates the bed from a respectful distance. b. The subject backs toward the bed without looking at it. c. The fully clothed subject waking up from a nap, gets out of the bed. d. If the subject is to actually be in the bed, homey non-exotic bed clothes must be used as in this natural wild-life motif.
In the bottom row the first example clarifies the kind of bed in which it would not be possible to place a subject. It clearly does not qualify as non-exotic. The next three would effectively mitigate the circumstances of an integrated subject.

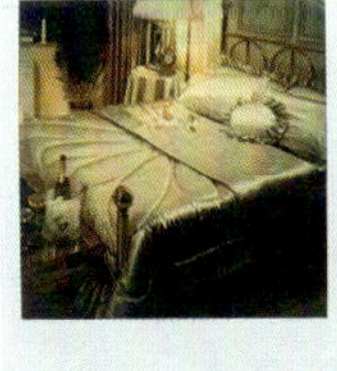 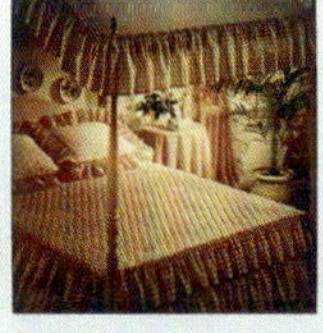 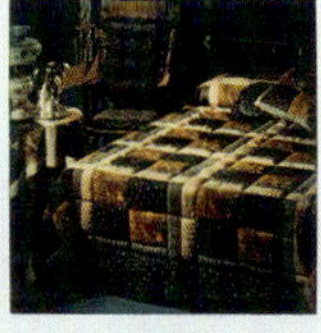 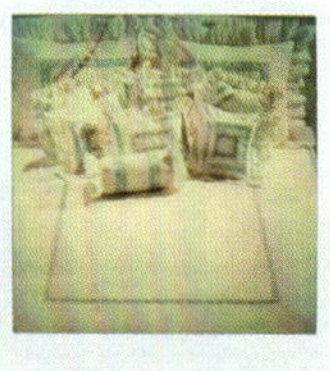

Hinrichen 1981

Lessons In Posing Subjects/(Beds)

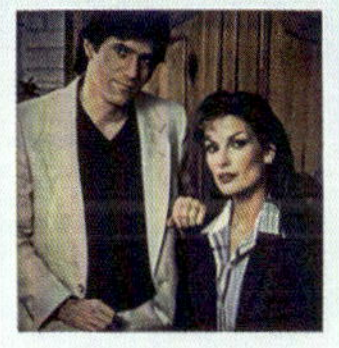 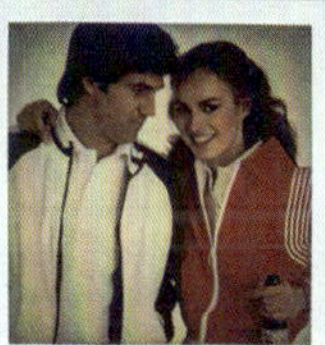 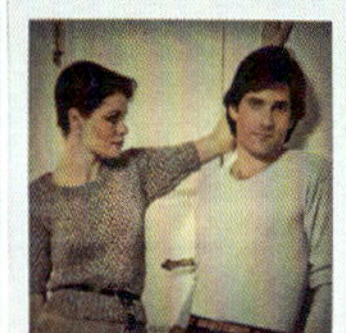

It is sometimes necessary to be able to instruct the subject to project a rather disinterested facial expression even though circumstances outwardly seem to be otherwise. In the top row the subject demonstrates this ability which is termed "distancing." In the bottom row he shows variations of how to achieve "distancing" without seeming to.

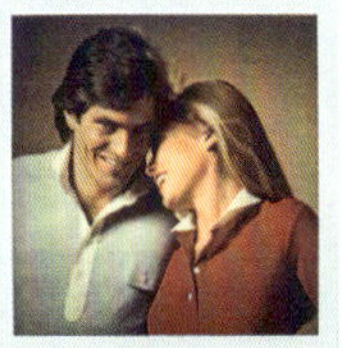 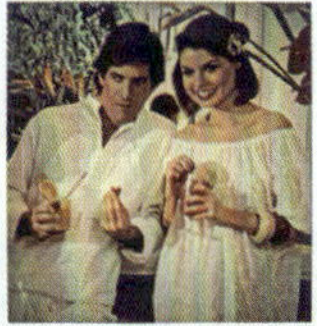 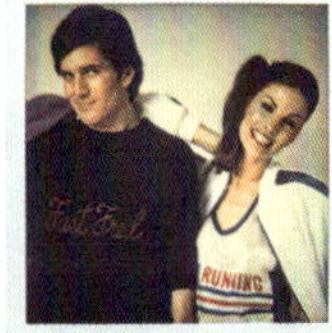

Lessons in Posing Subjects/Distancing

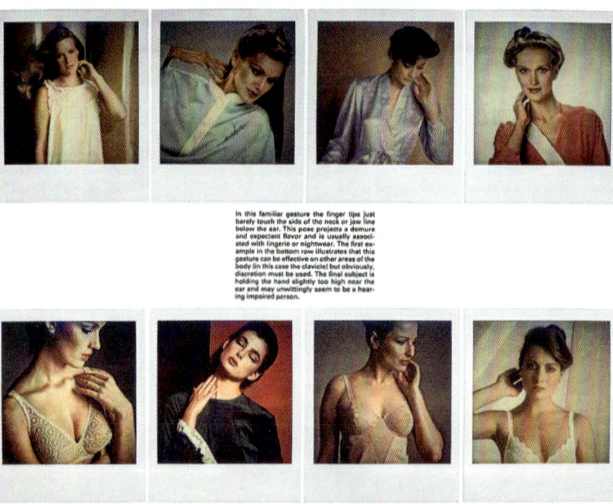

analysis of gender through the medium of photography.[37] First published in 1976 as a special issue of *Studies in the Anthropology of Visual Communication*, Goffman's analysis was republished by Harper and Row as a large-format book and marketed to a more general audience in 1979.[38] Around 60 percent of the volume comprised a pictorial section of photographs—primarily drawn from print advertising—depicting men, women, and children engaged in a variety of activities. Arranged in rows and columns and interspersed with short explanatory texts, these images repeated gestures, relationships, and props so as to suggest typologies of behavior that expressed gender. The sociologist focused on six different aspects of gender display: (1) relative size; (2) ways of touching or grasping; (3) "function ranking" (who takes the more controlling role in the depicted scene); (4) family relationships; (5) rituals of subordination (expressing a lesser status to another person); and (6) "licensed withdrawal" (not being fully present or aware in a situation). As he explained across three introductory chapters, photography—and in particular advertising photography—presented the ritualized appearances, expressions, behaviors, objects, contexts, and scenes through which gender was performed and constituted.

Already in his first book, *The Presentation of Self in Everyday Life* (1956), Goffman argued that the subject was in very fundamental ways socially constructed—formed through performances with other people in the context of everyday life.[39] We learned to become the people we were, first, by watching and listening to others, and then by engaging in social interactions in which we not only carried out everyday activities but also performed our social roles, acting out our age, gender, class, ethnicity, race, and profession to others who would then either accept or reject our performances. By focusing on human interaction, the co-presence of actors in small groups, and analyzing it in terms of concepts drawn from drama, games, and rituals, sociologists could discover the more fundamental structures that organized human societies.[40] One of the key concepts that emerged from this approach was "frame analysis," the disclosure of schemata of interpretation that allow people to identify strips of activity like events, deeds, and practices.[41] This idea of the frame through which we identified both natural and social situations and processes would become extremely useful for the analysis of the compressed and highly symbolic language and storytelling of advertising and the mass media. By interpreting experience in terms of common frames like the family dining room, the school, a restaurant, and a doctor's office, people knew what to expect and how to dress and act.

In *Gender Advertisements,* Goffman continued this approach to human interaction in the mid-1970s while radicalizing it in a number of ways. Although taking an interactionist perspective with regard to the analysis of social structure did not require one to embrace a fully social-constructionist concept of the subject, Goffman so stressed social behavior by this time that he seemed close to this position.[42] As he put it in *Gender Advertisements*:

> What the human nature of males and females really consists of, then,
> is a capacity to learn to provide and to read depictions of masculinity
> and femininity and a willingness to adhere to a schedule for presenting
> these pictures, and this capacity they have by virtue of being persons, not
> females or males. One might just as well say there is no gender identity.
> There is only a schedule for the portrayal of gender. There is no relation-
> ship between the sexes that can so far be characterized in any satisfactory
> fashion. There is only evidence of the practice between the sexes of choreo-
> graphing behaviorally a portrait of relationship.[43]

It is thus not surprising that Goffman's sociological concept of the self as a performer in the midst of everyday life has been seen as anticipating Judith Butler's philosophical claims that gender is performative and that it does not rest on a preexisting biological difference known as "sex."[44] Culture, not biology, is the determining factor for both authors, and they acknowledge that sociologists and philosophers must begin with what they observe, which is always culturally constructed.

In another book, his case study *Stigma: Notes on the Analysis of Spoiled Identity* (1963), Goffman distinguished "social identity," referring to the everyday ways people are identified and categorized, from "personal identity," which designated what makes someone distinct from other people, as well as from ego or "felt identity," which indicated the feelings one had about one's identity.[45] In *Gender Advertisements*, he suggested that these aspects of identity were always highly intertwined: the self was a continuous locus of mediation between both public and private, conscious and unconscious, drives, intentions, and mandates.

Goffman was furthermore at pains to articulate his method of visual analysis, distinguishing between lived reality, (unstaged) vernacular and documentary photographs, (staged) advertising photographs, and the broader structures he sought to expose. His account of his procedure is instructive: "The pictures reproduced were selected at will from newspapers and current popular magazines. . . . They were chosen to fit into sets, each set to allow the displaying, delineating, or mocking up of a discrete theme bearing on gender."[46] The isolated themes revealed visual gender typologies: "Different pictorial examples of a single theme bring different contextual backgrounds into the same array, highlighting untold disparities even while exhibiting the same design. It is the depth and breadth of these contextual differences which somehow provide a sense of structure, a sense of a single organization underlying mere surface differences."[47] Goffman used visual evidence, in other words, to both generate and support a conceptual mapping of the conventional aspects of gender display and behavior in the 1970s.

Far from serving as mere illustrations of his behavioral categories pertaining to gender, Goffman's typologies were thus designed to initiate his readers into a type of sociological visual analysis that they could direct toward a number of distinct fields of inquiry:

> The pictures I have un-randomly collected of gender relevant behavior can be used to jog one's consideration of three matters: the gender behavioral styles found in actual life, the ways in which advertisements might present a slanted view thereof, and the scene-production rules specific to the photographic frame. Although my primary interest is actual gender behavior, the pictures are accompanied by textual glosses that raise questions of any order that might be stimulated by the pictures.[48]

In addition to being open-ended about the goals of the visual analysis of gender display, the investigator could focus on real life, advertising, or the medium of photography itself. Goffman was also explicit about the lack of completeness of the visual evidence that he presented. Moreover, although he was focused on behavior and expressions that pertained to the differences between the sexes, he did not even concentrate on the most obvious of these. Instead, he often picked examples that reversed the expected display, arranging them at the end of the typological sequence, so as to somehow prove the rule by noting outliers or exceptions:

> By and large, I did not look for pictures that exhibited what seemed to
> me to be common to the two sexes, whether just in pictures or in reality
> as well. Nor for pictures that dealt with sex differences which I assumed
> were widely and well-understood. The vast amount of what is—at least to
> me—unremarkable in advertisements is thus vastly underrepresented. . . .
> *But given these limitations, once a genderism was identified as one worth
> mocking-up, almost all sex role exceptions and reversals I came across were
> selected.* . . . Also, in the case of each still, by imagining the sexes switched
> and imagining the appearance of what results, one can jar oneself into
> awareness of stereotypes. By keeping this switching task in mind, the
> reader can generate his own glosses and obtain a cue to the possible
> merit of mine.[49]

Not only was *Gender Advertisements* intended to help the viewer who was
also a reader see gender as culturally constructed, but it was designed to
encourage a type of visual practice that would search for idealizations and
stereotypes in both real life and the mass media.

At a fundamental level, Goffman wanted to draw attention to important structural similarities between real life and the idealized world
depicted by the mass media: both were based on performance and ritual,
and both were productive of the differences that they also represented.
Furthermore, as *Gender Advertisements* suggests, it was the medium
of photography that facilitated their ever-increasing interaction and
mutual influence:

> I want to argue now that the job the advertiser has of dramatizing the
> value of his product is not unlike the job a society has of infusing its social
> situations with ceremonial and with ritual signs facilitating the orien-
> tation of participants to one another. Both must use the limited "visual"
> resources available in social situations to tell a story; both must transform
> otherwise opaque goings-on into easily readable form. And both rely on
> the same basic devices: intention displays, microecological mapping of
> social structure, approved typifications, and the gestural externalization
> of what can be taken to be inner response. (Thus, just as a Coca-Cola ad
> might feature a well-dressed, happy looking family at a posh beach resort,
> so a real family of modest means and plain dress might step up their level
> of spending during ten days of summer vacation, indeed, confirming that a
> self-realizing display is involved by making sure to photograph themselves
> onstage as a well-dressed family at a posh summer resort.)[50]

As both a professional and an amateur practice, photography was teaching Americans to adjust their bodies to match the visual typologies that
circulated in their culture—gender (and other) ideals that were confirmed
and memorialized in their performances and that continued to produce a

wealth of new examples by which they could augment and develop their evolving individual identities.

As a result, by understanding the role that photography played in their lives, as well as the particular strategies both photographers and their subjects used to signal the various identities that pertained to the self, Americans in the 1970s might be better prepared to both utilize photography and control its effects. For this reason,

> when one looks, then, at the presentation of gender in advertisements, attention should be directed not merely to uncovering advertisers' stereotypes concerning the differences between the sexes—significant as these stereotypes might be. Nor only examine these stereotypes for what they might tell us about the gender patterns prevalent in our society at large. Rather one should, at least in part, attend to how those who compose (and pose for) pictures can choreograph the materials available in social situations in order to achieve their end, namely, the presentation of a scene that is meaningful, whose meaning can be read at a flash. For behind these artful efforts one may be able to discern how mutually present bodies, along with nonhuman materials, can be shaped into expression. And in seeing what picture-makers can make of situational materials, one can begin to see what we ourselves might be engaging in doing. Behind infinitely varied scenic configurations, one might be able to discern a single ritual idiom; behind a multitude of surface differences, a small number of structural forms.[51]

Goffman's ultimate goal, it thus seems, was to empower people in the new, media-saturated environment, helping them to understand photography and read the mass media as a way to improve their own performances of their personal and social identities. More than a way to comprehend the social construction of identity, *Gender Advertisements* was designed to foster a new understanding of the ways in which the contents of American magazines affected, controlled, and regulated the most intimate and seemingly fundamental aspects of American selfhood.

In light of Goffman's analysis of the visual production of gender difference, *Lessons in Posing Subjects* seems to have been both an homage and a critique. The works in the series that are the closest to Goffman's typologies were the last to be produced—montages like *Lessons in Posing Subjects #1–12,* all from 1982. As mentioned above, these are the most deadpan and least absurd, thus coming closest to Goffman's sociological study. In particular, Heinecken's montages that deal with women touching their own bodies—for example, *Lessons in Posing Subjects/Standard Pose #4 (Fingers/Neck)*—evoke the second set of Goffman's typologies, those that catalogue the theme of the "feminine touch."

For Goffman, the feminine touch indicates greater passivity or a more subordinate relationship to action:

> Women, more than men, are pictured using their fingers and hands to trace the outlines of an object or to cradle it or to caress its surface (the latter sometimes under the guise of guiding it), or to effect a "just barely touching" of the kind that might be significant between two electrically charged bodies. This ritualistic touching is to be distinguished from the utilitarian kind that grasps, manipulates, or holds.[52]

For Heinecken, on the other hand, the focus on touching emphasized the sensual and erotic aspects of clothing advertisements, not their subordinate connotations. Significantly, Heinecken's focus on lesbianism suggested that the man was no longer necessary. Once again, his ironic, pseudosociological visual gender analysis turned against the straight male gaze, undermining the patriarchal claim that men are positioned at the center of their societies. In addition, and perhaps even more important, Heinecken's use of the SX-70 photograph—with its connotations of amateurism and its connections to real life—as a tool for appropriation emphasized more strongly than Goffman's text how the medium of photography helped Americans objectify themselves in relation to the mass media. Although Heinecken cast doubt on the sociological truth of his typologies, he trenchantly documented how Americans were willingly turning themselves into clichés through the practices of amateur photography.

Sontag's *On Photography*

As Heinecken's work with the SX-70 process made abundantly clear, instantaneous photography was altering everyday life during the 1970s and early 1980s. Heinecken's engagement with Polaroid photography extended beyond the SX-70 process, however, and in this regard it intersected with another aspect of Polaroid's great legacy: the company's promotion of photography as an independent art. In 1978, Heinecken presented two large-scale portraits of Susan Sontag, whose *On Photography* (1977) had been published the previous year and was creating great controversy among both photographers and photography critics (Plate 6.10).[53] A complex and polemical analysis of the medium, which had its origins in a series of essays published in the *New York Review of Books*, *On Photography* criticized the instrument for its deceptive characteristics, its power to inflict violence, and its nature as a technology of mastery and control. "To photograph," Sontag wrote, is to appropriate the thing photographed. It means putting oneself into a certain relation to the world that feels like knowledge—and, therefore, like power. A now notorious first fall into alienation, habituating people to abstract the world into printed words, is supposed to have engendered that surplus of Faustian energy and psychic damage needed to build modern, inorganic societies. But print seems a less treacherous form of leaching out the world, of turning it into a mental object, than photographic images, which now provide most of the knowledge people have about the look of the past and the reach of the present. What is written about a person or an event is frankly an interpretation, as are handmade visual statements, like paintings and drawings. Photographed images do not seem to be state-ments about the world so much as pieces of it, miniatures of reality that anyone can make or acquire.[54]

Presenting photography as a paradigmatic expression of the capitalist and consumerist worldview produced by advanced industrial societies in the West,[55] Sontag argued that the medium reinforced the power of the status quo by promoting passivity and a lack of comprehension.[56]

Responding to Sontag's indictment of the medium, which accused it of beautifying violence and mystifying reality, Heinecken employed Pola-roid technologies to confound clear distinctions between author and subject, image and text—distinctions on which Sontag appeared to base her account. Titled *The S.S. Copyright Project "On Photography,"* Heinecken's work consisted of two collages of black-and-white Polaroid instant prints of various sizes stapled to a board, along with a one-page typewritten text.[57] Both portraits were appropriations of *On Photography*'s dustcover photograph of Sontag's face taken by Jill Krementz in 1974; both con-sisted of tiny fragments—some whole, some cut—of multiple prints assembled so as to reproduce a somewhat grainy (or pixilated) image of the author's visage.[58] The portraits differed, however, in terms of the source materials that were used to construct Sontag's face. The left por-trait was made up of (differently exposed) photographs taken from pages of text that appeared in *On Photography.* The right portrait consisted of photographs depicting Heinecken's studio and everyday environment; in addition to the studio shots, images of palm trees, cars, motorcycles, and posing figures—Heinecken and his friends—were featured.

Reading differently from close up and far away, Sontag's double portrait reminds the viewer that even photographs—supposedly direct traces taken from the real world—are constructed. Made from entirely different types of photographic subjects (printed text on the left and per-sonal images on the right), they stress the fact that photographs have the ability to signify in highly arbitrary and contradictory ways. The accompanying typewritten text, which enjoins the spectator to compare

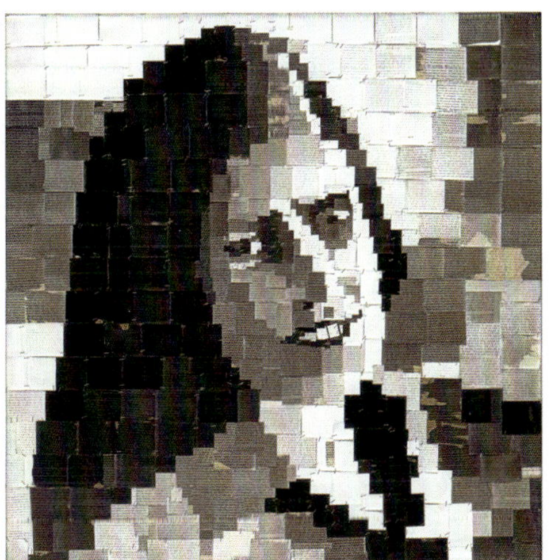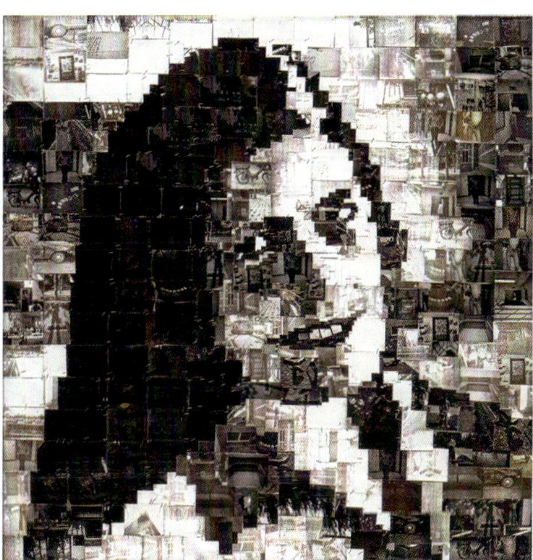

the two photographic collages and reflect on both their similarities and their differences, emphasizes the absurdity of a gaze that tries to decide which image is more meaningful, resolved, or artistic.[59] Asking a series of questions about the characteristics of each portrait, it suggests that the traditional distinctions that we use to classify photographs—for example, art versus document, professional versus amateur, or intentional versus arbitrary—often break down when applied.

In addition, the work's title, which evokes issues of copyright, raises questions of authorship: who is actually the author of this—and by implication, because of its mechanical nature, potentially any—photographic work? The associated text suggests a number of different possible answers. Heinecken claims authorship at the bottom of the page by asserting his own 1978 copyright of the work. At the same time, however, he also notes Jill Krementz's 1974 copyright of the photograph on which the two images were based. He also notes the "assistance" of Krementz and Hali Rederer in the production of his collages. Rederer was the photographer who made the source photographs of Heinecken and his environment for the right-hand Sontag collage, and although he does not give her credit as the author of the final work, she—like Krementz—is specifically acknowledged as having a hand in its production. Finally, Sontag is not credited at all, even though she is the author of all the text that makes up the left-hand collage portrait. Authorship, Heinecken's work suggests, is a complicated concept, particularly for works that are based on the works of others—like *The S.S. Copyright Project* itself, as well as Sontag's *On Photography,* which purported to be a work of critical commentary although it more closely resembled a high-level theoretical account of the primary roles that photography played in the development and functioning of modern consumer societies.

Although Heinecken's Sontag collages have been interpreted as being critical of her book and its account of photography's nature, the actual state of affairs is far more complex.[60] Instead of rejecting Sontag's positions, Heinecken responded with a work that engaged with many of her fundamental distinctions—word versus image, representation versus reality, authorship versus mechanical transcription, and truth versus propaganda—without resolving the issues that these distinctions raised in any definitive way. Instead, as he did when he was criticized in the late 1970s and 1980s for misogyny and promulgating a pseudo–left-wing critique, he countered elliptically, producing a work that seemed to amplify some of the very paradoxes with which Sontag sought to engage in her influential work. An understanding of photography, his double portrait seems to suggest, can only result from a bringing of overarching concepts together with specific examples—a practice that the highly theoretical Sontag was accused of avoiding.[61] And when one does so, what results is not the disclosure of some fundamental "essence" of photography but, rather, a series of concepts and practices that lead in a multitude of different directions.

Large-Format Polaroid Photography

If, as Heinecken's SX-70 work suggests, Polaroid was strongly associated with the vernacular and with amateurism in the 1970s, the corporation also had a highly technical and artistic side as well. Not only did Polaroid amass a large collection of art photography in the 1980s, but they also developed larger and larger cameras to take even more detailed photographs.[62] They were also continually innovating their unique direct-positive films, aiming for richer color, increased fidelity, and less grain, among other characteristics. In addition, the Polaroid Corporation invited select artists to use and experiment with their large-format cameras and film technologies, supplying equipment, technicians, and even funding for them to make new and innovative works. Polaroid, in short, wanted to be recognized as producing tools for artists: creative individuals who would "author" artworks. They also wanted renown for the verisimilitude and color of their products—as well as for their ability to rival artworks made in other media.

Heinecken was invited by Polaroid in 1983–84, 1985, and 1988 to explore their 24 x 24 inch camera, opportunities that he used to make three different types of work.[63] During his first visit, he worked with technicians at the company's headquarters and at the Museum of Photographic Arts, San Diego; during the second two grant periods, Heinecken worked at the School of the Museum of Fine Arts, Boston, where he was assisted by John Reuter.[64] Some of the series were developed over multiple visits.[65] One of the earliest was *Tuxedo Striptease* (1984), a horizonal film strip consisting of ten 24 x 20 inch Polacolor prints, depicting a series of different women and one male baby, all connected through their attire, which referenced male formal dress (Plate 6.11). As in the *Lessons on Posing Subjects* series, the various images were all catalogue appropriations, but the goal was not to create a typology. Instead, *Tuxedo Striptease* suggested a short scene in which a "woman" seemingly strips for a (presumably) male spectator.

Initially, the scene that *Tuxedo Striptease* constructs seems a very old, obvious, and sexist one. Although each model is different, the figures develop a progressive action when the spectator reads from left to right, a movement that partially unifies them. We interpret the women, in other words, as a single woman, a living individual, captured in a photographic sequence, progressively disclosing herself to us in an increasingly sexually explicit way. The final (rightmost) image comes as a surprise, but also perhaps as a crude joke that continues the sexual metaphor: the striptease culminates with the birth of a child. At the same time, there is something purposefully in bad taste about *Tuxedo Striptease,* a sterile obviousness that undermines its leering point of view. The images, although erotic, seem banal; and their artificial and airbrushed nature is emphasized by the fact that they are enlarged between eight and ten times their original scale. Allowed to examine the images in detail, we furthermore become aware of the fact that most of them are collaged. Heinecken has cut the figures out and placed them against different, sometimes monochromatic backgrounds. Thus although *Tuxedo Striptease* initially seems somewhat univocal and communicative of pernicious gender stereotypes—that the ideal woman is both sexually available and fertile—closer examination reveals this not to be the case. Not only does it confound clear gender distinctions by garbing a feminine striptease in masculine clothing, but it also provokes awareness of the mass media by blowing up the details of print production and the facture of montage. Once again, while summoning the straight male gaze, Heinecken also deconstructs it.

Heinecken also used the 24 x 24 inch Polaroid camera to make photograms of food, a practice he started more than a decade before in other photographic media. Already in 1971, he developed this new photogram technique, which in some ways seemed closer to the original technique of William Henry Fox Talbot and Anna Atkins. Moving away from the mass-media appropriation strategy that he developed for *Are You Rea* and used in *Mansmag,* he made black-and-white photograms of comestibles that he purchased from the local diner. Images that were taken directly from real, generally cooked objects, Heinecken's food photograms initially focused

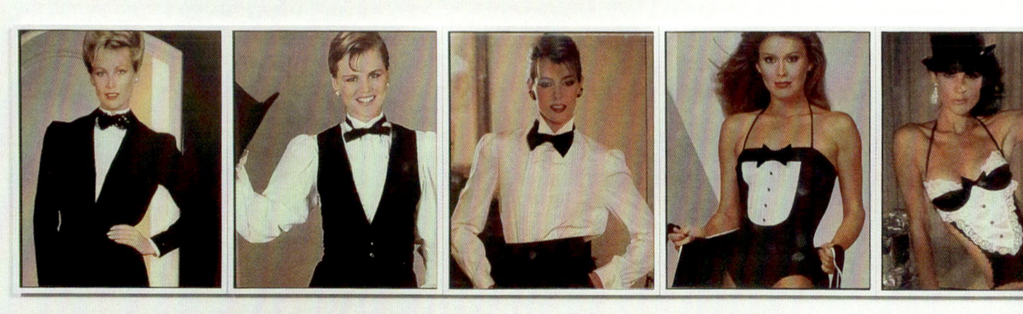

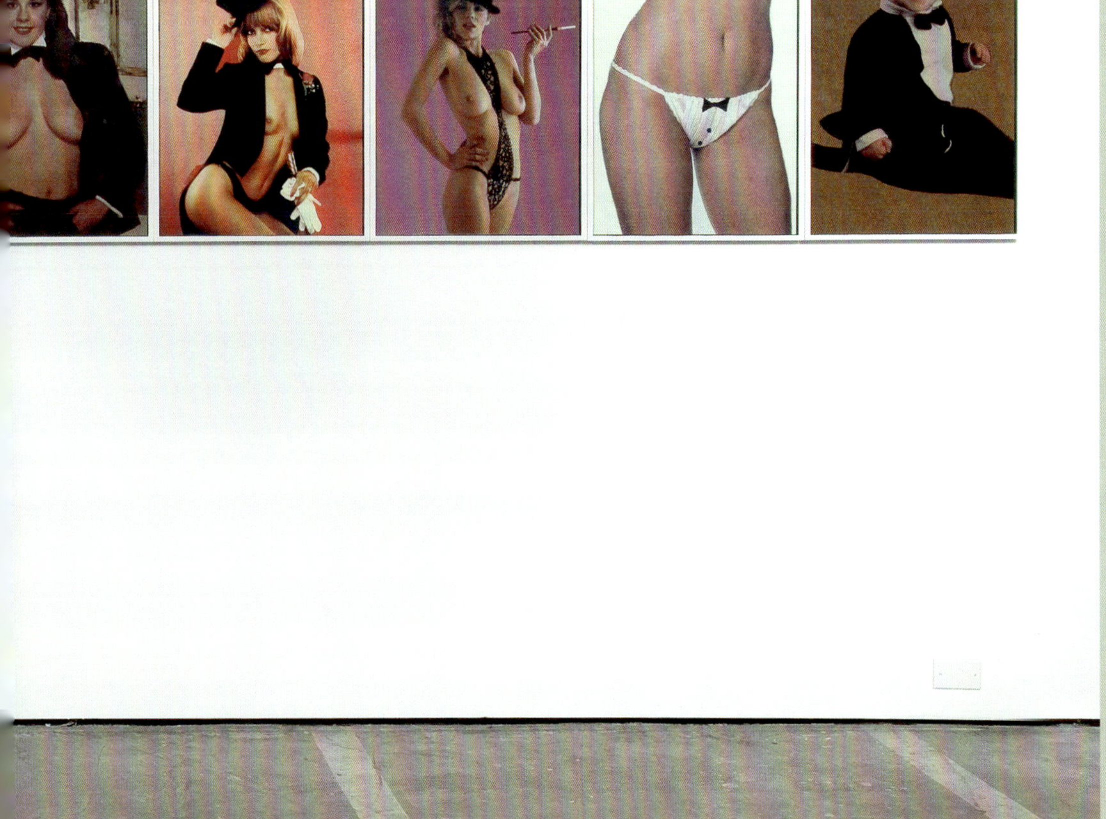

PLATE 6.11. Robert Heinecken, *Tuxedo Striptease* (1984). Ten internal dye diffusion transfer prints (Polaroid Polacolor), each 24 x 20 inches (61 x 50.8 cm). Private collection. COPYRIGHT 2022 THE ROBERT HEINECKEN TRUST, CHICAGO.

on the products of an iconic American institution, a facilitator of both urban and suburban community.

In early works such as *Documentary Photogram/Breakfast and Lunch* (1971), Heineken both evoked and parodied the early use of the photogram technique in service of natural science. In addition to either blocking or transmitting light, the various cooked materials also sometimes stained the paper, combining the effects of chemistry with that of light to produce a final image. This food photogram strategy took on an even more socio-logical character with the portfolio *Just Good Eats for U, Diner* (1971), in which Heinecken contact-printed different types of diner fare on gelatin silver paper and then transferred the image to lithographic plates.[66] As Heineken wrote in the introduction to the portfolio, "This suite of eight original lithographs . . . [was] printed by the artist using the offset method. The work represents five typical feeding times of the American middle class. Breakfast, Coffee Break, Lunch, Cocktails and Dinner."[67] A quasi-scientific presentation of the typical American meal, the portfolio seems like it was designed to function as part of a Goffmanian analysis explor-ing the frames that determine the sociality of everyday life. At the same time, however, it also recalls the botanical photograms of Anna Atkins and the mid-nineteenth-century scientific uses to which the process was put. Through its humor, *Just Good Eats* thus celebrates and undermines pho-tography's botanical and sociological gazes, defamiliarizing them, while at the same time provoking reflection on the increasing objectification of American society.

But it was only in the 1980s, when Heinecken returned to the food photogram technique, now working with direct-positive color papers, that its full material and sociological implications could emerge, insights that revealed class inequality in photography and art. Initially he worked in Cibachrome, which like the large-format Polaroid process produced a detailed and color-rich image. Then in 1984, Heineken created a series of photograms titled *Iconographic Art Lunches* in which he used the Polaroid 20 x 24 inch Land camera as a film processor to produce photograms depicting different arrangements of food (Plate 6.12). A series dedicated to documenting the parallel existences of two different groups of people associated with the Museum of Fine Arts, Boston, the affluent visitors to the museum and the art students enrolled at its school, these unique works juxtaposed student artist fare bought from a food truck nearby with visitor lunches purchased from the fancy museum cafeteria on the same day.[68] "The idea," Heinecken said, "is that the students are in the same context as the collectors but worlds apart."[69]

Although he developed the progression of works by exploring a ques-tion of class, Heinecken's interests were formal as well. Significantly,

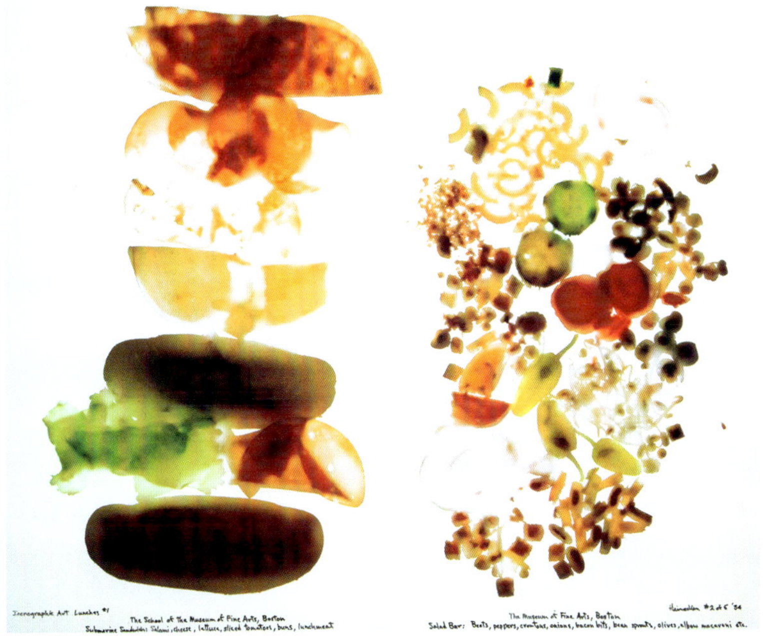

these photograms dropped all background imagery while preserving the general color of the specimens that were used to make them. In addition, the massive Polaroid camera was employed to create an indistinct photogram rather than a highly detailed lens-based image, and thus the cutting-edge photographic technology was turned against itself. As he described the process: "What's involved is very interesting, because the camera is also the processing device of this. In other words, when you pull the paper down out of it, the camera stays there. You photograph with it, the paper goes back up into the machine and is processed in the machine."[70] The logistical issues created by Heinecken's employment of the large-format Polaroid process were novel and Dadaist in character. As he continued:

> So to make a photogram of the food, it had to be figured out how to take the food, bring the paper down out of the thing onto the flat surface, and arrange the food on that paper. Later we put down Plexiglas so that it— But the ones without the Plexiglas are more interesting, because you've got the juices on there and the staining, and the stuff sticks to the paper and all of that. Then you remove the food, run the paper back up into the camera, and process it, which takes only a few minutes or something. Then you can see exactly what you've got. You can rearrange it, you can change the exposure— Because you have no idea what the exposure should be because of the density of the food. Who knows? So anyway, what this produces is a positive color but a transparent image. It's hard to describe. Light is

running through it, so it's showing the silhouette of the food. It makes the background all white so that there's no depth to it at all. It shows you the interior and the basic color of the food.[71]

As suggested by this description, Heinecken greatly enjoyed using photographic technologies against the dictates of common practice to explore photography's possibilities and to uncover aspects of vision that were generally overlooked.

In addition to its formal concerns, *Iconographic Art Lunches* integrated questions of the social construction of identity through consumption and interaction—different diners revealing their class positions vis-à-vis their eating habits within the museum—within a more overtly Marxist (class-based) framework. Like *Just Good Eats*, this series evoked a Goffmanian perspective: focusing on the body, eating, and the contexts of everyday life to explore the social construction of identity. More than *Just Good Eats*, however, the *Iconographic Art Lunches* stressed class division, pointing to the different lifestyles enjoyed by the producers and the consumers of art.

Heinecken's third series of large-format Polaroid photographs were superimpositions of newswomen, composite photographs whose implications will be explored in the next chapter. Head shots of famous news personalities, they were made by twice rephotographing paused videotape on a television screen, recording two different individuals on the same plate. Reflecting on the ever-increasing influence of television on American society and identity in the 1980s, they evince a desire to slow time down and to integrate the ephemeral with the symbolic and the historical.

As Heinecken understood it, large-format Polaroid photography connected verisimilitude with art in a very fundamental and unequivocal way. There was a story he liked to tell about how in later years Land attempted to save his company's fortunes by developing ever larger cameras, including a massive 40 x 80 inch apparatus, whose fidelity and detail were demonstrated to stockholders through a side-by-side comparison of a painting borrowed from the Boston Museum with a Polaroid print made from that very same painting.[72] And it was precisely this association that Heinecken's large-format Polaroid work consistently attacked. Heinecken recounted that the company's technicians actively resisted his directions; they simply could not understand why he would want to utilize their technology in the way he wanted to.[73] During the visit when he made the Polaroid newswomen composites, for example, Heinecken also enlarged an SX-70 photograph:

I had an SX-70, which is their material, and I wanted to blow that up to as big as it could be on their camera. It got down to, "Well, this is a grant that we're giving out for people to experiment with the camera, and you could do this with any camera. You just photograph with this SX-70 and you make a big picture." I said, "That's not the point here. I want to see exactly what the grain structure of that SX-70 is. I want to see the edge of where the paper doesn't quite fit down onto the image. I want it to be the world's biggest SX-70 picture." And they went, "Well—" Anyway, we finally got that done. It was just a horrible fight between my originality and imagination and this strict use of that camera. I learned something there about technology.[74]

And because of its fidelity and artistic claims, characteristics that his practice constantly attacked, Polaroid large-format photography could thus function for Heinecken as a set of technologies through which he could critically reflect upon television, a medium whose speedy movement helped to conceal the ideologies it disseminated.

As we have seen, Heinecken's exploration of Polaroid technologies revealed some of the profound effects that instantaneous and large-format photography technologies were having on the American psyche during the 1970s and 1980s. From the commodification of the self to radically rethinking the nature of both authorship and art, Polaroid provided Heinecken with the means to engage some of the most significant media issues of his time. And as always, it was the keen integration between Heinecken's forms and his content that made his work so important. Often though not exclusively evoking a straight male gaze, Heinecken used simple, ironic means to disrupt and call into question the dominant patriarchal values of his time. In particular, the SX-70 format with its close associations with amateur photography proved a perfect channel to explore and develop Goffman's radical concepts of gender performance. Connecting sociological concepts with specific media technologies, Heinecken engaged with Goffman's thinking, while questioning the development of his all-too-narcissistic moment.

Although I have traced Heinecken's work through a particular submedium of photography, this is not the only way to organize it. As we have seen, he pursued themes (for example, voyeurism, print media, or the battle between the sexes) and genres (for example, pinups and pornography) across different photographic media. The next chapter will focus on Heinecken's pursuit of a larger theme—broadcast media—across a number of different photographic technologies. Turning one area of lens-based reproduction onto another, Heinecken pursued shifts in American ideologies over the course of the 1980s, changes that revealed the affinities between consumerism and politics. At the same time, his exhibitions, though not without their supporters, were met with growing criticism from photographers and critics, and a different form of appropriationist photography was developing in New York, one that was to have a huge impact on contemporary art.

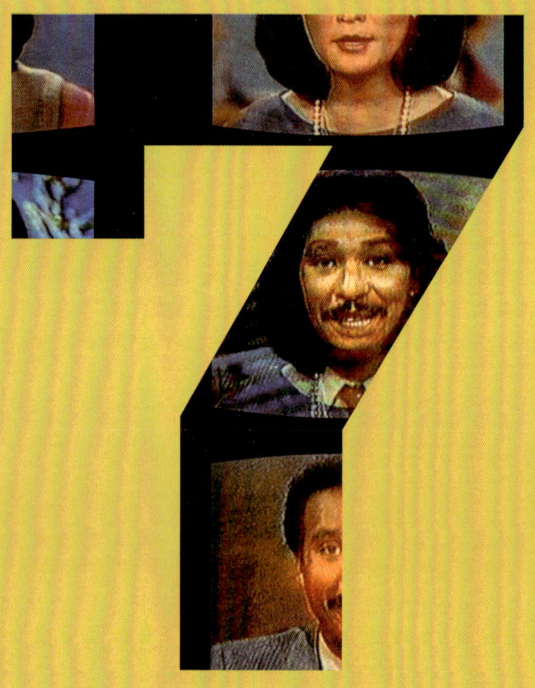

7

Ronald Reagan and the Newscasters

WHILE HEINECKEN'S INTEREST IN TV went back to the early 1970s, he focused on the subject most in the 1980s. During a decade in which television's broadcast era ended, and the oligopoly of NBC, CBS, and ABC was destroyed by the development of cable, satellite TV, VCRs, and remote controls, Heinecken homed in on the electronic environment and network news, exploring how electronic media affected identity, sexuality, and community in American society. By using photography, a much older medium, to explore the new technologies of electronic communication—the cathode ray tube, videotape, and electromagnetic broadcast infrastructure and practices—as well as the identities and situations that they solicited, Heinecken's television work demonstrated that the products of the mass media could be used critically to reveal their own techniques and biases. Employing a realistic yet static medium to selectively sample the broadcast media's ever-changing stream of information, he exposed prevailing U.S. ideologies as well as intimate connections among visual pleasure, consumption, and politics.

Heinecken was no doubt exposed to television as a teenager and while in the Marines, but it most probably did not become a significant technology in his life until 1960, when he and Janet moved out of UCLA housing into a suburban home in the Beverly Glen section of Los Angeles. It was in suburbia that they raised their three children, Geoffrey, Kathe, and Karol; and as was the case for many professionals at the time, a television set became part of their living room, a source of entertainment for the entire family. Like magazines, TV was basically an advertising device for Heinecken; its fundamental purpose was to stimulate the desire to consume a variety of different mass-produced products.[1] And it was this assumption—that the pleasure of television came from its ability to target desire and stimulate one's sense of uniqueness and personhood—that guided his investigation of the electronic medium.

Heinecken understood broadcast television to be a family leisure device, a locus within the home that linked it to the outside world by creating an environment designed to entertain while simultaneously propagandizing for commercial interests. This was a view that corresponded to the actual state of affairs in America at the time: television was a technology that almost exclusively served corporate and capitalist interests. Although its potential was (and is) much broader, TV was very much a mass-market and advertising-based medium throughout Heinecken's engagement with it— just as it remains today.[2] Although broadcasting commenced in the United States in the 1930s, the development of its television system only took off after World War II. Growing from a local to a regional medium during the 1940s and 1950s, with early centers in New York and Chicago, it had become "the centerpiece of national culture by the start of the 1960s," penetrating more markets (and reaching more demographics) than any other mass medium.[3] Television also supported the suburban boom, promoting a national mass culture at a time when more and more Americans were turning inward and commodifying themselves, their families, and homes.

Today, the history of broadcast television is often divided into three periods: the network era (1948–75), during which time NBC, CBS, and ABC grew to dominance while establishing TV's main genres and techniques; the cable era (1976–94), in which the three-network oligopoly was overcome through "narrowcasting" and the development of hundreds of niche television markets; and the digital era (since 1995), a time during which TV's audiences, genres, techniques, and practices further morphed and diversified, and what was experienced as broadcast and cable television has become part of a larger, much more complex and multinodal communication network.

Heinecken's engagement with television thus began during the height of the network era and extended into the cable era, but not beyond. This fact is significant because it means that his work deals with television as it was before the digital revolution, when it was still largely a one-way medium, with information flowing from a set of well-funded, institutional producers to a mass audience of consumers, whose control over the content was limited to the simple bestowing or withholding of attention (and purchasing power). Heinecken was initially most entranced by the electronic environment that television created and by the way it linked vision to consumption. Because of its environmental concerns, Heinecken's early TV work can thus be productively understood in terms of the popular media theory of Marshall McLuhan, with which it shares a number of similarities and differences. Heinecken then turned to a consideration of television's effect on news, history, and politics, an inquiry in which the fortieth President of the United States, Ronald Reagan, an actor-turned-politician, played a starring role. Parallel to this investigation, the photographer also examined network news and the ways in which it conveyed an appearance of truthfulness through surface qualities such as the attractiveness and connection of its actors. And in part by juxtaposing mass-media technologies developed in different centuries, Heinecken's TV work explored transformations in concepts of national identity and truth that were affecting Americans in the 1980s.

1970s

Some of Heinecken's first attempts to examine the medium of television focused very directly on consumption. Between 1970 and 1973, he made a series of mixed-media *TV Dinners,* photo-sculptural objects that evoked food's artificial nature as well as its illusionistic promises (Plate 7.1). Exact scale, black-and-white Images, printed in photographic emulsion on canvas, which was then partially crumpled and stiffened with resin, they also contained hand-coloring and sometimes objects like cigarettes. Literal, detailed, and slightly disgusting, they poked fun at the idea of art photography: why, viewers were compelled to ask, should they contemplate such a banal image? At the same time, these socially critical images also documented—and to some extent typologized—a new kind of product that had come, at least in part, to colonize Heinecken's everyday lifeworld. A *TV dinner* was a frozen prepackaged meal, generally containing a meat (or fish), starch, vegetable, and (sometimes) a dessert, in aluminum packaging originally designed to be heated in ovens. First a trademark for a brand of ready-made meal developed in 1953 by C. A. Swanson & Sons, the term was used generically in the 1960s and 1970s for any kind of frozen meal, before falling out of favor again for more contemporary terms like *microwave dinner.*[4]

TV dinners, as Heinecken recalled, were fundamentally labor-saving devices, ones that encouraged parents to turn the family into passive consumers: "What's good is you don't have to cook dinner; you heat this thing up and you go watch television. That's why it's called 'TV dinner.'"[5] And although he seemed a little uneasy about it, he embraced the product's convenience in the 1960s and 1970s. For many years, the artist was responsible for dinner while his wife was away at work, so "the kids and I probably ate a couple of hundred thousand of these things. . . . But

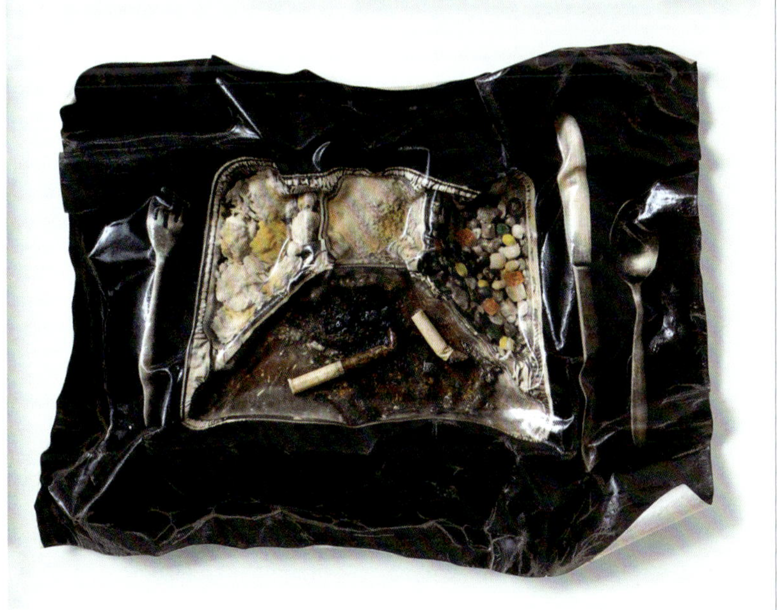

we didn't watch TV with it."[6] Mixed with Heinecken's fascination with TV, and the various forms of consumption that it encouraged, was a keen awareness of the medium's potentially deleterious effects. The artist's TV dinner magazines, photographs, and photo-sculptures—which combined typology, tactility, and deadpan illusionism to both document and criticize a mass-market consumer product—function as clear metaphors for the idea that the electronic media fundamentally treats its spectators as consumers, by stimulating their appetites and appealing to their senses.

Also in 1970, Heinecken created the first iteration of *TV/Time Environment,* a dark, dystopian installation that at first blush simulated a cozy, middle-class living room. In it an actual armchair, rug, lamp, and side table, with plastic plants and flowers, were juxtaposed with a constantly running television, its screen partially obscured by a high-contrast, black-and-white positive transparency depicting a nude torso (Plate 7.2).[7] The transparency was fashioned from a soft-core negative manufactured by The Latent Image, the company Heinecken had used before in the mid-1960s. First produced for an exhibition at the Downey Museum of Art in 1970, *TV/Time Environment* was reprised at the Pasadena Museum of Art in 1972, and at least four more times subsequently.[8] One of Heinecken's altered magazines was sometimes placed on the side table, and in at least one of these instances a Spiro Agnew mask was also situated there for the spectator to put on. The habitat—somewhat reminiscent of William Leavitt's contemporaneous environments—also recalled Edward Kienholz's found-object TV installations such as *The Eleventh Hour Final* (1968) and *The Commercial No. 2* (1971–73).[9] As curator Fred R. Parker said in 1973 about *TV/Time Environment,* "Here, two worlds collide with biting satire and urgency. The great American opiate, television, meets the great American fantasy, sex."[10] By affixing a Kodalith nude directly to

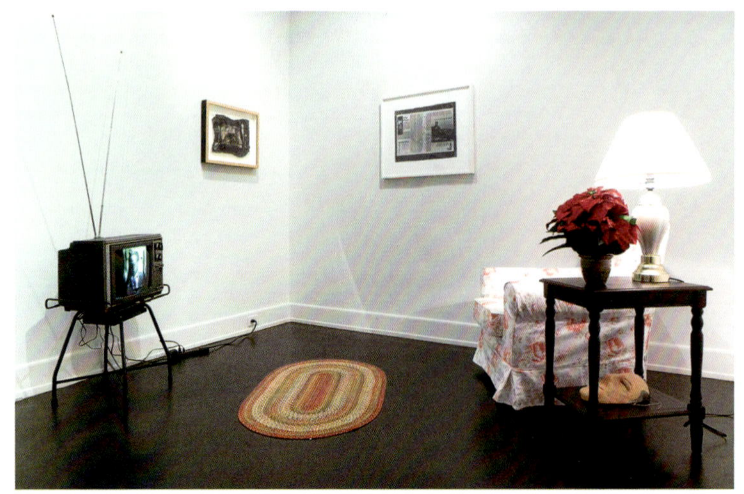

PLATE 7.2. Robert Heinecken, *TV/Time Environment* (1970). Functioning television set, film transparency, chair, rug, plastic plant, and related magazine, dimensions variable. 2016 re-creation, Petzel Gallery, New York. COPYRIGHT 2022 THE ROBERT HEINECKEN TRUST, CHICAGO.

the cathode ray tube's surface, Heinecken emphasized a new connected-
ness between broadcast content and generic frames, thus highlighting
television's character as a medium that does not simply transmit information but also selects and filters it. Both the content (programming) and
the advertisements of the new electronic medium, the transparency suggests, were designed to appeal to the same primal impulses and desires;
the real was never served up straight on American television but, rather,
abstracted, cut up, and recontextualized within new frames and narratives.

In its various iterations, *TV/Time Environment* would create an experience that was both temporal and critical. Spectators could stay as long
as they wanted, experiencing their "normal" television broadcast world
through an alienating screen filter. The installation, which sometimes
used a black-and-white TV and sometimes a color one, also included
other distancing devices: at times the volume was turned all the way
down, and in certain iterations framed photographs by Heinecken were
mounted on the walls, images in which TV dinners and more montaged
bodies could be seen. Situated within the gallery or museum space, their
movement temporarily frozen, visitors were thus provoked to reflexively
regard themselves as both subjects and objects of contemplation; from
this position, they were invited to consider their visual desires and their
place within a nexus of consumer identities. Perhaps paging through an
altered magazine, they would be reminded of the similarly filtering and
recontextualizing consumer-oriented character of the print media. And if
one was ready at hand, they could put on the visage of Nixon's vice president, a possibly disturbing experience since Agnew was by that time a
figure with whom few Americans would wish to identify.

In some of the iterations, Heinecken took photographs of the moving
television screen through the transparency with a 35mm camera, and a
few years later printed some of them as 3M prints (*Daytime Color TV Fantasy*, 1974–75) and four-color lithographs (*Daytime TV Fantasy*, 1976). As
suggested by these two series, there were six different transparencies—all
of a female nude cropped at her shoulders and thighs—that were used at
different times. And these works, which began their lives as photographs
taken of a television broadcast, serve as apt metaphors for the increasingly couch-potato character of life in the United States in the mid-1970s.
Even the photographer, they sardonically suggest, no longer bothers to get
up off the couch and leave the living room anymore.

Marshall McLuhan

Because of their focus on the electronic environment that was changing
the fabric of American identities and society, there are parallels between

Heinecken's television photographs, environments, and objects of the 1970s and the contemporaneous media theory of Marshall McLuhan. Although Heinecken never spoke directly of the Canadian cultural theorist, it seems very likely he was aware of McLuhan's ideas. McLuhan was a pioneer of media studies, developing an influential media theory and pedagogy at the University of Toronto between the early 1950s and late 1970s, the broad outlines of which became very popular and widespread between the mid-1960s and the mid-1970s. McLuhan's fundamental project was to develop media literacy within the general population, a comprehensive understanding of the new forms of communication that were transforming societies after World War II, combined with an ability to analyze the streams of audiovisual communications—like those that issued from the television set—that surrounded them in everyday life.[11]

McLuhan began from the assumption that all communications media were extensions of the body and consciousness, and as they developed across the world, they had a pervasive and often unnoted effect on the ways people thought, acted, and formed their societies.[12] "The medium is the message" was McLuhan's most famous turn of phrase, an adage that was designed to remind his growing mass audience that to understand the nature and effects of contemporary communications, they must first attend to the forms—and not the content—of the new mass media.

In his academic writing, McLuhan developed a media history that anchored his analyses of the contemporary audiovisual spectacle.[13] Fundamentally, for McLuhan shifts in worldview—orders of knowing and being—correlated with changes in the nature of human communications as indicated by transitions between oral, written, print, and, after World War II, electronic cultures. According to the historical narrative he developed, the act of writing down the spoken word that began in ancient cultures inaugurated a long process of instrumental thinking; by externalizing ideas, feelings, and experiences in repeatable media, human beings learned to penetrate, control, and transform their worlds. At the same time, this increase of instrumental and manipulative power came with a certain devaluation of everyday experience, a privileging of vision over a more multisensorial mode of apprehension that McLuhan identified with oral cultures.

The printing press revolutionized communication once again, by making both writing and books—traditionally elite sources of power and status—commodities; it thus popularized them and facilitated the spread of literacy. Through the growth of printing, a huge network of institutions and practices emerged that created vast wealth and new forms of knowledge in the modern world. And although it helped to propel the rise of capitalism, nationalism, and colonialism between the fifteenth and the nineteenth centuries, the print communication system was also fundamentally linked to the creation of new, more individualistic forms of subjectivity. As the Gutenberg Galaxy, as he called it, developed, novels, for example, encouraged a new sense of interiority and subjective awareness, while the rise of newspapers helped to construct broader concepts of group belonging (defined in terms of class, religion, nationality, ethnicity, race, and sex) with which individuals could identify, or from which they could distinguish themselves. Through print, people became more and more interlinked with an ever-expanding set of common affinities; these commonalities in turn facilitated new hybrid positions within a greater set of allegiances that were potentially different for each individual and that ranged from the local to the national to the global.

For McLuhan, the rise of radio and television in the twentieth century once again marked a fundamental transformation in consciousness, just as radical as those initiated by writing in the ancient world and by the printing press at the beginning of the modern era. In the post–1945 world, human beings were living through a clash of communications media in which the old literary order was being contested and overcome by a new electronic one. Writing and print culture lived on, but more and more they now existed as part of a broader "environment" in which tactile, haptic, architectural, and audio components were intermixed with these older visual forms of communication. McLuhan called this new environment "acoustic space," to emphasize the greater orality that it encouraged—or, better, communication's return to multisensory forms of experience.[14] He contrasted acoustic space with modern written culture, which he characterized as linear, as operating with fixed distinctions, and as predominantly visual. In contrast to print culture, the new media environment was always in flux and had no fixed boundaries. "Oral cultures and temperaments," he wrote in 1967, "are mobile and transitory in their moods."[15] Electronic space was primordial, stream-of-consciousness, and saturated with a multitude of competing historical meanings, a condition that encouraged creative responses.

The new media environment was also rapidly changing the modern conceptualization of both individual and group identity. In particular, although it continued the cultivation of individuality that flourished already in the modern era, the new media overcame barriers of space and time to create what McLuhan called a "global village."[16] As a result, peoples' sense of their group identities was no longer as tied to particular locations or eras, and new collectivities could be developed between individuals separated not only by language and race, but also by space and time.

For McLuhan, the potential effect that the new electronic communication media had on consciousness and society was enormous. As was the case with publishing in the modern world, the electronic media of his time primarily served commercial interests as well as the political status quo. It thus tended to reinforce hegemonic stereotypes of gender, race, class, and nationality, despite its potential to do the opposite as well. In comparison to the past, however, the promise that TV, radio, and other contemporary mass-media channels held out for different and novel forms of participation was much greater. Less and less, as McLuhan predicted, would mass communication remain a one-way medium. And this insight into the potential of the new media to promote new forms of individual expression, coupled with the idea of the global village, which held out possibilities for affinities beyond the familial, local, and national, remains one of the Canadian theorist's most important legacies.

When compared to McLuhan's media history and theory, Heinecken's TV work of the 1970s reveals a number of significant similarities and differences. In the first place, like McLuhan, Heinecken insisted that television was an environment. This was most apparent in *TV/Time Environment,* which in its various iterations provided a kind of stage set—or Goffmanian social frame—by means of which the spectator could reflect on the construction of identity through the broadcast media. But it was also apparent in Heinecken's mid-1970s lithographs made from images shot from a similarly augmented television screen, which implied that the photographer, too, now acted in an environment dominated by the electronic media. Even the *TV Dinners,* which suggested that television put its stamp on the most basic elements of everyday life, emphasized how much electronic communication surrounded individuals at that time.

Second, like McLuhan, Heinecken suggested that the new electronic environment did not eliminate modern forms of mass communication—books, newspapers, illustrated magazines, and the like—but, rather, that it incorporated them into a larger and more interconnected and open network. This can be seen in the ways in which Heinecken consistently juxtaposed different forms of visual representation—live TV, photography, illustrated magazines, and the like—in these 1970s TV works, and the ways in which he played their various material forms off one another in order to engender self-reflexive critique. "Artists in various fields," McLuhan wrote in *Understanding Media: The Extensions of Man,* "are always the first to discover how to enable one medium to use or to release the power of another"—something that Heinecken's television work demonstrated very well.[17]

Heinecken seemed to differ from McLuhan, however, in two fundamental respects. First, Heinecken placed much more emphasis on subject matter. McLuhan was rightly criticized for concentrating too much on the forms of modern and contemporary communications and largely ignoring the content of ideologies they transmitted.[18] Heinecken did not do this; instead, he balanced a reflexivity about form and apparatus with an enumeration of content—often in the form of typologies of gender, race, and class, but also by examining key historical figures and events. This focus on the gendered and racialized subjects selected by the electronic media comes to the fore in his television work of the 1980s. But significantly, due to Heinecken's more critical mien, it did not occur at the expense of reflexive formal analysis.

Second, Heinecken differed from McLuhan in that his work seemed less utopian about broadcast media than McLuhan's pronouncements. Supported by his Catholic faith, McLuhan imagined a better future, and he saw the new networked global village as offering tremendous potential for the improvement of humanity. Heinecken's work, on the other hand, was more cynical. The artist always focused on how the media brainwashed and manipulated the spectator, although longer contemplation of his work also suggests that he believed that there were ways of using the tools and products of the mass media to become self-aware and to situate oneself critically within the communication networks of consumer capitalism.

Videograms

In 1981, Heinecken's interest in television led him to what was perhaps his most significant formal innovation: the videogram, a contact print taken from the face of a cathode ray tube. Heinecken collaborated with Neimanas to make such prints of U.S. President Ronald Reagan during his first inauguration speech, which was held on January 20, 1981. As both Heinecken and Neimanas recall, there were two live television events, a rehearsal and an inauguration, and during each event, Heinecken, who was at UCLA, telephoned Joy in their Los Angeles studio and directed her when to begin and end the photogram.[19] Sitting in a darkened room, and following Heinecken's disembodied voice, Neimanas pressed 11 x 14 Cibachrome (dye bleach destruction) paper to the face of her television screen, turning the set on and off to create two-to-three-second exposures. As Heinecken remembered, the videograms took a lot of experimentation. Furthermore, they were based on chance; neither he nor Joy knew what image was going to appear; they just knew that Reagan's inauguration was going to be on the screen.[20]

This formal innovation resulted in *Inaugural Excerpt Videograms* (1981), a collection of at least seventy 10.5 x 13.5 dye bleach destruction prints, redacted into a selection of twenty-seven (and now twenty-four) works and originally displayed in a three-by-nine (and now a four-by-six) grid (Plate 7.3).[21] Single prints and groupings of the *Inaugural Excerpt Videograms* also exist, and all the works are unique (Plate 7.4). Each image was associated with a subtitle, which named the subjects (Ronald and Nancy Reagan, Warren Burger, Frank Sinatra, and others), and a phrase that Heinecken excerpted from Reagan's published speech the next day, a carefully selected metaphor that did not correspond to what the president actually said at the moment the videogram was made. For example, "(. . . is not for sale . . .)" is associated with an image of Burger administering the oath of office to Reagan while Nancy and other figures stand by.[22]

The resulting images—using what was then called Cibachrome, a dye bleach destruction positive-to-positive photographic print technology for its detail, color saturation, clarity, and stability—depict the president, first lady, government officials, and others as blurry and effulgent electronic specters. Predominantly bluish-green in color, and mostly very dark in tonality, the videograms present the public event, its main actors, and a few secondary characters drawn from its media framework (namely reporters, newscasters, and celebrities) as if in an underwater or outer space movie. The figures are often indecipherable, but nonetheless the identities of Ronald and Nancy (because of her red dress) come through. Overall, the prints remind viewers of the ritualized nature of presidential successions and the constructedness of Reagan's vaunted persona. Images of the new Republican president predominate, and as the famous pompadour and Midwestern bonhomie dissolve into electronic noise, we recall how they coded his appearances and allowed him to convey a convincing message. Both Heinecken's technique and his selection thus foreground the actor-president, a mouthpiece who sold "morning in America" in just the same way that sexy women sell products and that Reagan himself had sold General Electric TVs in the 1950s and early 1960s.

In terms of form, what is perhaps most interesting about the *Inaugural Excerpt Videograms* is their lack of moiré patterns—the jagged, linear distortion effects that often occur when either printed images or television broadcasts are rephotographed. Instead, there is a smoothness created by the subjects' motion blurs that gives the prints a great deal of indexical and organic presence. Also adding to these indexical qualities are their natures as photograms, unique images that were traditionally made through direct contact with originals, in relation to which they then stood as representations. By means of both form and technique, Heinecken thus marked the remote viewing of Reagan's inauguration as a fundamental event, as important as the twice-removed original that happened in Washington, D.C.

This reflexivity about spectatorship in a time of multiplying and overlapping media outlets is further stressed by the collaborative nature of

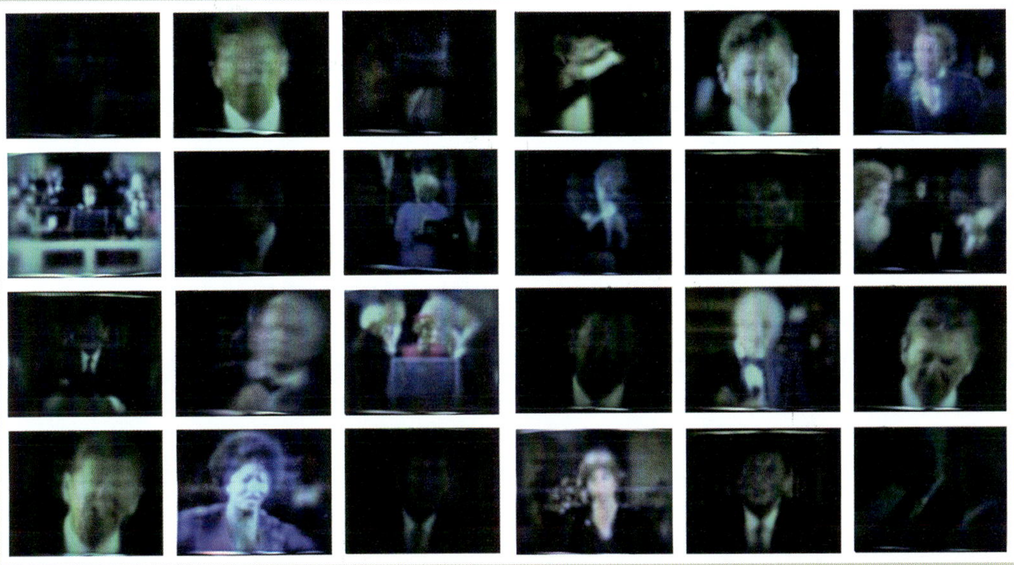

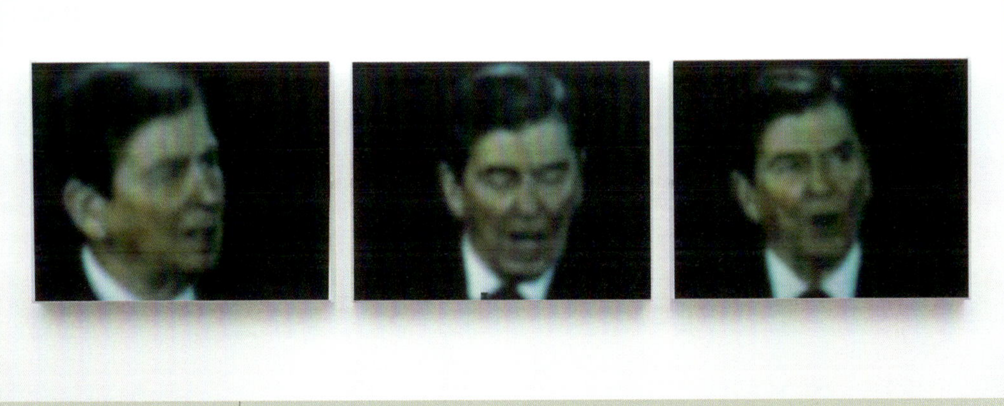

the creative technique in which Robert, watching the live event on one television set, worked together with Joy to make photograms on another set, communicating by means of a telephone. Not only does this strategy suggest the collective nature of television news production, but it also evokes László Moholy-Nagy's famous avant-garde telephone pictures, *EM 1, EM 2,* and *EM 3.* These were three porcelain enamel paintings on steel that were created in 1922–23 when Moholy telephoned a local enamel factory and ordered the panels to be produced by one of their artisans.[23] Abstract, formal investigations of Suprematist color and form, the painting strategy distanced Moholy's hand from the making of the artwork, emphasizing the idea over the production of the material objects. By mechanizing nonobjective painting, the telephone pictures heightened awareness about the relationship between advanced art and industry in the 1920s, while giving abstract painting a kind of repeatability previously only experienced in photography and printing.

In an analogous way, Heinecken's Reagan videograms explored the relationships among art, politics, and industry, wielding art to explore political communication in his new—and in comparison to Moholy's time— much more electronic moment. Heinecken's videograms drew attention to the ways in which television had changed politics since the 1950s.[24] As Heinecken was well aware, the first televised presidential debates, the Nixon–Kennedy contests of 1960, played an important role in Kennedy's narrow victory that year. They also demonstrated the importance of live broadcasts of political events at a time when significant portions of the broadcast schedule were taken up by shows that were fictional and prerecorded. The U.S. presidential debates also kicked off a period in which the image of leadership seemed to count for as much as a leader's specific policies did, with voters or supporters giving their assent to the person who seemed to most embody the personality traits they sought in a leader, qualities like strength, optimism, fairness, integrity, and vision. As JFK put it in 1959, in an article in *TV Guide*:

> Honesty, vigor, compassion, intelligence—the presence or lack of these
> and other qualities make up what is called the candidate's "image."
> While some intellectuals and politicians may scoff at these images—
> and while they may in fact be based only on a candidate's TV impression,
> ignoring his record, views and other appearances—my own conviction
> is that these images or impressions are likely to be uncannily correct.
> I think, no matter what their defenders or detractors may say, that the
> television public has a fairly good idea of what Eisenhower is really
> like—or Jimmy Hoffa or John McClellan or Vice President Nixon or
> countless others.[25]

For Kennedy, it was central to governance that the president project an image of leadership—particularly in live broadcasts, where the possibility of gaffes and misstatements that couldn't be edited out arose.

By the 1980s, there was already a long history of presidential television that affected the meaning of Reagan's inauguration, including the regular practice of televised national addresses, which began under Eisenhower, but also other ceremonies and, as Americans had discovered already in 1963, presidential funerals. Coverage of the Kennedy funeral ran continuously for four days and reached an estimated 140 million citizens. As Gary R. Edgerton notes, it transfixed the nation, "using the medium to process the unthinkable, mourn collectively, and cope with the feelings of shock, sadness, and disbelief that overwhelmed many in the face of this terrible and unexpected tragedy."[26] Presidential performances were thus extremely powerful; particularly during live broadcasts, they brought citizens together through an awareness that the entire audience was sharing a moment together in which something about their collective nature as a nation was being represented. In addition, because of their liveness, they also connoted authenticity: they produced a conviction, in other words, that U.S. citizens were seeing national politics enacted before their very eyes, something that resulted in a sense of intimacy and connection with their leaders.

Of course, the fact that it was Reagan's inauguration that Heinecken chose for one of his most important para-photographic gestures was no accident. Much more star-studded and fancy than that of President Jimmy Carter's, and criticized as such in the newspapers, the event suggested a change in the course of the nation. The inauguration marked a shift in political power in the United States from Democratic to Republican leadership that indicated not only the start of a new decade but also a significant move away from the social welfare state that had been growing since FDR.[27] Rejecting the perceived weakness of Jimmy Carter as well as the supposed "failures" of the Johnson, Nixon, and Ford administrations, Reagan promised "Morning in America" again: a renewal of American values, power, and optimism that would overcome the social, political, and economic malaise in which the United States had become mired in the 1970s. Embracing tax cuts, business deregulation, and military spending over his eight-year stint, the president also attempted to cut social programs, although he was not always successful in doing so. To accomplish his goals, he projected an affable, optimistic persona, one that was half-cowboy and half-grandfather, an iconic embodiment of a new, more paternal and powerful American president. As Reagan himself put it, "I place myself in the 'seller' category of leadership."[28] Heinecken's videograms evoked Reagan's mastery of presidential performance on the electronic screen while also insisting—through their sinister sci-fi movie connotations—on how powerfully Reagan's policies could affect the country.

As McLuhan noted, in the new electronic environment people see the present in terms of nostalgic representations of the past, an insight that reveals the appeal of Reagan's persona as well: "When faced with a totally new situation, we tend always to attach ourselves to the objects, to the flavor of the most recent past. We look at the present through a rear-view mirror. We march backwards into the future. Suburbia lives imaginatively in Bonanza-land."[29] Reagan, with his cowboy persona, represented precisely such a form of nostalgic rhetorical leadership; his was a media-oriented presidency in which often pernicious policy was cloaked by noble-sounding clichés. It was not for nothing that Reagan was called the Teflon president; more Americans liked him than believed him; and they approved of him even when they did not agree with all of his policies. And Heinecken's *Inaugural Excerpt Videograms* seem to home in on Reagan as a malleable creature of the electronic media as well as his menacing character as a mouthpiece for capitalism, militarism, and the cultivation of narcissistic self-interest.

Although Heinecken could not have foretold the events that would unfold under the Reagan administration, he was clearly familiar with Reagan's persona and policies, having lived in California while Reagan was governor from 1967 to 1975.[30] And in the years that followed that inauguration, a number of the menacing possibilities that Heinecken saw in Reagan's emergence as president were realized, with a reassertion of American military power abroad, union busting, deregulation, and other pro–corporate policies at home, and increasing income disparity that divided the nation, often along racial lines. In 1987, Heinecken returned to the subject of the television president, photographing Reagan with a 35mm camera as he spoke on television during the Iran-Contra scandal. This resulted in *Mr. President* (1987), a three-by-four grid of silver dye bleach prints, in which portraits of the talking president were again juxtaposed with fragments of one of his speeches. (Unlike the *Inaugural Excerpt Videograms*, these photographs of Reagan had the short texts inscribed directly on them as if they were subtitles.) Taking place between 1985 and 1987 during Reagan's second term, the Iran-Contra affair and the ensuing scandal were the greatest crisis of the Reagan presidency. By documenting Reagan's speech during a time when he was caught lying to the American public, Heinecken bore witness to the dark side of U.S. foreign policy in the 1980s, involving both anti-Communism in Latin America and antiterrorism in the Middle East.

The Iran-Contra affair was exposed in late 1986, when it was discovered that Reagan's senior staff had secretly facilitated weapons sales to

Iran, despite being prohibited from doing so by a previously enacted arms embargo. The administration had hoped thereby to gain release of several U.S. hostages being held in Lebanon, while simultaneously generating money that could be used to continue to back the Nicaraguan Contras, a U.S.–trained paramilitary group, in their fight against their country's socialist Sandinista government, funding that had been explicitly prohibited by the U.S. Boland Amendment. In response to the scandal, Reagan gave a series of television addresses in which he gradually revealed the truth about what happened, sometimes contradicting what he had said only a few months previously. Although Reagan—but not his senior officials—survived the scandal, he did so at the cost of seeming hopelessly out of touch with his own government. As he put it in his twelve-minute television address on March 4, 1987: "A few months ago I told the American people I did not trade arms for hostages. My heart and my best intentions still tell me that's true, but the facts and the evidence tell me it is not."[31] By picking an episode that revealed the mendacity and hollowness of the electronic chief executive, Heinecken's *Mr. President* photographs identified critical issues and problems having to do with the transformation of U.S. politics through broadcast television media.

Newscasters

Perhaps not surprisingly, after first concentrating on Reagan, the consummate electronic president, Heinecken next turned his attention to newscasters, those most notoriously plastic of public figures. Like Reagan, newscasters were mass communicators and figures in which people invested—or withheld—trust, attention, and belief. And like Reagan, they were aspirational: they represented an ideal, a type of American whom others often celebrated and desired to become. To explore the phenomenon of the newscaster, Heinecken first used Polaroid technologies. In 1983–84, he made a series of newswomen appropriations and composites with Polaroid's 20 x 24 inch camera, exposing paused videotape on a television screen, sometimes twice in order to capture two different individuals on the same plate. The resulting Polacolor prints, which are curiously blurry and detailed at the same time, include works like *Untitled Newswomen* and *Untitled Newswomen (Suite C#1),* both from 1983. The former consists of two prints: a headshot of Connie Chung positioned directly above a second headshot in which the same Chung image is merged with another—presumably white—newswoman. The latter presents a horizontal sequence, comprising Jane Pauley, Joan Lunden, Diane Sawyer, and then a composite of the three previous images (Plate 7.5). In other works, different typologies and combinations of newswomen

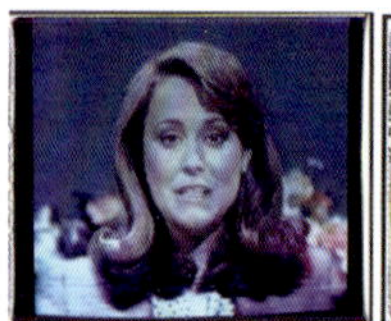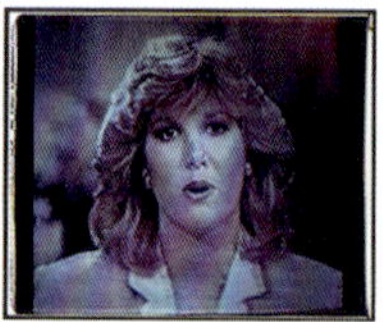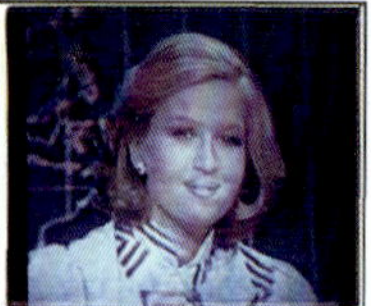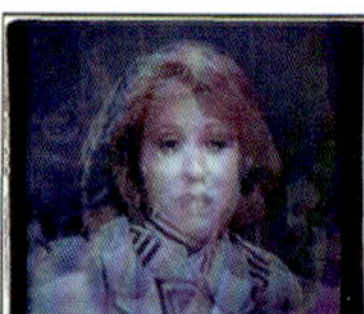

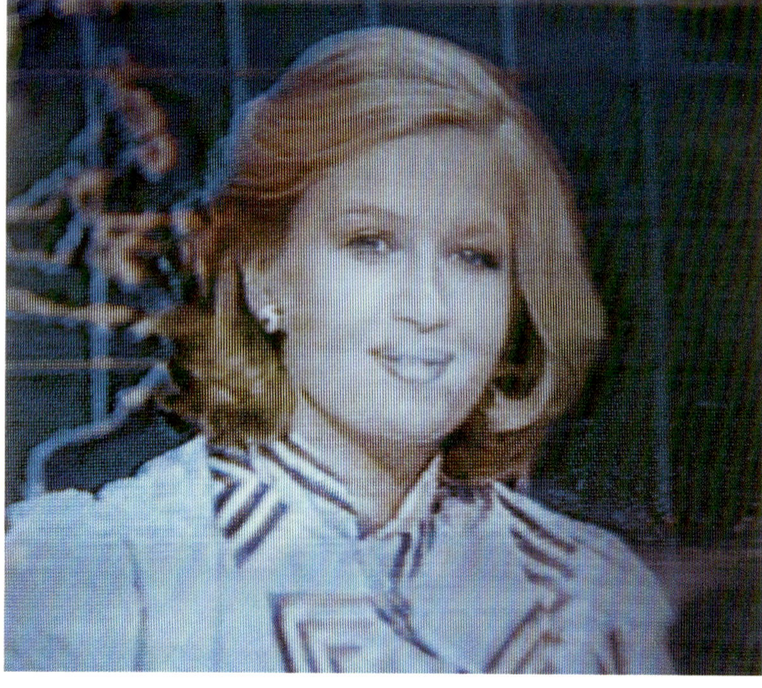

PLATE 7.5. *Top:* Robert Heinecken, *Untitled Newswomen (Suite C#1)* (1983). A sequence of four unique internal dye diffusion transfer prints (Polaroid Polacolor), comprising Jane Pauley, Joan Lunden, Diane Sawyer, and a composite, 20 ¾ x 25 inches (52.7 x 63.5 cm) each. *Bottom:* Detail *(Diane Sawyer).* COPYRIGHT 2022 THE ROBERT HEINECKEN TRUST, CHICAGO.

appear. But always, the effect is disturbing: in rows and grids, we are presented with the progressing alienation of the human visage through television and videotape.

In comparison to the Reagan videograms, which are blurrier and smoother, the Polacolor newswomen prints are harsher and more vibratory. Like Cibachrome, the Polacolor print technology was both detailed and saturated, and thus it captured a range of qualities in the electronic image that were generally not attended to. The electronic patterning created by the paused videotape—particularly horizontal lines produced by the cathode ray tube's electron gun—made the images seem more technologically mediated than the videograms of Reagan. Particularly in the composite images, the figures seem overtaken by a nexus of mechanized lines; it is as if we see them switching back and forth between a set of fixed positions like human beings stuck in the levers of a machine. Heinecken liked to tell the story about the resistance he got from the first Polaroid technicians with whom he worked. They simply could not understand why he wanted to photograph the television set because of the low saturation and resolution of the source material in relation to the capabilities of Polaroid's massive direct-positive film.[32] But as Heinecken's television work as a whole suggests, it was precisely by scrutinizing changes in human perception and behavior brought about by the electronic medium itself that new understandings of identity could be forged.

Like McLuhan, Heinecken seemed to think that a historical perspective was also needed. Electronic media could best be understood as the latest phase of a longer history of human communication; Heinecken's strategy of composite photography was intended to do just that—to evoke the historical practice of Francis Galton and his followers in the late nineteenth and early twentieth centuries. As scholars like David Green and Allan Sekula would articulate in the mid-1980s, Galton and his followers used multiple-exposure copy photography of precisely registered sets of portrait samples to produce images that they believed represented visual types or "averages."[33] Galtonian composite portraits, in other words, were made with—and tried to perpetuate—the assumption that photographic montage produced images depicting common traits shared by their set of sample subjects: visual characteristics that signaled their belonging to a more general family, race, class, or condition. As such, composite photographs were used at this time to illustrate scientific and popular literature in the fields of criminology and eugenics, providing visual evidence of hereditary and racial "essences" as well as the various "looks" of criminality, virtue, health, and disease (what Sekula called the "shadow archive").[34]

Heinecken's historical reference to Galton was designed to prod the viewer to think about mass media's long development from photography in the nineteenth century to television in the twentieth. By using earlier technologies or strategies, Heinecken's work demonstrated, photographers could slow down the speed of electronic communication and provoke reflection on its impact on individuals and societies. Because of its associations with pseudosciences like eugenics, physiognomy, and phrenology, composite photography was also a perfect strategy to cast doubt on the truthfulness of network news. As was the case with Heinecken's Reagan images, spectators were provoked to question the trust they placed in news anchors like Connie Chung and Diane Sawyer.

By linking nineteenth-century pseudoscientific practices, like composite photography, and bodies of knowledge, like physiognomy, to electronic journalism, these works made viewers aware of the nonverbal cues and assumptions that conditioned their understanding of truth. They got spectators to think about the visual characteristics that made people seem trustworthy—things like direct eye contact and an open expression, for example—and they also prompted them to consider how regular and attractive features could be read as signs of good or noble character. In this way, the newswomen photographs pointed to the changing nature of news in a time of electronic communication. Not only was the speed of news gathering and dissemination becoming faster, but the people employed to deliver this information were getting simultaneously more typical and more intermixed: a new "tribe" of trusted news professionals. The new shrinking of space and time accomplished by electronic mass media, in other words, as well as their construction of a new sense of the global village, seems in these works to have unmoored traditional distinctions between race, gender, and class.

The disruption of traditional stereotypes about race was a particularly important aspect of Heinecken's newscaster works. As the selection of Connie Chung suggests, racially diverse subjects were becoming a larger part of the television broadcast environment, a reflection of the changing demographic makeup of the United States. And as Heinecken's television works already implied in the 1980s, the media was an important channel through which the unquestioned whiteness of the American subject was being challenged. Asian and Black subjects appear with some frequency in Heinecken's work, and when he composited figures of different races or ethnicities together, his art allegorized the slow overcoming of hegemonic whiteness in American society, which continues to this day. Indeed, Heinecken's obsession with Connie Chung, whose appropriated visage he explored through a variety of different photographic techniques (including the same Cibachrome videogram process he had used on Reagan), suggests how powerful he found images of Asian American identity to be (Plate 7.6).[35]

The newswomen photographs culminated in a book, which contextualized the series by using text and sequencing to amplify its main themes. *1984: A Case Study in Finding an Appropriate TV Newswoman (A CBS Docudrama in Words and Pictures)* comprised eighteen pages with approximately seventy-nine four-color plates depicting male and female news anchors, a number of them composites (Plate 7.7).[36] Based on photographs shot with a 35mm camera from an active television screen, the book used an absurdist text to present Heinecken's TV photographs as part of a scientific visual analysis designed to help television executives pick the best female cohost for a morning news program. Many pages present two columns of three images; in each, the top portrait is a woman, the bottom a man, and the one in the middle is an uncanny androgyne created by layering one visage atop the other (Plate 7.8). Text running alongside explains a series of experiments in which composite photography is used to assess the ideal televisual couple. Through this strategy, marketing science is parodied and fixed categories of gender and race are pointedly undermined.

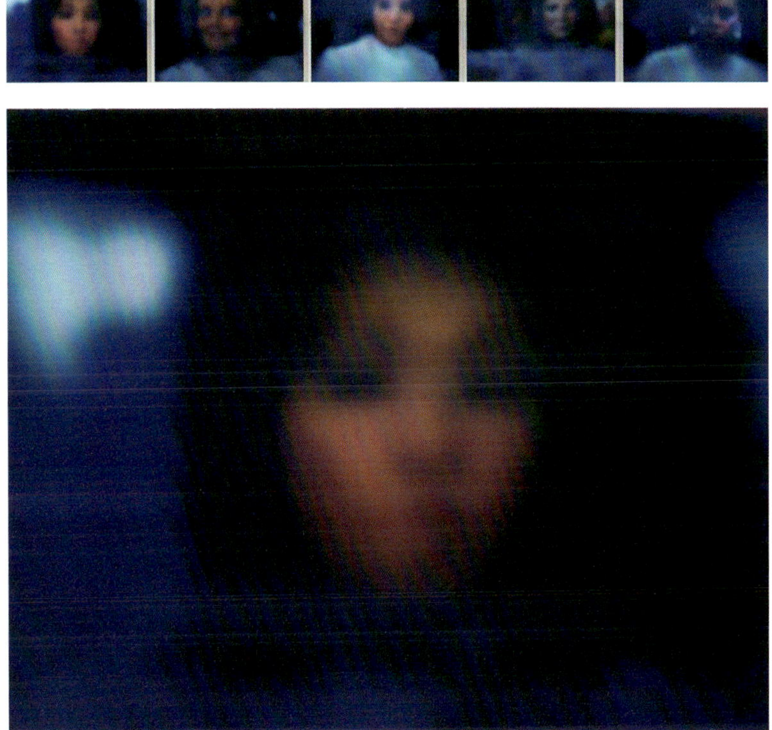

On the final page of the book, over a shot of Phyllis George speaking directly into the camera, Heinecken addresses the issue of physiognomy directly, suggesting that "the accelerating tendency to accept the basic physiognomic premise is predictable in technologically jaded cultures." Breaking out of the corporate address of the docudrama but speaking in a way that seems no more reliable, Heinecken insists on linkages between the nineteenth century and the mid-1980s, correspondences that demonstrate how photography and other lens-based media have consistently both determined and altered the truth.

The references to physiognomy, phrenology, and photography explicitly draw attention to Galton's practice of composite portraiture, reminding spectators that their understanding of how human vision functions continually lags behind the technologies of vision that human beings invent. While Galton believed that his combined portraits of soldiers, prisoners, and other human groups could reveal physiognomic types that defined fundamental differences of race, class, health, sickness, family, and so on, Heinecken's composites suggest the opposite. The newscasters, with their crossing of ages, races, and genders, all give the lie to the idea of fixed ideal types (Plate 7.9). Instead, what the spectator was prompted to consider was the growth of diversity in American life. In addition, the

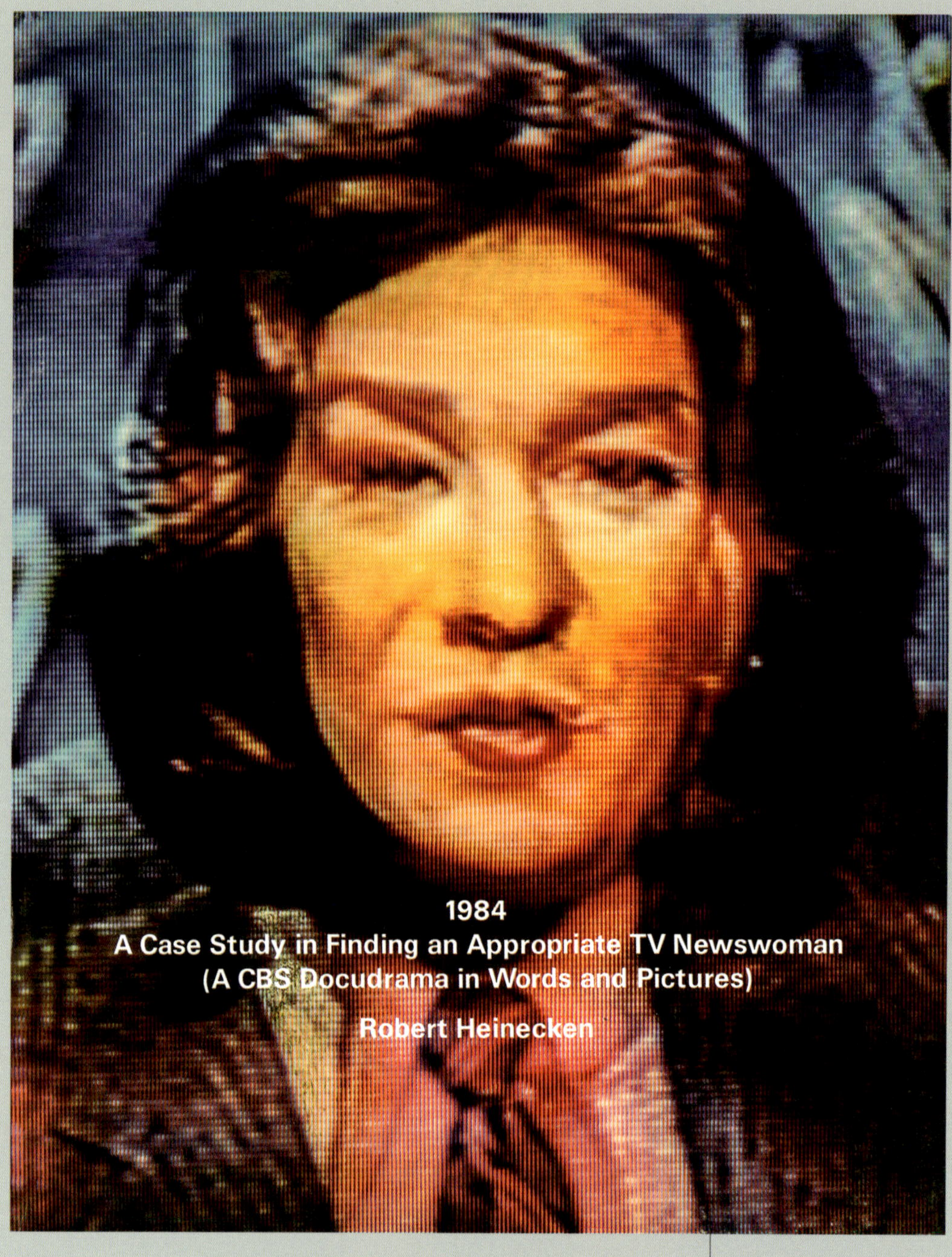

PLATE 7.7. Robert Heinecken, *1984: A Case Study in Finding an Appropriate TV Newswoman (A CBS Docudrama in Words and Pictures)*, Los Angeles: n.p. (self-published), 1985. Offset-printed staple-bound publication with pictorial wrappers and illustrations in black-and-white and color, 11 ¼ x 9 inches (28.6 x 22.8 cm), n.p. (sixteen pages). Edition of 2000, front cover. COPYRIGHT 2022 THE ROBERT HEINECKEN TRUST, CHICAGO.

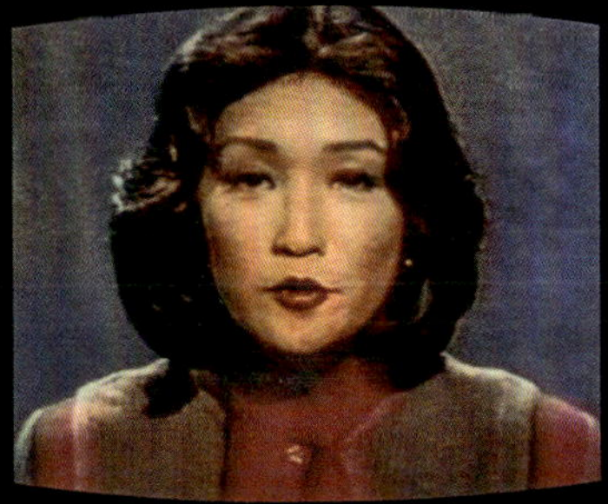
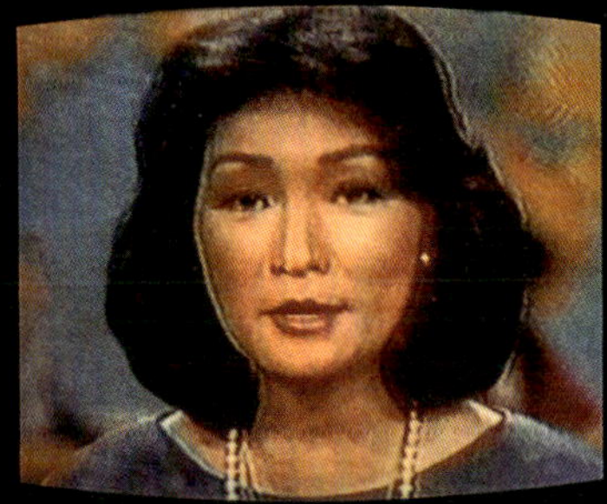
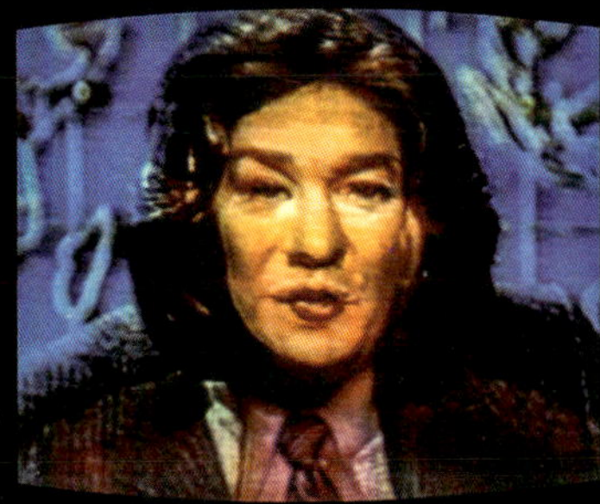
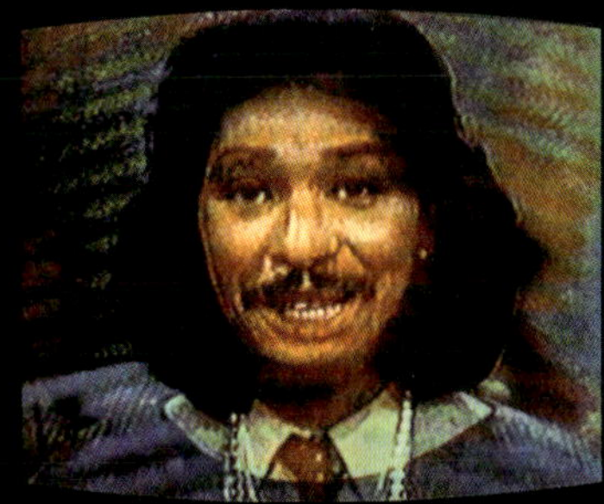
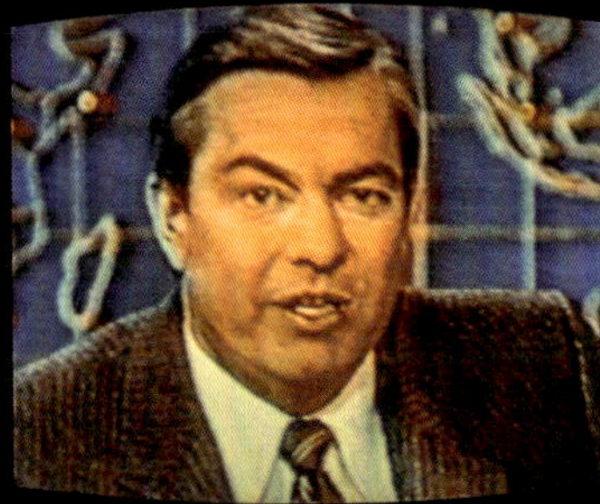
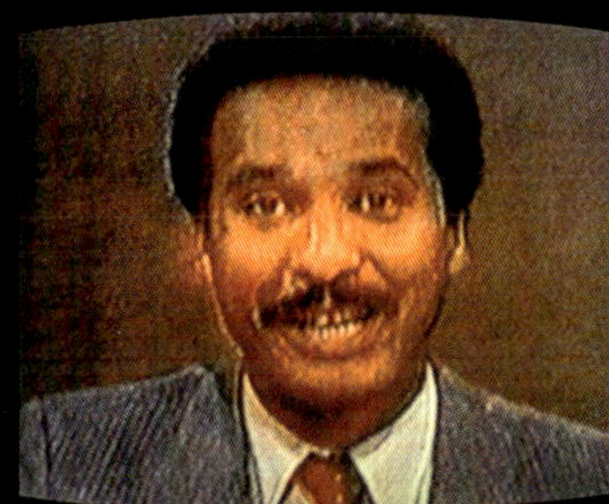

Fig. 12 Connie Chung / Bill Kurtis

Fig. 13 Connie Chung / Steve Baskerville

In their frustration management decided to follow the lead of NBC on which their clownish, heavy-set weatherman was often utilized in conjunction with Pauley and Gumbel. Steve Baskerville was the resident weatherman on the CBS *Morning News* and they elected to increase his visibility and integrate him into the team as much as possible. Being black it was expected that he would "round-out" whatever couple emerged and might prove to draw an increased audience. This change would also follow the ethnic casting policy at NBC where Bryant Gumbel functioned.

At this point, quite by accident, Connie Chung was up for a contract renewal at NBC where she was the regular replacement for Jane Pauley. She was contacted discretely and agreed to consider the CBS position if all discussions etc. could be accomplished in secret. The executives were awash in anticipation that they could be the first network to have an Asian woman in the morning slot and to create a gen-uine tri-racial team. I set out to visually test her in composite with Kurtis and Baskerville, who was now seen as a fixture on the team. However in both instances her classic Asian features seemed to dominate the men's and what was hoped would be exotic was grotesque instead. *(Figs. 12 and 13).* The entire high-blown fantasy had to be dismissed.

PLATE 7.8. Robert Heinecken, *1984: A Case Study in Finding an Appropriate TV Newswoman (A CBS Docudrama in Words and Pictures)*, Los Angeles: n.p. (self-published), 1985. Offset-printed staple-bound publication with pictorial wrappers and illustrations in black-and-white and color, 11 ¼ x 9 inches (28.6 x 22.8 cm), n.p. (sixteen pages). Edition of 2000, page 7. COPYRIGHT 2022 THE ROBERT HEINECKEN TRUST, CHICAGO.

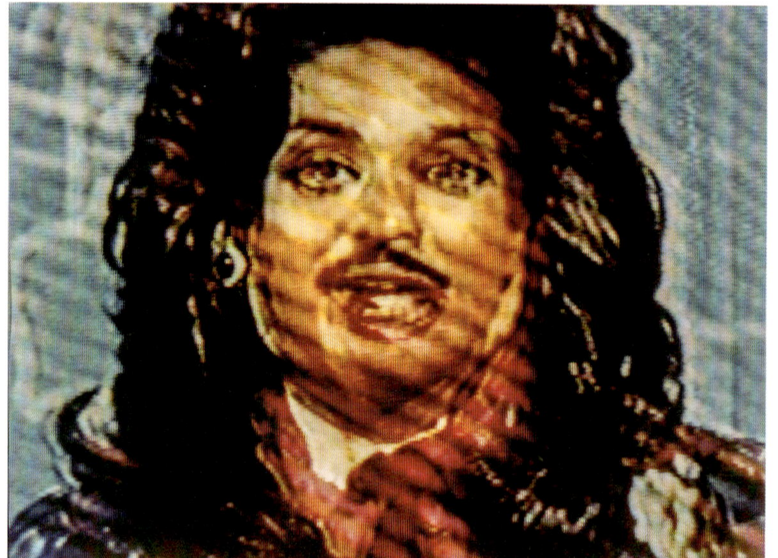

viewer was also encouraged to attend to the staging of the morning news show. Why did the networks work so hard to give audiences a couple who together would present the news? Were the big three broadcasting networks trying to evoke a family situation, subliminally encouraging viewers to see the presenters in light of a social frame in which many people invest their trust? And did a sexual dynamic or tension between news anchors increase interest or inspire greater audience identification? Finally, did cross-gender communication and banter make information more believable or more entertaining? All these questions, Heineken's book suggested, most likely could be answered in the affirmative.

The Yuppie Ideal

Viewed from the perspective of the 1980s, what possibly connected the newscaster images with those of the electronic president was the ideal of the yuppie: a new personality type embodied by the young urban profes-sional, an aspirational identity that linked an intense focus on success and self-development to an unbridled avidity for consumption. In comparison to the more intellectual and elitist understanding of the narcissistic per-sonality type of the 1970s, the American yuppie ideal of the 1980s was more diffuse and popular, emerging in mass marketing, the news media, films, and television. But the yuppie was also similar to the older narcissistic personality type in that it continued the narcissist's focus on individuation and pleasure. Indeed, the yuppies' primary difference from the 1970s nar-cissist was the fact that they were no longer conflicted or made anxious by their own self-centeredness and materialism. Unperturbed about their own rampant capitalism and consumerism, the yuppie further enshrined individualism over a concern for social equality or the collective good of the community.

As Gil Troy notes, the yuppie was a creature of the economic boom of the 1980s, which raised the affluence of many (but not all) Americans:

> In 1983 the great economic boom—the baby boom, the Reagan boom—began. It was a boom of service jobs, not manufacturing, of the Sun Belt and silicon chips, not the Rust Belt and smokestacks. It was also a boom with its own cultural institutions and accents. Just as the 1920s' boom became linked in the national imagination with the herky-jerky, grainy quality of the first "talkie" movies, this would be the boom of CNN twenty-four-hour news-reporting, *USA Today* trend-spotting, and MTV music video-watching; this would be the boom marking the debut of the modern network anchoring trinity of Dan Rather, Tom Brokaw, and Peter Jennings. The entrepreneurs of the moment such as Lee Iacocca, Donald Trump, and Ted Turner would join President Reagan in elevating the pursuit of wealth, the compulsion to consume, and the desperation to succeed from selfish acts of individualism into altruistic acts of patriotism. This brazen ethos, along with the slick sensibility and colorful graphics of an increasingly wired world, would be part of the Big Chillers' "yuppie" package.[37]

Although Heinecken, a member of the silent generation, was older than the typical baby-boomer yuppie, his interest in electronic media and focus on manufactured desire led him to engage with and explore this new ethos. He saw how the yuppie incorporated behaviors and traits characteristic of earlier American personality types, and he was thus aware of his own similarities to this newest of American ideals.

Yuppies, as Troy argues, had

> an addiction to building an identity around exotic food, trendy clothing, slick cars, and all of the other supposedly finer things in life. The archetypal yuppie built an identity on consuming rather than being, on things rather than relationships, on an aesthetic life rather than ascetic living. There was a fetishism to it, a competitive, status-oriented, and obsessive search for the right spice or accent piece. The yuppie church was the health club or bistro, the yuppie sacraments a rigorous exercise regime or the brilliantly idiosyncratic four-course meal.[38]

Yuppies were also technology obsessed, supporting the burgeoning consumer electronics market in computers, video cameras, VCRs, answering machines, pagers, and the Sony Walkman. As emblematized by the yuppie, the 1980s marked a huge uptick in consumer technology consumption:

In its January 3, 1983, issue, *Time* magazine violated its "Man of the Year" tradition, designating a 1982 "Machine of the Year"—the computer. With 2.8 million units purchased for $4.9 billion, in "1982 a cascade of computers beeped and blipped their way into the American office, the American school, the American home," heralding the "information revolution." By repudiating the 1960s with their march to materialism, yuppies became the shock troops of the Reagan restoration. Their excess reflected Reaganism's success, seeking salvation through prosperity.[39]

And the relationships that Americans built up with their familiar newscasters—avatars of the new, educated, specialized, and technologically savvy professional class—were important avenues that encouraged this shift toward increasing materialism and apolitical behavior during the Reagan years.

By the 1980s, as Heinecken's series revealed, newscasters had become celebrities in their own right. With their slick good looks and their increasingly affluent lifestyles, they were no longer mere conduits for information; instead, they had become famous, simply by reporting on other significant individuals and events. Because they tended to be younger than their male counterparts, newswomen in particular were exemplars of the yuppie stereotype, and they encouraged the decade's focus on appearance, materialism, and the cultivation of the self. Like the President of the United States, they needed to be viewed with suspicion, since merely consuming their images furthered the objectification of everyday life.

When viewed critically, on the other hand, Heinecken's newscasters could help diagnose the contradictions of the Reagan revolution.[40] As scholars have pointed out, actual yuppies made up a small percentage of all Americans.[41] However, as the ideal of the baby boomers, the generation that was then becoming ascendent in terms of power and influence, yuppies represented the specific ideological energies that powered the Reagan era. As Heinecken's television work revealed, the yuppie helped direct the 1980s by emblematizing a twisted, egalitarian ideal. A form that could be equally embodied by both men and women—and as suggested by Connie Chung's rise to megastardom, increasingly by Americans of all different ethnicities—the yuppie myth concealed the fact that the changes initiated by the rights revolutions of the 1960s and 1970s were beginning to run aground. And by incorporating a greater diversity of participants, the neoliberal yuppie ideal allowed its adherents to pretend that racism and sexism had been overcome by the 1980s, thus ironically supporting the growing structural racism and sexism of an increasingly postindustrial capitalist status quo.[42] By defamiliarizing both gender and race, Heinecken's newscaster composites could perhaps have reminded their spectators of this fact: that despite its greater tolerance of diversity, its rejection of racism and sexism on an individual level, the yuppie ideal allowed individuals to escape a feeling of culpability for the unequal systems in which they operated.

TV in the Late 1980s

In the later 1980s, Heinecken's TV work became environmental again, and in different artworks he critiqued the new yuppie consciousness that was taking form around him. Like *TV/Time Environment* (1970), *Waking Up in News America* (1986) was an installation simulating a living room with similar furniture; it was first installed at the Museum of Contemporary Art Chicago during the museum's Heinecken retrospective of 1986, and it was later re-created at Cherry and Martin Gallery in 2013 and the Museum of Modern Art in 2014 (Plate 7.10). Unlike *TV/Time,* the TV did not run in this installation, and two manikins were positioned in the room, to some extent usurping the space of the spectator who entered the exhibition. (A female figure was seated in the armchair; a male figure stood near to her, hugging the rear wall; both appeared to watch TV.) Everything in the environment—including the manikins, floor, and ceiling—was covered with photolithographs of newswomen photographs, all surrounded by the same appropriated TV console frame. Suggesting that Americans were becoming the very news subjects they consumed, *Waking Up* was much more static than *TV/Time,* and much less interactive as well.

Fragments of a phrase were distributed across the floors, ceilings, walls, figures, and objects: "Waking up in News America with mostly blue-eyed blondes. Pretending another Occidental sunrise. Sensing the technologic banzai." These clips simulated subtitles to an unheard soundtrack articulated by the frozen female celebrities. In the text, the evocation of whiteness through hair and eye color is undermined by the suggestion that the continuing ascendency of the Western world was a pretense, while technological "banzai" implied a mixing of Eastern and Western cultures as well as a sudden electronic attack. In contrast to *TV/Time,* which got the visitor to focus on their own temporal aleatory experience in relation to images and sounds, *Waking Up* provoked the spectator to focus more on the TV as a frame—an underlying interpretive structure that conditions how people process experience.

Another work, *Surrealism on TV* (1986), on the other hand, was much more radical, a Dadaist masterpiece that simultaneously seemed both simple and profound. The work took the form of a three-channel slide projection, comprising some two hundred 35mm color slides—appropriated

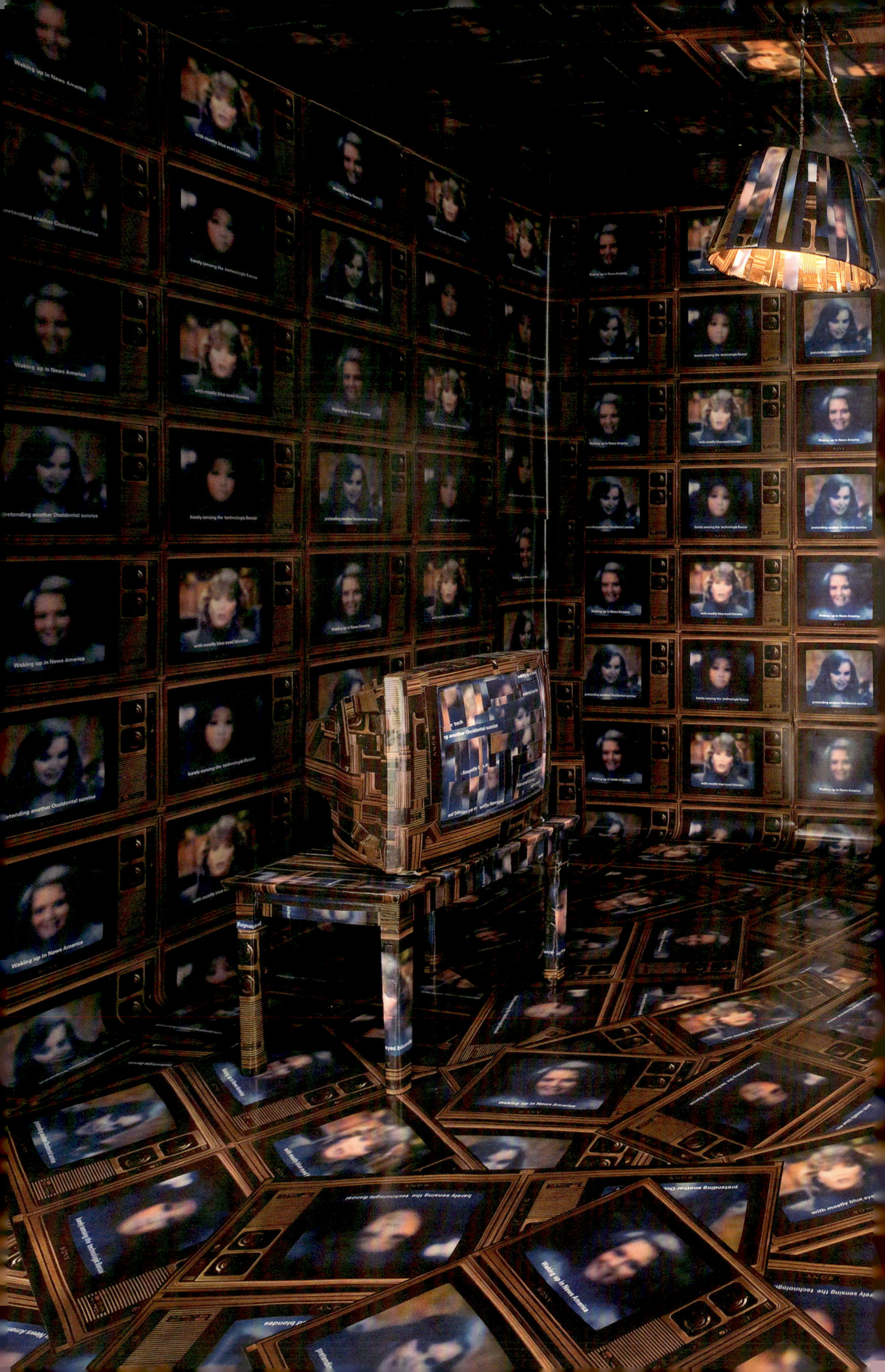

Waking up in News America
with mostly blue eyed blondes
pretending another Occidental sunrise
barely sensing the technologic flaw

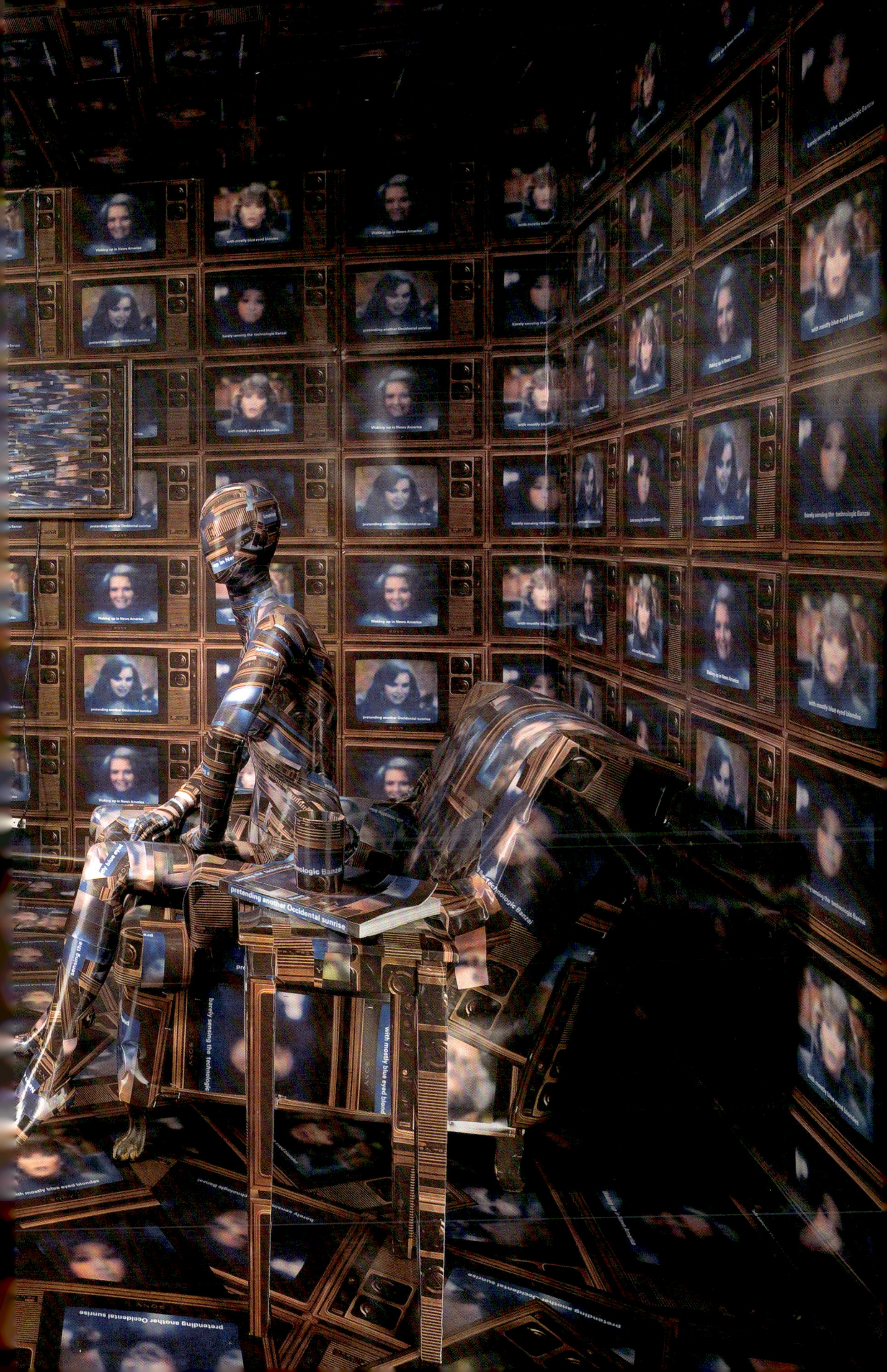

Waking up in News America
with mostly blue eyed blondes
pretending another Occidental sunrise
barely sensing the technologic Banzai

images depicting fires, newswomen, pet food commercials, aerobics instructors, sunsets, and religious/motivational figures (Plate 7.11). This cache of images was divided among three machines, each advancing its slides at a slightly different rate. The setup, producing seemingly endless combinations of images, was a mechanical approximation of the surrealist game of Exquisite Corpse transposed into the Ektachrome slide age. Sometimes multiple examples of the same type appeared—three perfectly coiffed blondes, for instance, or two cats and a newswoman. At other times the images were wholly heterogeneous. The work was also durational and aleatory: the spectator was invited to stay and consume image combination after image combination, the sustained contemplation of which provoked self-reflection at the same time as the work also focused attention on the common capitalist stereotypes that supported both Reagan and the yuppie mindset.

Mixing typology with chance, *Surrealism on TV* effected an uncanny simulacrum of television in the United States during Ronald Reagan's second presidential term. It also embodied what was best about Heinecken's work: his materiality, his concern for history, and his dialectical inventiveness. From the point of view of today, the work's trenchant historical materialism was particularly acute. Its emphasis on juxtaposition in particular seemed designed to provoke the spectator to think about the television remote and the way that this device would begin to transform experience in the 1980s. As Jimmie Reeves and Michael Epstein note, remotes—along with VCRs and other forms of audiovideo recorder and playback devices—fostered a more personal, aleatory, and associational attitude to the consumption of television:

> Along with the VCR (and other new media technologies such as videodisc players and video games) came remote control keypads. These small, handheld devices were first introduced in the mid-1950s, but they did not become commonplace in most American homes until the widespread adoption of cable and VCRs during the 1980s. "There's no doubt that the remote control switch revolutionized the way we watched TV in the '80s," announced David Lachenbruch in *TV Guide* in January 1990. By 1991, at least 37 percent of all domestic viewers admitted that they preferred channel surfing (or quickly flipping through the 33.2 channels they now received on average) than just turning their television sets on to watch one specific program.[43]

Corresponding to the shift from broadcasting to narrowcasting, the remote marked the rise of cable TV, with its twenty-four-hour news cycle, its more distracted mode of viewing, and its incubation of specialized programming, which significantly increased the number of content producers.[44]

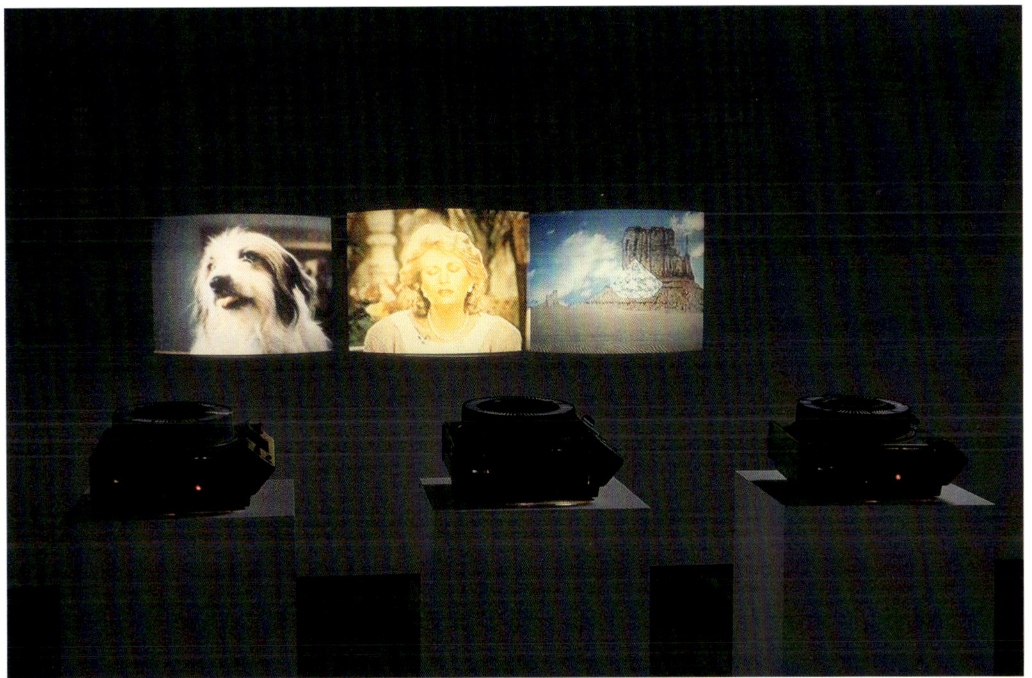

As *Surrealism on TV* suggested, the remote allowed spectators to create their own montage of the broadcast stream, a new capacity that had enormous effects in the cable TV era and after. It made television more personal, subservient to the spectator's ever-changing desires and interests; and it made the broadcast medium less one-way, potentially less hegemonic in relation to individual consumers. Simultaneously, with the proliferation of the remote, the spectator was also being granted access to a broadcast environment that was becoming ever more variegated; niche markets were growing at a staggering pace, and the potential for increasingly bizarre juxtapositions was steadily increasing. Although the power of the mass media to instill passivity and provoke consumption continued to grow, as *Surrealism on TV* suggested, one of its central devices, the montage, was also a key to its creative potential. Not only could the remote and the cable system liberate the viewer by allowing them to imagine new behaviors and identities outside of traditional ones: the television stream also contained the potential for disruptive montage within itself.

Heinecken believed that along with the conformist behaviors and identities conveyed by television, the medium also contained naturally occurring moments of disruptive juxtaposition. The premise behind his book *1984: A Case Study in Finding an Appropriate TV Newswoman* was this naturally occurring electronic moment of montage. He described his process in a self-published brochure that advertised the volume:

The subject of this work is the process by which "CBS Morning News"
determines which woman will be hired to fill the vacant slot as the morning anchorperson. The docudrama premise which evolves is based on
the "fact" that when the TV studio cameras cut from one person's head to
another's, there is a brief instant when the visages of two individuals are
exquisitely fused in superimposition. At that moment the TV audience subliminally perceives a single combinational person. In this way the viewers'
judgement of the image as being attractive vs. grotesque etc. is formed
unconsciously without their knowledge.[45]

Although the montage instant that Heinecken described did indeed take place in the TV broadcast stream, it is unclear if all his 1984 composites were actually made this way. Their precision, as well as their connections to the male and female portraits from which they were derived, suggests that this was probably not the case, and that they were instead made by combining or printing two separate slides. What is clear, however, is that montage was central to Heinecken's belief in the productive power of television, and this concern is one of the reasons that his work from this time endures.

Although Heinecken's art continued to be shown in significant venues throughout the 1980s, it was criticized more and more. In addition, despite the fact that his practice had for two decades explored the very issues that seemed most pertinent to the advanced artists of the 1980s, no mention of Heinecken was made in the criticism surrounding contemporary art, and in particular postmodern photography. In retrospect, this can seem surprising, because Heinecken's work in many ways fit critical notions about postmodernism in photography, and postmodern photography during this time became critically and commercially accepted. Not only did Heinecken's materials resemble those of the "pictures generation" of artists who emerged in the 1980s, but so did his devices—appropriation, allegory, and the mixing of mediums.[46] His themes, including sexuality, violence, and the mass media's impact on identity, were also similar.

There is not enough space here to elaborate at length on Heinecken's relationship to postmodern photography, nor is it necessary to do so.[47] Instead, a few key similarities with the first-generation postmodern pho-tographers will only be described in outline. Like Richard Prince, as we have seen, Heinecken created works consisting of appropriated magazine photographs—constellations of images that formed media typologies and thus allowed their viewers to consider stereotypes of gender, race, class, and sexuality.[48] And like Barbara Kruger, Heinecken repurposed the strat-egies of consumer advertising, consistently merging image and text to inspire spectator self-consciousness and a rejection of the status quo.[49] Moreover, as suggested by some of his *He:/She:* works, Heinecken, like

Cindy Sherman, used photographic self-portraiture to demonstrate the performative and socially constructed character of human identity.[50] Furthermore, like Laurie Simmons and others, he photographed dolls and children's toys to examine how psyche and identity were formed within the context of the family. And like Sherrie Levine, Heinecken used appropriation to interrogate the concept of copyright in U.S. capitalist society. These similarities, both formal and conceptual, demonstrate the tremendous growth of the strategies and issues that Heinecken had pursued since the early 1960s.

That Heinecken was not better recognized as an earlier practitioner of many of these postmodern concerns during the 1980s was a result of the relative hegemony of the New York art market at the time, an economy that was invested in its local artists and galleries, and that looked for legitimation to the postmodern theory that was emerging then as well.[51] It seemed self-evident in New York that Heinecken was not part of "critical" postmodernism, and the fact that he anticipated much of its most radical aspects became easier to ignore.[52] Yet to ignore Heinecken was to miss out on an important and critical body of art. As demonstrated by the correspondences between Heinecken's television work of the 1970s and 1980s and McLuhan's ideas about the new electronic environment and the global village that the mass media was helping to bring about, postmodernism was not the only discourse in which appropriation art could be productively discussed. In addition, Heinecken's critical representations of contemporary figures like Reagan and broadcast newscasters were shockingly prescient—symbolizing the 1980s with its unbridled capitalism, materialism, and electronic manipulation of truth, while anticipating the post-truth "fake news" era of today. In the final chapter, we will follow Heinecken as he responded to the early 1990s through a series of new and recycled artistic techniques. During this time, questions of diversity were to become more prominent in his art.

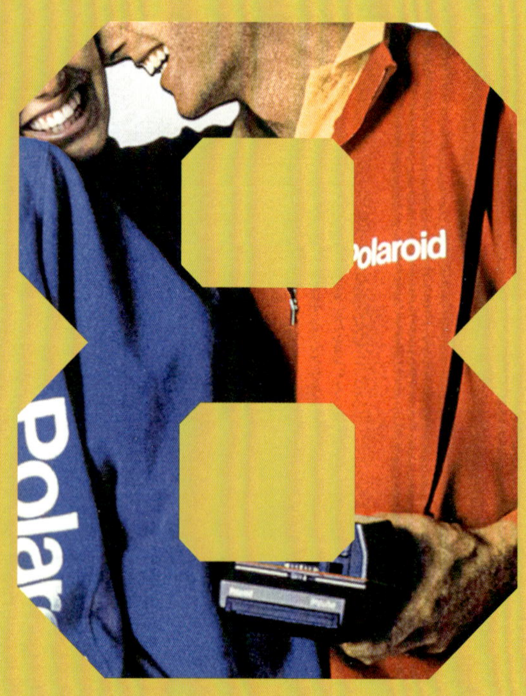

8

APPROPRIATION IN THE 1980s AND 1990s

History and the Body at the End of the Analog Era

THROUGHOUT THE LATE 1980S AND 1990S, Heinecken continued to innovate, developing new forms of hybrid practice including
three-dimensional collages and freestanding photographic figures that
combined the human body with logos and mass-produced products. The
former referenced Heinecken's ancestry, exploring hybrid identity and
consumption, while the latter interrogated advertising and media subcultures like home videotaping. In other works of this time period, Heinecken
returned to his earlier strategies of the magazine photogram and the
collaged magazine, albeit with significant changes. In these works, he
challenged the prevailing stereotypes of the United States in the Bush
and early-Clinton eras, deconstructing ideals of masculinity, femininity,
class, and race with both ferocity and humor.[1]

As his creativity continued to flourish in the 1980s and early 1990s, so
did Heinecken's career as an artist. In addition to numerous solo shows
in U.S. university art museums and centers, Heinecken also presented
substantial one-person exhibitions in important commercial photography galleries, such as Fahey/Klein Gallery in Los Angeles (1987, 1992),
Gallery MIN in Tokyo (1986, 1990), and Pace/McGill Gallery in New York
(1989, 1992). Heinecken's association with Light Gallery ended in 1981
with solo shows in New York and Los Angeles that year.[2] Heinecken also
commanded a growing presence in Europe and Asia, and most important,
he began to garner solo exhibitions at major art museums in the United
States, for example, the Art Institute of Chicago, in 1987, with a show
titled *Television/Source/Subject.* But perhaps because of his connections
to the commercial photography market, it would take another decade for
Heinecken's career to advance to the next level, when he was recognized
as an artist first and foremost, and not just a somewhat suspect albeit
well-known photographer.

This transformation in Heinecken's reputation—the change from photographer to artist—mostly occurred after Heinecken's death in 2006,
corresponding with a series of new shows and retrospectives, events
that created both enthusiasm and debate. Major exhibitions were produced, beginning with *Robert Heinecken: Photographist, A Thirty-Five Year
Retrospective* at the Museum of Contemporary Art in Chicago, in 1999, a
show that traveled to the Los Angeles County Museum of Art in 2000.[3] In
2006, the Smart Museum of Art in Chicago put on an exhibition focused
on Heinecken's magazines; the Museum of Contemporary Photography
in Chicago followed in 2007 with another retrospective, *Robert Heinecken
1932–2006: Sex and Food, A Memorial Exhibition.*[4] In 2014, the Museum of
Modern Art in New York presented *Object Matter,* Heinecken's most extensive retrospective until then, an exhibition that traveled to the Hammer
Museum in Los Angeles and remained on view until early 2015.[5] Also

indicative of the shift in Heinecken's reputation was the change in dealers: instead of being represented by specialized photography galleries as he was up to the early 1990s, Heinecken began to be shown by mainstream contemporary art galleries that presented work in a variety of different media. His first exhibition at Rhona Hoffman Gallery in Chicago occurred in 1999; it was followed by Marc Selwyn Fine Art in Los Angeles, who has represented him since 2008; and Cherry and Martin in Los Angeles and Friedrich Petzel in New York, both of which began representing the artist in 2011. (Cherry and Martin closed in early 2018.) Although the discussion of postmodern photography in New York tended more and more to ignore Heinecken, and even edit him out of the conversation, his stature as a contemporary artist continued to grow.

Photo-Sculptural Work in the Late 1980s and 1990s

Beginning in 1987, Heinecken returned to the question of the photographic object, exploring the relationship between photography and sculpture through new avenues of practice. He began by making relief collages consisting primarily of color magazine pages, which he crumpled, stiffened with varnish, and mounted onto board, sometimes adding paint. Appropriating clothing and product advertising, he folded and scrunched carefully cut out, two-dimensional images that were banal and airbrushed in content, morphing them into slightly tumescent shapes that he then assembled into much larger configurations. For the most part in Heinecken's compositions, one or two hybrid figures appeared, embedded within a seemingly flickering, patterned environment that was composed of multiple, smaller figures and objects. Interacting with the larger figures, these configurations of commodities and persons suggested environments populated by products and screens: media-saturated spheres in which the spectator's body and their experience of their own physical environment was always also simultaneously connected to a variety of different outside objects and situations.

As the series evolved, Heinecken increased its heterogeneity on a number of different levels. In earlier works like *Upper Middle Class Nuclear Family* (1987), *First Class Male* (1987), and *Credit Card Witch* (1987), the artist focused on specific (sometimes peculiar, but still recognizable) identity stereotypes, deconstructing them through three-dimensional facture and the incorporation of nonhuman, nonbodily image fragments. In these works, the figures are only partially present: mangled, amputated forms set off against a dark background. They appear as dismembered social types, broken figures that suture together flesh and consumer products in traumatic configurations.

As Heinecken developed the series, the chimerical figures grew larger and more complete; they thus increased in physical presence while retaining their disturbing mangled qualities. (This was the case in part because scale contrasts between different components of the collages were magnified in the new configurations.) In addition, the titles of the relief collages started to reference South Asian Hindu deities; and the poses of the main figures became based on dance- and yoga-inspired forms of traditional Indian religious sculpture, a change that introduced a multicultural, multiethnic significance to the tableaus. These references to Hindu religion and culture were a way for the artist to focus on a partic-ular aspect of his own identity: according to his family history, Heinecken had South Asian ancestry. His paternal grandfather, Friedli Heinecken, a missionary preacher, married a mixed-race Indian woman, who gave birth to Robert's father in Berlin before the entire family emigrated to the United States.[6] Toward the end of his life, increasingly fascinated with his mixed ethnicity—which represented for him his grandfather's rejection of his northern European identity and culture—Heinecken used the relief collages to interrogate aspects of his self-image and self-understanding that were radically distinct from the rest of his family's white Lutheran heritage. As suggested by works like *Shiva Manifesting as a Single Mother* (1989), *Shiva, the Lord Whose Half Is Woman* (1990), *"Shiva and Parvati Seated, Embracing" and Their Son Ganesha* (1991), and *"Shiva, King of Danc-ers" Manifesting as a Transvestite* (1992), this exploration was both socially critical and deeply personal. Resulting as it did in preposterous mash-ups of gender and race, images that were banal and striking at the same time, the work evoked the growing multiculturalism of the moment, as well as the tensions globalism provoked (Plate 8.1).

The complex mixing of ethnicity and gender in Heinecken's later relief collages was particularly significant. Although composed of banal, airbrushed representations of mostly white models, they seemed to under-mine many of the distinctions that traditionally supported white identities within the United States. Not only were clear separations between different genders broken down, undermining the patriarchal and heteronormative ideology that supported whiteness, but supposedly Caucasian skin was shown to have a range of different hues and tonalities as well as striking affinities with the skins of animals and consumer products. As a result, attentive viewers were left with a sense of the porousness and indetermi-nacy of white identity, a sense that whiteness was performed, and perhaps also an awareness of whiteness's multiethnic history. As suggested by these relief collages, as successive waves of immigrants became American, certain groups—previously defined by their ethnic or national origin—were assimilated into a white U.S. society that was never very pure (Plate 8.2).[7]

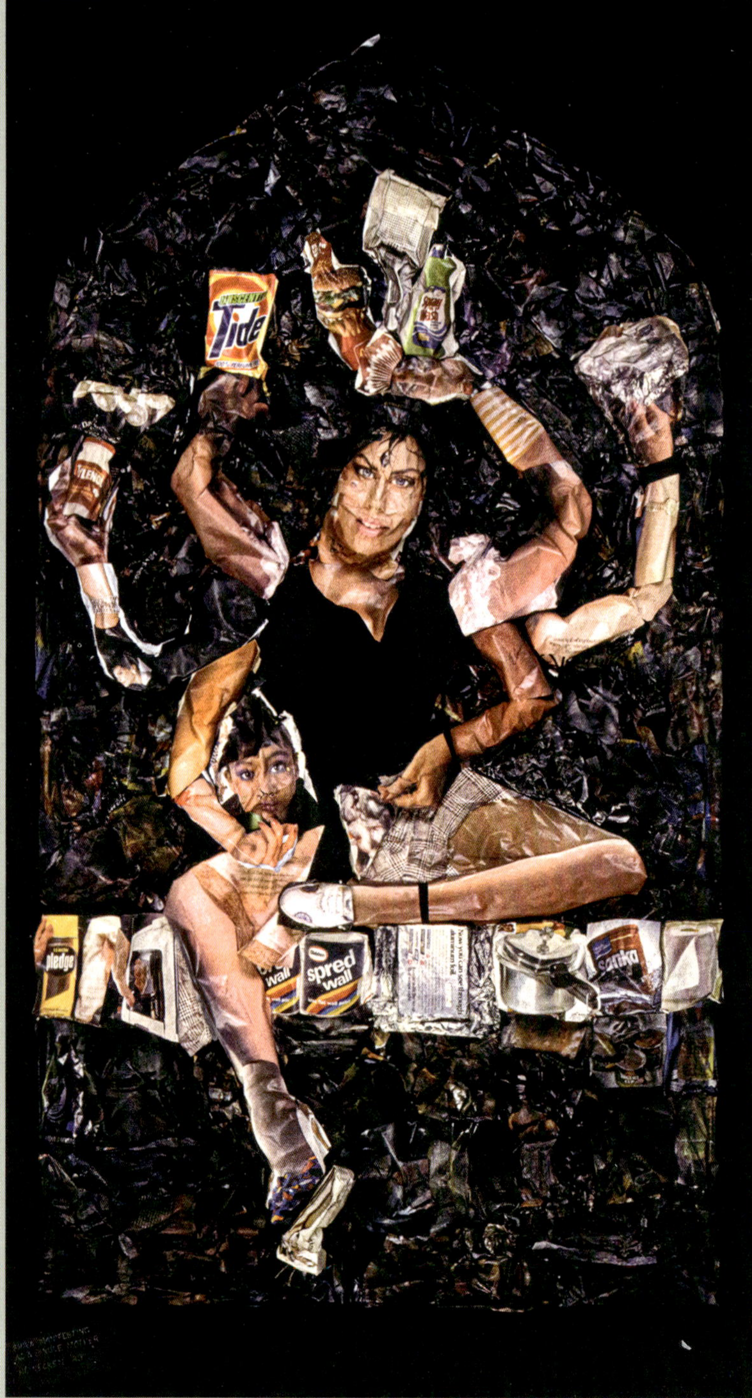

◄ **PLATE 8.1.** Robert Heinecken, *Shiva Manifesting as a Single Mother* (1989). Magazine paper, paint and varnish, 84 x 48 inches (213.4 x 121.9 cm). Collection Philip F. Denny, Chicago. COPYRIGHT 2022 THE ROBERT HEINECKEN TRUST, CHICAGO.

➤ **PLATE 8.2.** Robert Heinecken, *Shiva, the Lord Whose Half Is Woman* (1990). Magazine paper, paint and varnish, 83 $\frac{7}{10}$ x 48 x 3 ½ inches (212.7 x 121.9 x 8.9 cm). Private collection. COPYRIGHT 2022 THE ROBERT HEINECKEN TRUST, CHICAGO.

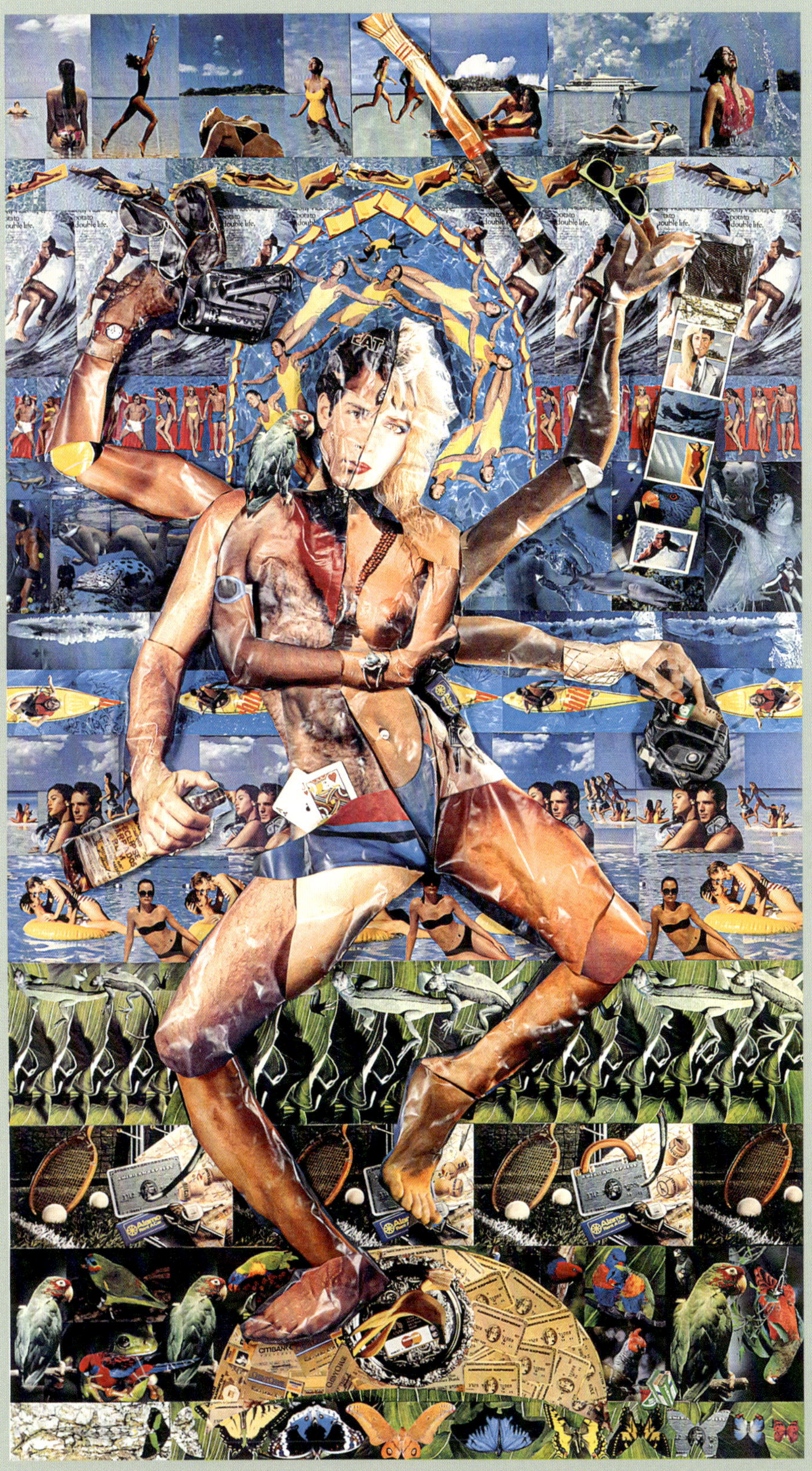

Even more destabilizing was the polymorphous sexuality that ran strongly through these works. In combination with the evocation of multiple ethnicities and the description of the United States as a melting pot of immigrants from different countries, they suggested that attraction and desire were powerful forces for the overcoming of social, racial, and political differences. Sex connected bodies to larger, often global networks, and as a result people become more and more open to nontraditional affinities and associations through their erotic and sexual interests and behaviors. As Heinecken noted in the late 1990s:

> The love of sex, the poetry of sex, is so much tied into the Hindu religion unlike any other religion I know of. My grandfather and my father broke the taboos of their religion. Both were Lutheran ministers who left their clerical positions, lived the secular life, repented, and then were forgiven and welcomed back into the fold. I think you can find sexuality in everything, if you look closely enough, and I think it's there in all my work.[8]

And this almost religious sense of desire and sexuality promoting cross-racial and multiethnic identities, so particular to the artist's retrospective self-image, permeates these late relief collages.

If some of Heinecken's photo-sculptural works, like the relief collages, actually imagined new forms of multiracial identity, others simply critiqued the ideals of whiteness that continued to circulate in American culture. At the end of the 1980s, Heinecken began working on a second series of sculptural objects that followed this latter path; these consisted of life-size, cutout figures of humans and animals, collaged with other mass-market images that he sometimes assembled into larger tableaus. Appropriations of the figural advertising displays that record, film, and video companies in particular (and also many other forms of corporation) regularly sent to retail outlets in the 1980s and 1990s, these flat, standing figures raised consequential questions about the relationship of consumers to visual culture in general. As he developed the series in the 1990s, Heinecken began to (re)photograph the standing, collaged figures, cutting them out at a life-size scale and mounting them on foam core. Throughout his investigation, he focused on the two-dimensional figure as a metaphor for the increasingly plastic and generic nature of white identity in the sex- and celebrity-obsessed 1990s: the mass media, these works suggested, asked a hegemonic white society to identify with cardboard cutouts.

Certain works, like *Rum and Coke Woman* (1989) and *Seated Figure/ Martini* (1991), are almost indistinguishable from the original liquor displays they appropriate.[9] In the former, it is only the figure's upraised-middle-finger gesture that gives Heinecken's editing away; in the latter, it is through the addition of a lock and chain that the artist transforms the mundane photographic object into a statement. The works, which initially appear trite and banal, become mysterious with contemplation. "What are these figures selling?" they ask us, and "Why do they consistently attract and repulse us at the same time?" In both cases, the spectator is invited to make eye contact with a figure that is both life-size and completely flat, a form of intimacy with an obviously nonhuman cardboard object. Other works, like *Polaroid Couple* (1992) and *Couple with Porno Tapes* (1992), are more obviously manipulated.[10] In both cases, the added images make the couples' relationships more overtly sexual, thus emphasizing the ways in which advertisers use sexually suggestive poses and gestures to sell their products.

Cybill Shepherd, the model who portrayed the Kodak girl for the company in 1972, appears repeatedly in this series, thus adding a self-reflexive element—a reference to the manufacturer and thus to the history of the

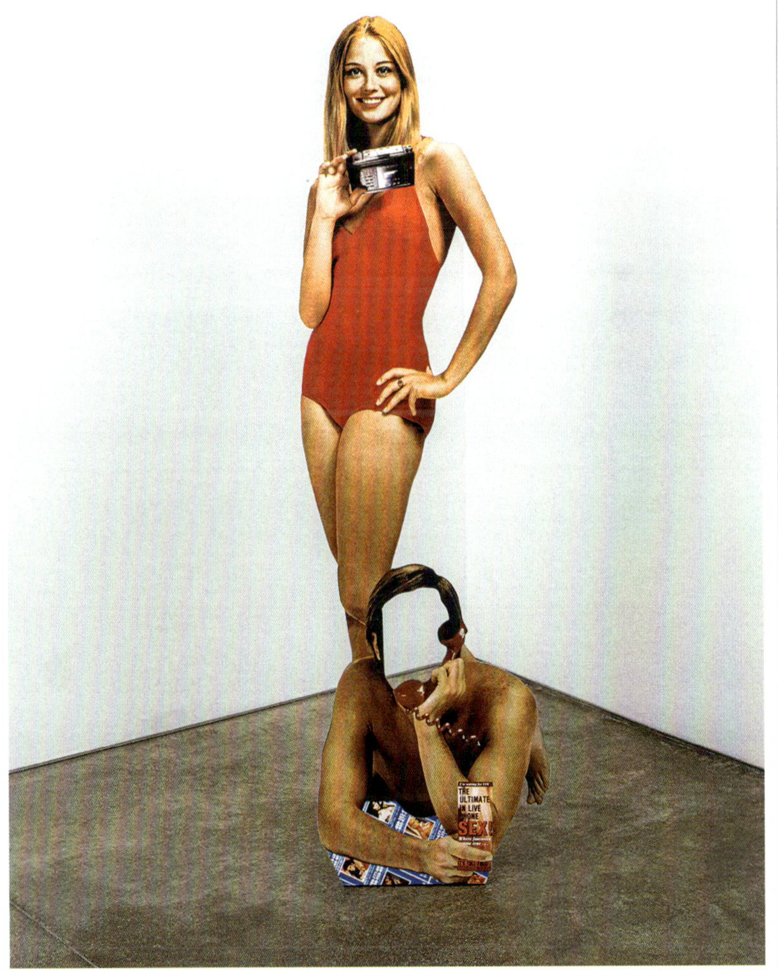

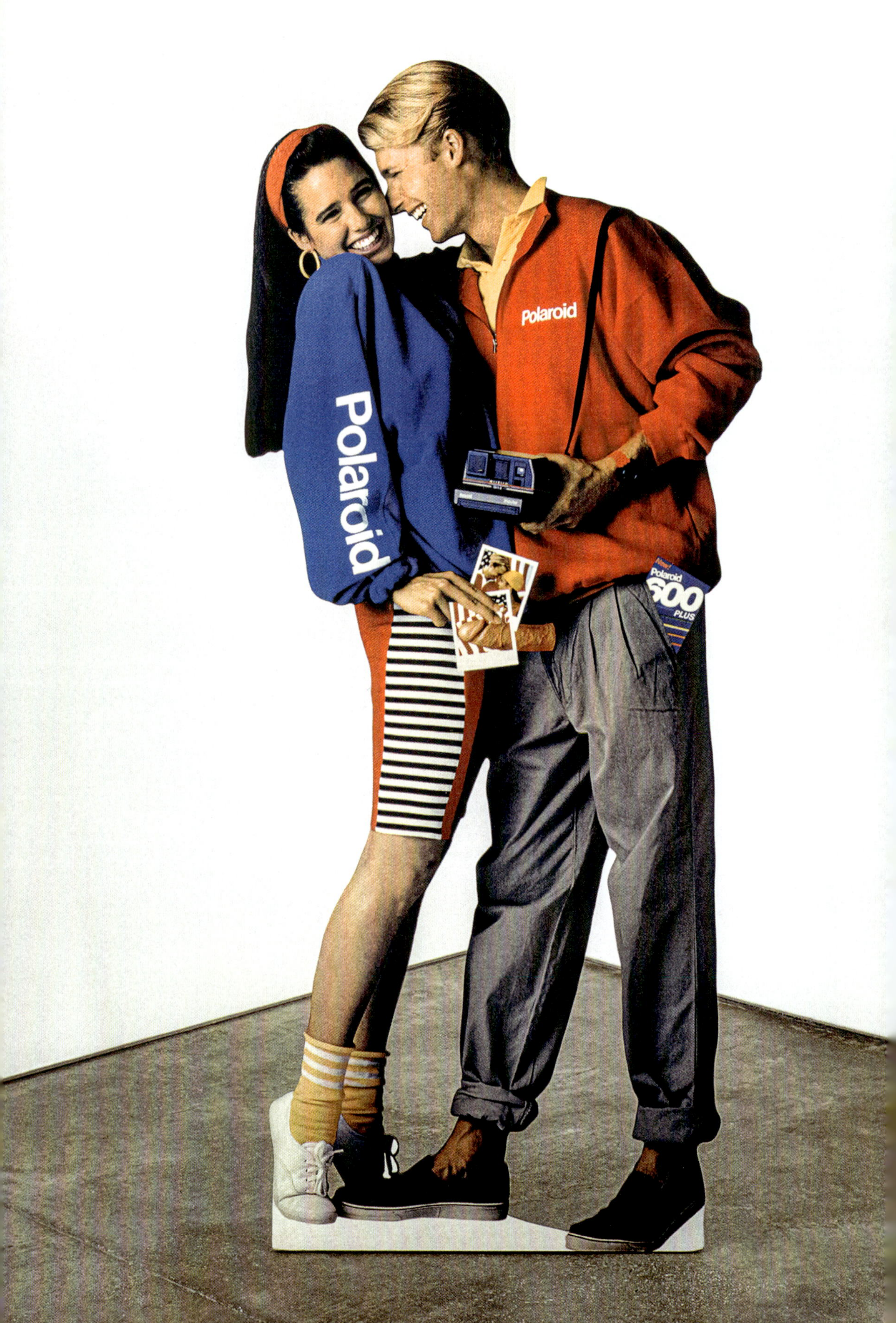
Polaroid
Polaroid
Polaroid
New!
Polaroid
600
PLUS

medium—to Heinecken's photographic sculptures.[11] Featured since the 1970s as an ideal embodiment of white female beauty, Shepherd was by the 1990s a well-known film and TV actress: a romantic lead and a symbol of the all-American girl of everybody's dreams. In *Cybill Shepherd/ Phone Sex* (1992), a life-size flat image mounted on foam core, the actress holds a camera, a prostrate man at her feet; faceless, he grasps a telephone in his left hand and circulars for telephone sex numbers in his right (Plate 8.3). As a whole the tableau suggests that sexuality is being transformed, moving from a physical to a virtual level. Although Shepherd and the anonymous male model physically touch, the couple does not seem to concentrate on one another but instead appear intensely focused on the spectator as well as technologies that extend their sight or their hearing. Like their bodies, their interest in their partner has flattened, attenuated. In *Cybill Shepherd and Bicycle* (1994), the celebrity straddles a handbag-bedecked bicycle, again evoking a sexual pairing between human and machine.[12] Finally, in *Woman Holding a Gun* (1997), the actress appears again, this time exposing her breasts and casually grasping a weapon.[13] Here, the all-American girl seems to embody both sexuality and violence, suggesting that—as mass media abstracts, reduces, and stereotypes human conduct—these two very different types of behavior draw closer and become more interchangeable.

Most of Heinecken's two-dimensional figures are comedic: there is something ironic between their cosmeticized perfection and the elements that have been added or removed. Heinecken also made proportionally sized baby and cat figures, and as the series developed, they were mobilized to construct uncanny tableaus and environments. Not unlike Heinecken's altered magazines of the 1990s, the depicted celebrities and models seem to crowd one another when assembled in the artist's tight configurations, undermining the fantasy of a one-on-one relationship with the spectator. Heinecken populated his growing universe with curious assemblages of people and types, including mermaids, security guards, sales workers, Elvira (Cassandra Peterson, the TV horror-movie hostess), Andre Agassi, and George H. W. Bush. Significantly, and in contrast to the relief collages, almost all of his cutout standing figures are white, evoking an American racial homogeneity that no longer existed in the United States. Both alone and in groups, the figures project a powerful sense of disquiet: they are overbearing and deadened at the same time, a frozen, commodified civilization on its last legs.

There is a reflexivity about photo-reproductive media in the standing figure series that extends beyond the selection of Kodak Girl Cybill Shepherd. In addition to food, booze, and tennis rackets, characters grasp cameras, X-ray films, and videotapes. By including an erect penis that extends from a young man's crotch through a SX-70 print held by a smiling woman who stares at the viewer, *Polaroid Couple* (1992) alludes to the growth of amateur pornography over the 1970s and 1980s (Plate 8.4). First the SX-70 system and then video, Heinecken's tableau suggests, allowed more and more consumers to see themselves as pornographic subjects, to objectify themselves for fame or profit (or for other reasons as well). *Couple with Porno Tapes* (1992) evokes the other side of this process: with the development of home video—the viewing of videotapes through VCR players hooked up to television sets—the consumption of pornography became even more widespread. Just as mainstream video stores introduced consumers to the advertising displays that Heinecken satirized, other types of these stores, generally the small, family-owned, or independent operations, acquainted them with X-rated content through back rooms in which adult material was kept. In the 1980s and 1990s, more and more Americans were being exposed to an ever-greater fund of pornographic representations, the long-term effects of which were still unknown. Flat, montaged chimeras, Heinecken's cutout figures were disturbing reminders of a rapid transformation in patterns of human sexuality that were taking place in the United States at this time.

Later Magazine Work

In the early 1990s, Heinecken returned to an intensive engagement with the American magazine. A brilliant example of this concern was *150 Years of Photojournalism* (1990), a "compromised magazine," as he now called them, which was created as an edition of eight, plus at least five artist proofs.[14] The work was an appropriation of the news magazine's commemorative issue on photojournalism from its origins to the present day. Consisting of seventy-five pages plus front and back covers, each iteration of the series was a simple re-presentation of the original mass-market object, changed only by the fact that parts of the pages were cut out allowing other images on the pages underneath to peek through. Appearing in the fall of 1989, the popular issue was a celebration of the magazine's own medium and genre. Employing the archaeological excision technique that he developed with *Periodical #9* (1972), Heinecken created an edition of roughly identical but nevertheless handmade copies, issues that disclosed how the famous news magazine (and the tradition of photojournalism that it represented) transformed the messy and ambiguous, constantly changing world into a clearly defined set of personalities and events.

The magazine was divided into an introduction titled "Icons" and five chapters. Beginning in 1839, the year of photography's invention, it covered

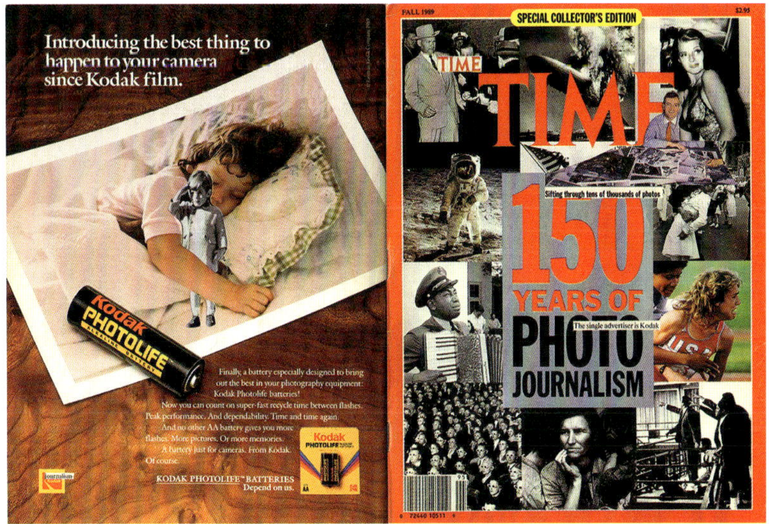

a trajectory that ran from the origins of documentary through the contemporary moment. Both the introduction and the subsequent chapters were arranged chronologically, and Heinecken's montages exploited this structure to present iconic yet surreal worlds in which past and future were consistently intermixed. These compromised magazines fit into the tradition of photomontage, but the technique was not practiced in the traditional avant-garde manner—namely, as a cutting up and mixing of photographs and other elements that could be repositioned freely on a new background. Instead, Heinecken created montage juxtapositions as a kind of archaeology: he removed shapes on bound pages to let the adjacent texts and images show through. As a result, the surreal images were not simple edits and recombinations chosen by the artist without constraint, but—because Heinecken had to discover significant juxtapositions that already existed—marvelous finds or profane illuminations, things that allegorized the larger moment as if they were artistically shaped.[15] And it was this aspect of Heinecken's practice of photomontage in his last great *Time* magazine work that gave the edition its uncanny power.

The cover, which presented *Time*'s characteristic title logo and red border as well as the subject of the special issue also included a grid of ten iconic images, visual previews of what the collector's edition contained (Plate 8.5). Heinecken's only changes to *Time*'s cover were two cuts. The first revealed a *Time* picture editor sitting at a table covered with photographs above the text "Sifting through tens of thousands of photographs." The second was a horizontal excavation revealing the line "The single advertiser is Kodak." Together, these visual and linguistic fragments formed a shorthand suggesting the incredible power that a select group of technology and media companies held over the common perception

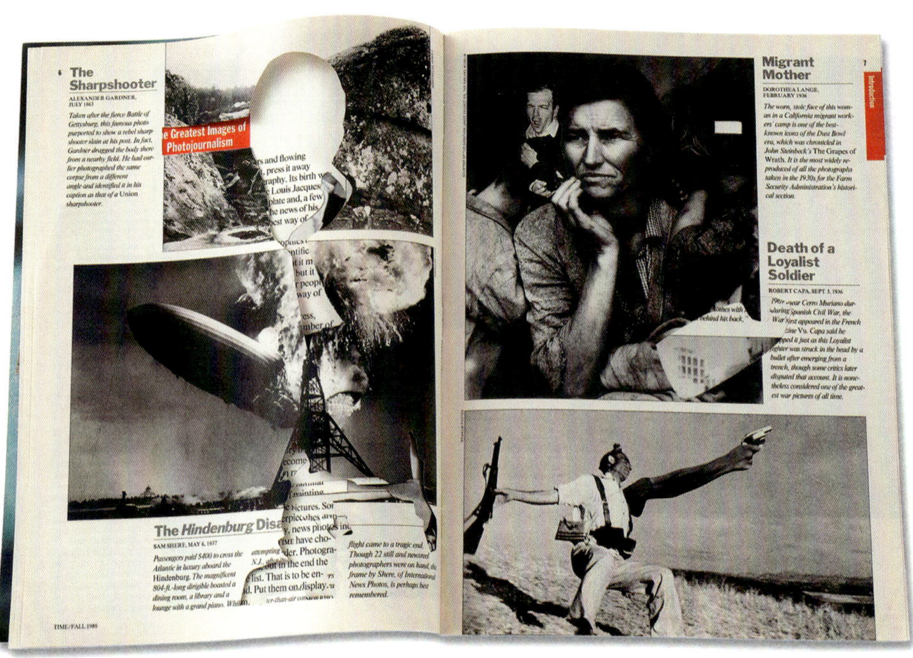

The Sharpshooter

ALEXANDER GARDNER, JULY 1863

Taken after the fierce Battle of Gettysburg, this famous photo purported to show a rebel sharpshooter slain at his post. In fact, Gardner dragged the body there from a nearby field. He had earlier photographed the same corpse from a different angle and identified it in his caption as that of a Union *sharpshooter.*

The *Hindenburg* Disaster

SAM SHERE, MAY 6, 1937

Passengers paid $400 to cross the Atlantic in luxury aboard the Hindenburg. *The magnificent 804-ft.-long dirigible boasted a dining room, a library and a lounge with a grand piano. When...*

Migrant Mother

DOROTHEA LANGE, FEBRUARY 1936

The worn, stoic face of this woman in a California migrant workers' camp is one of the best-known icons of the Dust Bowl era, which was chronicled in John Steinbeck's The Grapes of Wrath. *It is the most widely reproduced of all the photographs taken in the 1930s for the Farm Security Administration's historical section.*

Death of a Loyalist Soldier

ROBERT CAPA, SEPT. 5, 1936

...near Cerro Muriano during Spanish Civil War, the War first appeared in the French ...zine Vu. *Capa said he ...ped it just as this Loyalist fighter was struck in the head by a bullet after emerging from a trench, though some critics later disputed that account. It is nonetheless considered one of the greatest war pictures of all time.*

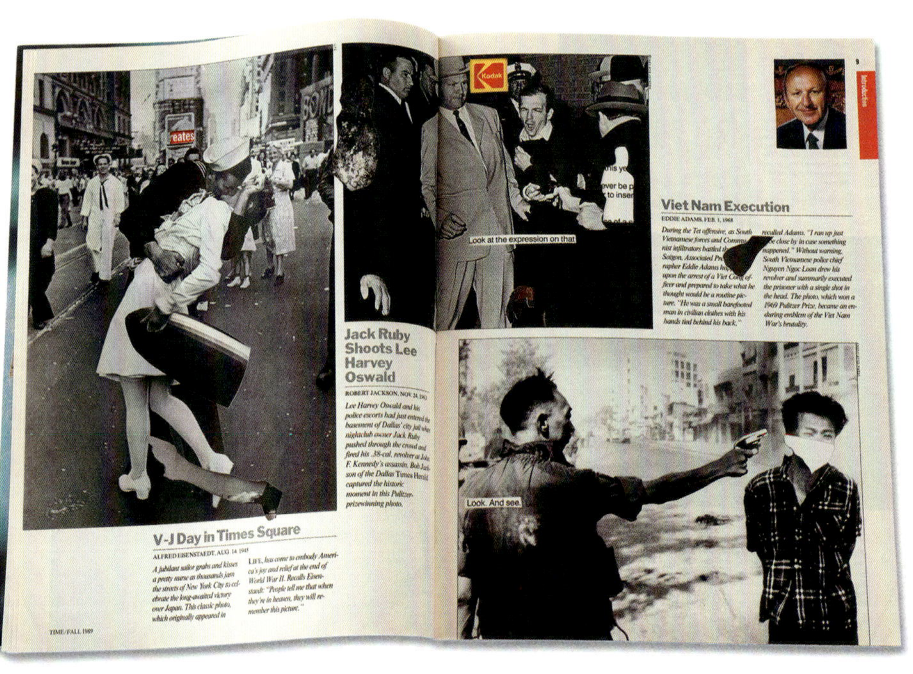

V-J Day in Times Square

ALFRED EISENSTAEDT, AUG. 14 1945

A jubilant sailor grabs and kisses a pretty nurse as thousands jam the streets of New York City to celebrate the long-awaited victory over Japan. This classic photo, which originally appeared in LIFE, *has come to embody America's joy and relief at the end of World War II. Recalls Eisenstaedt: "People tell me that when they're in heaven, they will remember this picture."*

Jack Ruby Shoots Lee Harvey Oswald

ROBERT JACKSON, NOV. 24, 1963

Lee Harvey Oswald and his police escorts had just entered basement of Dallas' city ... nightclub owner Jack Ru... pushed through the crow... fired his .38-cal. revolver ... F. Kennedy's assassin, Bob Jackson of the Dallas Times *Herald captured the historic moment in this Pulitzer-prizewinning photo.*

Viet Nam Execution

EDDIE ADAMS, FEB. 1, 1968

During the Tet offensive, as South Vietnamese forces and Communist infiltrators battled th... Saigon, Associated Press photographer Eddie Adams hap... upon the arrest of a Viet Cong officer and prepared to take what he thought would be a routine picture. "He was a small barefooted man in civilian clothes with his hands tied behind his back," recalled Adams. *"I ran up just to be close by in case something happened." Without warning, South Vietnamese police chief Nguyen Ngoc Loan drew his revolver and summarily executed the prisoner with a single shot in the head. The photo, which won a 1969 Pulitzer Prize, became an enduring emblem of the Viet Nam War's brutality.*

of the past. And through this simple form of montage, which Heinecken repeated throughout the issue, the American mass media, an industrial medium of capitalist propaganda, appeared to unmask itself by revealing its guiding narrative tropes and stereotypes.

As the reader pages through the magazine, the cuts create a sense of figures and situations morphing into one another. On pages 4 and 5, for example, part of the background surrounding the Marine figure group from Joe Rosenthal's *Raising the Flag at Iwo Jima* (1945), is cut away, revealing the forearm, hand, and head of Dorothea Lange's *Migrant Mother* (1936), on page 7 beneath. The Marines seem to elevate the migrant mother along with the American flag, while beneath them another figure from the previous decade, Robert Capa's falling combatant from *Death of a Loyalist Soldier* (1936), drops away from the squad as if he were their murdered companion. What is striking about Heinecken's technique is how the disparate images merge together despite the scale differences and their fixed orientation in the image field due to their nature as components of a bound periodical. This creates an uncanny effect in that the images seem true, despite the fact that they violate both logic and historical knowledge. Notwithstanding the morphing of scales, events, and individuals—and in the face of Heinecken's playful rewriting of history—the connections disclosed come across as somehow real or as expressing something true. The reader can imagine that the artist has found preexisting moments of convergence and has used his X-Acto knife to excavate them like an archaeological discovery.

The iconic, yet morphing individuals and events also repeat, forming new uncanny clusters and combinations. On page 7, Robert Capa's loyalist soldier topples again, now sprouting a new left arm, the limb of Nguyen Ngoc Loan in Eddie Adams's *Saigon Execution* (1968), which emerges from page 9 underneath (Plate 8.6). Above the Vietnam execution on page 9, Oswald pops up behind the migrant mother, only to be shot by Jack Ruby in Robert Jackson's *Jack Ruby Shoots Lee Harvey Oswald* (1963) (Plate 8.7). Excavations are made exposing texts below that seem to comment on the action: the Kodak logo above Oswald's head; the phrase "Look at the expression on that," over which his clenched body crumples; and "Look and see" across the back of the South Vietnamese executioner below him. Written language once again links historical actors and events to technology, consumerism, and a kind of augmented but disjunctive vision. Although *Time*'s editors attempted to form history into a coherent framework of actors, contexts, and events in the original magazine, Heinecken's edits disrupted their simplistic narratives and enforced continuities, imagining possible worlds and alternative developments that the popular historians could not envision.

The continuation of people and events across timeframes also implies the persistence of particular states of affairs or conditions over long periods.[16] As Heinecken's montage juxtapositions suggest, just as war and social violence seem to be constants across time, so does economic exploitation—something that is evoked by his merging of Jakob Riis's *Children Sleeping on Mulberry Street (Street Arabs in Sleeping Quarters)* (1889) on page 23 with Lewis Hine's *Breaker Boys in Coal Mine, South Pittston, PA* (1911) on page 25. If popular history relies on cause-and-effect relationships, the assumption of fundamental conflicts, and the belief that individuals and groups are motivated by goals, ideas, and emotions, then Heinecken's cross-temporal events suggest that these narrative conventions conceal as much as they reveal. Historical "truth" is always much more multicausal and complex.

Heineken did a dry run for his *Time* project several years earlier, with the compromised *Newsweek, October 21, 1974* (1974), a regular issue of *Time*'s primary competitor that contained a nineteen-page cover story on photography, an article that examined mostly contemporary manifestations and discussed the medium's documentary and artistic aspects.[17] Here, he also used the archaeological form of montage that he started in *Periodical #9* and would use to great effect in *150 Years.* Speaking about his compromised *Newsweek* (while noting that he began the altered magazines in the late 1960s while bedridden and recovering from chickenpox), Heinecken recalled:

> I tried to use whatever my feelings told me about the material that was being presented to the public and alter it in a specific rather than a random way. So by putting an African person into an Ansel Adams landscape or by relating William Buckley to war or by giving Diane Arbus, who committed suicide, a censor's mark, I attempted to expand a sickbed idea into something more expressive.[18]

This expressivity is highly apparent in *150 Years,* in which Heinecken used his archaeological method of photomontage to open up the associative meanings of the magazine's historical subjects. And by creating ruptures, historical discontinuities that allowed different moments to speak to one another, the work promoted an alternative view of American history and the guiding ideologies through which the nation evolved.

On page 37, a shouting, bare-chested Muhammad Ali appears as a character in Dorothea Lange's *White Angel Breadline, San Francisco* (1932), perhaps leading the unemployed men from the Great Depression beyond the barricades that hem them in (Plate 8.8). Like the head of a more contemporary looking girl below him, which is sutured to the shoulders of the daughter of a Depression-era farmer in Walker Evans's *Floyd Burroughs*

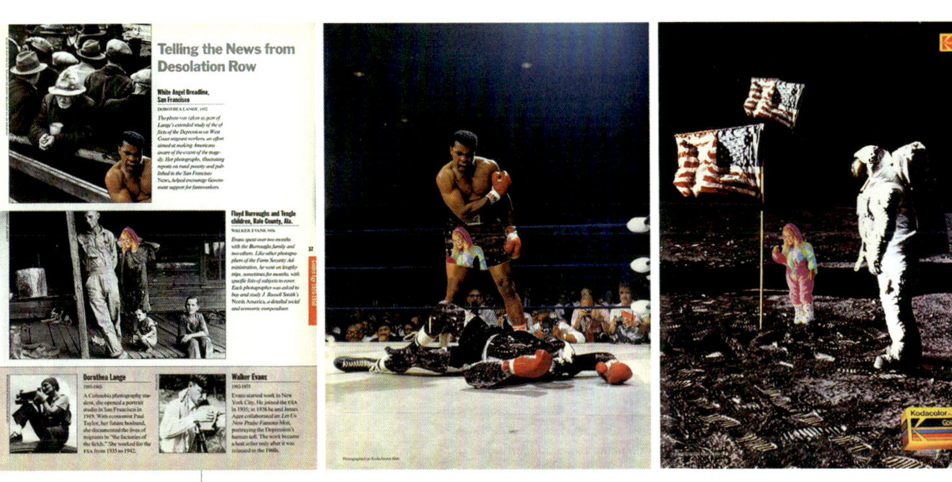

and Tengle Children, Hale County, AL (1936), Ali is photographed in color and thus distinguished from the past, which is represented in black and white. This complex juxtaposition concludes the original magazine's chapter on photojournalism between 1920 and 1950, titled "Golden Years"; it leads to a multipage sequence in which Heinecken deconstructed the central advertisement of the magazine. Here, Kodak, the sponsor of the special edition, placed itself in the tradition of great documentary photography that the editors of *Time* so concisely constructed.[19]

In this sequence, the company juxtaposed four photographs across six pages, all shot on Kodak film; they are (in normal reading order): Neil Leifer's iconic shot of the twenty-three-year-old Muhammad Ali, the defending heavyweight champion, standing over the prostrate Sonny Liston in the first round of their rematch on May 25, 1965 (page 39); Neil Armstrong's photograph of *Apollo 11* astronaut Edwin "Buzz" Aldrin posed next to an American flag on the moon on July 20, 1969 (page 41); and separate images of an anonymous boy and girl, both dressed in sporting outfits (pages 42–43). Facing Ali's page is a blank white page with the text "Time and time again" (page 38); facing Aldrin another blank page appears, this time with "the world's great pictures" (page 40). On the following double-page spread featuring the boy and girl, the photos of Ali and Aldrin appear again, this time above the images of the boy in boxing gloves and the girl in a snow suit (pages 42–43). Text below the montages reads "are trusted to the same brand of film. Kodak," and "Why trust your memories to anything less?" On the bottom-right corner of the last page, an image of a Kodacolor Gold film box appears, with the text "true colors" hovering above it; at the top-right corner, the red-and-yellow Kodak logo appears once again.

In the unaltered sequence of the original magazine, Kodak's strategy was both elegant and effective. Through the combination of images with texts, the company linked its technologies to the achievement of greatness in sports, exploration, and photography. It then addressed the American consumer directly, suggesting that they should use the same products used by the highest achievers in their culture. The children's outfits, which correspond to those of the adult exemplars above them, emphasized the role that emulation plays in human development. The boy could grow up to be a world-class boxer, Kodak suggested, and the girl, an intrepid astronaut.

On the altered pages of Heinecken's appropriated magazine, on the other hand, the cuts and new juxtapositions exposed Kodak's market-oriented consumer ideology, while at the same time emphasizing the radical aspects of the company's message. Turning the page to reveal Ali's full image, the reader also discovers the girl again, now silhouetted against an otherworldly background, like an ultrasound readout or a tele-vision broadcast taking place in the boxer's abdomen and thighs (page 39) (Plate 8.8). Evoking both male pregnancy and the broadcast medium that helped make Ali a hero to tens of millions of Americans, the excisions—which also include the unclothed parts of Liston's body—disrupt a smooth reading of Kodak's message, while also raising questions about the trans-formative effects that technologies of visualization and dissemination were having on the human body. When one pages forward again to Aldrin, the girl appears for a third time, now as a completely excavated figure, standing on the moon with Aldrin and seeming to hold a second flag, which hovers above her like a balloon (page 41) (Plate 8.8). (In the orig-inal magazine, Aldrin's photo was repeated on the page beneath where it first appeared and Heinecken excavated the same flag, which makes the image seem like it is flickering or moving in his version.) In addition, Heinecken excised a red-and-yellow Kodak logo and Kodacolor Gold film box, and these branded images repeat on the picture's right edge; they will appear on the following page as well.

By the time the reader turned to the final double-page spread of Kodak's main advertising sequence in Heinecken's compromised maga-zine, the company's strategies would have been made even more apparent through the slowing down of the viewing process and the introduction of edits that emphasized the technologies that supported the mass media. The spectator was made aware of how powerful instruments like lenses, cameras, video recorders, and electromagnetic transmission devices were used to affect cognition and desire. By capturing the images of exemplary individuals, repeating them over time, and disseminating them to millions, the American media encouraged a wide variety of standardized behav-iors and forms of consumption. Magazines and television, Heinecken reminded the viewer, raised and instructed the American child as much as the country's parents, schools, and religious institutions did—if not more. In addition, however, Heinecken's edits, which helped to undermine fixed distinctions between race, class, and gender, also pointed to the progressive aspects of Kodak's address to the consumer. In particular, the image choices remind the spectator of Ali's appeal to white as well as Black audiences (as exemplified in part by his famous relationship with the sports newscaster Howard Cosell), as well as women's increasing chances of reaching the pinnacles of professional life by the late 1980s. By setting Kodak's assertion of its place in the history of photography into a larger context, Heinecken both criticized the mass media and revealed its progressive potentialities. And by opening up radical fissures within iconic bodies and contexts, he stressed the mutability of reality and the idea that powerful historical trajectories could be altered.

Like the mass-produced consumer object it appropriated, Heinecken's compromised magazine focused on central historical icons and events that were commonly believed to have helped form and exemplify the United States. Moving through images from World War II and the Cold War, Heinecken's montage appropriations then explored the rise of postwar popular culture, sports, and entertainment before turning to the turmoil and political violence of the 1960s; over a series of remarkable pages, the murders of JFK, RFK, and Martin Luther King Jr. merge with civil rights demonstrations and the Vietnam War. Globalization and environmental disaster are also treated, before the survey concludes with the Tiananmen Square protests, AIDS, and John Lennon and Yoko Ono. (Photographed by Annie Liebowitz only hours before his murder by a deranged fan, Lennon poses nude, his body enfolding the clothed Ono.) On the last page, John F. Kennedy Jr. appears, saluting at his father's funeral. In Heinecken's altered reality, the president's son then returns on the back cover, now nestled in the arm of a sleeping toddler and inscribed within a photographic border (Plate 8.5). Serving as an unexpected component in an ad for Kodak-branded alkaline batteries, John Jr. salutes under a text stating, "Introducing the best thing to happen to your camera since Kodak film." The embodiment of tragedy sells, as Heinecken suggested, and people often tend to remember history through its most violent expressions and disasters. In the materialist, yuppie- and Reagan-dominated United States of the late 1980s and early 1990s, it was as if the entire past had become a product of a single corporation.

As David Pagel noted in 1999, Heinecken's engagement with the American magazine was intense: "From 1969 to 1974, Heineken made nineteen collaged and overprinted magazines, in editions ranging from one to nineteen. From 1989 to 1994, he produced eighteen more compromised and revised magazines, in editions of one to seventeen."[20] The number is actually higher, as new works and editions have been discovered in Heinecken's archive at the Center for Creative Photography in Tucson and in his trust in Chicago. As Pagel's incisive description and analysis of this body of work suggest, the power, complexity, and radicality of Heinecken's magazine work increased from the 1960s to the 1990s. On one level, the other revised magazines of the 1990s seem less radical than *150 Years,* in that Heinecken's photomontage practice was no longer archaeological. These later magazines, in other words, were not based on single, complete issues that were appropriated whole cloth. Instead, like the periodicals of the 1970s, different pages from different magazines were excised and rebound into new configurations before the archaeological cuts were made. Yet these works were radical, nonetheless, because of the complex ways in which they integrated form with content. At a moment when Photoshop was radically displacing the physical cut-and-paste approach to photomontage, Heinecken's adherence to analog practices created a reflexivity about visual signification that had few rivals.

Heinecken employed a variety of different photocollage techniques in his revised magazines of the 1990s. Contrasting with his earlier magazine work, many of these new periodicals played down text and instead presented decontextualized American images in terms of strong, dialectical oppositions. Indeed, some of Heinecken's strangest magazines of the 1990s dispensed with language almost entirely. *Revised Magazine: Billy Graham/Time, Nov. 15, '93* (1993), for example, was a series of loose, double-sided pages consisting of cropped color images.[21] Based on an issue of *Time* with a Graham cover story ("A Christian in Winter"), it explored and undermined the glossy image of the American televangelist through a series of dialectical and typological juxtapositions. Early on Heinecken paired an alert profile of the seventy-five-year-old minister, then at the height of his power and influence, with a cheesecake image of a woman's derriere. The preacher's mind, the conjunction suggested, was not where it should have been. Or perhaps Heinecken's implication was that sexual and religious messages appealed to similar desires and instincts. On later pages, Heinecken combined representations of Graham with images of Arlington National Cemetery as well as with Paul Watson's indelible photograph taken for the Associated Press of the mutilated body of a U.S. soldier being dragged through the streets of Mogadishu, Somalia, in 1993—both references to the televangelist's frequent pro-military pronouncements. Altered close-up ads for preppy clothing, evoking affluent, often yuppie lifestyles, round out the magazine, connecting this version of Graham to the rampant American materialism that continued unabated in the 1990s. By cropping all text from the images, Heinecken decontextualized his contemporary Christian subject, making Graham and his work seem ominous and strange. Because the expected textual narrative that supported the images had been excised, spectators were led to question what they really knew about the man.

Other revised magazines from this period used a much more elaborate form of photomontage—one in which pages and page elements were more freely recombined. In a series of works that he made synthesizing the subjects of jungle prints, cuts, and straight pornography, Heinecken created crowded, diverse worlds that were both instantly recognizable and completely unfamiliar (Plate 8.9). The cut-image sequences, in which Heinecken sometimes paired a male figure that looked vaguely like him with diverse fashion and mainstream porn images, used the device of the animal print pattern to unite the figures into larger, seemingly flickering and mobile spaces—hybrid environments in which scales shifted and the boundaries between humans, animals, and machines broke down. The animal patterns tended to integrate male and female figures, subverting clear-cut distinctions between genders as well. And while the edits on the right-hand pages often seemed to unite pictorial space, those on the left-hand pages—which showed more randomly cut images—frequently violated it, emphasizing the artificial and constructed nature of the magazines.

In another series of compromised works, Heinecken used incision and recombination to destabilize gender and allegorize his moment as a time in which divisions between public and private, leisure and labor were breaking down (Plate 8.10). Collating Maidenform ads, incising them, and combining them with ads for men's clothing as well as cigarettes, Heinecken created a completely commercial universe in which men

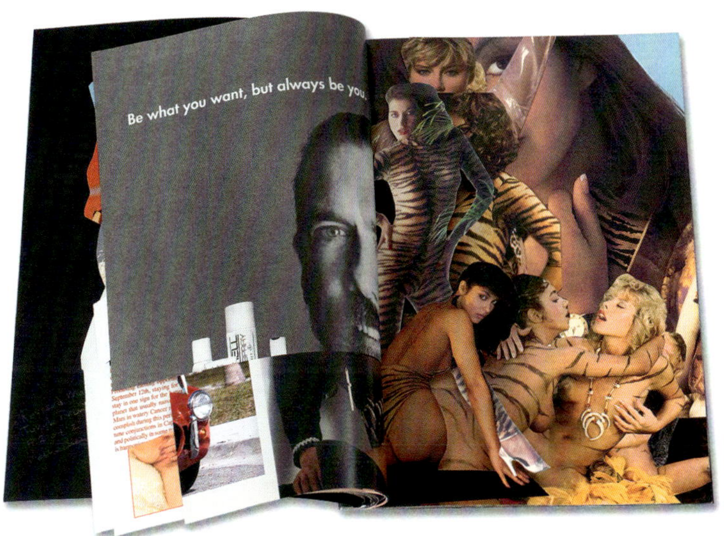

PLATE 8.9. Robert Heinecken, *Revised Magazine: Jungle Prints/ Cuts/Porno* (1993). Artist bound and collated incised found magazine pages, 10 ¾ x 8 inches (27.31 x 20.32 cm). 2 of 2. Private collection. COPYRIGHT 2022 THE ROBERT HEINECKEN TRUST, CHICAGO.

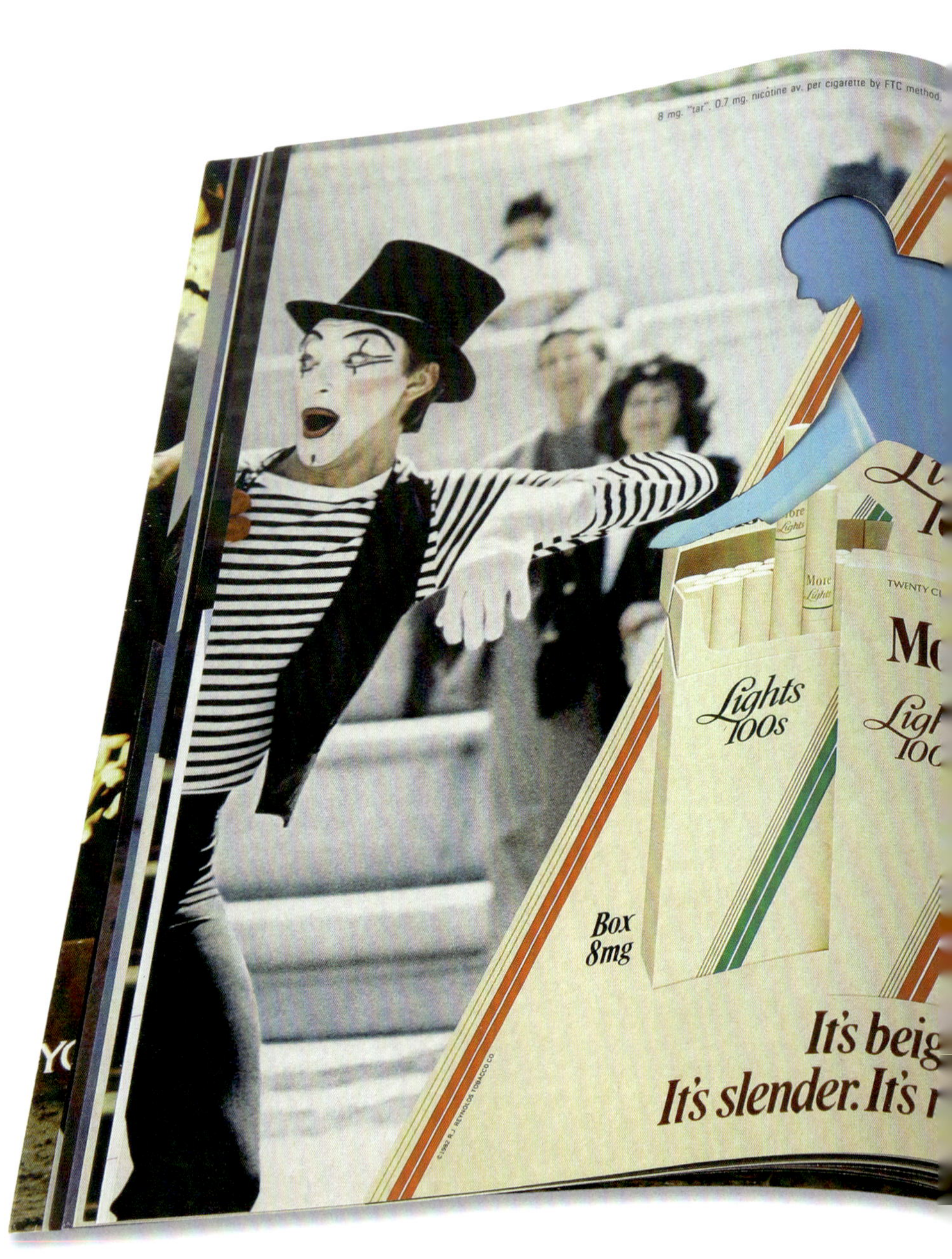

8 mg. "tar", 0.7 mg. nicotine av. per cigarette by FTC method.
More
Lights
More
Lights
Lights
100s
Mo
Ligh
100
TWENTY C
Box
8mg
It's beig
It's slender. It's m
© 1983 R.J. REYNOLDS TOBACCO CO

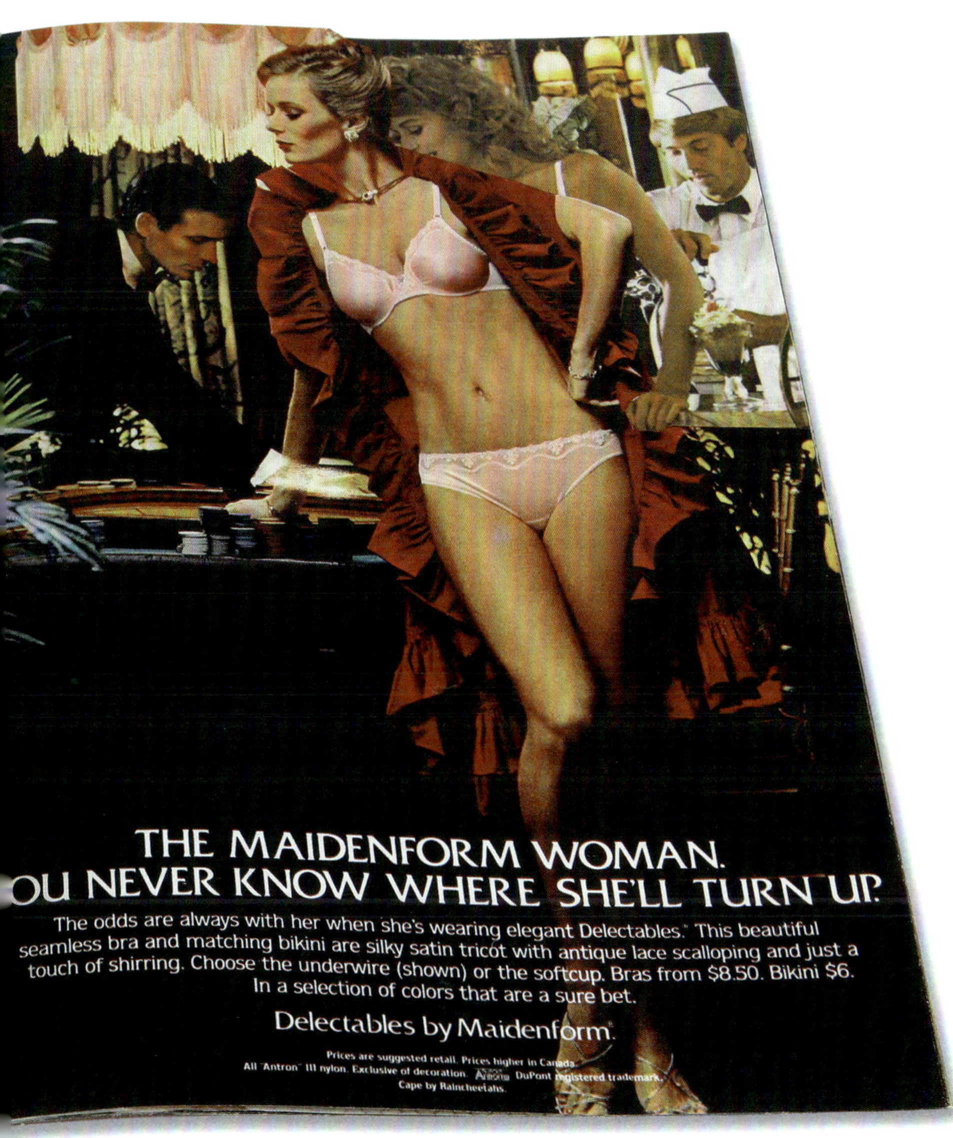

PLATE 8.10. Robert Heinecken, *Revised Magazine: Maidenform* (1993). Artist bound and collated incised found magazine pages, 10 ¾ x 8 inches (27.31 x 20.32 cm), 52 pages, 2 of 3. Private collection. COPYRIGHT 2022 THE ROBERT HEINECKEN TRUST, CHICAGO.

wore makeup and acted feminine, while women went out wearing nothing but their underwear.[22] In this way, novel worlds were envisioned that suggested that Americans in the 1990s were emulating old and new stereotypes simultaneously. In still other revised magazines, Heinecken repeated an easily recognizable type of image, a typology that consistently juxtaposed two different kinds of ideal subjects: Virginia Slims and Marlboro; beer and cigarettes; whiskey and cigarettes; and women and cigarettes.[23] These double typologies were fundamentally dialectical: they evoked not one but two overarching products or types, and thereby they provoked their readers to imagine various forms of similarity and difference. In yet other revised magazines, profiles of well-known individuals, from Richard Avedon to Lani Guirnier, were disrupted and made strange; just as he did to visuals of Billy Graham, Heinecken remixed their official images with uncanny effects.[24] Although clearly altered, Heinecken's revised magazines seemed less like works of art and more like things that people would find in their everyday environments; because of this, they retained a subversive aspect. They were ordinary, mundane even, but also surprisingly constructed, and thus jarring, provocative, and critical of the traditional stereotypes and frames through which American magazine readers in the 1990s understood one another and their collective worlds.

As the magazines of the 1990s developed, Heinecken became more and more interested in the distinction between color and black-and-white images, and the changing significance of this opposition over time. Emerging in compromised magazines that included "B+W" in the title and culminating in an astonishing series of works that appropriated perhaps the most famous fashion advertising campaign of the early 1990s, the Gap's iconic Who Wore Khakis ads, Heinecken explored black-and-white photography as a frame that signified a nostalgic past.[25] This central critical intervention was brilliantly demonstrated in *Revised Magazine: Gap New York Headaches* (1995) and *Gap Magazine* (1994–99), both editions of five variants that consisted of bound, collated, and incised found magazine pages.[26] It probably reached its apogee, however, in Heinecken's book *. . . Wore Khakis* (1999), which consisted of spiral-bound page proofs on heavy cardstock.[27] Consisting of twenty identical copies of sixty pages with fifty-six separate hand-cut images, *Wore Khakis* did more than undermine the Gap's message and intentions: Heinecken's work stands as a potent allegory of its time, one that it represented as growing increasingly narcissistic, elitist, and nostalgic (Plate 8.11).

When Heinecken appropriated their ad campaign, the Gap was one of the most dominant retail fashion-clothing companies in the world. Originally an outlet that sold Levi's jeans and records to teenagers in malls, the company morphed in the 1980s into a brand known for its simple,

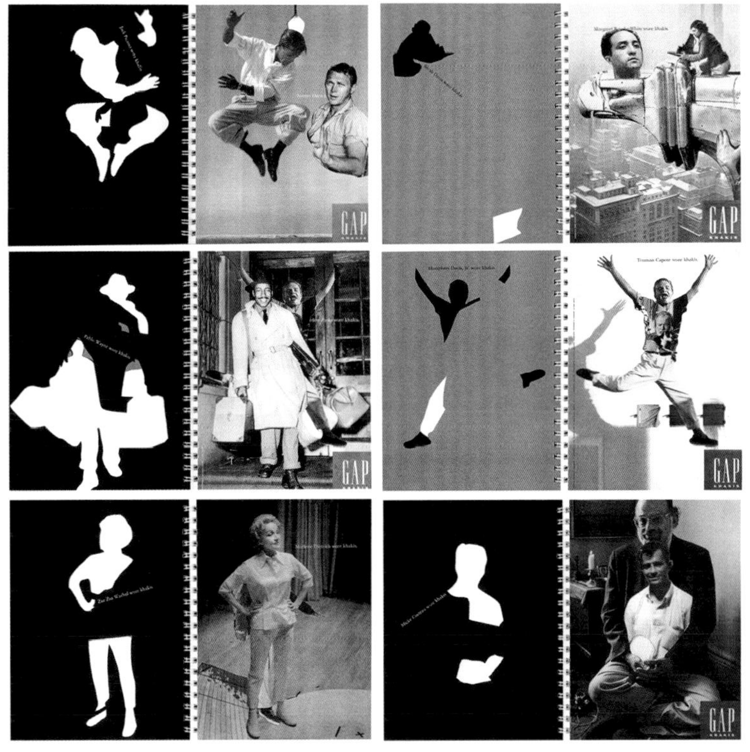

minimalist casual wear that appealed to a variety of different consumers from teens and young adults to aging baby boomers and even seniors. Using the tagline ". . . wore Khakis," the 1993 Gap campaign defined the affordable brand as both hip and elite. It featured iconic celebrities from the past including Amelia Earhart, John Wayne, Pablo Picasso, Isamu Noguchi, James Dean, Marilyn Monroe, Ernest Hemingway, Sammy Davis Jr., Steve McQueen, Truman Capote, Muhammad Ali, and Andy Warhol, all wearing khakis.[28] Restrained, minimal, and completely black-and-white, the ads invited consumers to identify with actors, artists, and intellectuals of all stripes, a largely American pantheon that defined both high achievement and the enjoyment of the good life. The Gap's print ads were hugely successful, with the phrase entering mainstream conversations and references being made to it in popular culture and entertainment. They also gave the company significant revenue growth by popularizing one of its central products, a pair of pants intended to supplant blue jeans—an item of clothing that had signified the counterculture of the 1960s and 1970s and that had by the 1980s become a ubiquitous uniform and thus no longer fashionable or cool.[29] In part through these advertisements, the Gap made khakis the jeans of the 1990s. Despite the diversity of its appeal—not only did the Gap attract multiple generations of consumers, but its ads featured people of a variety of different races and ethnicities—it continued to project a very traditional elite vision of the good life, one that was associated with the preppy White Anglo-Saxon Protestant (WASP) culture that had dominated American culture, society, and politics for most of the nation's existence.

When attentive viewers paged through Heinecken's *Wore Khakis* book, the Gap's vision of American success and celebrity was called radically into question. The right-hand pages carry the image and Gap logo, while the left-hand pages carry cutout black (and sometimes gray) backgrounds and parodic text in which the names of the celebrities get mixed up. In contrast to the original ads, which contained one (spatially and temporally) unified image of a single celebrity with the Gap logo and tagline, Heinecken's appropriations contained a multiplicity of different figures and implied contexts. As David Pagel wrote in an essay accompanying Heinecken's artist book, *Wore Khakis* destroyed the bond of intimacy between the celebrity depicted in the advertisement and the audience who desired to emulate them, a negation of the one-to-one relationship between model and consumer that was so fundamental to the appeal of contemporary advertising:

> Heinecken shatters this fantasy by creating a sequence of images in which one celebrity always intrudes into another's ad. On each subsequent page, the previous page's intruder is likewise intruded upon by another celebrity. . . . Paired, the celebrities tip the fragile balance established by the original ads, and viewers are no longer able to even unconsciously imagine that such images might offer some sort of fantastic transport out of our mundane lives and into the glamorous world of adventure, fame, and fortune.[30]

While robbed of the ad's fantasy, viewers were not left defeated; instead, they were empowered as new, less stereotypical possibilities of human existence and relationship were allowed to emerge.

Although it celebrated diversity, *Wore Khakis* also attempted to warn its spectators about the tight complicity between capitalism and exploitation. The book's final image did not come from a Gap campaign. Rather, it was a personal photograph of the artist wearing his Marine Corps khaki flight suit, an image that linked the iconic fashion item to the military and warfare. It thus potentially reminded the spectator that khaki cloth had its origins in the British colonial occupation of India in the nineteenth century, and that the power of American and European nations in the nineteenth and twentieth centuries continued to be linked very strongly to colonial exploitation. The preppy look promoted by the Gap, Ralph Lauren, Calvin Klein, and others in the 1990s was in a certain way democratic. Particularly in the case of the Gap, it was designed to be affordable, while offering its customers access to a more affluent and desirable look. The Gap ads reflected this intended mass appeal by addressing an audience that was not simply rich and white. At the same time, to take on an elite appearance did nothing to alter the status quo. Although more Americans could look like they were successful, they were not necessarily getting ahead.

In conjunction with the pronounced black-and-white qualities of the book, Heinecken's presentation of khakis as an emblem of colonialism thus prompts questions about the advancement of African Americans during the 1990s and the ways in which U.S. capitalism and racism intersected. Heinecken did not simply focus on the Gap's use of black-and-white photography to link its products to an idealized and aestheticized past filled with celebrities and great accomplishments; he also emphasized the opposition between black and white by the often black left-hand pages, which are completely opaque, other than the cut-out areas and the short line of text. These blank black pages—the cutout areas of which often trace human silhouettes—contrast with the pages of black-and-white photographs, thus multiplying the meanings of *blackness* and *whiteness*.[31] The heightening of focus around what it means to be Black and what it means to be white in turn intersected with the meaning of khaki pants, creating questions that spectators needed to answer for themselves.

As Jane Tynan has argued, after being developed during the colonial occupation of India, the khaki military uniform came to represent the entire British army by World War I, and shortly thereafter it became the standard dress for the armies of the world.[32] Designed to camouflage soldiers by making them less distinguishable from their environments, cotton khakis were distinct from earlier, more aristocratic battle dress that used material, color, and ornament to signify the wearer's status and heroism and to allow them to stand out on the battlefield.[33] Khaki cloth did not come in a single color; rather, it was dyed with different drab earth hues from yellow to gray to olive to brown. When cut into a standard, mass-produced uniform, it became one of the primary signifiers of the modern mass army. Here, it helped socialize soldiers by deindividualizing them and by binding them together into organized units. The khaki uniform also served a disciplinary function, constituting part of the look and comportment of the masculine military ideal to which real male bodies were supposed to conform themselves.[34] As Heinecken's *Wore Khakis* documents, Americans in the 1990s were being encouraged to identify with a cloth that signified both the military and colonialism—a new uniform that was intended to replace the countercultural blue-jean work clothing of the 1960s and 1970s. In a framework that raised questions about the relationships between black and white, Heineken's book also challenged its spectators to attend to the exploitative aspects of

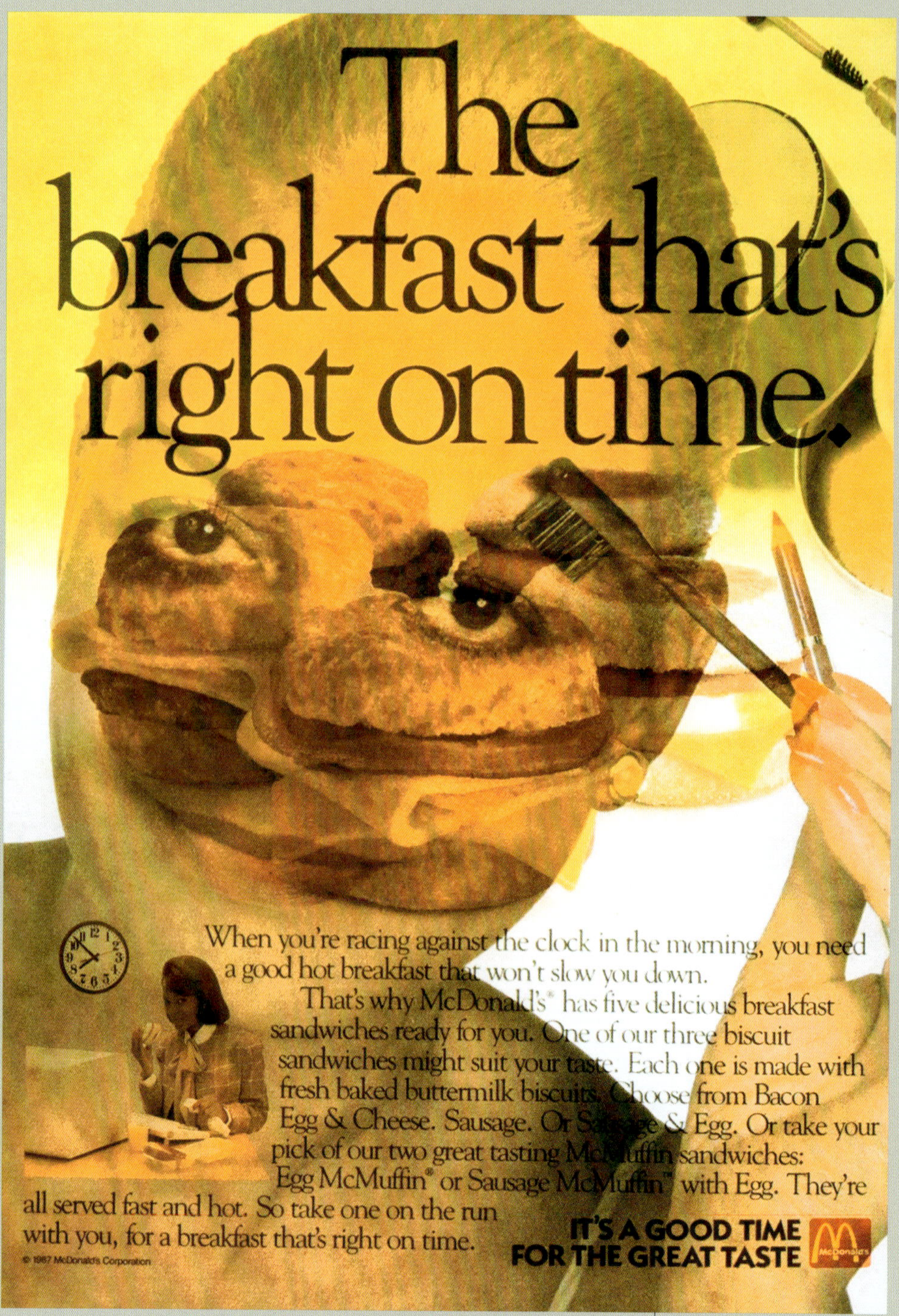

PLATE 8.12. Robert Heinecken, *PP/Surrealism G* (1987). Dye bleach destruction print (Cibachrome) photogram, 14 x 11 inches (35.56 x 27.94 cm). Edition of 5. Private collection. COPYRIGHT 2022 THE ROBERT HEINECKEN TRUST, CHICAGO.

the capitalist system that continued to structure their everyday lives. Despite the diversity of the Gap's khaki wearers, capitalism's structural inequities continued.

The Late Photograms

In the late 1980s, Heinecken returned to the photogram practice for a final time. In these late photograms, he continued his early strategy combining appropriation with montage, but once again with a decisive shift in photographic technology. Between 1987 and 1991, the artist created approximately 125 different Cibachrome photograms, which he produced in editions of one to fifty, using *Vogue, Harper's Bazaar,* and other contemporary magazines. He issued these under a number of series titles, including *Possible Prints (PP), Recto/Verso, Whiskey and Cigarettes,* and *Move to Malibu,* among others. Unlike the *Are You Rea* photograms, these color photograms were positive images, and thus although similarly morphed, they were generally much more legible. Unlike the color food photograms of the 1970s and 1980s, but like those of *Are You Rea,* these Cibachrome photograms were focused on the mass media: surreal manufactured documents of the people, objects, and events that different specialized magazines conjoined in Heinecken's contemporary moment.

Because of their materiality, the late photograms were also more disturbing than either *Are You Rea* or the food photograms. The Cibachrome process blended the two sides of the magazine leaf with greater variation of tone and color, and as a result, human bodies merged convincingly with one another as well as with processed foods and other forms of consumer products, producing exuberantly grotesque chimeras. In addition, Heinecken consistently chose pages that contained advertising on both sides, thus implicating the media to an even greater degree. The Cibachrome photogram works bespeak not only the tastes and excesses of the period but also the financial crisis following the '87 crash and the AIDS crisis—as well as a sense that all aspects of humanity can be bought and sold. Taken together, they form a powerful vision of the fears and anxieties coursing through the media-saturated society of the United States at the end of the age of analog photography.

In *PP/Surrealism G* (1987), for example, Heinecken mixed a McDonald's ad promoting the chain's breakfast sandwiches with an advertisement for eye makeup to create an uncanny chimera that evoked the massive growth of the service economy in the 1980s and the social problems that were developing as a result (Plate 8.12). As the U.S. Department of Commerce admitted in 1992:

The industrial restructuring of the economy from basically a goods-producing economy to a service-producing economy has been going on for many years, but recently it has become a cause of concern among some economists. This is because earnings, on average, tend to be lower in the service-producing industries than in the goods-producing industries. Furthermore, earnings in the service-producing industries are subject to greater variation. Indeed, the growth in income inequality among the Nation's households has been linked to these developments.[35]

This growth in the numbers of low-paid American service workers, and their precarious product-like existences, is apparent in Heinecken's image. Here, the larger woman's face contains Egg McMuffins that merge seamlessly with her eyes, mimicking interior organs in a semitransparent representation of a human head.[36] Lodged in the larger woman's throat, a Black woman in office attire munches on a McDonald's meal in front of a computer screen; from the clock on the wall, she is at work before 8 a.m. In Heinecken's image, it seems like anything that can be seen or touched can be consumed, incorporated into another gestalt within a shifting image field. Excessively concerned with appearances, Americans spend more and more time at work. Their bodies have morphed into fast-food products; and through their occupations and leisure-time activities, they have become assimilated into larger, mostly disembodied institutional structures.

In *PP/Surrealism—B* (1990), distinctions between human bodies and manufactured products break down once again, while at the same time symbolically the U.S. financial system is exposed to critique and reflection (Plate 8.13). Merging an ad for *The Economist,* the London-based, neoliberal newsweekly, with one for a VW sedan, the image evokes linkages between globalization, mass production, sexuality, and finance. Through Heinecken's found montage, the contradictions of the original ads become more pronounced. The deliberatively provocative financial magazine ad, which compares itself to an adult magazine that must be wrapped in brown paper before being sent through the mail, seems to explode through the car's impact. The figure of the rapacious corporate raider, immortalized by Michael Douglas as Gordon Gekko in Oliver Stone's classic 1987 film *Wall Street,* is perhaps evoked: a persona who celebrates greed and who covets people—like possessions—as tools or as markers of status. Once again, the human form has become something to be manipulated and consumed, its broken parts replaced by mass-produced components. In addition, although the ad is for *The Economist*'s American edition—as indicated by the New York address at the bottom of the image—both products depicted are essentially foreign imports. Just as U.S. manufacturing was undermined since the 1970s by cheap (or sometimes better) overseas products, the foreign media was by then also firmly entrenched in American soil.[37]

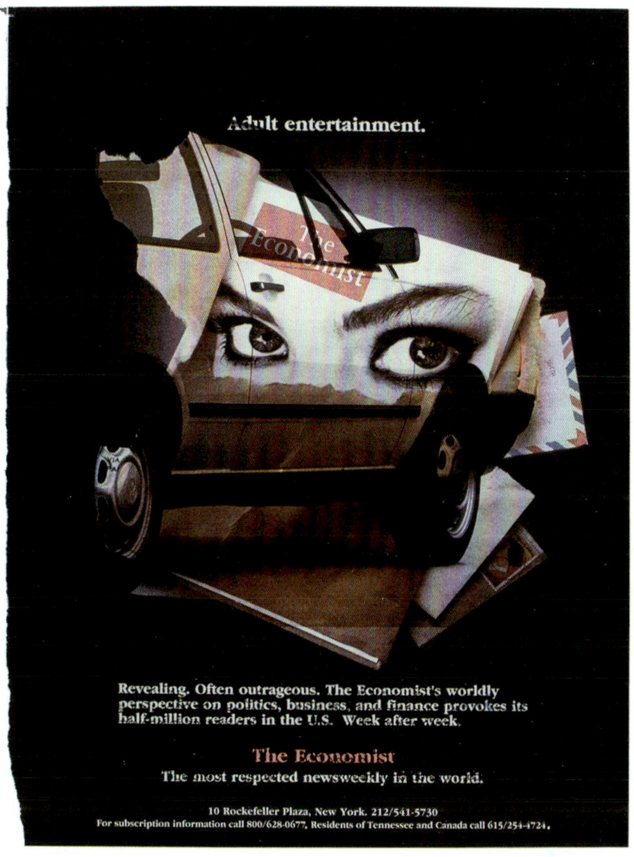

Heinecken released a *Recto/Verso* portfolio in 1989, which consisted of twelve Cibachrome photographs, all from 1988, which he culled from his archive of magazine page negatives, a compendium that was produced in an edition of fifty. In this work, he focused exclusively on images of women, exploring a variety of different themes evoked by the fashion industry, including objectification and the gendering of the gaze. Heinecken invited twelve writers to contribute a paragraph about a selected image; the text was then printed on a transparency and sequenced before its corresponding photograph in the portfolio. In this way, the critics' words introduced (and also protected) the images, a gesture that Heinecken performed to relinquish his own authorial control, empower the viewer, and encourage a variety of different interpretations. Various photographs in the portfolio combine humans with animals, products (both natural and manmade), or other humans, and most mix a variety of scales and contexts. As Rod Slemmons notes, there is an undertone of violence in some of the selected images.[38] This comes, at least initially, from the blood-red colors favored by fashion advertising, which when superimposed on parts of human bodies that are not lips evoke seeping or gushing wounds. In *Recto/Verso #4*, for example, which is preceded by a text by Irene Borger, the main figure seems to stab herself in the arm and chest with a large bullet or missile; in *Recto/Verso #11*, introduced by A. D. Coleman, a plume of blood seems to explode upwards from an aloof model's neck.

An undertone of dread and disaster is also evoked by the seamlessness of Heinecken's uncanny *Recto/Verso* chimeras (Plate 8.14). Their combinations of parts are clearly impossible, unnatural, and overwhelmingly bizarre; but at the same time their components seem so integrated and the monstrous figures seem very alive. The erotic yet violated appearances of Heinecken's figures recall the body horror of 1980s films such as David Cronenberg's *Videodrome* (1983), *The Fly* (1986), and *Dead Ringers* (1988); like Cronenberg's films, Heinecken's photograms emphasize biological reproduction gone awry.[39] In addition, there is a strong sense of fluidity and underwater life—a result of the semitransparency of the figures, the way that forms seem to float in suspension, and the backgrounds, which are often dark or greenish-blue.

Because of the overall emphasis on blood, eroticism, fluids, and horror in relation to the human body, the *Recto/Verso* portfolio as well as many of Heinecken's late magazine photograms evoke the AIDS crisis, which by the end of 1989 had claimed nearly ninety thousand lives—including those of the photographers Peter Hujar and Robert Mapplethorpe.[40] Although Heinecken's evocation of the crisis was not explicit, it is present in the Cibachrome photograms as a whole given the emphasis in the imagery on sexuality in conjunction with signs indicating the vulnerability and porousness of the human body (Plate 8.15). For a heterosexual man who had for a time embraced the sexual revolution of the 1960s and 1970s, he must have been aware that his age had perhaps allowed him to dodge a bullet. Although AIDS was a sexually transmitted disease that then was still erroneously perceived as affecting gay men and minority groups the most, it was clear by the late 1980s that it was also being communicated quite easily by heterosexual populations. The fashion industry furthermore, which had already suffered through the deaths of some of its brightest contributors, is also quietly memorialized in *Recto/Verso*.

In 2006, Heinecken came out with his final *Recto/Verso* compendium, a hardcover book consisting of twenty-four duotone reproductions of Cibachrome photograms in an edition of one thousand.[41] In contrast to the earlier portfolio, the *Recto/Verso* book was more like *Are You Rea* in that it included more narrative and text as well as a wider selection from Heinecken's archive of late photograms. Comprising depictions of both genders, the various images evoked Goffmanian social frames

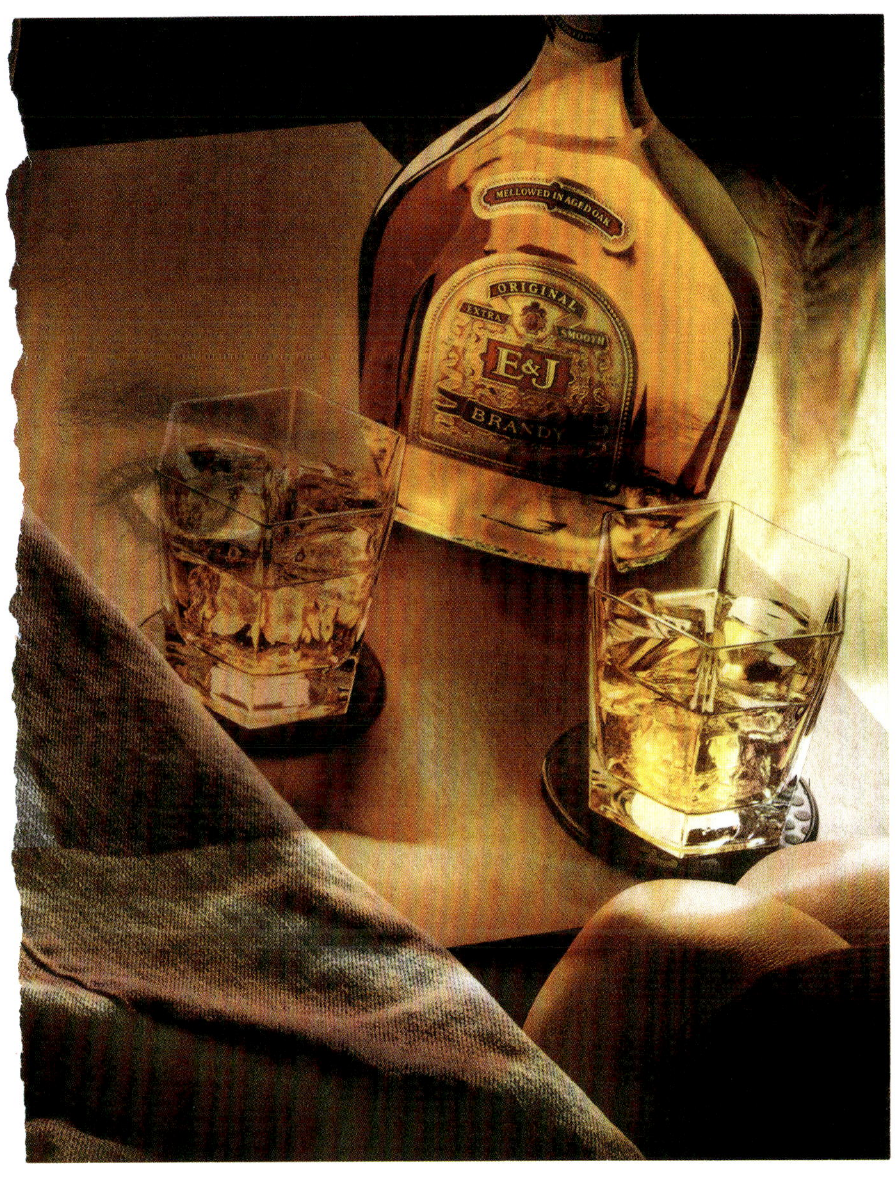

PLATE 8.14. Robert Heinecken, *PP/Whiskey—Figures/E* (1991). Dye bleach destruction print (Cibachrome) photogram, 14 x 11 inches (35.56 x 27.94 cm). 3 of 3. Private collection. COPYRIGHT 2022 THE ROBERT HEINECKEN TRUST, CHICAGO.

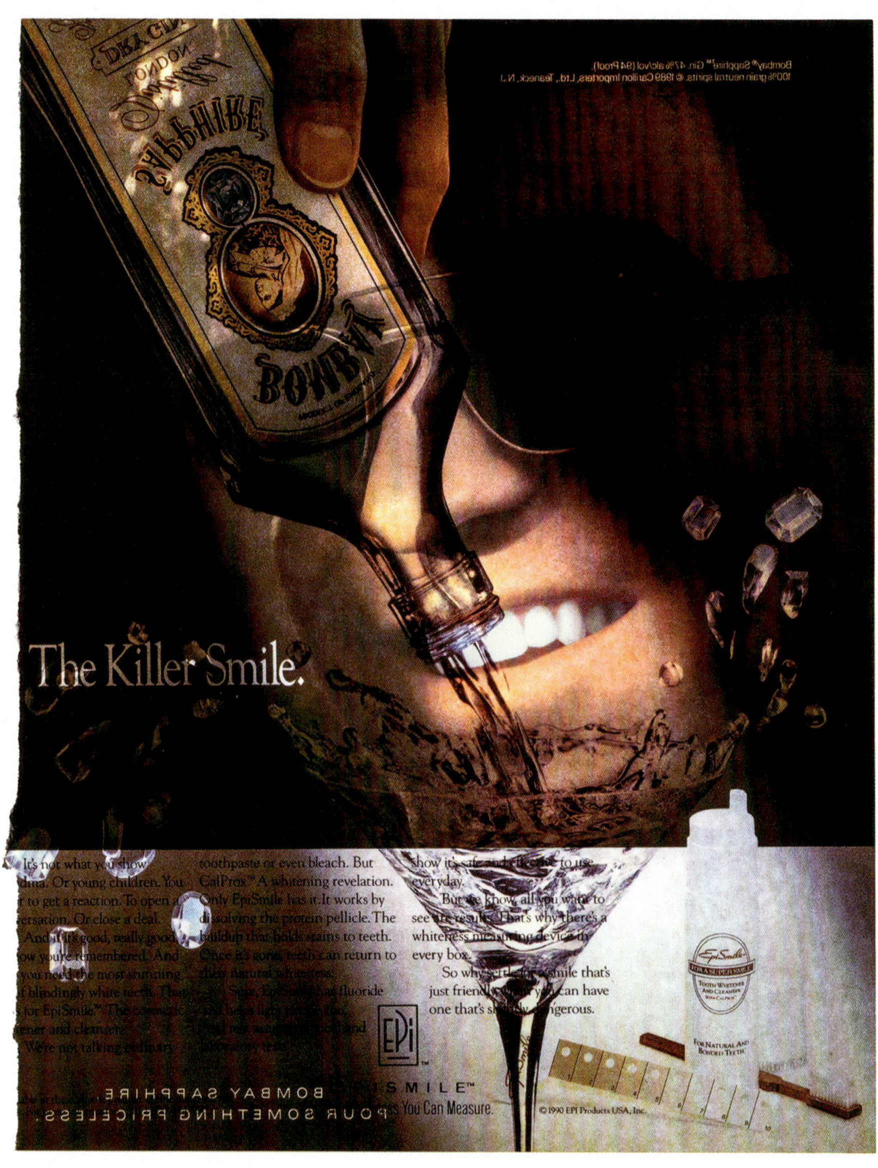

PLATE 8.15. Robert Heinecken, *PP/Whiskey—Figures/E* (1991). Dye bleach destruction print (Cibachrome) photogram, 14 x 11 inches (35.56 x 27.94 cm). A.P. #1. Private collection. COPYRIGHT 2022 THE ROBERT HEINECKEN TRUST, CHICAGO.

and actions—family and social situations, ritualistic contexts, modes of engagement and withdrawal, and forms of touching—in which gender roles were played out. Although the body horror of the earlier portfolio was more subdued, it was still present, evoked by the bizarre juxtapositions of human flesh, nonhuman object, and printed text. In addition, much more than in the Cibachrome portfolio, fixed gender roles were undermined and contested in the *Recto/Verso* book, an aspect of Heinecken's practice that was to become one of his most enduring legacies.

By referencing photography's origins at the end of the analog age, Heinecken's late photograms provoked reflection on the distance that photography had traveled since the nineteenth century. An overpowering engine of visual representation, photography was, as Heinecken's work suggested, a force for the objectification of human identity that transcended time, space, and language. At the dawn of the photographic era, out of the twenty-four photographic images illustrating William Henry Fox Talbot's *The Pencil of Nature* (1844–46), four were photograms: a leaf of a plant (Plate VII); a facsimile of an antiquarian printed book page (Plate IX); a delicate sheet of lace with a floral pattern (Plate XX); and an Italian master drawing (Plate XXIII).[42] In his text, Talbot discusses these photograms in order to define different types of photographic practice: photographic printing, the positive-negative process, and the differences between camera-less pictures and images made in the camera obscura. Talbot also noted that while two-dimensional objects can already be viewed well as negatives, in the case of anything three-dimensional, a positive image needed to be made.[43] And by making direct positive photograms from magazine pages, Heinecken adopted Talbot's first photographic technique in a way that allowed the three-dimensional world to enter the (camera-less) contact print, a transformation that helped to make his merging of photographic bodies and spaces so uncanny.[44] Finding chance poetic combinations as well as signs of social breakdown through the appropriation of mass-media detritus, Heinecken's late photograms allegorized an anxious time, a moment in which analog practices were giving way to the digital.

Perhaps for this reason the body vacillates powerfully and uncannily in Heinecken's late Cibachromes, cycling between positive and negative, and between print, X-ray, and cathode ray tube. Consistently in these works, the pleasure of consumption is linked to the horror of violence, a critique that these works raise but do not attempt to solve. Here also there is a deep awareness of the history of photography and of photography's institutions and effects. In the end, Heinecken's use of the photogram technique to explore consumption as simultaneous pleasure and violence in American culture was a prescient move, recalling the ontological promise of the first photographs, their capacity to connect the viewer with the real.

Heinecken's Significance

Robert Heinecken died on May 19, 2006, in a nursing home in Albuquerque, New Mexico, the city where he and Joy had bought a house a few years previously. Heinecken was seventy-four years old, and he died of pneumonia, after suffering from Alzheimer's disease since 1994.[1] As a result of his physical decline, the artist's output declined significantly in his last decade, but even so, his importance and influence grew. Heinecken left behind an extensive body of work that was extremely prescient and significant, and his reflexivity about form, consumption, and identity in photography-based media still speaks to central concerns of today. Also important was Heinecken's trajectory as an artist: namely, his public development from a quirky and problematic photographer, to a contemporary artist who was only recognized as such at the end of his career (since the late 1990s).

The fact of Heinecken's belated artistic presence has important implications for traditional narratives about contemporary art. It contradicts the myth of newness around the development of postmodern photography and the pictures generation in the 1980s, and it challenges the belief that an understanding of the self as socially constructed and performative did not exist in contemporary art before that time. In relation to the postmodern theory of Douglas Crimp and Craig Owens that was in part developed to explain the significance of postmodern photography, Heinecken's practice points to an entirely different corpus of literary, historical, and theoretical sources that can be productively clustered around mass-media appropriation in art: models of history, society, and identity that help to elucidate distinctive appropriative concerns, ones that were more documentary and sociological in nature. Heinecken's importance does not invalidate the significance of such breakthrough postmodern photographers as Cindy Sherman, Barbara Kruger, Richard Prince, and, slightly later, Carrie Mae Weems, all of whom are much better known. Nor does his output make them less innovative and important. Rather, what Heinecken's example brings to twentieth-century art is an awareness of an expanded creative sphere in which fine art and mass culture were always—and continuously—in close dialogue, and where similar questions could be pursued in different artistic media, often without knowledge of the parallels. Supported by developments in North American media theory and sociology, as well as high and low culture of all types, this expanded creative sphere reveals that artistic development in the twentieth century was always more complex and more interconnected than traditional histories of modern and postmodern art have allowed.

The semiotic understanding of postmodern appropriation as articulated by Crimp and Owens elucidates aspects of Heinecken's allegorical montage process: its Dadaist attack on originality and fine art; its reflexivity and gestures of institutional critique; and its undermining of distinctions between art and life, art and mass culture, and the art of different mediums. In addition, it helps to explain Heinecken's interest in environments and site specificity, as well as important characteristics of his work such as impermanence, accumulation, discursivity, and hybridization. Their theorization of postmodernism's allegorical impulse, however, gives short shrift to the documentary aspects of appropriated media images, the initial public meanings and original contexts of the likenesses that are scavenged.

As Heinecken's work demonstrates, appropriation—even in its allegorical forms—can also support a documentary impulse and a sense that reality, though socially constructed, is never completely fictional or immaterial. And as Heinecken's work reminds us, even if the real is constructed, it is not an ephemeral fiction but, rather, material, physical, impactful, and most importantly shared. As we have seen, one of Heinecken's great strengths was his specificity—his references to known figures and events, to clear actions and situations, and to his own perspective in relation to the work. His artworks provoke their viewers to dig below their surfaces and to explore the histories of the fragmented, stolen representations they contain.

Another aspect of Heineken's importance that was occluded by the postmodern model of appropriation was the radicality of his depictions of sexuality and violence. By revealing the omnipresence of such images in American culture—and their transformative effect on everyday life—Heinecken raised central questions about the specific ways in which lens-based technologies were changing both people and societies in his contemporary moment. His art did not celebrate the male gaze but acerbically criticized it; and his analysis of its tendencies and obsessions not only revealed its fundamental contradictions but also imagined strategies through which new nonbinary viewpoints could emerge.

A final aspect of Heinecken's importance that remains obscured by the postmodern theory of appropriation was his interest in manipulating his materials, his willingness to change them and thus inflect and direct their meanings. Heinecken's ironic interventions mark the beginnings of an ongoing activity of historical questioning and never its end. Although Heinecken's work was mysterious and ambiguous, it was never unequivocal: one senses an intelligence and a point of view behind the appropriative montage practices. And Heinecken's willingness to editorialize—to spin—asserts the importance of the individual as a locus of cultural performance. Although we are all culturally constructed, we are neither powerless nor all the same. Challenging us to live actively within the society of the spectacle, to assert specific identities through the performance of cultural stereotypes, to celebrate consumption while criticizing its deleterious effects—this, perhaps, is Heinecken's most enduring legacy.

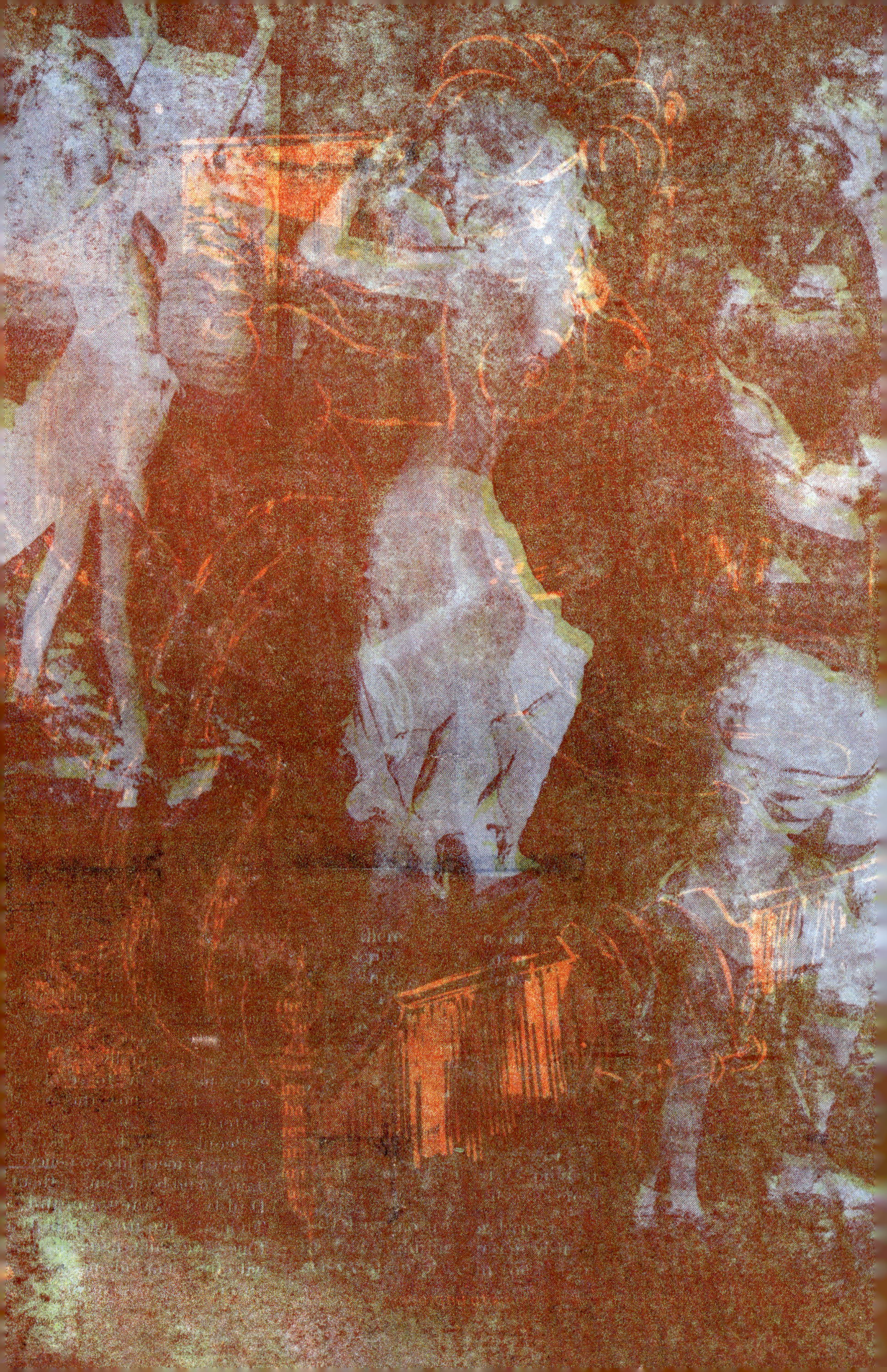

ACKNOWLEDGMENTS

This book owes its existence to many benefactors. First, I refer readers to my notes for the artists and scholars who mattered most to this endeavor. I thank Michelle Kuo and *Artforum* for supporting my first engagements with Robert Heinecken in 2011. Since then, my research and writing have greatly benefited from an Ansel Adams Research Fellowship at the Center for Creative Photography, a Michigan Humanities Award at the University of Michigan, and an Ailsa Mellon Bruce Senior Fellowship at the Center for Advanced Study in the Visual Arts at the National Gallery of Art. Sabbatical leave from the University of Michigan also supported different chapters, as did research funds from the Department of the History of Art as well as from the university at large. To my friends and colleagues at all these institutions, I am most grateful for your engagement and support. I would also like to thank the various institutions that invited me to lecture on Robert Heinecken, including the Museum of Modern Art, the National Gallery of Art, the University of Virginia, Cranbrook Academy of Art, and the University of Florida, as well as the audiences that responded there.

Many friends, colleagues, and interlocutors, both at the University of Michigan and beyond, lent me meaningful support while I was working on Heinecken. I would particularly like to thank Ed Dimendberg, Joan Kee, and Alex Potts for their long-standing friendship as I wrestled with the issues that guided this project over the past ten years. I am grateful to Dora Apel, Luke Batten, Phong Bui, A. D. Coleman, Milton Curry, Luke Gartlan, Andreas Kalyvas, Donald Kuspit, Grant Mandarino, Roxana Marcoci, Philip Martin, Joyce Neimanas, Elizabeth Otto, Lane Relyea, Eva Respini, Jennifer Robertson, Kristin Schroeder, Graham Smith, Sheida Soleimani, Leslie Squyres, Jason Stanley, and Andrés Mario Zervigón, all of whom contributed in different ways.

Finally, this project would not have been completed without the love and support of my spouse, Beverly Fishman, and Juliane Biro, my mother. Without either of these two extraordinary women, I wouldn't be here. This book is dedicated to Bev, because she—more than anyone else—has been my inspiration for the past eighteen years.

NOTES

INTRODUCTION

1. The change happens over the course of the 1970s. On the resistance of the U.S. art world to (pure) photography being understood as art, see A. D. Coleman, "'From Today Painting Is Dead': A Requiem" (1974), in Coleman, *Light Readings: A Photography Critic's Writings, 1968–78*, 2d ed. (Albuquerque: University of New Mexico Press, 1998), 182–94.

2. On the assimilation of photographic practices into contemporary art, see David Campany et al., *Art and Photography* (London: Phaidon Press, 2003); Giovanni Anselmo et al., *The Last Picture Show: Artists Using Photography 1960–1982* (Minneapolis: Walker Art Center, 2003); Maria-Christina Villasenor et al., *Moving Pictures: Contemporary Photography and Video from the Guggenheim Collection* (New York: Guggenheim Museum, 2003); and Nancy Burns, ed., *Photo Revolution: Andy Warhol to Cindy Sherman* (Worcester, Mass.: Worcester Art Museum, 2020).

3. On the work of these photographers, see Regis Durand et al., *Cindy Sherman* (Paris: Flammarion, 2007); Johanna Burton, ed., *Cindy Sherman* (Cambridge, Mass.: MIT Press, 2006); Nancy Spector et al., *Richard Prince* (New York: Guggenheim Museum, 2007); and Barbara Kruger et al., *Thinking of You* (Los Angeles: Museum of Contemporary Art, 1999).

4. Heinecken preferred the term *para-photographer* to describe himself, emphasizing the fact that, although his photographs were materially hybrid, his subject matter was the medium of photography and the society of goods and spectacles in which it played a major role. See James Enyeart, ed., *Heinecken* (Carmel, Calif.: Friends of Photography, with Light Gallery, 1980), 8. All subsequent quotations from this book are from lectures and interviews given by Heinecken between 1973 and 1980. Here Enyeart is paraphrasing Heinecken.

5. An understanding of photography as both a technology that produced an objective representation of the world and a medium that extended and created self-consciousness about the nature of human vision was a cornerstone of straight photography from the very beginning; see, for example, Paul Strand, "Photography," *Seven Arts* 2 (August 1917), 524–25. On Paul Strand, see *Paul Strand: Sixty Years of Photographs* (1976) (New York: Aperture, 2005); and Maren Stange and Alan Trachtenberg, eds., *Paul Strand: Essays on His Life and Work* (New York: Aperture, 1990).

6. On Alfred Stieglitz and pictorialism, see Sarah Greenough, *Alfred Stieglitz: The Key Set—Volumes I and II: The Alfred Stieglitz Collection of Photographs* (New York: Harry N. Abrams, 2002); Sarah Greenough et al., *Alfred Stieglitz: Photographs and Writings* (Washington, D.C.: National Gallery of Art, 1983); and Christian A. Peterson, *After the Photo-Secession: American Pictorial Photography, 1910–1955* (New York: Norton, 1997). On straight photography, see Nancy Newhall, ed., *The Daybooks of Edward Weston*, 2 volumes (New York: Aperture, 1961); and Mary Street Alinder et al., *Ansel Adams: Letters and Images, 1916–1984* (Boston: Bulfinch, 1988). See also Jonathan Green, *American Photography: A Critical History 1945 to Present* (New York: Harry N. Abrams, 1984), 53–67; and Mary Street Alinder, *Group f.64: Edward Weston, Ansel Adams, Imogen Cunningham, and the Community of Artists Who Revolutionized American Photography* (New York: Bloomsbury, 2014).

7. On previsualization and the craft of photography, see, for example, Minor White, *Zone System Manual: Previsualization, Exposure, Development, Printing*, 4th ed. (New York: Morgan & Morgan, 1967).

8. On Weston's realism, see Newhall, ed., *Daybooks of Edward Weston*, 1: 55.

9. On photojournalism since the 1960s, see Christian Caujolle and Mary Panzer, *Things As They Are: Photojournalism in Context since 1955* (New York: Aperture, 2006).

10. On social documentary in the 1960s, see Nathan Lyons, *Contemporary Photographers: Toward a Social Landscape* (New York: Horizon Press and George Eastman House, 1966); Green, *American Photography*, 81–129; and Joel Meyerowitz and Colin Westerbeck, *Bystander: A History of Street Photography* (Boston: Bulfinch, 1994), 351–64, 373–403. See also Sarah Greenough et al., *Robert Frank: Moving Out* (Washington, D.C.: Scalo Publishers and National Gallery of Art, 1994); Elisabeth Sussman et al., *Diane Arbus: Revelations* (New York: Random House, 2003); Jeffrey Fraenkel et al., *The Man in the Crowd: The Uneasy Streets of Garry Winogrand* (San Francisco: Fraenkel Gallery, 1999). For a good account of how the various terms used to define the photographic document continued to remain in flux in the mid-1980s, see A. D. Coleman, "Documentary, Photojournalism, and Press Photography Now: Notes and Questions" (1986), in Coleman, *Depth of Field: Essays on Photography, Mass*

Media, and Lens Culture (Albuquerque: University of New Mexico Press, 1998), 35–52.

11. Heinecken took the term *photographist* from Arthur C. Danto, who used it to describe the work of artists such as Andy Warhol, Robert Rauschenberg, Joseph Beuys, Gerhard Richter, Sigmar Polke, Peter Roehr, and Hans-Peter Feldmann, who were using photographs "in art" as opposed to making photographs "as art." See Arthur C. Danto, "Photographism in Contemporary German Art," in Danto, *Embodied Meanings: Critical Essays and Aesthetic Meditations* (New York: Farrar Straus Giroux, 1994), 304–11. For Heinecken's discussion of the term, see Stephen K. Lehmer, *Photographist Oral History Transcript, 1996: Robert F. Heinecken*, vol. 2 (Los Angeles: Oral History Program, University of California, 1998), 361.

12. Heinecken, interview with Charles Hagen, 1976, in Enyeart, ed., *Heinecken*, 110.

13. Heinecken, "Statements about Work," circa 1963, in Kevin Moore et al., *Robert Heinecken: Copywork* (London: Ridinghouse, 2012), 5.

14. Martha Rosler, "Lookers, Buyers, Dealers, and Makers: Thoughts on Audience," *Exposure* 17, no. 1 (Spring 1979): 22.

15. Colin Westerbeck, "Tongue in Cheek: The Strange Relationship between Robert Heinecken and Wallace Berman," in Claudia Bohn-Spector and Sam Mellon, *Speaking in Tongues: Wallace Berman and Robert Heinecken 1961–1976* (Pasadena, Calif.: Armory Center for the Arts, 2011), 7, n. 13.

16. Carol Squiers, "Photography: Tradition and Decline," *Aperture* 91 (Summer 1983): 75.

17. Mark Alice Durant, *Robert Heinecken: A Material History* (Tucson: Center for Creative Photography, University of Arizona; New York: Distributed Art Publishers, 2003), 84–86. The review to which he refers is Nadine L. McGann, "Dumb Luck at SPE," *Afterimage* 19, no. 10 (May 1992): 3.

18. Martha Gever, who also reports that Heinecken's work was perceived as "sexist" in the early 1980s, notes Heinecken's interest in discussing the broader implications of the use of pornographic images in art. In an exchange with Susan Sontag, Heinecken "asked Sontag to explain the political exemptions granted women artists and refused men like him or [David] Heath. She feinted, replying she had missed his presentation the previous afternoon." See Gever, "The Neurotic Erotic: Debating Art and Pornography," *Afterimage* 10, nos. 1–2 (Summer 1982): 5.

19. Durant, *Robert Heinecken*, 86.

20. Charles Hagen, "Robert Heinecken: An Interview," *Afterimage* 3, no. 20 (April 1976): 11.

21. Robert Heinecken, "I Am Involved in Learning to Perceive and Use Light," 1974, in Moore et al., *Robert Heinecken: Copywork*, 8.

22. All the works were created in 1974. The first permutation was as a unique work, a constellation of photographs and handwritten text (Center for Creative Photography [CCP] 79.46.9). The second permutation was as a lithograph in an edition of three hundred, an image presented in the context of a broader sequence of five lithographs by Heinecken of a woman's torso superimposed with a television screen, a sequence that formed part of a portfolio of fifty images by ten different artists (CCP 76.271.50). The third permutation was as a gelatin silver print with a Polaroid photo montaged on top in an edition of thirty (CCP 93.3.25; Los Angeles County Museum of Art, The Audrey and Sydney Irmas Collection, AC1992.197.66). The order of the permutations is based on Heinecken's statement that the photograph was made from the same plate that was used for the lithograph; see Robert Heinecken, "CCP Seminar #5," videotape, 1995, Box 40, Robert Heinecken Archive, AG 45, Center for Creative Photography, University of Arizona, Tucson.

23. Stephen K. Lehmer, *Photographist Oral History Transcript, 1996: Robert F. Heinecken*, vol. 1 (Los Angeles: Oral History Program, University of California, Los Angeles, 1998), 1–27, 90–112.

24. Lehmer, *Photographist*, 1: 113–16.

25. They were married in 1955. See Lehmer, *Photographist*, 1: 107.

26. Lehmer, *Photographist*, 1: 138–41.

27. Lehmer, *Photographist*, 1: 37–38.

28. Owing to the Polaroid process by which they are made, SX-70 prints are unique images. However, the same Polaroid appears in each of the thirty iterations of the gelatin silver print series of *Evolution*, revealing that Heinecken created multiple SX-70 copies by rephotographing the same image multiple times.

29. On Ruscha's photography and books, see Sylvia Wolf, *Ed Ruscha and Photography* (New York: Whitney Museum of American Art, 2004); and Cécile Whiting, *Pop L.A.: Art and the City in the 1960s* (Berkeley and Los Angeles: University of California Press, 2008), 63–105. On Graham's *Homes for America* and its various iterations, see Dan Graham, "Homes for America: Early Twentieth Century Possessable House to the Quasi-Discrete

Cell of '66," *Arts Magazine* 41, no. 3 (December 1966–January 1967): 21–22; Graham, "My Works for Magazine Pages: 'A History of Conceptual Art,'" in Graham, *Two-way Mirror Power*, Alexander Alberro, ed., (Cambridge, Mass.: MIT Press, 1999), 10–13; "In Conversation: Dan Graham and Michael Smith," *Artforum* 42, no. 9 (May 2004): 184–89; and Craig Buckley et al., *Dan Graham's New Jersey* (New York: Lars Muller Publishers; Graduate School of Architecture, Planning, and Preservation, Columbia University), 2012.

30. Heinecken's title implies a comparative study of visual conventions, and thus it also evokes the visual anthropology of John A. Collier Jr., who was influential in San Francisco between the 1950s and the 1980s as a theorist, photographer, and educator. See Collier, *Visual Anthropology: Photography as a Research Method* (1967), rev. ed. (Albuquerque: University of New Mexico Press, 1986). Heinecken was aware of Collier's work; see Lehmer, *Photographist*, 2: 369, 428–29.

31. Heinecken also commented on how his own personal photographs both revealed and disguised the truth as well as how they both confirmed and subverted dominant stereotypes. Referring to the fourth image in row three, he noted that he was permitted to wear a beard at one point while flying because he had chickenpox and could not shave. Likewise, referring to the fourth image in row one, the first "adult" image, which shows him posed in mask and flight suit about to enter his plane, he stated that it was totally "false." Although it looks like he is about to fly his plane, it is actually his introductory flight school photograph taken before he has taken his first flying lesson; see Heinecken, "CCP Seminar #5," videotape, 1995, Box 40, R. Heinecken Archive, AG 45, Center for Creative Photography, University of Arizona, Tucson.

32. Roland Barthes, *Camera Lucida: Reflections on Photography,* trans. Richard Howard (New York: Hill and Wang, 1981), 13.

33. On the history of the concept of appropriation, see David Evans, ed., *Appropriation* (London: Whitechapel Gallery, 2009).

34. David Joselit, *Infinite Regress: Marcel Duchamp 1910–1941* (Cambridge, Mass.: MIT Press, 1998); Thierry de Duve, *Kant after Duchamp* (Cambridge, Mass.: MIT Press, 1998); Amelia Jones, *Postmodernism and the Engendering of Marcel Duchamp* (New York: Cambridge University Press, 1994); Ecke Bonk, *Marcel Duchamp: The Box in a Valise,* trans. David Britt (New York: Rizzoli, 1989); Anne D'Harnoncourt and Kynaston McShine, eds., *Marcel Duchamp* (New York and Philadelphia: Museum of Art and Philadelphia Museum of Art, 1973); Arturo Schwarz, *The Complete Works of Marcel Duchamp,* rev. ed. (London and New York: Thames & Hudson, 1970).

35. Marcel Duchamp, "The Creative Act," in Michel Sanouillet and Elmer Peterson, eds., *The Writings of Marcel Duchamp* (New York: DaCapo Press, 1989), 138–40.

36. Lehmer, *Photographist,* 2: 316.

37. Lehmer, *Photographist,* 2: 418.

38. Lehmer, *Photographist,* 2: 419.

39. See Craig Owens, "The Allegorical Impulse: Toward a Theory of Postmodernism" (1980), in Owens, *Beyond Recognition: Representation, Power, and Culture* (Berkeley: University of California Press, 1992), 52–87, esp. 54.

40. On *Still Life with Chair Caning* as the first cubist collage, see William Rubin, *Picasso and Braque: Pioneering Cubism* (New York: Museum of Modern Art, 1989), 36–37, 58. On the conceptualization of the arbitrary nature of the visual sign in Picasso's Cubism, see Yve-Alain Bois, "Kahnweiler's Lesson," in Bois, *Painting as Model* (Cambridge, Mass.: MIT Press, 1990), 65–97, esp. 72–74. See also Rosalind E. Krauss, "In the Name of Picasso," in her *The Originality of the Avant-Garde and Other Modernist Myths* (Cambridge, Mass.: MIT Press, 1985), 23–40; as well as Krauss's and Bois's later essays in Lynn Zelevansky, ed., *Picasso and Braque: A Symposium* (New York: Museum of Modern Art, 1992).

41. On the development of cubism, see William Rubin, *Picasso and Braque.*

42. Krauss, *The Originality of the Avant-Garde,* 37.

43. Rubin, *Picasso and Braque,* 36.

44. Lehmer, *Photographist,* 2: 512–13. On the impact of surrealist art in California after World War II, see Susan M. Anderson, "Journey into the Sun: California Artists and Surrealism," in Paul J. Karlstrom, ed., *On the Edge of America: California Modernist Art, 1900–1950* (Berkeley: University of California Press, 1996), 180–203. See also Susan Ehrlich, *Pacific Dreams: Currents of Surrealism and Fantasy in California Art, 1934–1957* (Los Angeles: Armand Hammer Museum of Art and Cultural Center, University of California, Los Angeles, 1995).

45. On Heinecken's appreciation of Dada art and in particular the photomontages of John Heartfield, see Alan G. Artner, "Adventures in Dada," *Chicago Tribune* (October 24, 1999). http://www.chicagotribune.com/news/ct-xpm-1999-10-24-9910240356-story.html

46. On how the Berlin Dada artists used art to imagine new forms of hybrid identity, see Matthew Biro, *The Dada*

Cyborg: Visions of the New Human in Weimar Berlin (Minneapolis: University of Minnesota Press, 2009).

47. See Roman Jakobson, "Shifters, Verbal Categories, and the Russian Verb," in Roman Jakobson, *On Language*, ed. L. Waugh and M. Monville-Burston (Cambridge, Mass.: Harvard University Russian Language Project, 1990 [1957]), 386–92. Rosalind Krauss introduces the idea of the fundamental indexicality of U.S. art in the 1970s through a discussion of the role of shifters in the works of Vito Acconci and Marcel Duchamp. See Krauss, "Notes on the Index: Seventies Art in America," *October* 3 (Spring 1977): 68–81.

48. See, in particular, Douglas Crimp, "Pictures," *October* 8 (Spring 1979): 75–88; and Crimp, "The Photographic Activity of Postmodernism," *October* 15 (Winter 1980), 91–101. For Crimp's arguments about the photography and the museum, see Crimp, *On the Museum's Ruins* (Cambridge, Mass.: MIT Press, 1993).

49. Walter Benjamin, *The Origin of German Tragic Drama* (1925/1928), trans. Josh Osborne (New York: Verso, 1990).

50. Craig Owens, "The Allegorical Impulse: Toward a Theory of Postmodernism," *October* 12 (Spring 1980): 67–86; and Owens, "The Allegorical Impulse: Toward a Theory of Postmodernism (Part 2)," *October* 13 (Summer 1980): 58–80. Both essays are reprinted in Craig Owens, *Beyond Recognition: Representation, Power, and Culture* (Berkeley: University of California Press, 1992).

51. Owens, *Beyond Recognition*, 54.

52. Owens, *Beyond Recognition*, 55–58.

53. Owens, *Beyond Recognition*, 53–54.

54. For example, Abigail Solomon-Godeau, one of postmodern photography's most incisive critics, argues, "seriality and repetition, appropriation, intertextuality, simulation or pastiche: these are the primary devices employed by postmodernist artists." Despite Heinecken's extensive use of all these strategies in the 1960s and 1970s, he is nowhere mentioned in Solomon-Godeau's important writings on postmodern photography. See Solomon-Godeau, "Photography after Art Photography," in Brian Wallis, ed., *Art after Modernism: Rethinking Representation* (New York and Boston: New Museum of Contemporary Art and David Godine, 1984), 80. See also Solomon-Godeau, *Photography at the Dock: Essays on Photographic History, Institutions, and Practices* (Minneapolis: University of Minnesota Press, 1991); and Solomon-Godeau, *Photography after Photography: Gender, Genre, History* (Durham, N.C.: Duke University Press, 2017).

55. The great collectors Walter and Louise Arensberg lived in Los Angeles between the 1920s and the 1950s, amassing one of the city's most important collections of modern art, which included significant works by cubist, Dada, and surrealist artists. They were strong supporters of Marcel Duchamp as well as the (soon-to-be) curator Walter Hopps, who would give Duchamp his first retrospective at the Pasadena Art Museum in 1963. On the presence of Duchamp and his art in Los Angeles, as well as the impact of his work on artists, curators, and the public, see Rebecca Peabody et al., eds., *Pacific Standard Time: Los Angeles Art 1945–1980* (Los Angeles: Getty Research Institute, 2011), 11–12, 135. Man Ray lived in Los Angeles between 1940 and 1951, showing his work frequently there as well; see Peabody et al., eds., *Pacific Standard Time*, 11, 14–16. A few LA galleries showed surrealist art during the 1940s and 1950s; these movements had a strong effect on art produced in Los Angeles in the 1950s and 1960s; see Peabody et al., eds., *Pacific Standard Time*, 16–21. Heinecken also remembers seeing a Kurt Schwitters collage, possibly at an exhibition at UCLA, wherein the glue had turned a theater ticket translucent. In retrospect, he thought that it might have been one of his inspirations for the *Are You Rea* series; see Lehmer, *Photographist*, 2: 404–405.

56. Lehmer, *Photographist*, 2: 314–16, 417–19, 422–23.

57. Lehmer, *Photographist*, 1: 274.

58. On the relationship of the surrealists to Sigmund Freud, see Maurice Nadeau, *The History of Surrealism*, trans. Richard Howard (Cambridge, Mass.: Harvard University Press, 1965 [1944]), esp. 23, 24, 48–49, 61, 79–84; Hal Foster, *Compulsive Beauty* (Cambridge, Mass.: MIT Press, 1993); and Donald Kuspit, *Signs of Psyche in Modern and Postmodern Art* (Cambridge: Cambridge University Press, 1993), 51–85. On the relationship of the surrealists to Georges Bataille, see Rosalind Krauss et al., *L'Amour fou: Photography and Surrealism* (New York: Abeville, 1985), 60, 64–65, 74, 165–75, 197–99; and Rosalind Krauss, "No More Play," in her *Originality of the Avant Garde*, 42–85.

59. On French colonial postcards, see Malek Alloula, *The Colonial Harem*, trans. Myrna Godzich and Wlad Godzich (Minneapolis: University of Minnesota Press, 1986).

60. Sigmund Freud, "The Uncanny" in Sigmund Freud, *Collected Papers*, 5 vols.,trans. Joan Riviere (New York: Basic Books, 1959), 4:378.

61. Freud, "The Uncanny," 378.

62. Freud, "The Uncanny," 382–86.

63. Freud, "The Uncanny," 387.

64. Freud, "The Uncanny," 390–91.

65. Freud, "The Uncanny," 393–94.

66. Freud, "The Uncanny," 394.

67. Freud, "The Uncanny," 398.

68. Freud, "The Uncanny," 403.

69. See Rosalind E. Krauss, "The Photographic Conditions of Surrealism," in her *Originality of the Avant-Garde*, 87–118, esp. 103–12. See also Biro, *Dada Cyborg*, 81–82.

70. On the construction of identity through the consumption of images, objects, and texts, I am indebted not only to Dada and surrealist art and their conceptual sources but also to scholarship on the production of identity in a number of different fields, including Jennifer Scanlon, *Inarticulate Longings: The* Ladies' Home Journal, *Gender, and the Promise of Consumer Culture* (New York: Routledge, 1995); Carolyn Kitch, *The Girl on the Magazine Cover: The Origins of Visual Stereotypes in American Mass Media* (Chapel Hill: University of North Carolina Press, 2001); Michael S. Kimmel, *Manhood in America: A Cultural History*, 2d ed. (New York: Oxford University Press, 2006). I am also building here on arguments about the production of individual and collective identity through art and visual culture that I made in my earlier books, *Anselm Kiefer and the Philosophy of Martin Heidegger* (New York: Cambridge University Press, 1998); and *Dada Cyborg*.

71. Lehmer, *Photographist*, 1: 37.

72. Lehmer, *Photographist*, 1: 38.

73. Lehmer, *Photographist*, 1: 38–39.

74. Lehmer, *Photographist*, 1: 16, 24–25.

75. Lehmer, *Photographist*, 1: 75–88.

76. Lehmer, *Photographist*, 1: 51.

77. Lehmer, *Photographist*, 1: 56–57.

78. Lehmer, *Photographist*, 1: 43–49.

79. Lehmer, *Photographist*, 1: 48.

80. Lehmer, *Photographist*, 1: 75.

1. ARTIST AND EDUCATOR

1. On the locations where Heinecken shot these photographs, see Robert Heinecken, "CCP Seminar #1," videotape, 1995, Box 40, Robert Heinecken Archive, AG 45, Center for Creative Photography, University of Arizona, Tucson.

2. On the more subjective or personal documentary practices that gained ascendency in the United States in the 1960s, see Cornelia H. Butler et al., *The Social Scene: The Ralph M. Parsons Foundation Photography Collection at the Museum of Contemporary Art, Los Angeles* (Los Angeles: Museum of Contemporary Art, 2000).

3. On Brassaï's photographs of graffiti, see Brassaï, *Brassaï Graffiti* (Paris: Flammarion, 2002). On Atget's photographs of commercial signage and urban locations, see John Szarkowski and Mary Morris Hambourg, *The Work of Atget*, 4 vols. (New York: Museum of Modern Art, 1981–85).

4. CCP Heinecken, Teaching Files, AG45:13, Sabbatical Applications and Reports (1966–87). Stephen K. Lehmer, *Photographist Oral History Transcript, 1996: Robert F. Heinecken*, vol. 1 (Los Angeles: Oral History Program, University of California, Los Angeles, 1998), 125–33.

5. Lehmer, *Photographist*, 1: 122–23.

6. On the economic rise of LA, see Steven P. Erie, *Globalizing L.A.: Trade, Infrastructure, and Regional Development* (Stanford, Calif.: Stanford University Press, 2004).

7. On the postwar evolution of Los Angeles, see Mike Davis, *City of Quartz: Excavating the Future in Los Angeles* (London: Verso, 1990); and Mike Davis, *Ecology of Fear: Los Angeles and the Imagination of Disaster* (New York: Vintage, 1999).

8. Other gelatin silver prints of this time that seem to criticize the postwar economic growth and suburbanization characteristic of Los Angeles include *Over, Baby Meto, Los Angeles, Ladies Heels, Chessman*, and *Broken Fence*, all from the early 1960s. See *Robert Heinecken Photographs* (Tucson, Ariz.: Center for Creative Photography, 2010), 72–77.

9. Stephen K. Lehmer, *Photographist Oral History Transcript, 1996: Robert F. Heinecken*, vol. 2 (Los Angeles: Oral History Program, University of California, Los Angeles, 1998), 512–13.

10. On modernist photography in San Francisco, see Stephanie Comer, Deborah Klochko, and Jeff Gunderson, *The Moment of Seeing: Minor White at the California School of Fine Arts* (San Francisco: Chronicle Books, 2006).

11. Turbans and other forms of "oriental" dress were sometimes used to give nude figures artistic connotations in nineteenth-century photography; see Michael Koetzle, *1000 Nudes: Uwe Scheid Collection* (Cologne: Benedikt Taschen, 1994), 57, 71, 90, 94, 118, 120, 162,

175, 189, 190, 203–205, 210, 299, 340–41, 344–47, 352, 422, 468, 471, 473–74, 476–79; and Serge Nazarieff, *Early Erotic Photography* (Cologne: Taschen, 2002), 50–51, 167, 185.

12. On allegory see Matthew Biro, *The Dada Cyborg* (Minneapolis: University of Minnesota Press, 2009), 16, 147, 156–60, 217, 288n122, 290n8, 290n14, 290n16.

13. On the use of photography to define and classify human beings in terms of different general qualities or characteristics, see Allan Sekula, "The Body and the Archive," *October* 39 (Winter 1986): 3–64; John Tagg, *The Burden of Representation: Essays on Photographies and Histories* (Minneapolis: University of Minnesota Press, 1993 and 2021 [1988]); and Jonathan Finn, *Capturing the Criminal Image: From Mug Shot to Surveillance Society* (Minneapolis: University of Minnesota Press, 2009).

14. Elaine Tyler May, *Homeward Bound: American Families in the Cold War Era* (New York: Basic Books, 1988). For an interesting recent analysis of the 1950s (nuclear) family ideal and its subsequent decrease in influence (and the concomitant return of the extended family), see David Brooks, "The Nuclear Family Was a Mistake," *The Atlantic* (March 2020). https://www.theatlantic.com/magazine/archive/2020/03/the-nuclear-family-was-a-mistake/605536/.

15. On the suburban home, television, and the family, see William Douglas, *Television Families: Is Something Wrong in Suburbia?* (Mahwah, N.J. and London: Lawrence Erlbaum, 2003).

16. May, *Homeward Bound,* 9–11.

17. See David R. Roediger, *Working toward Whiteness: How America's Immigrants Became White* (New York: Basic Books, 2005).

18. May, *Homeward Bound,* 174–97.

19. After they started a family, the Heineckens initially lived at a Marine family base in Laguna Beach, as well as at other Marine bases around the country. When Robert returned to UCLA, they first lived in family housing and later, in 1960, they moved to Beverly Glen (Lehmer, *Photographist,* 1: 105–106, 140–44). In 1963, they moved to a larger house on Viretta Lane, also in Beverly Glen. Claudia Bohn-Spector, "Rearguard Revolutionaries: Wallace Berman and Robert Heinecken," in Claudia Bohn-Spector and Sam Mellon, eds., *Speaking in Tongues: The Art of Wallace Berman and Robert Heinecken, 1961–1976* (Pasadena, Calif.: Armory Center for the Arts, 2011), 11.

20. See William H. Whyte, *The Organization Man* (New York: Simon and Schuster, 1956).

21. On Heinecken's struggle to establish photography as a fine art (as well as a graduate program) against the view of some of his fellow pictorial arts faculty members, see CCP Heinecken, Teaching Files, AG45:13, Sabbatical Applications and Reports (1966–87). See also Lehmer, *Photographist,* 1: 125–33.

22. Robert Heinecken, "The Photograph, Not a Picture of, But an Object about Something," UCLA (1965), 4 (pamphlet). The essay was also published that year in *Twenty-First Annual Art Directors Show* (Los Angeles: Art Directors Club of Los Angeles, 1965), n.p.

23. Heinecken, "The Photograph," 9.

24. Heinecken, "The Photograph," 7.

25. On indexes as anti-intentional, "empty," or meaningless, see the essays collected in James Elkins, ed., *Photography Theory* (New York and London: Routledge, 2007), many of which focus on the antihuman characteristics of the index.

26. Heinecken, "The Photograph," 4.

27. Lehmer, *Photographist,* 1: 223.

28. Robert Heinecken, "American Image Ideal," mixed media, 1963, Boxes 20 and 21, R. Heinecken Archive, AG 45, Center for Creative Photography, University of Arizona, Tucson.

29. It was designed to grapple directly with the theme of the conference, organized by Charles and Ray Eames, "Design and the American Image Abroad." On the conference, see Justus Nieland, *Happiness by Design: Modernism and Media in the Eames Era* (Minneapolis: University of Minnesota Press, 2020), 337.

30. Foreign students were asked about their conceptions of America around issues having to do with religion, war and peace, music and art, women, teenagers, and mass media such as Westerns and films. Heroes, Hollywood, crime, sex, clothing, the family, and money were also discussed.

31. Daniel Boorstin, *The Image: A Guide to Pseudo-Events in America* (New York: Vintage, 1992 [1961]). On the influence of Boorstin and Marshall McLuhan on Heinecken's work, see A. D. Coleman, "'I Call It Teaching': Robert Heinecken's Analytical Facture," in Irene Borger et al., *Robert Heinecken, Photographist: A Thirty-Five-Year Retrospective* (Chicago: Museum of Contemporary Art, 1999), 8.

32. Boorstin, *The Image,* 185.

33. Boorstin, *The Image,* 198.

34. Boorstin, *The Image,* 240.

35. Boorstin, *The Image*, 240–41.

36. See 93.17.12 *Venice Alley*, 1963. Gelatin silver print, 13⅜ x 19⁹⁄₁₆ inches (34.0 x 48.8 cm).Center for Creative Photography, University of Arizona: Robert Heinecken Archive/Gift of the artist. 81.107.2 *Venice Alley*, 1963. Photo-etching, 14 x 19¼ inches (35.5 x 48.9 cm). Center for Creative Photography, University of Arizona: Robert Heinecken Archive/gift of the artist.

37. On surrealist Paris as a forest of signs, see David Hopkins, *Dada and Surrealism: A Very Short Introduction* (Oxford: Oxford University Press, 2004), 59–60.

38. Hopps left Ferus in 1962. Ferus Gallery operated on La Cienega Boulevard between 1957 and 1966. See Rebecca Peabody et al., eds., *Pacific Standard Time: Art in L.A., 1945–1980* (Santa Monica, Calif.: Getty Research Institute, 2011), 11–16.

39. Peter Plagens, *Sunshine Muse: Contemporary Art on the West Coast* (New York: Praeger, 1974), 74.

40. On assemblage art in California, see Lizzetta LeFalle-Collins, ed., *19 SIXTIES: A Cultural Awakening Re-evaluated, 1965–1975* (Los Angeles: California Afro-American Museum, 1989); Anne Ayres et al., *Forty Years of California Assemblage* (Los Angeles: Wight Art Gallery, University of California, Los Angeles, 1989); Richard Cándida Smith, *The Modern Moves West: California Artists and Democratic Culture in the Twentieth Century* (Philadelphia: University of Pennsylvania Press, 2009), 141–64; and Peabody et al., eds., *Pacific Standard Time*, 66–123.

41. On Berman's *Veritas Panel*, see Richard Cándida Smith, *Utopia and Dissent: Art, Poetry, and Politics in California* (Berkeley: University of California Press, 1995), 217–21. On Kienholz's *Roxy's*, see Alex Potts, "Edward Kienholz's *Roxy's*," in Rebecca Peabody et al., eds., *Pacific Standard Time*, 121–23.

42. See Jess, *O! Tricky Cad and Other Jessoterica*, ed. Michael Duncan (Los Angeles: Siglio Press, 2012), esp. 16–439.

43. On Bruce Conner, see Rudolf Frieling and Gary Garrels, eds., *Bruce Conner: It's All True* (San Francisco: San Francisco Museum of Modern Art; University of California Press, 2016); and Matthew Biro, "Bruce Conner: It's All True," *The Brooklyn Rail* (October 2016): 42.

44. On the connection of assemblage with "dirtiness," see Plagens, *Sunshine Muse*, 87–89, 94.

45. Richard Cándida Smith, *The Modern Moves West*, 147.

46. Richard Cándida Smith, *The Modern Moves West*, 150.

47. Richard Cándida Smith, *The Modern Moves West*, 153.

48. Berman left Los Angeles for San Francisco after his arrest on obscenity charges in 1957, and he returned in 1961. Bohn-Spector, "Rearguard Revolutionaries," 9–10. On Berman, see Eduardo Lipschutz-Villa et al., *Wallace Berman: Support the Revolution* (Amsterdam: Institute of Contemporary Art, 1992).

49. Bohn-Spector, "Rearguard Revolutionaries," 12.

50. See Andy Grundberg, "Review/Photography; Reminders of the 60's in Collage and Montage," *New York Times*, October 19, 1990. http://www.nytimes.com/1990/10/19/arts/review-photography-reminders-of-the-60-s-in-collage-and-montage.html.

51. Because of its nature as a copying machine, its reduction of color and detail, and its connections to the work done in corporate offices, the Verifax seemed at first blush a very unlikely medium for artistic image creation. It was thus even more antiart than Andy Warhol's silkscreen strategy, despite the fact that Warhol's subject matter was cooler, more matter-of-fact, and less poetic than Berman's (and thus more antiart than Berman in another way). On Warhol's mechanization of painting and its relationship to the modernist tradition, see Benjamin H. D. Buchloh, "Andy Warhol's One-Dimensional Art: 1956–1966," in Kynaston McShine, ed., *Andy Warhol: A Retrospective* (New York: Museum of Modern Art, 1989), 39–61.

52. See *Life* 56 (24) (June 12, 1964): R12.

53. On *Semina*, see Michael Duncan and Kristine McKenna, eds., *Semina Culture: Wallace Berman and His Circle* (New York: D.A.P./Santa Monica Museum of Art, 2005); and Johan Kugelberg, ed., *Semina 1955–1964: Art Is Love Is God* (New York: Boo-Hooray Gallery, 2014).

54. Bohn-Spector, "Rearguard Revolutionaries," 12.

55. Heinecken identified the slides that were projected on the models' bodies for this series as coming from the Aspen conference. See Heinecken, "CCP Seminar #2," videotape, 1995, Box 40, R. Heinecken Archive, AG 45, Center for Creative Photography, University of Arizona, Tucson.

56. As Heinecken later described their process of creation, he used four to six models, both male and female, and seven or eight slide projectors. Everybody took off their clothes, including Heinecken. The models moved around, dancing in and out of the images transmitted by the slide projectors, while the machines ran automatically. Approximately ten rolls of film were shot. See Heinecken, "CCP Seminar #1," videotape, 1995, Box 40, R. Heinecken Archive, AG 45, Center for Creative Photography, University of Arizona, Tucson. All slide projection images emerged from one, possibly

two, sessions. Both Heinecken and the models made the photographs, and then he selected the best images. An effort was made to have the projected image fit or mirror the body; see Heinecken, "CCP Seminar #2," videotape, 1995, Box 40, R. Heinecken Archive, AG 45, Center for Creative Photography, University of Arizona, Tucson.

57. Thomas Hobbes, *Leviathan,* ed. Edwin Curley (Indianapolis: Hackett, 1994 [1651/1668]), 76.

58. Lehmer, *Photographist,* 2: 472–74.

59. See "We Wade Deeper into Jungle War," *Life* 54 (4) (January 25, 1963): 22–30 (with photographs by Larry Burrows); Milton Orshefsky, "Despite Battlefield Setbacks There Is Hope—With Caution," *Life* 54 (4) (January 25, 1963): 31–33; "A Little War, Far Away— And Very Ugly," *Life* 56 (24) (June 12, 1964): 34–44C. The latter issue also contained the Sony advertisement from which Wallace Berman appropriated his famous transistor radio (R12).

60. On the connections between war and sexual violence, see Susan Brownmiller, *Against Our Will: Men, Women, and Rape* (New York: Simon and Schuster, 1975), 31–113. As Brownmiller notes, "The American military got into the prostitution business by degrees, an escalation process linked to the escalation of the war. Underlying the escalation was the assumption that men at war required the sexual use of women's bodies" (93–94). "In 1965 the Marine Corps base at Danang began experimenting with organized battalion trips to town on a once-a-month basis. . . . A shantytown of brothels, massage parlors and dope dealers, known as Dogpatch, soon ringed the base" (94). Describing how rape could become an accepted practice during the Vietnam War, Brownmiller notes: "Despite the intense propaganda throughout the long war, our American soldiers did not believe that they were 'liberating' anyone, nor were they perceived as liberators. . . . As [Peter] Arnett described it, 'There were no fixed targets, no objectives, no highways to take . . . . Anything outside the perimeter of the base camp . . . was enemy territory, and all civilians were treated as enemy. It was so easy to rape on a squad level. . . . Any American could grab any woman as a suspect and there was little or no recourse to the law by the people'" (97–98).

61. Wallace Berman, *Untitled* (1964). Verifax collage mounted on plywood, 45 x 45 inches (114.3 x 114.3 cm). Los Angeles County Museum of Art.

62. In the 1980s, Heinecken began to add lithographic frames shaped like television sets to some of his photographs, in particular those of newswomen. See, for example, *Waking Up in News America* (1986), discussed in chapter 7.

63. Bohn-Spector, "Rearguard Revolutionaries," 14.

64. See René Magritte, *Le Viol (Rape)* (1934). Oil on canvas. Menil Collection, Houston. Also Magritte, *Le Viol (Rape)* (1934), drawing on the cover of André Breton's *Qu'est-ce que le Surréalisme?* (1934). See also Man Ray, *Torso,* gelatin silver print. Museum of Modern Art, New York.

65. On the torso in Surrealist photography, see Kristen A. Hoving, "Man Ray's Disarming Venuses: Deconstructing the Classical Torso in Surrealist Photography," *History of Photography* 29 (2) (Summer 2005): 123–34.

66. Heinecken, "CCP Seminar #2," videotape, 1995, Box 40, R. Heinecken Archive, AG 45, Center for Creative Photography, University of Arizona, Tucson.

67. Multiple versions of each photograph exist.

68. Lehmer, *Photographist,* 1: 105–6.

69. See Malcom Green and Hans Bellmer, *Hans Bellmer: The Doll* (London: Atlas Press, 2013).

70. On Bellmer's relationship to models of instinct and desire drawn from psychoanalysis, see Hal Foster, *Prosthetic Gods* (Cambridge, Mass.: MIT Press, 2004), 230–39.

71. We read this figure as the bridegroom because of his positioning in the center of the photograph next to the bride as well as the adjective *eager,* which implies that he was so excited that he forgot to dress.

2. DOCUMENTS OF MANUFACTURED EXPERIENCE

1. Robert F. Heinecken, *Are You Rea, 1964–1968* (N.p.: self-published), i. Introductions are indicated by i and ii; images by 1–25.

2. On the politics of postwar consumer culture in the United States, see Lizabeth Cohen, *A Consumers' Republic: The Politics of Mass Consumption in Postwar America* (New York: Vintage, 2003); on its relationship to counterculture, see Joseph Heath and Andrew Potter, *Nation of Rebels: Why Counterculture Became Consumer Culture* (New York: Harper Collins, 2004).

3. Heinecken, "Autobiographical Sketch," September 1974, mimeograph of a typed manuscript, n.p., in Heinecken's Biographical Materials, 1954–1994, Box 1, Folder 4, R. Heinecken Archive, AG 45, Center for Creative Photography, University of Arizona, Tucson.

4. Heinecken, untitled manuscript. Mimeograph of
a typed manuscript in a loose-leaf binder, n.p., in
Heinecken's UCLA Teaching Files, Box 42, Book 5,
R. Heinecken Archive, AG 45, Center for Creative
Photography, University of Arizona, Tucson.

5. Stephen K. Lehmer, *Photographist Oral History Transcript, 1996: Robert F. Heinecken*, vol. 1 (Los Angeles:
Oral History Program, University of California, 1998),
132–33, 189–90, 194–202.

6. Although successful, the photography program
was always small. While Heinecken was involved
with it, there were never more than two full-time
faculty members at once. Other than Heinecken, most
of the continuity was supplied by Mark McFadden,
Mark Durant, and Robert Fichter (Lehmer, *Photographist*, 1: 228).

7. On Heinecken's influence on the Grunwald Center
for the Graphic Arts and the Frederick S. Wight
Gallery, both at UCLA, see James Welling, "A Fine
Experiment: A Tribute to Robert Heinecken," exhibi-
tion brochure, (Los Angeles: Hammer Museum, 2006).
The five photography exhibitions that Heinecken
curated or co-curated while at UCLA were *Bullock/
Davidson/Frank/Lartigue/Siskind*, UCLA Art Galleries,
1965; *Contemporary Photographs*, UCLA Art Galleries,
September–October, 1968; *William Doherty*, UCLA Go
Gallery and Ohio Silver Gallery, Los Angeles; 1973;
UCLA Collection of Contemporary American Photographs,
Frederick S. Wight Art Gallery, 1976; and *Celebrating
Two Decades in Photography: Recent Work by UCLA MFA
Recipients*, UCLA Grunwald Center for the Graphic
Arts, 1985; see Heinecken, untitled manuscript (1985),
mimeograph of a typed manuscript, n.p., in Heineck-
en's UCLA Teaching Files, Box 42, Book 5, R. Heinecken
Archive, AG 45, Center for Creative Photography, Uni-
versity of Arizona, Tucson.

8. On the 1960s as a cultural moment, see Arthur
Marwick, *The Sixties: Cultural Transformation in Britain,
France, Italy and the United States, c. 1958—c. 1974* (New
York: Oxford University Press, 1998); David Farber, *The
Age of Great Dreams: America in the 1960s* (New York:
Hill and Wang, 1994); and David Farber, *The Sixties:
From Memory to History* (Chapel Hill: University of
North Carolina Press, 1994).

9. Among the photographers and artists who produced photograms during the practice's long history,
we find some of the most famous of the nineteenth
and twentieth centuries including William Henry Fox
Talbot, Sir John Herschel, and Anna Atkins between
the 1830s and the 1850s; Christian Schad, Man Ray,
László Moholy-Nagy, Kurt Schwitters, and El Lissitzky

in the teens and 1920s; and since the 1950s figures as
diverse as Robert Rauschenberg, Bruce Conner, Sigmar
Polke, Adam Fuss, and James Welling. The photogram's documentary side was already represented at
the beginnings of its history between the 1830s and
1850s by figures such as Talbot and Atkins, whereas
its artistic side first emerged most prominently in the
1920s in surrealism and New Vision photography, with
figures like Man Ray and László Moholy-Nagy, who
used the technique to allegorize reality in a manner
similar to the way Heinecken would use it in his
practice. On the photogram, see William Henry Fox
Talbot, Michael Gray, Arthur Ollman, Carol McCusker,
*First Photographs: William Henry Fox Talbot and the
Birth of Photography* (New York: Powerhouse, 2002),
134–35; William Henry Fox Talbot, *The Pencil of Nature*,
fascimile ed. (New York: Da Capo Press, 1969 [1844–
46]), n.p.: plates VII, IX, XX, XXIII; Larry J. Schaaf, *The
Photographic Art of William Henry Fox Talbot* (Princeton,
N.J.: Princeton University Press, 2000), 42–50; Larry
J. Schaaf, ed., *Sun Gardens: Cyanotypes by Anna Atkins*
(Munich: Prestel, 2018); Man Ray, *Les Champs délicieux*
(Paris: 1922); Renate Heyne and Floris M. Neusüss,
with Hattula Moholy-Nagy, eds., *László Moholy-Nagy:
The Photograms; Catalogue Raisonne* (Ostfildern, Ger.:
Hatje Cantz, 2009).

10. Given that the "Amerian Image Ideal" predates the
earliest *Are You Rea* gelatin silver prints by about a
year, Heinecken's adoption of the photogram technique
seems to have arisen from his work with slides and
projection, which likewise played between index and
allegory, although they did not really make this dialectic explicit. A. D. Coleman remembers a slide show
that Heinecken produced in 1965 wherein he projected
fragments of newspapers mounted into slide holders—
another channel through which he explored the
relationship of reality to its photographic and textual
representation. A. D. Coleman, "Heinecken: A Man for
All Dimensions," *New York Times* (August 2, 1970), 83.

11. Although Heinecken determined a particular order
for his images, he did not number the plates. Thus
the portfolio can lose its original order quite quickly,
and even museums differ in their precise organization of *Are You Rea*. Compare, for example, the order
found in the following catalogues: Irene Borger et al.,
*Robert Heinecken: Photographist—A Thirty Five Year
Retrospective* (Chicago: Museum of Contemporary Art,
1999), 52–59; and Eva Respini, ed., *Robert Heinecken:
Object Matter* (New York: Museum of Modern Art, 2014),
50–59. Regardless, there is a fair amount of uniformity in the presumed order of the portfolio, and the
following description does not significantly differ from
the sequences presented by these two museums. I

describe the portfolio in its presumed intended order because Heinecken understood this to be part of *Are You Rea*'s content. As he put it, "It's sequenced in such a way where you look at three or four pictures in a row. I don't identify them this way, but you'll see that they're all a woman and a woman for three pictures. Then suddenly it's got text in it; it's about rioting or something. If you're really smart you can sense the sequencing of the twenty-five pictures as being the content. It's not the pictures, but the order in which they're being revealed to you in terms of social phenomena. . . . I didn't—and this was a mistake—number the pages, because as soon as someone owns this thing, if it gets out of order then you don't have those groupings. So, they're in there, obviously, but they're not in sequence to show you the three or four." Stephen K. Lehmer, *Photographist Oral History Transcript, 1996: Robert F. Heinecken,* vol. 2 (Los Angeles: Oral History Program, University of California, 1998), 414–15.

12. The identities of the figures and objects in the *Are You Rea* lithographs, which are sometimes hard to discern, were checked by consulting the original production materials—the excised magazine pages that were used to make the photograms. See Box 37, R. Heinecken Archive, AG 45, Center for Creative Photography, University of Arizona, Tucson.

13. See the reproduction of the original magazine page, Respini, ed., *Robert Heinecken: Object Matter,* 13.

14. The numbers in parentheses here refer to the pages or plates in Heinecken's portfolio as they appeared in their original order. They are to be distinguished from the plate numbers in this chapter, which are always preceded by the word *Plate.*

15. For Prince's cowboy imagery, see, for example, Nancy Spector et al., *Richard Prince* (New York: Guggenheim Museum, 2007), 86–101.

16. J. Courtney Sullivan, "How Diamonds Became Forever," *New York Times,* May 3, 2013, ST23. http://www .nytimes.com/2013/05/05/fashion/weddings/how -americans-learned-to-love-diamonds.html?_r=0.

17. Although the magazine article that contained the source for this image cannot be determined, the news story that it describes can be identified by consulting the original (trimmed) page at the Center for Creative Photography from which the photogram was generated. This story, which concerns the murder of two New York police detectives, James Donegan and Salvatore Potenza, when they responded to a domestic abuse complaint in the Flatlands section of Brooklyn on October 15, 1964, does not have any obvious racial overtones. Heinecken's transformation of his source,

however, gives the image a palpable racial charge, mutating it into an allegory about police violence against civil rights demonstrators. It thus shows how a news article from 1964 can be reshaped into an emblem for a slightly later moment, possibly 1968, a year that saw horrible racial violence in the wake of the assassination of the Reverend Martin Luther King Jr. on April 4. See Walter Carlson, "Wife of Slayer of Two Detectives Read Bible as He Took Own Life," *New York Times,* October 16, 1964, L29. http://mobile .nytimes.com/1964/10/16/wife-of-slayer-of-two -detectives-read-bible-as-he-took-own-life.html.

18. The terms *male gaze* and *female gaze* emerged in film theory in the 1970s and 1980s; I am here particularly indebted to feminist film and cultural theorist Laura Mulvey, who used the former term to model the heterosexual male subject position that was created by classical Hollywood cinema in the 1950s and 1960s. See Laura Mulvey, "Visual Pleasure and Narrative Cinema," *Screen* 16 (3) (Autumn 1975): 6–18; see also the essays collected in Laura Mulvey, *The Visual and Other Pleasures* (Bloomington: Indiana University Press, 1989). Since Mulvey, the concepts of male and female gazes have been significantly developed in relation to Hollywood and independent cinema, both from psychoanalytic and materialist perspectives; see, for example, E. Ann Kaplan, *Women and Film: Both Sides of the Camera* (New York: Methuen, 1983); Teresa de Lauretis, *Technologies of Gender: Essays on Theory, Film, and Fiction* (Bloomington: Indiana University Press, 1987); Mary Ann Doane, *The Desire to Desire: The Woman's Film of the 1940s* (Bloomington: Indiana University Press, 1987); Kaja Silverman, *The Acoustic Mirror: The Female Voice in Psychoanalysis and Cinema* (Bloomington: Indiana University Press, 1988); and Lorraine Gamman and Margaret Marshment, *The Female Gaze: Women as Viewers of Popular Culture* (Seattle: Real Comet Press, 1989). As the terms are used here, *male gaze* at times means a selection of imagery that suggests a heterosexual and active male point of view, while *female gaze* can sometimes signify a straight and passive female mode of spectatorship. But these standpoints, it should be noted, are abstractions—extremes that indicate opposite endpoints of a continuum of different subject positions. In cinema, art, and popular culture, evocations of gendered perspectives intersect with other forms of group belonging that involve identity categories such as sexuality, race, ethnicity, class, and generation. Thus as this study shows in relation to Heinecken's work, there are multiple types of male and female gaze as well as subject positions that do not fit under these categories.

19. On the U.S. counterculture in the 1960s, see Todd Gitlin, *The Sixties: Years of Hope, Days of Rage* (New York: Bantam, 1987); and Terry H. Anderson, *Movement and the Sixties: Protest in America from Greensboro to Wounded Knee* (New York: Oxford University Press, 1996).

20. Cécile Whiting, *Pop L.A.: Art and the City in the 1960s* (Berkeley and Los Angeles: University of California Press, 2006), 9.

21. Whiting, *Pop L.A.*, 66.

22. Whiting, *Pop L.A.*, 71.

23. See Mark Alice Durant, *Robert Heinecken: A Material History* (Tucson: Center for Creative Photography, University of Arizona; New York: Distributed Art Publishers, 2003), 106.

24. Lewis Kachur et al., *Robert Rauschenberg: Transfer Drawings from the 1960s* (New York: Jonathan O'Hara Gallery, 2007), 8.

25. Heinecken, "CCP Seminar #11," videotape, 1995, Box 41, R. Heinecken Archive, AG 45, Center for Creative Photography, University of Arizona, Tucson. See also Kevin Moore et al., *Robert Heinecken: Copywork* (London: Ridinghouse, 2012), 26–27; and Irene Borger et al., *Robert Heinecken, Photographist: A Thirty-Five-Year Retrospective* (Chicago: Museum of Contemporary Art, 1999), 47.

26. On Rauschenberg's transfer drawings, see Lewis Kachur et al., *Robert Rauschenberg: Transfer Drawings from the 1960s* (New York: Jonathan O'Hara Gallery, 2007); Branden W. Joseph, *Random Order: Robert Rauschenberg and the Neo-Avant-Garde* (Cambridge, Mass.: MIT Press, 2003), 173–207; Mary Lynn Kotz, *Robert Rauschenberg: Art and Life* (New York: Harry N. Abrams, 1990), 98–101; and Götz Adriani, *Robert Rauschenberg: Zeichnungen, Gouachen, Collagen, 1949 bis 1979* (Munich/Zurich: R. Piper & Co. Verlag, 1979).

27. On Rauschenberg's combines, see Paul Schimmel, ed., *Robert Rauschenberg: Combines* (Los Angeles: Museum of Contemporary Art, 2005); on his silkscreen paintings, see Roni Feinstein et al., *Robert Rauschenberg: The Silkscreen Paintings, 1962–64* (New York: Whitney Museum of American Art, 1990).

28. Arthur C. Danto, *Andy Warhol* (New Haven, Conn.: Yale University Press, 2009), 31, 38.

29. Danto, *Andy Warhol*, 135–36.

30. Danto, *Andy Warhol*, 136.

31. Danto, *Andy Warhol*, 36–37.

32. Danto, *Andy Warhol*, 143–44.

33. Benjamin H. D. Buchloh, "Andy Warhol's One-Dimensional Art: 1956–1966," in Annette Michelson, ed., *Andy Warhol* (Cambridge, Mass.: MIT Press, 2001), 11

34. Buchloh, "Andy Warhol's One-Dimensional Art," 35.

35. Buchloh, "Andy Warhol's One-Dimensional Art," 26.

36. Buchloh, "Andy Warhol's One-Dimensional Art," 36–37.

37. Thomas Crow, "Saturday Disasters: Trace and Reference in Early Warhol," in Michelson, ed., *Andy Warhol*, 49.

38. Crow, "Saturday Disasters," 51, 53.

39. Crow, "Saturday Disasters," 51.

40. Crow, "Saturday Disasters," 55.

41. Crow, "Saturday Disasters," 57.

42. Crow, "Saturday Disasters," 58.

43. Crow, "Saturday Disasters," 60.

44. There is also a transparency with a grass background. Heinecken, "CCP Seminar #5," videotape, 1995, Box 40, R. Heinecken Archive, AG 45, Center for Creative Photography, University of Arizona, Tucson.

45. See the original supplement in Heinecken's production materials, Box 32, R. Heinecken Archive, AG 45, Center for Creative Photography, University of Arizona, Tucson.

46. On the War Babies, see Cécile Whiting, "California War Babies: Picturing World War Two in the 1960s," *Art Journal* 69 (3) (2010): 40–61.

3. THE PHOTOGRAPHIC OBJECT

1. Robert Heinecken, "Manipulative Photography," *Contemporary Photographer* 5, no. 4 (Winter 1967). Reprinted in Eva Respini, ed., *Robert Heinecken: Object Matter* (New York: Museum of Modern Art, 2014), 156. Text originally delivered at an SPE meeting circa 1964.

2. Heinecken, "Manipulative Photography," 156.

3. Heinecken, "Manipulative Photography," 156.

4. Robert Heinecken, "The Photograph: Not a Picture of, but an Object about Something," in *21st Annual Art Directors Show* catalogue (Los Angeles: Art Directors Club of Los Angeles, 1965). See Respini, *Robert Heinecken: Object Matter*, 155.

5. Hilton Kramer, "Modern Museum Displays Photography as Sculpture," *New York Times*, April 9, 1970.

6. On the terms *blocks* and *stacks*, see Stephen K. Lehmer, *Photographist Oral History Transcript, 1996: Robert F. Heinecken*, vol. 2 (Los Angeles: Oral History Program, University of California, 1998), 397.

7. Respini, ed., *Robert Heinecken: Object Matter*, 40. Cat. 13.

8. For *Figure in Six Sections*, see Respini, ed., *Robert Heinecken: Object Matter*, 41. Cat. 14. For *Transitional Figure Sculpture*, see Respini, ed., *Robert Heinecken: Object Matter*, 42–43. Cat. 15.

9. Respini, ed., *Robert Heinecken: Object Matter*, 44. Cat. 16. See also Respini, ed., *Robert Heinecken: Object Matter*, 47. Cat. 21.

10. See Respini, ed., *Robert Heinecken: Object Matter*, 11–13.

11. Willème began developing his process in 1859 and patented it in France in 1860–61. The technique only became practical in 1863, however, when Willème's Paris studio was completed. Although briefly popular, photo-sculpture was not a financial success, and he closed his studio in 1867. Attempts to promulgate the practice in England (by Antoine Claudet) and the United States (by Huston & Kurtz) during the mid-1860s were similarly short-lived. On the photo-sculpture of Willème, see Beaumont Newhall, "Photosculpture," *Image*, 7 (5) (May 1958): 100–105; Gillian Greenhill, "Photo-Sculpture," *History of Photography*, 4 (3) (1980): 243–45; and Robert Sobieszek, "Sculpture as the Sum of Its Profiles: François Willème and Photosculpture in France, 1859–1868," *Art Bulletin*, 62 (4) (December 1980): 617–30.

12. Sobieszek, "Sculpture as the Sum of Its Profiles," 617–18, 629–30.

13. James Enyeart, ed., *Heinecken* (Carmel, Calif.: Friends of Photography, with Light Gallery, 1980), 116.

14. Respini, ed., *Robert Heinecken: Object Matter*, 45. Cat. 17. See description of the process in Jennifer Jae Gutierrez, "Pinups, Photograms, Polaroids, and Printing Plates: Iterations in Robert Heinecken's Work Process," in Eva Respini, ed., *Robert Heinecken: Object Matter*, 146–48.

15. Respini, ed., *Robert Heinecken: Object Matter*, 45. Cat. 18.

16. Respini, ed., *Robert Heinecken: Object Matter*, 46. Cat. 19 and Cat. 20.

17. Respini, ed., *Robert Heinecken: Object Matter*, 48. Cat. 22.

18. Respini, ed., *Robert Heinecken: Object Matter*, 39. Cat. 12. For the original image, see Respini, ed., *Robert Heinecken: Object Matter*, 12, figure 4.

19. See Rosalind Krauss, "No More Play," in Krauss, *The Originality of the Avant-Garde and Other Modernist Myths* (Cambridge, Mass.: MIT Press, 1985), 73.

20. Krauss, "No More Play," 73–74.

21. Krauss, "No More Play," 83.

22. Krauss, "No More Play," 85.

23. Robert J. McMahon, "Turning Point: The Vietnam War's Pivotal Year, November 1967–November 1968," in *The Columbia History of the Vietnam War*, ed. David L. Anderson (New York: Columbia University Press, 2011), 191–92.

24. Heinecken used the cover image from the *Life* magazine issue of November 4, 1966, as one of the last images of *Are You Rea*, 1964–68.

25. See David Farber, *The Age of Great Dreams: America in the 1960s* (New York: Hill and Wang, 1994), chap. 8.

26. Kodalith film is a high-contrast, ortho-chromatic medium that is used to transfer photographs, line art, and text to printing plates. (When photographs requiring tonal values are reproduced, then a halftone screen is also employed.) Transparencies were used in printing for type as well as to combine word and image. When used on images they increase contrast and make subjects more abstract. See John Ross, Clare Romano, and Tim Ross, *The Complete Printmaker: Techniques, Traditions, Innovations* (New York: Free Press, 1990), 260–61.

27. Robert Heinecken, "CCP Seminar #5," videotape, 1995, Box 41, R. Heinecken Archive, AG 45, Center for Creative Photography, University of Arizona, Tucson.

28. Numerous installation photographs exist of the *Large Glass*—also known more officially as *The Bride Stripped Bare by Her Bachelors, Even* (1915–1923)—which was purchased from the artist by the collector Katherine Dreier around 1918 and photographed even before its initial completion in the early 1920s. It was first exhibited in 1926 at the Brooklyn Museum and later broken in transit and repaired by the artist, who deemed it completed by this chance event. The *Large Glass* became a part of the Philadelphia Museum of Art's permanent collection in 1953. Heinecken would have seen it firsthand in 1963, at the Pasadena Museum (now the Norton Simon

Museum) in Los Angeles County, when the institution gave Duchamp his first major U.S. retrospective, October 9–November 3.

29. Respini, ed., *Robert Heinecken: Object Matter*, 60. Cat. 26.

30. Respini, ed., *Robert Heinecken: Object Matter*, 61. Cat. 27.

31. Respini, ed., *Robert Heinecken: Object Matter*, 61. Cat. 28.

32. Respini, ed., *Robert Heinecken: Object Matter*, 62. Cat. 29.

33. Respini, ed., *Robert Heinecken: Object Matter*, 63. Cat. 30.

34. For more on TLI, see Library of Congress, *Catalog of Copyright Entries*, third series (1971): January–June (1973), 244.

35. Respini, ed., *Robert Heinecken: Object Matter*, 16.

36. See *Catalogue for The Latent Image*, 1960s. Robert Heinecken Trust, Chicago. Reproduced in Respini, ed., *Robert Heinecken: Object Matter*, 17, fig. 13.

37. Erving Goffman, *The Presentation of Self in Everyday Life* (Edinburgh: University of Edinburgh Social Sciences Research Centre, 1956).

38. On the pinup, see Ellen Wright, "Female Sexuality, Taste and Respectability: An Analysis of Transatlantic Media Discourse Surrounding Hollywood Glamour and Film Star Pin-Ups during WWII," doctoral dissertation (University of East Anglia, 2014), Despina Kakoudaki, "Pinup: The American Secret Weapon in World War II," in Linda Williams, ed., *Porn Studies* (Durham and London: Duke University Press, 2004), 335–69; Charles G. Martignette and Louis K. Meisel, *The Great American Pin-Up* (Köln, Ger.: Taschen, 2012); and André Bazin, "Entomology of the Pin-Up Girl" [1946], in his *What Is Cinema?*, vol. 2, trans. Hugh Gray (Berkeley: University of California Press, 1971), 158–62.

39. Cited in Shirley Christian, "But Is It Art? Well, Yes; A Trove of Pinups at the University of Kansas Is Admired by All Sorts, Including Feminists," *New York Times* (November 25, 1998).

40. See, for example, Kakoudaki, "Pinup," 358–63.

41. On changes in concepts of manhood and masculinity in the post–World War II context, see Kyle A. Cuordileone, *Manhood and American Political Culture in the Cold War* (New York: Routledge, 2005).

42. On the Tet Offensive and its relationship to politics, the press, and public opinion in the United States, see McMahon, "Turning Point: The Vietnam War's Pivotal Year," 191–216.

43. Chester J. Pach Jr., "And That's the Way It Was: The Vietnam War on the Network Nightly News," in David Farber, ed., *The Sixties: From Memory to History* (Chapel Hill: University of North Carolina Press, 1994), 69–89.

44. Pach, "And That's the Way It Was," 81.

45. Lehmer, *Photographist*, 2: 472–74.

46. On the history of People's Park, see Jon David Cash, "People's Park: Birth and Survival," *California History* 88 (1) (2010): 8–29, 53–55; and Peter Allen, "The End of Modernism? People's Park, Urban Renewal, and Community Design," *Journal of the Society of Architectural Historians* 70 (3) (September 2011): 354–74.

47. Anna Feigenbaum, "100 Years of Tear Gas," *The Atlantic*, August 16, 2014. http://www.theatlantic.com/international/archive/2014/08/100-years-of-tear-gas/378632/.

48. See MoMA online exhibition archive. https://www.moma.org/calendar/exhibitions/2694?locale=en.

49. See MoMA online exhibition archive. https://www.moma.org/calendar/exhibitions/2686?locale=en.

50. Mary Statzer, ed., *The Photographic Object 1970* (Oakland: University of California Press, 2016), 146.

51. Quoted in Kenneth R. Allan, "Understanding Information," in Michael Corris, ed., *Conceptual Art: Theory, Myth, and Practice* (New York: Cambridge University Press, 2004), 148.

52. See Lucy R. Lippard and John Chandler, "The Dematerialization of Art," *Art International* 12 (2) (February 1968): 31–36; and Lucy R. Lippard, *Six Years: The Dematerialization of the Art Object from 1966 to 1972* (New York: Praeger, 1973).

53. Kynaston L. McShine, "Information," MoMA Press Release, no. 69, 1970, 1.

54. Kynaston L. McShine, ed., *Information*, exhibition catalogue (New York: Museum of Modern Art, 1970), 57. See also "Information," MoMA Exhibition 0934 Master Checklist, 1970, 9.

55. Irene V. Small, *Hélio Oiticica: Folding the Frame* (Chicago: University of Chicago Press, 2016), 117–19.

56. Anonymous, "Photography Featured in MOMA Summer Exhibition," MoMA Press Release No. 69-I, 1970, 1.

57. McShine, ed., *Information,* 20–21. MoMA Exhibition 0934 Master Checklist, 4.

58. McShine, ed., *Information,* 69. MoMA Exhibition 0934 Master Checklist, 12.

59. As Kosuth wrote: "Works of art are analytic propositions. That is, if viewed within their context—as art—they provide no information what-so-ever about any matter of fact. A work of art is a tautology in that it is a presentation of the artist's intention, that is, he is saying that a particular work of art *is* art, which means, is a *definition* of art. Thus, that it is art is true *a priori* (which is what Judd means when he states that 'if someone calls it art, it's art')." Joseph Kosuth, "Art after Philosophy," in his *Art after Philosophy and After* (Cambridge, Mass.: MIT Press, 1991), 20.

60. "Photography into Sculpture," 1970, MoMA Exhibition 0934 Master Checklist, 7.

61. For a list of the cities, see Peter C. Bunnell, "Photography into Sculpture," *Artscanada* 27 (3) (June 1970): 25. See also Mary Statzer, *The Photographic Object 1970,* 214, n. 23.

62. Bunnell, "Photography into Sculpture," 21–23.

63. Bunnell, "Photography into Sculpture," 23.

64. Statzer, *The Photographic Object 1970,* 13.

65. Statzer, *The Photographic Object 1970,* 11.

66. "Photography into Sculpture," MoMA Exhibition 0925 Master Checklist, 1970, 2.

67. Statzer, *The Photographic Object 1970,* 28.

68. On Prince's process, see Jain Kelly, ed., *Darkroom 2* (New York: Lustrum Press, 1978), 97–109.

4. MAGAZINE WORK

1. Heinecken made nineteen of these magazines from 1969–74, and then eighteen more from 1989–94, with edition sizes ranging from one to nineteen; see David Pagel, "Pictures Turned Inside Out: Robert Heinecken's Homemade Magazines," in Irene Borger et al., *Robert Heinecken, Photographist: A Thirty Five Year Retrospective* (Chicago: Museum of Contemporary Art, 1999), 29. See also Mark Alice Durant, *Robert Heinecken: A Material History* (Tucson: Center for Creative Photography, University of Arizona; New York: 2003), 64–71; Kevin Moore, *Robert Heinecken: Copywork* (London: Ridinghouse, 2012), 29–74; and Eva Respini, ed., *Robert Heinecken: Object Matter* (New York: Museum of Modern Art, 2014), 71–94. Many significant production materials—including overprinted pages and complete magazines, printing plates, and stamps—related to Heinecken's magazine work may be found in his archive at the Center for Creative Photography; see Boxes 23–35, R. Heinecken Archive, AG 45, Center for Creative Photography, University of Arizona, Tucson.

2. See Tom Wolfe, "The 'Me' Decade and the Third Great Awakening," *New York* magazine (August 23, 1976), 27–48; and Christopher Lasch, *Culture of Narcissism: American Life in an Age of Diminishing Expectations* (New York: W. W. Norton, 1979).

3. Respini, ed., *Robert Heinecken: Object Matter,* 14.

4. On Coolidge's comic foregrounds (not named as such in the patent but only subsequently), see C. M. Coolidge, "Processes of Taking Photographic Pictures," U.S. Patent Number 149, 724, patented April 14, 1874; see also Jordan Bear and Albert Narath, "Head Trips: The Social Inversion of the Comic Foreground," *Cabinet* 33 (Spring 2009). http://www.cabinetmagazine.org/ issues/33/bear_narath.php. Coolidge is best known for his paintings of anthropomorphic dogs pursuing human pastimes (for example, poker or baseball), images that were designed to satirize the material life and social mores of the American middle class in the late nineteenth and early twentieth centuries. On Coolidge, see Moira F. Harris, "It's a Dogs' World According to Coolidge," *Antiques & Collecting Magazine* 102, no. 1 (March 1997): 26–31; Dan Barry, "Artist's Fame Is Fleeting, but Dog Poker Is Forever," *New York Times,* June 14, 2002, A1, 44; James McManus, "Play It Close to the Muzzle and Hands on the Table," *New York Times,* December 3, 2005, D8; William D. Moore, "Riding the Goat: Secrecy, Masculinity, and Fraternal High Jinks in the United States, 1845–1930," *Winterthur Portfolio* 41, no. 2/3 (Summer/Autumn 2007): 161–88, esp. 170–74; Elena Martinique, "Beloved by All but the Art World: The Dogs Playing Poker Painting by Cassius Marcellus Coolidge," *Widewalls,* April 21, 2020. https://www .widewalls.ch/magazine/dogs-playing-poker-painting.

5. On The Latent Image, see Respini, ed., *Robert Heinecken: Object Matter,* 16–17.

6. Sammya Johnson and Patricia Prijatel, *The Magazine from Cover to Cover* (New York: Oxford University Press, 2007), 72.

7. Johnson and Prijatel, *The Magazine from Cover to Cover,* 72–73.

8. In the 1970s, *Time*'s departments ranged from hard news—nation, world, business, health, and education—to arts and entertainment, sports, and people, thus addressing both genders; see, for example, *Time*

95 (14) (April 6, 1970)—a special issue titled *Black America 1970.*

9. On the concept of a photographic typology—a group of photographs that present different instances of the same type or ideal form—in the Bechers' work, see Susanne Lange, *Bernd and Hilla Becher: Life and Work,* trans. Jeremy Gaines (Cambridge, Mass.: MIT Press, 2007), 35, 44–45, 51–54. On the different ways that photographs have been assembled into larger works (including typologies), see Charles Stainback, *Photographic Collections: The Photographic Order from Pop to Now* (New York: International Center of Photography, 1992).

10. Respini, ed., *Robert Heinecken: Object Matter,* 71–84.

11. Mark Alice Durant, *Robert Heinecken: A Material History,* 69–70.

12. As David Campany suggests, the ambiguity of the figure's nationality is central to its effect; see Campany, *Art and Photography* (London: Phaidon, 2003), 153. This is correct, although I argue that this is only one of this figure's central ambiguities.

13. See "Grisly Trophies," *Time* (February 1, 1971), 25.

14. For a good overview of the white patriarchal stereotypes that circulated around Asian men and women in U.S. culture, see Yen Le Espiritu, *Asian American Women and Men: Labor, Laws, and Love,* 2nd ed. (Lanham, Md.: Rowman and Littlefield, 2008), 97–122. If we use the typology that Espiritu outlines, the Cambodian soldier could be read in terms of the threatening Asian male of the Yellow Peril trope, the dangerous and unassimilable Other bent on the destruction of the United States, or if we identify him as a soldier of America's South Asian allies, as a proto- type for the effeminate Asian male sidekick or servant figure of American culture who is partially assimilated, though decidedly not as an equal. As mobilized by Heinecken, however, the Cambodian soldier under- mines both stereotypes through the uncanny merging of characteristics that the dominant tropes seek to hold apart.

15. Stephen K. Lehmer, *Photographist Oral History Transcript, 1996: Robert F. Heinecken,* vol. 2 (Los Angeles: Oral History Program, University of California, 1998), 474–75.

16. Lehmer, *Photographist,* 2: 475.

17. Lehmer, *Photographist,* 2: 476.

18. "Everybody understands what a TV dinner is because you've eaten them all the time. Now you ask a kid, 'TV dinner?' and they don't know the term. They know that there's a frozen meal, but it's not a 'TV dinner.' What's good is you don't have to cook dinner; you heat this thing up and you go watch television. That's why it's called 'TV dinner.'" Lehmer, *Photographist,* 2: 421.

19. Lehmer, *Photographist,* 2: 420.

20. On the American magazine, see Amy Janello and Brennon Jones, *The American Magazine* (New York: Harry N. Abrams, 1991); David Abrahamson, *Magazine- Made America: The Cultural Transformation of the Postwar Periodical* (Cresskill, N.J.: Hampton Press, 1996); David Reed, *The Popular Magazine in Britain and the United States, 1880–1960* (Toronto: University of Toronto Press, 1997); Carolyn Kitch, *The Girl on the Magazine Cover: The Origins of Visual Stereotypes in American Mass Media* (Chapel Hill: University of North Carolina Press, 2001); Carolyn Kitch, *Pages from the Past: History and Memory in American Magazines* (Chapel Hill: University of North Carolina Press, 2005).

21. Abrahamson, *Magazine-Made America,* 16.

22. For more discussions on the rise of the mass consumer market in the nineteenth century and its relationship to American identity that are contempo- raneous to Heinecken's magazine work, see Daniel J. Boorstin, *The Americans: The Democratic Experience* (New York: Random House, 1973). For more recent histories of the development of American consumer society in the nineteenth and early twentieth centuries, see Susan Strasser, *Satisfaction Guaranteed: The Making of the American Mass Market* (New York: Pantheon, 1989); Richard S. Tedlow, *New and Improved: The Story of Mass Marketing in America* (New York: Basic Books, 1990); Pamela Laird, *Advertising Progress: American Business and the Rise of Consumer Marketing* (Baltimore: Johns Hopkins University Press, 1998); and Lisa Jacobson, *Children and the American Mass Market in the Early Twentieth Century* (New York: Columbia University Press, 2004).

23. On the *Ladies' Home Journal* and the crafting of female identity through illustrated advertising as well as fiction and advice columns in the teens and 1920s, see Jennifer Scanlon, *Inarticulate Longings: The* Ladies' Home Journal, *Gender and the Promise of Consumer Culture* (New York: Routledge, 1995).

24. Johnson and Prijatel, *The Magazine from Cover to Cover,* 60–61.

25. Abrahamson, *Magazine-Made America,* 21.

26. On modernist graphic design in America, see Philip B. Meggs and Alston W. Purvis, *Meggs' History of Graphic Design,* 6th ed. (Hoboken, N.J.: Wiley, 2016), chap. 17–20; and Steven Heller and Greg D'Onofrio, *The*

Moderns: Midcentury American Graphic Design (New York: Abrams Books, 2017).

27. Abrahamson, *Magazine-Made America,* 17.

28. This would quickly be overcome. As Lizabeth Cohen argues, mass culture in general is a force that over time created ever greater segmentation and diversification of American identities, particularly along the lines of race, class, and gender. See Lizabeth Cohen, *A Consumers' Republic: The Politics of Mass Consumption in Postwar America* (New York: Knopf, 2003), 292–344.

29. Abrahamson, *Magazine-Made America,* 2, 19.

30. Abrahamson, *Magazine-Made America,* 25–26.

31. Abrahamson, *Magazine-Made America,* 56–59.

32. See, for example, Tom Pendergast's study of the diversification of and dialogue among different forms of masculinity in American magazines during the first half of the twentieth century. Tom Pendergast, *Creating the Modern Man: American Magazines and Consumer Culture, 1900–1950* (Columbia: University of Missouri Press, 2000).

33. Abrahamson, *Magazine-Made America,* 27–28.

34. Abrahamson, *Magazine-Made America,* 29–30.

35. Daniel Bell, "The Cultural Contradictions of Capitalism," *The Public Interest* 21 (Fall 1970): 20.

36. Abrahamson, *Magazine-Made America,* 50–53.

37. On the seventies, see Peter N. Carroll, *It Seemed Like Nothing Happened: America in the 1970s* (New Brunswick, N.J.: Rutgers University Press, 1990); Bruce J. Schulman, *The Seventies: The Great Shift in American Culture, Society, and Politics* (New York: Free Press, 2001); Judith Stein, *Pivotal Decade: How the United States Traded Factories for Finance in the Seventies* (New Haven, Conn.: Yale University Press, 2010); Jefferson Cowie, *Stayin' Alive: The 1970s and the Last Days of the Working Class* (New York: New Press, 2010); and Dominic Sandbrook, *Mad As Hell: The Crisis of the 1970s and the Rise of the Populist Right* (New York: Knopf, 2011).

38. On deindustrialization and globalism as marking the end of New Deal liberalism and progressivism in the United States and the beginning of a new, deregulated, and increasingly stratified economy, see Judith Stein, *Pivotal Decade: How the United States Traded Factories for Finance in the Seventies* (New Haven, Conn.: Yale University Press, 2010).

39. As Rand Richards Cooper argues, Wolfe introduced certain fictional techniques into his new journalism—including irony, interior monologue, and vivid description—in order to emulate (and thereby emphasize, satirize, and critique) the solipsistic character of his contemporary moment; see Cooper, "Tom Wolfe, Material Boy: Embellishing a Doctrine," in Harold Bloom, *Tom Wolfe* (Broomall, Penn.: Chelsea House, 2001), 173.

40. Tom Wolfe, "The 'Me' Decade and the Third Awakening" (1976), reprinted in Wolfe, *The Purple Decades: A Reader* (New York: Farrar, Straus and Giroux, 1982), 271.

41. Wolfe, *The Purple Decades,* 272–74.

42. Wolfe, *The Purple Decades,* 290.

43. As Louis Menand argues, Lasch was not nostalgic about the 1950s or 1960s as somehow better moments than the 1970s; instead, he "was diagnosing a condition . . . that originated in the nineteenth century." Louis Menand, "Christopher Lasch's Quarrel with Liberalism," in John Patrick Diggins, ed., *The Liberal Persuasion: Arthur Schlesinger, Jr., and the Challenge of the American Past* (Princeton, N.J.: Princeton University Press, 1997), 239.

44. Christopher Lasch, *The Culture of Narcissism: American Life in an Age of Diminishing Expectations* (New York: W. W. Norton, 1979), 154.

45. Lasch, *Culture of Narcissism,* 238. See also Lasch, *Haven in a Heartless World: The Family Besieged* (New York: Basic Books, 1977).

46. Lasch, *Culture of Narcissism,* 239.

47. Lasch, *Culture of Narcissism,* 248.

48. Lasch, *Culture of Narcissism,* 176.

49. Lasch, *Culture of Narcissism,* 68.

50. Lasch, *Culture of Narcissism,* 189.

51. Lasch, *Culture of Narcissism,* 190.

52. Lasch, *Culture of Narcissism,* 205.

53. On the gendered character of Lasch's narcissistic personality, as well as feminist critiques of his model, see Miriam Dixson, "The Ideal Type, the Sociologist and the Contemporary Historian: A Case Study in a Feminist Appropriation of Psychoanalysis," *British Journal of Sociology* 39 (4) (December 1988): 545–53.

54. On Lasch as a critic of liberalism, see Menand, "Christopher Lasch's Quarrel with Liberalism," 233–50; and Kenneth Anderson, "Heartless World Revisited: Christopher Lasch's Parting Polemic against the New Class," *The Good Society* 6 (1) (Winter 1996): 36–39.

55. Lasch, *Culture of Narcissism,* 67–68.

56. Daniel C. Hallin, *The "Uncensored War": The Media and Vietnam* (London: Oxford University Press, 1986), 190, 211.

5. ART, PORNOGRAPHY, PAINTING

1. Stephen K. Lehmer, *Photographist Oral History Transcript, 1996: Robert F. Heinecken,* vol. 2 (Los Angeles: Oral History Program, University of California, 1998), 463.

2. Lehmer, *Photographist,* 2: 464–65.

3. "You're feeling things, you're looking at things," he explained. See Lehmer, *Photographist,* 2: 464.

4. Lehmer, *Photographist,* 2: 465.

5. Lehmer, *Photographist,* 2: 465.

6. By 1974, the phrase had become so widespread that Volkswagen parodied it in a magazine ad for their cars ("Different Volks for different folks"); see *Sports Illustrated* (November 25, 1974). https://vwsage.com/advertising/html/slide/vwb7599.htm.

7. To trace the development of gay male objectification over time when Heinecken was working, see Wayne E. Stanley, *The Complete Reprint of Physique Pictorial, 1951–1990* (Los Angeles: Taschen, 1996). This publication, whose editor/photographer was Bob Mizer, was probably the most prominent gay male illustrated magazine produced in LA at the time. On the history of the gay porn film, see Jeffrey Escoffier, *Bigger Than Life: The History of Gay Porn Cinema from Beefcake to Hardcore* (Philadelphia: Running Press, 2009).

8. Lehmer, *Photographist,* 2: 299.

9. Lehmer, *Photographist,* 2: 299.

10. For a representative compendium of classic Western landscape photographs in the United States, which includes the work of Timothy O'Sullivan, William Henry Jackson, John Hillers, Ansel Adams, and others, see Jerome Prescott, *The Unspoiled West: The Western Landscape As Seen by Its Greatest Photographers* (New York: Smithmark, 1994). On the distinctive graphic, informational style of Western landscape photographs and their relationship to U.S. geological and geographic surveys of the second half of the nineteenth century, see Robin Kelsey, *Archive Style: Photographs and Illustrations for U.S. Surveys, 1850–1890* (Berkeley: University of California Press, 2007).

11. See, for example, David Harris, *Eadweard Muybridge and the Photographic Panorama of San Francisco, 1850–1880* (Cambridge, Mass.: MIT Press, 1993).

12. See, for example, John Coplans, *A Body* (New York: PowerHouse Books, 2002).

13. See Alain Robbe-Grillet, *The Voyeur,* trans. Richard Howard (New York: Grove Press, 1958).

14. Roland Barthes, "Objective Literature," in *Critical Essays,* trans. Richard Howard (Evanston, Ill.: Northwestern University Press, 1972), 14.

15. On the concept and history of photographically based pornography—by which I mean both photographs and film, and which is itself a part of a larger set of technologies, industries, and practices—I am particularly indebted to the following works: Patchen Barss, *The Erotic Engine* (Toronto: Doubleday Canada, 2010); Alan McKee, Kath Albury, and Catharine Lumby, *The Porn Report* (Carlton, Victoria, Aust.: Melbourne University Press, 2008); Shira Tarrant, *The Pornography Industry: What Everyone Needs to Know* (New York: Oxford University Press, 2016); and Linda Williams, *Hard Core: Power, Pleasure, and the "Frenzy of the Visible"* (Berkeley: University of California Press, 1989).

16. See Patchen Barss, *The Erotic Engine,* 41–49, esp. 43.

17. *Golden age* is used to refer to the cultural moment of the 1970s, when porn films became more ambitious narratively, their budgets and technical sophistication increased, and the films and their actors achieved a level of popular fame closer to that of Hollywood movies and stars. By the 1980s, this moment was largely over. See Carmine Sarracino and Kevin M. Scott, *The Porning of America: The Rise of Porn Culture, What It Means, and Where We Go from Here* (Boston: Beacon Press, 2003), 172, 175; and Barss, *The Erotic Engine,* 68.

18. On debates about pornography in the 1970s in relation to the family and American values, see Dominic Sandbrook, *Mad As Hell: The Crisis of the 1970s and the Rise of the Populist Right* (New York: Knopf, 2011), 65–79. On the relationship of pornography to greater permissiveness about sexuality in the 1970s, see Peter Braunstein, "'Adults Only': The Construction of an Erotic City in New York during the 1970s," in Beth Bailey and David Farber, eds., *America in the 1970s* (Lawrence: University Press of Kansas, 2004), 129–56.

19. On photography's realism, see, for example, André Bazin, "The Ontology of the Photographic Image," trans. Hugh Gray, *Film Quarterly* 13 (4) (Summer 1960): 4–9.

20. For compelling arguments on the harm that pornography causes women, see Andrea Dworkin and Catharine MacKinnon, eds., *In Harm's Way: The Pornography Civil Rights Hearings* (Cambridge, Mass.: Harvard University Press, 1997). *Roth v. United States*

(1957) cites arguments that pornography has a capacity to "deprave or corrupt," see 354 U.S. 476 (1957) *Roth v. United States*. No. 582. Supreme Court of United States. https://scholar.google.com/scholar_case?case =14778925784015245625&q=Roth+v.+United+States +1957&hl=en&as_sdt=80000006&as_vis=1.

21. Robin Morgan, "Theory and Practice: Pornography and Rape" (1974), in Laura Lederer, ed., *Take Back the Night* (New York: William Morrow, 1980), 134–40.

22. For a sophisticated analysis of the changing representations of female identity in film contemporaneous with Heinecken's magazine work, see Molly Haskell, *From Reverence to Rape: The Treatment of Women in the Movies* (New York: Holt, Rinehart and Winston, 1974).

23. See McKee, Albury, and Lumby, *The Porn Report*, 9. For the text of the Comstock Act, see this online source. https://memory.loc.gov/cgi-bin/ampage?collId=llsl& fileName=017/llsl017.db&recNum=0639.

24. On the history of obscenity and censorship in the United States, see Edward de Grazia, *Girls Lean Back Everywhere: The Law of Obscenity and the Assault on Genius* (New York: Random House, 1992); Marjorie Heins, *Sex, Sin, and Blasphemy: A Guide to America's Censorship Wars* (New York: New Press, 1993); and Marjorie Heins, *Not in Front of the Children: "Indecency," Censorship, and the Innocence of Youth* (New York: Hill and Wang, 2001).

25. De Grazia, *Girls Lean Back Everywhere*, 12, 30–31, 192–94, 266–69; Heins, *Sex, Sin, and Blasphemy*, 20; and Heins, *Not in Front of the Children*, 28–29, 32–36.

26. On the case of *Ulysses*, see de Grazia, *Girls Lean Back Everywhere*, xi-xii, 9–39, 74, 144–45, 223–24, 320; Heins, *Sex, Sin, and Blasphemy*, 29–30, 118; and Heins, *Not in Front of the Children*, 40–41, 44–46.

27. On *Roth v. United States* and *Miller v. California*, see de Grazia, *Girls Lean Back Everywhere*, 273–326, 561–76; Heins, *Sex, Sin, and Blasphemy*, 15, 20–25, 30–31, 34; and Heins, *Not in Front of the Children*, 58–66, 68–69, 85–87.

28. *Miller v. California*, 413 U.S. 15 (1973).

29. U.S. Commission on Obscenity and Pornography, *The Report* (New York: Random House, 1970). On the Lockhart report, see de Grazia, *Girls Lean Back Everywhere*, 531–32, 551–65; Heins, *Sex, Sin, and Blasphemy*, 147–148; and Heins, *Not in Front of the Children*, 79–80, 86. See also Jon Lewis, "Presumed Effects of Erotica: Some Notes on the Report of the Commission on Obscenity and Pornography," *Film International* 6 (6) (2008): 7–16.

30. De Grazia, *Girls Lean Back Everywhere*, 562.

31. This can be identified by another work in the series, *Porno Film Strip #4*, where the brand name appears on the left edge; see Kevin Moore, *Robert Heinecken: Copywork* (London: Ridinghouse, 2012), 84.

32. Williams, *Hard Core*, 58–92.

33. Williams, *Hard Core*, 82–83.

34. Williams, *Hard Core*, 80.

35. Williams, *Hard Core*, 86.

36. Williams, *Hard Core*, 91.

37. Williams, *Hard Core*, 91.

38. Tarrant, *The Pornography Industry*, 22.

39. On how first-wave feminists used clothing as a form of protest, see Peter N. Carroll, *It Seemed Like Nothing Happened: America in the 1970s* (New Brunswick, N.J.: Rutgers University Press, 1990), 28; and Karen Heller, "The Year Women Refused to Stay Silent, Tossed Their Bras and Redefined Politics," *Washington Post*, May 23, 2018. https://www.washingtonpost.com/ national/the-year-women-refused-to-stay-silent -tossed-their-bras-and-redefined-politics/2018/05/23/ bf37606e-495c-11e8-827e-190efaf1f1ee_story.html.

40. Dennis Oppenheim, *Reading Position for Second Degree Burn, 1970, Jones Beach, New York, Stage #1 and Stage #2*. Skin, book, solar energy. Exposure time: five hours. Color photography and text, 85 x 60 inches (215.9 x 152.4 cm).

41. Lynne Warren, ed., *Encyclopedia of Twentieth-Century Photography* (New York: Routledge, 2005), 682.

42. See 81.5–81.5.9 *Artists and Models Ball in Yosemite*, September 1974. Ten photographic prints. Negatives by Joanne Callis, Virgil Mirano, and Robert Heinecken, Center for Creative Photography, University of Arizona: Robert Heinecken Archive. On extended loan from the artist.

43. Stephen K. Lehmer, *Photographist Oral History Transcript, 1996: Robert F. Heinecken*, vol. 1 (Los Angeles: Oral History Program, University of California, 1998), 152.

44. Lehmer, *Photographist*, 1: 155.

45. Lehmer, *Photographist*, 1: 156.

46. Lehmer, *Photographist*, 1: 156.

47. Lehmer, *Photographist*, 1: 157.

48. Lehmer, *Photographist*, 1: 158.

49. Lehmer, *Photographist*, 1: 159.

50. Eva Respini, ed., *Robert Heinecken: Object Matter* (New York: Museum of Modern Art, 2014), 20.

51. The review of the 1992 SPE conference by Nadine L. McGann that Respini cites is both detailed and thoughtful. From it, it is clear that McGann's judgment about Heinecken as educator is based on his art, and not his actual service as a teacher and administrator. It is also clear from McGann's review that Heinecken's work was not recognized in feminist photographic circles as critical of the male gaze. Instead, McGann insists on quite the opposite. See Nadine L. McGann, "Dumb Luck at SPE," *Afterimage* 19, no. 10 (May 1992): 3.

52. Martha Rosler, "Lookers, Buyers, Dealers, and Makers: Thoughts on Audience," *Exposure* 17, no. 1 (Spring 1979): 22. Although the reference to Heinecken remained through a number of reprintings of the essay, it was cut when Rosler republished it in her first comprehensive essay collection in 2004; see Rosler, *Decoys and Disruptions: Selected Writings, 1975–2001* (Cambridge, Mass.: MIT Press, 2004), 40. See also Carole Squiers, "Photography: Tradition and Decline," *Aperture* 91 (Summer 1983): 72–76.

53. James R. Hugunin, "Robert Heinecken's Neo-Physiognomy," *Spot* (Summer 1987): 5–6.

54. Allan Sekula, letter, *Spot* (Spring 1988): 24–25.

55. Sekula, letter, 24.

56. The *Spot* debate continued over the course of 1988, with a missive from photography critic Max Kozloff defending Heinecken against Sekula's charges, and Sekula responding with a second letter; see *Spot* (Summer 1988): 23; and *Spot* (Fall 1988): 22, respectively. Heinecken finally responded in the next issue in a very ironic and ambiguous way; his main point was that "a determination of context is crucial to an understanding of intended meaning." See *Spot* (Winter 1988): 22.

57. Indeed, since the late 1970s, there has been very important engagement with pornographic imagery by feminist photographers, many of whom, like Heinecken, employ extremely sophisticated strategies of appropriation and montage to engage in social and political critique; see, for example, the work of Linder (Linder Sterling), Natalia LL (Natalia Lach-Lachowicz), or, much more recently, Sheida Soleimani. See Dawn Ades, *Linder* (London: Ridinghouse, 2015); and Matthew Biro, "Sheida Soleimani, Cyborg: Photomontage in an Expanding Network," *History of Photography* 43 (2) (2019): 169–90. Like Heinecken, Soleimani also utilizes performance—as does Annie Sprinkle, another key porn-friendly feminist photographer: see Annie Sprinkle, *Annie Sprinkle: Post-Porn Modernist* (Jersey City, N.J.: Cleis Press, 1998). Since the 1970s, feminist painters have also engaged with pornography in important and critical ways; among the most significant are Betty Tompkins (since the early 1970s) and Marilyn Minter (since the 1980s). See Betty Tompkins, *Fuck Paintings Etc.* (New York: Dashwood Books 2011); and Bill Arning et al., *Marilyn Minter: Pretty/Dirty* (New York: Gregory R. Miller, 2015).

6. THE POLAROID EXPERIENCE

1. On the Polaroid Corporation and Edwin Land, see Peter Buse, *The Camera Does the Rest: How Polaroid Changed Photography* (Chicago: University of Chicago Press, 2016); Christopher Bonanos, *Instant: The Story of Polaroid* (New York: Princeton Architectural Press, 2012); Nuno Pinheiro, "Camera: Instant or Polaroid," in Lynne Warren, ed., *Encyclopedia of Twentieth-Century Photography* (New York: Routledge, 2005), 221–23; Stacy McCarroll, "Polaroid Corporation," in Warren, ed., *Encyclopedia*, 1279–82; and Peter C. Wensberg, *Land's Polaroid: A Company and the Man Who Invented It* (Boston: Houghton Mifflin, 1987).

2. Stephen K. Lehmer, *Photographist Oral History Transcript, 1996: Robert F. Heinecken*, vol. 2 (Los Angeles: Oral History Program, University of California, 1998), 444–45.

3. Stephen K. Lehmer, *Photographist Oral History Transcript, 1996: Robert F. Heinecken*, vol. 1 (Los Angeles: Oral History Program, University of California, 1998), 164.

4. Lehmer, *Photographist*, 1: 166. Robert Heinecken, *He:/She:* (Chicago: A Chicago Book, 1980), 47.

5. Lehmer, *Photographist*, 1: 159.

6. Lehmer, *Photographist*, 1: 161, 182.

7. Lehmer, *Photographist*, 1: 160.

8. Lehmer, *Photographist*, 1: 183.

9. Lehmer, *Photographist*, 1: 173–74.

10. Lehmer, *Photographist*, 1: 166–67.

11. Lehmer, *Photographist*, 1: 184–85.

12. Lehmer, *Photographist*, 1: 161, 182.

13. Lehmer, *Photographist*, 1: 168–69.

14. Lehmer, *Photographist*, 1: 170.

15. Heinecken quotes two lines from Mishima's *The Damask Drum* in the introduction to *He:/She:* He notes:

"These two fertile lines are the inspiration for this work, and my memory, its reason." Heinecken, *He:/She:*, introduction. See also Yukio Mishima, *Five Modern Noh Plays*, trans. Donald Keene (Tokyo: Tuttle Publishing, 1967), 48.

16. Susan E. Cohen, "Robert Heinecken's Photography: Confrontation and Assessment," in Suzanne E. Pastor and Susan E. Cohen, *Robert Heinecken: Food, Sex and TV* (Kassel, Ger.: Fotoforum, 1983), n.p.

17. The view that the women are all different is Irene Borger's; see, Irene Borger, "Relations: Some Work by Robert Heinecken," in Irene Borger et al., *Robert Heinecken, Photographist: A Thirty-Five-Year Retrospective* (Chicago: Museum of Contemporary Art, 1999), 37.

18. Borger et al., *Robert Heinecken, Photographist*, 76.

19. Borger et al., *Robert Heinecken, Photographist*, 78.

20. Devrim Bayar, "Robert Heinecken: Lessons in Commercial Realism," in *Robert Heinecken: Lessons in Posing Subjects* (Brussels: WIELS and Triangle Books, 2014), n.p.

21. Joyce Neimanas, interview with author, Albuquerque, New Mexico, July 24–26, 2014.

22. Mark Alice Durant, *Robert Heinecken: A Material History* (Tucson: Center for Creative Photography, University of Arizona, 2003), 79.

23. Durant, *Robert Heinecken: A Material History*, 79.

24. Borger et al., *Robert Heinecken, Photographist*, 77.

25. Durant, *Robert Heinecken: A Material History*, 75.

26. Eva Respini, ed., *Robert Heinecken: Object Matter* (New York: Museum of Modern Art, 2014), 121.

27. The second variant of this work is even more psychological: "He: How did you get started modeling? She: For my father, when I was a little girl. He: Did you like it? She: Very much. It made us closer. He: How do you feel about it now? She: People don't realize that it is really exhausting work. He: In what way? She: Holding the same pose, perfectly still—over and over again." See Borger et al., *Robert Heinecken, Photographist*, 80.

28. Pastor and Cohen, *Robert Heinecken: Food, Sex, TV* (Kassel, Ger.: Fotoforum, 1983), n.p.

29. See Bayar, "Robert Heinecken: Lessons in Commercial Realism," n.p.

30. Robert Heinecken, *He:/She:* (Chicago: A Chicago Book, 1980). Heinecken also created a run of fifteen special editions of the book the same year, in which original Polaroids of different models were pasted.

31. Heinecken, *He:/She:*, 11.

32. Heinecken, *He:/She:*, 15.

33. Heinecken, *He:/She:*, 19.

34. See Bill Johnson, "Robert Heinecken (Polaroid Project III)," *Knute Rockne Oasis Newsletter and Journal of Critical Opinion* 1 (3) (December 1983). Reprinted online in 2012. https://vintagephotosjohnson.com/2012/12/12/robert-heinecken-polaroid-project-iii/. See also Susie Cohen and Bill Johnson, "The Polaroid Project 1983–2014: Notes from the Knute Rockne Oasis," *Afterimage* 42 (1) (July/August, 2014): 20–27.

35. See A. D. Coleman et al., *Robert Heinecken: Photographist* (Chicago: Museum of Contemporary Art, 1999), 82–85; and Nancy Spector et al., *Richard Prince* (New York: Guggenheim Museum, 2007), 102–11.

36. Heinecken was always careful to distinguish himself from postmodernism—and embrace aspects of modernism—despite his focus on appropriation: "I've never made anything, no matter how automatic it might seem, that isn't looked at and changed or discarded because of its look. So I'm tied to that, I guess, as a modernist idea. The structure of it is what makes it interesting to make, not the quotation of it. Well, it's part of both, I guess." Lehmer, *Photographist*, 2: 272.

37. See, for example, Devrim Bayar, "Robert Heinecken: Lessons in Commercial Realism," n.p.

38. Erving Goffman, "Gender Advertisements," *Studies in the Anthropology of Visual Communication* 3 (2) (1976): 69–154; and Erving Goffman, *Gender Advertisements* (New York: Harper and Row, 1979).

39. Erving Goffman, *The Presentation of Self in Everyday Life* (Edinburgh: University of Edinburgh, 1956).

40. On Goffman, I am indebted to Greg Smith, *Erving Goffman* (New York: Routledge, 2006); and Thomas J. Scheff, *Goffman Unbound: A New Paradigm for Social Science* (Boulder, Colo.: Paradigm Publishers, 2006).

41. See Erving Goffman, *Frame Analysis: An Essay on the Organization of Experience* (Boston: Northeastern University Press, 1986 [1974]).

42. As Goffman argued in his major essay on gender, "The Arrangement between the Sexes": "Women do and men don't gestate, breast-feed infants, and menstruate as a part of their biological character. So, too, women on the whole are smaller and lighter boned and muscled than are men. For these physical facts of life to have no appreciable social consequence would take a little organizing, but, at least by modern standards, not much. Industrial society can absorb new ethnic groups

bearing raw cultural differences, a year or so of isolating military service for young men, vast differences in educational level, business and employment cycles, the wartime absence of its adult males in every generation, appreciable annual vacations, and countless other embarrassments to orderliness. That our form of social organization has any necessary features is, I take it, rather questionable. More to the point, for these very slight biological differences—compared to all other differences—to be identified as the grounds for the kind of social consequences felt to follow understandably from them requires a vast, integrated body of social beliefs and practices, sufficiently cohesive and all-embracing to warrant for its analysis the resurrection of unfashionable functional paradigms. . . . It is not, then, the social consequences of innate sex differences that must be explained, but the way in which these differences were (and are) put forward as a warrant for our social arrangements, and, most important of all, the way in which the institutional workings of society ensured that this accounting would seem sound." Goffman, "The Arrangement between the Sexes," *Theory and Society* 4 (3) (Autumn 1977): 301–302.

43. Goffman, "Gender Advertisements," 76.

44. See Greg Smith, *Erving Goffman*, 94. For Butler's arguments on the performativity of gender, see Judith Butler, *Gender Trouble: Feminism and the Subversion of Identity* (New York: Routledge, 1990).

45. Erving Goffman, *Stigma: Notes on the Analysis of Spoiled Identity* (Englewood Cliffs, N.J.: Prentice-Hall, 1963).

46. Goffman, "Gender Advertisements," 92.

47. Goffman, "Gender Advertisements," 93.

48. Goffman, "Gender Advertisements," 93.

49. Goffman, "Gender Advertisements," 93. Emphasis in original.

50. Goffman, "Gender Advertisements," 95.

51. Goffman, "Gender Advertisements," 95.

52. Goffman, "Gender Advertisements," 97.

53. For a concise overview of the debates around Sontag's book, see Michael Starenko, "Sontag's Reception," *Afterimage* 25 (5) (March–April, 1998): 1–6. See also A. D. Coleman, "Susan Sontag: Off Photography," in Coleman, *Light Readings: A Photography Critic's Writings 1968–1978*, 2nd ed. (Albuquerque: University of New Mexico Press, 1998), 294–303.

54. Susan Sontag, *On Photography* (New York: Farrar, Straus and Giroux, 1977), 2.

55. See Victor Bockris's interview with Sontag, "Susan Sontag: The Dark Lady of Pop Philosophy," *High Times* (March 1978): 36.

56. "Marx reproached philosophy for only trying to understand the world rather than trying to change it. Photographers, operating within the terms of the Surrealist sensibility, suggest the vanity of even trying to understand the world and instead propose that we collect it." Sontag, *On Photography*, 64.

57. The text is sometimes shown with the collages but not always.

58. Heinecken describes an exercise in one of his introductory classes that used the same technique as the one he used to make *S.S. Copyright Project "On Photography."* Lehmer, *Photographist*, 1: 236–37.

59. The text can be found online: https://www.moma.org/collection/works/50348.

60. For example, according to Michael Starenko, like critical reviews by Dru Shipman, Colin L. Westerbeck Jr., and Michael Lesey, Heinecken's photomontage portrait was an attempt "to discredit Sontag's book." Starenko, "Sontag's Reception," 1.

61. See Coleman, *Light Readings*, 299.

62. On Polaroid and art, see Mary-Kay Lombino and Peter Buse, *The Polaroid Years: Instant Photography and Experimentation* (Munich: DelMonico Books and Prestel, 2013).

63. Lehmer, *Photographist*, 1: ix; Lehmer, *Photographist*, 2: 430; William A. Ewing et al., *The Polaroid Project: At the Intersection of Art and Technology* (Ft. Worth, Tex.: Amon Carter Museum of American Art, 2017).

64. Lehmer, *Photographist*, 2: 431.

65. Bill Johnson, "Robert Heinecken (Polaroid Project III)," n.p.

66. Robert Heinecken, *Just Good Eats for U, Diner* (November 1971). Eight offset lithographs, a descriptive text, and a screen-printed menu case. 13 ⅜ x 11 ⁷⁄₁₆ x ³⁄₁₆ inches (34 x 29 x 0.5 cm). Edition of 100. Reproduced in Robert Heinecken and Mark Johnstone, *Heinecken: Selected Works 1966–1986* (Tokyo: Gallery Min, 1986), n.p; and Borger et al., *Robert Heinecken, Photographist*, 48.

67. Heinecken, *Just Good Eats for U*, colophon.

68. Heinecken's *Iconographic Art Lunches* were assisted by John Reuter, at the School of the Museum of Fine Arts, Boston; see Lehmer, *Photographist*, 2: 431.

69. Lehmer, *Photographist*, 2: 433.

70. Lehmer, *Photographist,* 2: 430.

71. Lehmer, *Photographist,* 2: 431.

72. Lehmer, *Photographist,* 2: 437–38.

73. Lehmer, *Photographist,* 2: 433–35.

74. Lehmer, *Photographist,* 2: 435–36.

---

7. SURREALISM ON TV

1. Stephen K. Lehmer, *Photographist Oral History Transcript, 1996: Robert F. Heinecken,* vol. 2 (Los Angeles: Oral History Program, University of California, 1998), 420.

2. On the history of television, see Gary R. Edgerton, *The Columbia Encyclopedia of American Television* (New York: Columbia University Press, 2007); and Alexander B. Magoun, *Television: The Life Story of a Technology* (Baltimore: Johns Hopkins University Press, 2009).

3. Edgerton, *Columbia Encyclopedia of American Television,* 321.

4. On TV dinners, see Jamie Horwitz, "Eating at the Edge," *Gastronomica* 9 (3) (Summer 2009): 44; Eric Burns, *Invasion of the Mind Snatchers: Television's Conquest of America in the Fifties* (Philadelphia: Temple University Press, 2010), 39–40; Andrew F. Smith, *Eating History: Thirty Turning Points in the Making of American Cuisine* (New York: Columbia University Press, 2009), 165–73.

5. Lehmer, *Photographist,* 2: 421.

6. Lehmer, *Photographist,* 2: 421–22.

7. Eva Respini, "Not a Picture of, but an Object about Something," in Eva Respini, ed., *Robert Heinecken: Object Matter* (New York: Museum of Modern Art, 2014), 19.

8. Zachary Austin Pfahler, "Robert Heinecken's *TV/Time Environment,*" master's thesis, University of California, Riverside (2012), 3.

9. On Edward Kienholz's brilliant work with televisions, much of which was created with his wife, Nancy Reddin Kienholz, see Edward Kienholz et al., *Kienholz Televisions* (Venice, Calif.: L. A. Louver).

10. Fred R. Parker, "Robert Heinecken, " in *Untitled* 5 (1973).

11. Among McLuhan's most important writings are *The Mechanical Bride: Folklore of Industrial Man* (London: Gerald Duckworth & Company, 2011 [1951]); *Understanding Media: The Extensions of Man* (Cambridge, Mass.: MIT Press, 1994 [1964]); and *Laws of Media: The New Science,* with Eric McLuhan (Toronto: University of Toronto Press, 1988). In my reading of McLuhan, I have been guided by Donald F. Theall, *The Virtual Marshall McLuhan* (Montreal: McGill Queen's University Press, 2001); and Janine Marchessault, *Marshall McLuhan: Cosmic Media* (London: SAGE Publications, 2005).

12. See, for example, Marshall McLuhan and Quentin Fiore, *The Medium Is the Massage: An Inventory of Effects* (New York: Bantam, 1967), 26.

13. See, in particular, Marshall McLuhan, *The Gutenberg Galaxy: The Making of Typographic Man* (Toronto: University of Toronto Press, 1962).

14. Marshall McLuhan et al., *Verbi-Voco-Visual Explorations* (New York: Something Else Press, 1967), n.p, section 14. See also Marchessault, *Marshall McLuhan,* 91–92, 117.

15. McLuhan et al., *Verbi-Voco-Visual Explorations,* section 7.

16. See Marshall McLuhan and Quentin Fiore, *War and Peace in the Global Village* (New York: Bantam, 1968).

17. Marshall McLuhan, *Understanding Media: The Extensions of Man* (Cambridge, Mass.: MIT Press, 1994 [1964]), 54.

18. Marchessault, *Marshall McLuhan,* 177–78.

19. See Andy Grundberg, "Robert Heinecken: Asking Provocative Questions," *New York Times,* June 7, 1981. They also shot the celebrity gala that preceded the inauguration.

20. The screen was covered with a neutral density filter; without it, the light was too bright. Robert Heinecken, CCP Seminar VHS tape #5 (1995) (0:52:30—1:05:17), series 9, audiovisual materials, boxes 40–41.

21. See Respini, "Not a Picture of," 22–23; and Susan E. Cohen, "Robert Heinecken's Photography: Confrontation and Assessment," in Suzanne E. Pastor and Susan E. Cohen, *Robert Heinecken: Food, Sex, and TV* (Kassel, Ger.: Fotoforum, 1983), n.p.

22. See Irene Borger et al., *Robert Heinecken, Photographist: A Thirty-Five-Year Retrospective* (Chicago: Museum of Contemporary Art, 1999), 88–89.

23. Eleanor M. Hight, *Picturing Modernism: Moholy-Nagy and Photography in Weimar Germany* (Cambridge, Mass.: MIT Press, 1995), 7, 27.

24. See Mary Ann Watson, "Television and the Presidency: Eisenhower and Kennedy," in Edgerton, *Columbia History of American Television,* 205–33.

25. John F. Kennedy, "A Force That Has Changed the Political Scene," originally published in *TV Guide,*

November 14, 1959. Reprinted in *TV Guide's Fifty Years of Television* (New York: Crown, 2002), 98–99.

26. Edgerton, *Columbia History of American Television,* 204.

27. On the political shifts of the 1980s, see David Sirota, *Back to Our Future: How the 1980s Explain the World We Live in Now—Our Culture, Our Politics, Our Everything* (New York: Ballantine, 2011); Bradford Martin, *The Other Eighties: A Secret History of America in the Age of Reagan* (New York: Hill and Wang, 2011).

28. Gil Troy, *Morning in America: How Ronald Reagan Invented the 1980s* (Princeton, N.J.: Princeton University Press, 2005), 69.

29. McLuhan and Fiore, *The Medium Is the Massage,* 74–75.

30. Mark Alice Durant describes the attitudes about Reagan that circulated in Heinecken's photographic milieu: "Early in his political career, Ronald Reagan was taken less than seriously; how could a second-tier Hollywood actor have the authority and depth necessary to lead? Reagan later quipped that he did not see how a man could be president and not be an actor. Reagan became a master manipulator of the electronic image, a god of the media age—remote, profoundly indifferent, yet appearing in front of us with a smiling, self-effacing benevolence." Mark Alice Durant, *Robert Heinecken: A Material History* (Tucson: Center for Creative Photography, the University of Arizona, 2003), 80.

31. Troy, *Morning in America,* 250.

32. Lehmer, *Photographist,* 2: 433–36.

33. See David Green, "Veins of Resemblance: Photography and Eugenics," *Oxford Art Journal* 7 (2) (1984): 3–16; and Allan Sekula, "The Body and the Archive," *October* 39 (Winter 1986): 3–64.

34. See Sekula, "The Body and the Archive." As he defined it, the "shadow archive" produced by photography is "a generalized, inclusive archive [. . .] that encompasses an entire social terrain while positioning individuals within that terrain" (10). It "necessarily contains both the traces of the visible bodies of heroes, leaders, moral exemplars, celebrities, and those of the poor, the diseased, the insane, the criminal, the nonwhite, the female, and all other embodiments of the unworthy" (10). Sekula distinguishes the shadow archive from real archives, which, he argues, "became the dominant institutional basis for photographic meaning" between 1880 and 1910, when archives incorporating photographic materials sprung up in multiple disciplines and institutions including criminology, the military, medicine, anthropology, architecture, and art history, to mention only a few (56).

35. As Yen Le Espiritu notes, "The preference for white male–Asian female [combinations] is also prevalent in contemporary television news broadcasting, such as in the successful 1993–1995 pairing of Dan Rather and Connie Chung as co-anchors of the *CBS Evening News.*" As an Asian American, Chung was thus one of the least threatening figures through which nonwhiteness and cross-racial affinities could be portrayed in American culture at the time. See Yen Le Espiritu, *Asian American Women and Men: Labor, Laws, and Love,* 2nd ed. (Lanham, Md.: Rowman and Littlefield, 2008), 108. Despite this fact, as Heinecken's representations of Chung in the 1980s suggest, her broadcast success marked a shift in the collective American ideology, one that indicated that Americans no longer saw whiteness as essential to the pinnacles of national achievement.

36. Robert Heinecken, *1984: A Case Study in Finding an Appropriate TV Newswoman (A CBS Docudrama in Words and Pictures)* (Los Angeles: Robert Heinecken [self-published], 1985). Sixteen pages plus front and back covers. 11 ¼ x 9 inches (29.85 x 22.86 cm).

37. Troy, *Morning in America,* 117.

38. Troy, *Morning in America,* 122.

39. Troy, *Morning in America,* 122.

40. Although Troy's sketch of the yuppie is very useful as it is presented here, it could possibly suggest a mere demographic. To the contrary, as I use it, the yuppie is both a demographic and a guiding ideal comprising a fundamental set of beliefs that include social liberalism and an uncritical view of postindustrial capitalism. On the yuppie as both real and symbolic, see John L. Hammond, "Yuppies," *Public Opinion Quarterly* 50 (4) (Winter 1986): 487–501; Emily Friedman, "The All-Frills Yuppie Health Care Boutique," *Society* 23 (July 1986): 42–48; Jerry Savells, "Who Are the Yuppies? A Popular View," *International Journal of Comparative Sociology* 27 (3–4) (January 1986): 234–41; William Roseberry, "The Rise of Yuppie Coffees and the Reimagination of Class in the United States," *American Anthropologist* 98 (4) (December 1996): 762–75; and Kevin L. Ferguson, *Eighties People: New Lives in the American Imagination* (New York: Palgrave Macmillan, 2016), 79–108.

41. See Michael Delli Carpini and Lee Sigelman, "Do Yuppies Matter? Competing Explanations of Their Political Distinctiveness," *Public Opinion Quarterly* 50 (4) (Winter 1986): 502–18.

42. See Richard Lowy, "Yuppie Racism: Race Relations in the 1980s," *Journal of Black Studies* 21 (4) (June 1991): 445–64.

43. Jimmie L. Reeves and Michael M. Epstein, "The Changing Face of Television: Turner Broadcasting System," in Edgerton, *Columbia History of American Television*, 314.

44. Reeves and Epstein, "The Changing Face of Television," 332.

45. Heinecken, self-published brochure for *1984: A Case Study in Finding an Appropriate TV Newswoman (a CBS Docudrama in Words and Pictures)* (Culver City, Calif.: 1985). Color offset cardstock sheet printed recto and verso, 11 x 8 ½ inches (27.94 x 21.59 cm).

46. On the *pictures generation*, a term that historicizes postmodern photography in terms of a broader, multimedia and institutional development, see Douglas Eklund, *The Pictures Generation, 1974–1984* (New York: Metropolitan Museum of Art, 2009); see also Margaret Iverson, "Pictures without Theory," *Art Journal* 69 (3) (Fall 2010): 128–31.

47. On postmodern photography, see Douglas Crimp's writings, in particular "Pictures," *October* 8 (Spring 1979): 75–88; "The Photographic Activity of Postmodernism," *October* 15 (Winter 1980): 91–101; as well as other essays, many of which are now collected in Crimp, *On the Museum's Ruins* (Cambridge, Mass.: MIT Press, 1993). See also Abigail Solomon-Godeau, "Living with Contradictions: Critical Practices in the Age of Supply-Side Aesthetics," *Social Text* 21 (1989): 191–213; Solomon-Godeau, "Playing in the Fields of the Image," in her *Photography at the Dock: Essays on Photographic History, Institutions, and Practices* (Minneapolis: University of Minnesota Press, 1991), 86–102; and Linda Andre, "The Politics of Postmodern Photography," *Minnesota Review* 16 (Fall 1984): 17–35.

48. On Prince, see Nancy Spector et al., *Richard Prince* (New York: Guggenheim Museum, 2007); and Lisa Phillips et al., *Richard Prince* (New York: Whitney Museum of American Art/Abrams, 1992).

49. On Kruger, see Barbara Kruger et al., *Thinking of You* (Los Angeles: Museum of Contemporary Art, 1999); and Arthur C. Danto, "Barbara Kruger," in Arthur C. Danto, *Unnatural Wonders: Essays from the Gap Between Art and Life* (New York: Farrar, Straus, and Giroux, 2005), 61–68.

50. On Sherman, see Paul Moorhouse, *Cindy Sherman* (London: Phaidon, 2014); Régis Durand et al., *Cindy Sherman* (Paris: Flammarion, 2007); Johanna Burton, ed., *Cindy Sherman* (Cambridge, Mass.: MIT Press, 2006); and Lisa Phillips and Peter Schjeldahl, *Cindy Sherman* (New York: Whitney Museum of Art, 1987). Like Heinecken, but in a very different way, Sherman also explored the subversion of pornography and the male gaze; see Lisa Phillips et al., *Cindy Sherman: Centerfolds* (New York: Skarstedt Fine Art, 2003); and Moorhouse, *Cindy Sherman*, 64–71.

51. For an account of the development of the New York market in postmodern photography, one that distinguishes between critical and affirmative forms of work, see Solomon-Godeau, "Living with Contradictions," 191–213.

52. For critics who wrote about postmodern artists like Craig Owens, Crimp, and Solomon-Godeau, it was important to distinguish critical postmodernism from its more affirmative and market-friendly forms; see Craig Owens, *Beyond Recognition: Representation, Power, and Culture* (Berkeley: University of California Press, 1992), 54, 111, 182, 315; Crimp, *On the Museum's Ruins*, 71–75; and Solomon-Godeau, "Living with Contradictions," 193–94.

8. APPROPRIATION IN THE 1980s AND 1990s

1. On social, cultural, political, and technological changes in the 1990s, see Gil Troy, *The Age of Clinton: America in the 1990s* (New York: St. Martin's Press, 2015); Bradford Martin, *The Other Eighties: A Secret History of America in the Age of Reagan* (New York: Hill and Wang, 2011); and David Sirota, *Back to Our Future: How the 1980s Explains the World We Live in Now—Our Culture, Our Politics, Our Everything* (New York: Ballantine, 2011).

2. See Eva Respini, ed., *Robert Heinecken: Object Matter* (New York: Museum of Modern Art, 2014), 180–82.

3. See Irene Borger et al., *Robert Heinecken, Photographist: A Thirty-Five-Year Retrospective* (Chicago: Museum of Contemporary Art, 1999).

4. On the latter exhibition, see Alan G. Artner, "Two of Heinecken's Themes: Sex and Food," *Chicago Tribune* (March 8, 2007).

5. See Respini, ed., *Robert Heinecken: Object Matter*.

6. Stephen K. Lehmer, *Photographist Oral History Transcript, 1996: Robert F. Heinecken*, vol. 1 (Los Angeles: Oral History Program, University of California, 1998), 5–8.

7. On whiteness as a construct that assimilated certain ethnic groups in the United States in the twentieth century while excluding others, see David R. Roediger, *Working Toward Whiteness: How America's Immigrants Became White, The Strange Journey from Ellis Island to the Suburbs* (New York: Basic Books, 2005).

8. Heinecken, in conversation with A. D. Coleman, December 3–5, 1998; see Coleman, "'I Call It Teaching': Robert Heineken's Analytical Facture," in Borger et al., *Robert Heinecken, Photographist*, 7.

9. See Borger et al., *Robert Heinecken, Photographist*, 104; Kevin Moore et al., *Robert Heinecken: Copywork* (London: Ridinghouse, 2012), 182.

10. See Borger et al., *Robert Heinecken, Photographist*, 103; Respini, ed., *Robert Heinecken: Object Matter*, 142; and Moore et al., *Robert Heinecken: Copywork*, 179.

11. On Shepherd as the Kodak Girl, see Nancy Martha West, *Kodak and the Lens of Nostalgia* (Charlottesville: University of Virginia Press, 2000), 53.

12. Moore et al., *Robert Heinecken: Copywork*, 180.

13. Moore et al., *Robert Heinecken: Copywork*, 181.

14. Robert Heinecken, *Time: 150 Years of Photojournalism*, 1990. Incised found bound magazine, edition of 8. 11 x 8 ¼ inches (27.94 x 20.96 cm).

15. On profane illumination in relation to surrealism and photography, see Walter Benjamin, "Surrealism: The Last Snapshot of the European Intelligentsia" (1929), in Walter Benjamin, *Reflections: Essays, Aphorisms, Autobiographical Writings*, trans. Edmund Jephcott (New York: Harcourt Brace Jovanovich, 1978), 177–92.

16. We also see this with the tragic figure of the nurturing mother, Tomoko Uemura, from Eugene W. Smith's epic series *Minimata* (1971) as well as with other iconic personalities known from the history of photography, such as Aristide Briand, Muhammad Ali, John F. Kennedy, and John F. Kennedy Jr.

17. Robert Heinecken, *Newsweek, October 21, 1974*, 1974. Incised found magazine, 12 x 9 inches (30.5 x 22.9 cm). Edition unknown, at least 3.

18. Quoted in James Enyeart, ed., *Heinecken* (Carmel, Calif.: Friends of Photography, 1980), 92.

19. Editors of *Time, Time: 150 Years of Photojournalism* (special collector's edition) (Fall 1989): 38–43.

20. David Pagel, "Pictures Turned Inside Out: Robert Heinecken's Homemade Magazines," in Borger et al., *Robert Heinecken, Photographist*, 29.

21. See Robert Heinecken, *Revised Magazine: Billy Graham/Time, Nov. 15, '93* (1993), reassembled found magazine pages, dry-mounted, loose-bound, portfolio case, 10 ⅝ x 7 ¾ inches (26.99 x 20.96 cm) (40 pages), edition of 10 unique variants; see also, illustrated in Moore et al., *Robert Heinecken: Copywork*, 129–37.

22. See Robert Heinecken, *Revised Magazine: Maidenform* (1993); illustrated in Moore et al., *Robert Heinecken: Copywork*, 138–44.

23. See, for example, Robert Heinecken, *Revised Magazine: Cigarette Ads/Women* (1993); illustrated in Respini, ed., *Robert Heinecken: Object Matter*, 94.

24. See Robert Heinecken, *Revised Magazine: Avedon* (1993), incised found magazine, edition of 10 unique variants, 10 ½ x 8 ¼ inches (26.67 x 20.96 cm); illustrated in Respini, ed., *Robert Heinecken: Object Matter*, 93.

25. See, for example, Robert Heinecken, *Compromised Magazine: B+W/Pairs* (1993), artist bound and collated found magazine pages, edition of 8 variants, 10 ¾ x 8 inches (27.31 x 20.32 cm); and Robert Heinecken, *Compromised Magazine: B+W / Cut, 1994*, artist bound and collated incised found magazine pages, edition of 17, 10 ¾ x 8 inches (27.31 x 20.32 cm); illustrated in Moore et al., *Robert Heinecken: Copywork*, 155–60.

26. See Robert Heinecken, *Gap Magazine* (1994–99), artist bound and collated incised found magazine pages, edition of 5, 10 ¾ x 8 ¼ inches (27.31 x 20.96 cm); and Heinecken, *Revised Magazine: Gap New York Headaches* (1995), reassembled found magazine pages, dry mounted, incised, 10 ½ x 7 ¾ inches (26.67 x 18.42 cm) (24 pages); illustrated in Moore et al., *Robert Heinecken: Copywork*, 163–70.

27. Robert Heinecken, . . . *Wore Khakis* (Portland, Ore.: Nazraeli Press, 1999), publisher's proof edition of 20 copies, unpaginated (60 pages), 10 ½ x 8 ⅝ inches (26.67 x 21.9 cm).

28. The khakis pictured in the ads were in fact not designed by the Gap, which was founded in 1969, long after most of the celebrity photos that were used in the campaign were taken.

29. See Genevieve Buck, "Gap Shows Us Who Wears the Pants," *Chicago Tribune*, November 20, 1994. https://www.chicagotribune.com/news/ct-xpm-1994-11-20-9411200368-story.html.

30. David Pagel, "The Gaps in the Ads: Robert Heinecken's Sabotaged GAP Ads," in Robert Heinecken, . . . *Wore Khakis*, n.p.

31. For an incisive analysis of African American identity in conceptualist American art of the late 1980s and early 1990s, a theorization that stresses the mobility and complexity of Blackness, as well as its multiple wellsprings and its antiessentialist characteristics, see Huey Copeland, *Bound to Appear: Art, Slavery, and the Site of Blackness in Multicultural America* (Chicago: University of Chicago Press, 2013).

32. Jane Tynan, *British Army Uniform and the First World War: Men in Khaki* (New York: Palgrave Macmillan, 2013).

33. See Amy Miller, *Dressed to Kill: British Naval Uniform, Masculinity, and Contemporary Fashions, 1748–1857* (London: National Maritime Museum, 2007).

34. Tynan, *British Army Uniform*, 22–23.

35. U.S. Bureau of the Census, *Current Population Reports*, Series P-70, No. 27, "Job Creation During the Late 1980's (Data from the Survey of Income and Program Participation)" (Washington, D.C.: U.S. Government Printing Office, 1992), 8. https://www2.census.gov/library/publications/1992/demographics/p70-27.pdf.

36. On semitransparent representations of the human body in the influential work of physician-author Fritz Kahn, see Michael Sappol, *Body Modern: Fritz Kahn, Scientific Illustration, and the Homuncular Subject* (Minneapolis: University of Minnesota Press, 2017).

37. On the deindustrialization of the United States, see Judith Stein, *Pivotal Decade: How the United States Traded Factories for Finance in the Seventies* (New Haven, Conn.: Yale University Press, 2010).

38. Rod Slemmons, "On Robert Heinecken and *Recto/Verso*," in Robert Heinecken, *Recto/Verso*, ed. Luke Batten and Jonathan Sadler (Portland, Ore.: Nazraeli Press, 2006), n.p.

39. On David Cronenberg, see William Beard, *The Artist as Monster: The Cinema of David Cronenberg* (Toronto: University of Toronto Press, 2006).

40. For a good timeline on the AIDS crisis, see Foundation for AIDS Research's "HIV/AIDS: Snapshots of an Epidemic" (https://www.amfar.org/thirty-years-of-hiv/aids-snapshots-of-an-epidemic/); see also Kathy S. Stolley and John E. Glass, *HIV/AIDS* (Santa Barbara, Calif.: Greenwood, 2009), 172–89; and Jamal Jones and Laura Salazar, "A Historical Overview of the Epidemiology of HIV/AIDS in the United States," in Eric R. Wright and Neal Carnes, eds., *Understanding the HIV/AIDS Epidemic in the United States: The Role of Syndemics in the Production of Health Disparities* (Basel, Switz.: Springer International, 2016), 19–41.

41. See Robert Heinecken, *Recto/Verso*, ed. Batten and Sadler, n.p.

42. See William Henry Fox Talbot, *The Pencil of Nature* (New York: Da Capo, 1969 [1844–46]).

43. See Talbot's text discussing his photogram depicting a piece of lace, in Talbot, *Pencil of Nature*, n.p., Plate XX.

44. On Talbot's photograms as his "first photographs," predating those taken in a camera obscura, see William Henry Fox Talbot, Michael Gray, Arthur Ollman, Carol McCusker, *First Photographs: William Henry Fox Talbot and the Birth of Photography* (New York: Powerhouse, 2002), 134–35.

CODA

1. Joyce Neimanas, interview with author, Albuquerque, New Mexico, July 24–26, 2014.

MATTHEW BIRO is professor of modern and contemporary art at the University of Michigan. He is author of *Anselm Kiefer and the Philosophy of Martin Heidegger* and *The Dada Cyborg: Visions of the New Human in Weimar Berlin* (Minnesota, 2009).